ACHIEVING PERCEPTUAL-MOTOR EFFICIENCY

A SPACE-ORIENTED APPROACH TO LEARNING

by **RAY H. BARSCH**

volume 1 of a
PERCEPTUAL-MOTOR CURRICULUM

Standard Book Number **87562-009-4**

Library of Congress Catalog Card Number **68-282**

© 1968 SPECIAL CHILD PUBLICATIONS
4535 Union Bay Place N.E.
Seattle, Washington 98105

Printed in the United States of America

DEDICATION

To my son, Jeff, who taught me

the full meaning of Movigenics.

ACKNOWLEDGEMENTS

Many years of clinical confrontation with children whose problems in learning did not lend themselves to precise and neat categorization according to existing models of thought have preceded the writing of this book. In the search for answers which would support a meaningful approach to the resolution of those problems a winding path through the literature and a series of personal encounters with dedicated and profound behavioral scientists marked the trail to the setting forth of these ideas on the printed page.

It is difficult to assess in any objective manner the relative degrees of influence which various respected people have exerted on the cognitive modeling of the chapters in this book. Those who have exerted such influence will undoubtedly recognize threads and strands of their own thinking which have been woven into the fabric of Movigenics. The list of people to whom a cognitive debt is owing would form an impressive and lengthly litany. The writings of many great thinkers have had their influence but on a very personal level the many long "learning hours" spent with Dr. Darrel Boyd Harmon, Dr. A. M. Skeffington and Dr. G. N. Getman have had a very special influence. I am grateful to them for generating the integrating forces. They will most clearly see the mark of their influence upon the pages of this manuscript.

The completion of this volume is in large measure due to the dedicated efforts of a core of enthusiastic graduate students from the University of Wisconsin and other colleges who must be considered as "charter Movigenicists" both in deed and spirit.

A final acknowledgement must be accorded to the thousands of classroom teachers and parents who persistently urged that these concepts be set forth in printed form.

1   A PERSPECTIVE ON
                    EDUCATION   17

2   BASIC CONSTRUCTS OF
                    MOVIGENICS   33

3   THE CONCEPT OF SPACE   67

4   MUSCULAR STRENGTH   85

5	DYNAMIC BALANCE	**103**
6	BODY AWARENESS	**115**
7	SPATIAL AWARENESS	**123**
8	TEMPORAL AWARENESS	**149**

9	THE PERCEPTO-COGNITIVE MODES	**167**
10	THE GUSTATORY MODE	**179**
11	THE OLFACTORY MODE	**195**
12	THE TACTUAL MODE	**203**

13	THE KINESTHETIC MODE	**219**
14	THE AUDITORY MODE	**231**
15	THE VISUAL MODE	**253**
16	DEGREES OF FREEDOM—BILATERALITY	**289**

17	RHYTHM	**299**
18	FLEXIBILITY	**313**
19	MOTOR PLANNING	**321**
20	DEFINING A CURRICULUM	**329**

BIBLIOGRAPHY 335

1

A
PERSPECTIVE
ON
EDUCATION

Man considered not merely as an organized being but as a rational agent and a member of society is perhaps the most wonderfully contrived and to us the most interesting specimen of Divine wisdom that we have any knowledge of.

Whately

The concept of explorations into outer space by manned space vehicles capable of rendezvous, landing on other planets and advancing man's knowledge of the Universe has passed from the pages of science fiction to science reality in the short span of little more than a decade. The imagination of an entire world has been captivated by the exploits of the astronauts and the cosmonauts. Another frontier of ignorance is giving way to man's irrepressible desire to know his universe and understand his relationship to it. Historians have already christened this era in mankind's time as the Age of Space and every school child has incorporated a wide assortment of "space" terms into his everyday vocabulary.

Space exploration is another miracle of modern science. Remarkable as these astronautic adventures may be from a scientific viewpoint they are surpassed by the prosaic daily miracle of the newborn infant's conquest of terrestrial space.

While the collective genius of man combined to achieve the technological advances necessary to explore "outer space" and claim it's conquest, the world of "inner space" has always been his domain.

Every infant born can be considered a "terranaut" automatically receiving such a commission as a human birthright. His exploits in space will rival those of the astronauts in comparative complexity. In his exploration of terrestrial space each child will conquer the spatial mysteries of climbing stairs, running uphill, pedaling a bicycle, batting a ball, skating on blades or wheels, writing his name, drawing a form and will resolve thousands of other spatial dilemmas. Each "terranaut" leads an extremely busy exploratory existence. He moves to seek objects, transports objects from one place to another, experiments with height, depth and width, circumvents obstacles———moving constantly to acquire information. Each infant is a space pioneer. Each discovers within the laboratory of human experience Newton's Laws of Motion. He learns that his toy will drop to the floor when he releases it from his grasp—that his wagon will not move unless he pushes it or pulls it—he learns to accelerate and decelerate his own body in running and walking—he learns a system of thrusting and counter-thrusting in his own body parts if he is to move in balance. Each of Newton's Laws are vital to the development of rockets and space flight and equally vital to the movement of the human organism in all of its encounters in space.

The thrill experienced by the infant when he achieves independent walking across space must be as exhilarating to him as a "walk in space" is to the astronaut. Once the infant achieves erect locomotive skill his vistas for exploration are tremendous. Vision steers him, audition alerts him and touch excites him. The whole world stretches before him to be discovered bit by bit in increasing complexity.

Man has been a space-oriented being from the beginning of time. Exquisitely designed to move in order that he might act, every man from infancy to his demise is an explorer of space. He moves in space according to the directions of his intelligence and thus directed moves from a state of ignorance to a state of knowledge about his universe.

The marvel of the spaceship launching, orbiting and re-entering the atmosphere for safe landing is an engineering design masterpiece which perhaps more than any other discovery of man has required the synthesis of countless individual discoveries from many previous centuries of man's efforts to understand his Universe.

Every previous generation of man in some manner contributed some bit of knowledge about the Universe which has found its way into the synthesis we now refer to as astronautical engineering. Space ships are designed to conform to the Laws of Nature. The movement pattern of the Universe is also the foundation for terranautics.

The design of the human organism as a mobile unit, perfectly engineered for economical movement capable of communicating its thoughts to other members of its species, loving, hating, rejecting, criticizing, praising, inventing, planning, increasing in size, acquiring reproductiveness and achieving a peak of maturity has fascinated scientists for centuries. The mystery of the Universe and the mystery of the human organism existing in that Universe have been the scientific frontiers from the beginning of time. As the scientist has come to understand portions of one mystery he has been led inevitably to the revelation of portions of the other. Discoveries in one have been reciprocally interwoven in the other. As the mysteries of the Universe have unfolded so also have the mysteries of the human come to light.

Each generation can only hope to add to Man's body of knowledge but no generation can expect to complete the task. Whatever man may currently understand about his own nature he must always face the inevitable fact that the generations to follow will be more knowledgeable. There is always a point in time to be considered. Man is constantly learning. Man is constantly exploring. Mystery is a challenge to man's intellect.

All men are explorers of mystery. As they explore they learn. They learn in order to improve the efficiency of future explorations. The greater efficiency they achieve through learning the greater is their explorative proficiency. Each infant terranaut explores his world in preparation for his preschool advancements which lead him to his elementary and secondary years of exploration and then onward to his vocational, marital, social, economic and citizen explorations. The journey from infancy to seniority passes through many worlds of space. The ease with which it is accomplished by most youngsters is a credit to the basic design of the "capsule" and the manner in which each one is programmed for transport. The human organism is designed for efficiency. The Great Architect conceived a remarkable being. The manner in which that design is dynamically expressed from infancy through adulthood constitutes the concern of this book.

Three major terrains of space must be travelled by every terranaut—(1) the Primary terrain mapped out from infancy to his entry into the second major locale of (2) Academic space bounded by the markers of elementary, secondary and collegiate schooling in preparation for his lengthy journey on the terrain of (3) Adulthood.

The Primary Terrain

The infancy period of man is devoted to the establishment of those patterns of cognitive and physical movements which will support a lifetime of adaptation—to teach the organism the rules and regulations governing "human beingness." The new organism is provided with a dual guide system in the form of a mother and father. Both parties having reached adulthood are presumed by biologic maturity to be prepared to act as guides in teaching the "lessons of the world" to the neophyte. In the earliest organization of the family unit the task of the parent was to prepare the offspring to eventually assume an adult role in the existing society. Whatever the tribal rules may have been according to geography, religion, economics and so on the obligation of the parent in primitive society as well as modern Space Age society has always been the same— to transmit the culture.

Sears (1957) has described the parents of America as the "conveyor belts of society" developing a product to enter the socio-economic stream of our nation. While a small percentage of the nation's parents may legitimately be accused of neglect, rejection and deliberate negative influence the vast majority of our parents try to do the best possible job of rearing their children.

Behavioral scientists have accumulated a significant list of what might generally be termed "the wrong things to do to a child", but this effort has not been matched by an equal amount of investigation on the topic of the "right things to do to a child". This listing of "rights" must usually be inferred from the listing of "wrongs." It is safe at this time to state that an appropriate child-rearing curriculum has not been defined. There is evidence from the Sears (1957) study on child-rearing practices among parents of normal children and the Barsch (1967) study on child-rearing practices among the parents of handicapped children which indicates that the average parent tends to rely upon a trial and error approach to rearing a child as a primary method followed in second place by parental models, i.e., the way their own parents reared them, and in third place, to be guided by "peer example", i.e., utilizing the same techniques as the "lady next door." Most parents probably rely upon all three approaches at one time or another.

As a consequence of this rather random process, there is probably relatively little understanding of what constitutes an appropriate set of life experiences during the first five years of life to guarantee that a child will arrive at the kindergarten doorstep experientially prepared according to the desires of the educational system. Preschool and kindergarten teachers will quickly attest to the shaping process which they must undertake to convert a youngster into a pupil. No adequate system of preparing a child for school has as yet been communicated to the parents of our nation. In general we seem to rely upon faith in the average parent to provide a suitable five year period of basic training for an academic career.

The vast majority of our nation's parents have a dedicated interest to rearing their children for achievement in school. Every parent hopes his child will sail smoothly and safely on academic seas. The multiplicity of experiences and activities required to ensure a successful voyage must be delineated to guide parents in their task.

The infancy and preschool period may be characterized as a truly remarkable period in the Ages of Man. Within this four to five year period the human organism constructs a physical and cognitive experiential foundation for movement efficiency which will serve him throughout a lifetime. Through movement and exercise he acquires sufficient strength of muscle to support his own weight and to push, pull and lift within the limits of his total size. He learns to move in balance using both sides of his body as reciprocally interweaving halves to jump, run, skip, kneel, crawl, roll and ride a tricycle. He becomes aware of his own body parts and the nature of their relationship one to another as well as achieving a recognition of how each part may serve him in his personal adaptation to the world in which he lives. Within that period of time he acquires a basic orientation of his own position in space in relation to all other objects which he might encounter. He achieves some recognition of time and its relation to him in terms of his rewards, goals and desires. He learns to see in order that he might see to learn. He learns to hear so that he might listen to learn. He learns to talk in order that he might express in communication with others the uniqueness of his own "being-ness". He learns to move his body parts so that he may move efficiently to secure the information he needs. He learns to touch so that he may learn from contact with his world. He develops his sensitivity to smell so it may serve him in the discrimination of the attractive and unattractive odors in his world.

He acquires grace and ease in his movements and progressively becomes more rhythmic. He tries to utilize both sides of his body to acquire a proficiency at manipulation. In the bitter laboratory of early childhood he learns that all events cannot occur exactly as he may desire and acquires some form of response to disappointment. He learns to plan his moves to strategically achieve his intended goal progressively becoming more adept at circumventing and avoiding obstacles. Washing hands, bathing, dressing, throwing a ball, building blocks, winding a toy, dancing to rollicking records, talking to friends, talking to strangers, going for a walk, visiting grandma, planning a birthday — the list of learnings and accomplishments are endless.

Each achievement advances his proficiency as a traveler in terrestrial space. The canvas of development is the working surface.

Development paints a dynamic portrait of a man, plotting an organization of space, sketching in crude pencil lines the earliest outline of a particular detail and then progressively, adds body and depth with shading and nuances to evoke its proper relationship to all other portions of the portrait — it builds in perspective through time and eventually fills in the space.

Securing his development and insuring his readiness to cope with the multiplicity of problems which are yet to confront him in the next sixty to seventy years — his parents stand by enlisted in the service of his development giving active help when needed, quietly observing his independent struggles to achieve mastery and wisely noting the time for adult intervention versus the time to allow for independent exploration. Through it all he is moving. From birth to year one and to each succeeding birthday he is moving bit by bit toward the complexity of adulthood. Each advancement serving only as an introduction to some more complicated learning which must follow to fulfill his commitment to adulthood.

The societal obligation of the parent is to establish, define and structure the basic rules of living. Most parents address themselves to this task with a sincere dedicated effort. In the light of their effort, most parents feel reasonably confident that they have achieved a proper preparation of their offspring by the time he reaches kindergarten age. It has become a comfortable pastime among diagnosticians to point an accusing finger at the parent for some omission in the child-rearing procedure when a child reaches a point of failure during elementary years. Since there is common agreement on the importance of the learning in those first five years and since the parent is the natural party of responsibility the diagnosis of a child problem which defies explanation on physical or intellectual grounds leads inevitably to a search for parental omissions to account for the current situation. The evidence is too overwhelming to deny that such an accusation is frequently justified. While it is perhaps possible in the orientation of some clinicians to achieve such an explanation even though the psychological "fit" is difficult the possibility of explaining some of the failure patterns experienced by children on other bases than psychologic dysfunction of parents must certainly be considered.

Few parents are aware that they have borne a "terranaut"—an explorer of space. They discover it when he moves into forbidden places, climbs to dangerous heights, insists on experimenting and must "have his fingers into everything" but rarely do they attribute such exploration to a search for spatial orientation. Many well-intended parents fail to help a child acquire a system for building generalizations of space and building new concepts of space.

Most parents find that their little terranaut tends to conform to the expected standards learning to walk, talk, feed, dress, bathe and run according to the norms. A certain percentage of parents will face the problem of rearing a child whose development does not conform to expected standards for various reasons. These special children eventually receive a label to designate their developmental problem. The little terranauts whose fledgling explorations are complicated by physical, neurologic, emotional or sensory impairments have their own special problems in establishing a spatial proficiency on which to build a lifetime of progressive complexity. Their parents require a special awareness and assistance in guiding their child-rearing practices. The special child is no less a space explorer than the unimpaired child. The commitment of the parent is not reduced. The lessons of life must still be taught. The infancy and early childhood of the terranaut deserves a spatial perspective from both research and practice if the journey into other life spaces is to be made comfortably and expeditiously. Biology provides the launching pad and the parents provide the original directional guidance system. Their briefing for their mission must therefore inform them of the full and abiding nature of the traveler born into their charge.

The School Period

It is the customary practice in our American society to register the five year old for enrollment in the kindergarten of his neighborhood school to initiate the formal process of instruction leading to graduation as an intelligent, contributing, vocationally successful, economically independent, emotionally mature, socially adaptive, and politically sensitive and concerned member of society. For most children the kindergarten year represents an introduction to a form of group experience which they have never before encountered. In their own families they have associated with siblings of varying ages, either more mature or less than they. They may have spent happy hours playing with neighborhood children of the same age. But it is unlikely that they have experienced a group of 25-35 boys and girls of their own age in the same setting involved in the same activity.

The kindergarten year is the first full test for the terranaut. For the first time in a very real way he or she is asked to demonstrate in a peer-comparison setting the results of his five year program of basic training. All of the lessons of basic motor performance, oral language structure, form perception, color discrimination, independent toileting and dressing, "sharingness", conformity to patterns, ability to follow auditory and visual directions and many, many more functions in a seemingly endless list are expected to be properly organized, defined and integrated. According to the general rules of his society he has now moved into the social institution of a school to enter the next significant stage of preparation for adulthood. From the day he releases his mother's hand to greet the lady whom he will come to call "my teacher" until the time some thirteen years later when he is photographed in cap and gown proudly clutching a high school diploma approximately one third of all of his waking hours will be devoted to school. From September to June each of the thirteen years he will be "employed" for approximately six to seven hours per day five days per week. His schedule will be regular and his "off" days are carefully defined. His occupation can be listed as an "apprentice citizen."

During that space he will become familiar with all previous explorations of man delving into the history of man, cultural developments, basic fundamentals of all sciences, great literature, mathematical systems—all systematized and attractively packaged for his consumption by those who have gone before. He will cognitively explore man's past, evaluate man's present accomplishments and critically evaluate man's future. Like a world traveler with a thirteen year itinerary he will move from knowledge to knowledge, cognitively enriching his awareness of the world around him. The boundaries and obligations of **his** apprenticeship are identical to those of his peers. He is a learner. The product yield of his apprenticeship is an education. By definition he is systematically led from the darkness of ignorance to the bright open fields of knowledge for the purpose of eventually contributing to the expansion of those same fields as a constructive thoughtful adult. Magellan, Columbus, Cortez, Alexander the Great, Pythagoras, Newton, the Pilgrims, Shakespeare, Einstein, Madame Curie, Audubon, Sir Walter Scott———thousands and thousands of explorers, inventors, contributors will all march before his eyes and ears to excite his imagination, stir his own explorative desires and present him a composite of what Man has learned about himself and his Universe and what has remained a mystery.

The path from naivete to sophistication is not a solo flight. The terranaut is not alone. Two parents and a teacher share the responsibility for the optimal outcome of his spatial apprenticeship. Many other guides may also be enlisted along the route. However each guide may express his or her influence along the way the net objective is to achieve an optimal progression toward a sophisticated maturity. The community school system is a major terrain for the aspiring terranaut. In historical perspective the child as an academic learner entitled to an education as a birthright within a free society is a new entity. In terms of "mankind time" the community elementary school is in the toddler stage of development regardless of the present state of complexity. We must keep in mind that the young child did not achieve status as a "research subject in learning experiments" until 50-60 years ago. Prior to that time he simply learned or did not and very little attention was paid to how the processes of learning took place.

Our society is committed to a principle of free public education for all of its members and is further committed to a principle of literacy. Every young child is entitled to the opportunity to learn to read, write and compute along with many other activities offered by the schools. This commitment must be honored, and it is in the honoring of that commitment and conviction that we find theoretical disagreement, contradictory research, and confusion of thought and practice. We are still in our novitiate as a teaching society and there are yet many things to be learned about learning.

The space world of the modern community school system is composed of three basic types of children. The first type enters school at the appropriate age and systematically achieves expanded mastery of school subjects year after year. As the curriculum has been plotted and becomes available to them, they grasp what is offered, integrate the new comfortably into the composite of their previous learnings, explore new cognitive horizons and progress from grade to grade, filling their mental containers with the proper amounts of knowledge year after year. They are sometimes anxious and sometimes frightened. They learn to read in the prescribed amount of time and steadily improve and expand their reading through the grades. They grasp the concepts of quantity and progressively become more competent "arithmetickers". They spell and write according to expectancy. This is the **integrating learner group** which seems to ideally represent the model on which the curriculum was based. This is the group that literally learns "as the textbook said they would". Their periodic achievement tests reflect the steady expansion of their academic knowledge. Perhaps it would be better to refer to this group as the CURRICULUM MODEL group. The percentage of this type of child varies in every classroom, building and system in the nation. Most authorities in education seem to agree that this group is in the majority in every school system. As long as this group remains in the majority the curriculum of the school system can be regarded as appropriate to society's demand that the school serve as the institution to prepare its children for adult competency.

The second population of children may be designated as the Special Education group. For a variety of reasons, they are unable to survive on a day-by-day basis in the mainstream of education and require a special curriculum to meet their needs. The deaf, blind, physically handicapped, mentally retarded, aphasic, emotionally disturbed and culturally disadvantaged compose this category.

The firmament of Special Education is filled with many constellations. Despite the labels and the diagnostic scramble, the fundamental truth on which school provisions for this population are based is one of failure. A school decision is made, at times upon entry or later after the child has been given the opportunity to achieve, to the effect that the child is not benefiting from the curriculum of the mainstream and special provisions are necessary. This it not to condemn the child as a failure in a general sense, but rather to indicate that the unique needs of this child have demanded some other form of curricula than the majority form.

The complexity of the human organism in its vulnerability to disease, injury, neglect, deprivation, psychic trauma and metabolic error has consistently been the cause of educational dilemnas. Children have frequently appeared on the Special Education doorstep with multiple problems and the educational classifier has been forced to decide which of the child's problems should take precedence over the others for purposes of school placement.

Harnessed by the artificial construct of "homogeneous groups" as the major administrative device at his disposal, the educator has been forced to form groups with the "greatest possible homogeneity that can be obtained". This enables the class to operate under the conventional wisdom that children with similar physical, mental or sensory problems will be similar in their learning. This assumption borrowed easily as a cup of sugar from the next door neighbor of elementary education has proven to be a constant migraine headache for the Special Educator, since homogeneity for classroom learning has not been easy to attain. The typical outcome of this difficulty has been the formulation of various sub-classifications within each of the major disability groups seeking to more clearly define elements of homogeneity that would permit optimal benefit from a school experience.

This second population of Special Education children is a variable percentage according to most authorities because each community school system is free to establish as many or as few special units as it may deem necessary. Throughout the nation, the complex of special units in a school system is variable from town to town and state to state. The per cent size of this second child group has been estimated from 3-20%. In consideration of the improvement in diagnostic sensitivity leading to more discrete identifications, we are inclined to accept the 20% figure as operational for Special Education.

For the sake of argument we shall arbitrarily at this moment assign a 50% figure to the population we have called the CURRICULUM MODEL group. This leaves a figure of 30% to be accounted for in the third child population. Perhaps the most apt designation for this population is that of the REMEDIAL group.

In general practice this group of children has virtually become a "limbo" group floating in mid-space between the mainstream of education and the specialized units. This group indicates an adequate intelligence when measured by currently available instruments, demonstrates no gross sensory impairment, appears to be culturally advantaged, and while perhaps exhibiting some signs of emotional problems is not seriously disturbed. They cannot truly be classified in any of the existing Special Education categories, and yet they do not learn at the pace and with the same efficiency as the "mainstream" demands. This "limbo" group is progressively achieving identification as the Learning Disabilities population.

The community educator is painfully aware of that gnawing 30% which seems to be an inevitability. Each September eager tens of thousands of children embark upon the first grade journey towards reading competency and each following September there is little doubt that the previous nine months of school experience will have produced a **high, middle** and **low** reading group. By the time the middle and low group have struggled through another year, the referral forms for Remedial Reading service begin.

The same phenomenon of grouping may occur in arithmetic, spelling, writing, and so on. The CURRICULUM MODEL group proceeding according to schedule begins to draw further and further away from the stumbling, hesitant, confused remedial group. The Remedial group loses the cadence and is out of step in the march. Their only hope lies in a form of emergency educational first-aid to bolster their reading, arithmetic or whatever position of the academic anatomy may be wounded and returning them to the frontlines with the Model group. This first-aid corps is composed of the classroom teacher providing extra help or special assignments, the Remedial tutor removing the child from class several periods per week, the Speech Correctionist, or any others the school may add to the roster. The general thinking here is that the child is only a minor casualty and can eventually be restored to full battle status. Sometimes the first-aid is highly successful and such restoration is achieved, but many times the remedial plasma still leaves the child with an academic limp on which he hobbles for the remainder of his academic life.

These are the three child populations served by the school from age 5-18 as a general rule. There is yet a fourth population whose constellation of problems is sufficiently severe to deny them admission to a classroom program. There remains a small percentage of children who are so severely damaged physically, mentally or emotionally that they are unschoolable.

Perhaps the percentage split of 50-50 between those who achieve curricular competency and the two problem groups in the Special and Remedial categories appears to be an overstatement of the case. The figures are illustrative and intended to establish a perspective and should not be considered to have been derived from statistics. Neither should they be considered as a fictitious exaggeration. The true statistic will probably always be open to debate and question, but all community educators will attest to a growing percentage of children in each of the two problem groups. Educators will also admit that the services in any school system are rarely astride the needs.

We have almost reached a point where half the effort of a community school system is devoted to the CURRICULUM MODEL child, and the other half is devoted to the Special child in one category or another.

In the battle for educational survival the casualty rate is impressive. Every child born today will five years hence be counted in one of those three school groups. He has five years from his first cry to his kindergarten entry to make all necessary preparations to ensure his assignment to the CURRICULUM MODEL group.

Another type of educational problem which has received little attention in the literature may be termed the "diminishing achiever". Educators throughout the nation are acquainted with the problem of the child who is judged to be an adequate achiever for the first three grades of school and begins to demonstrate learning problems in his fourth grade year. The child who has been doing well until fifth grade and then begins to encounter serious difficulty is a known figure. The shift to junior high school regimen usually produces a number of learning problems among students who have previously performed at adequate levels. Senior high school also produces another percentage who become failing students after a prior record of adequacy. This phenomenon is also noted at the college level. Most colleges and universities are highly selective in their admission policies taking in only those students who have already demonstrated academic adequacy in their secondary years. The reasons for college failure may be numerous, such as immaturity, social excess, psychological problems, etc. Some segment of the college dropout percentage, however, is traceable to inadequate study habits, poor reading ability, inability to sustain a high quality effort and other perceptocognitive difficulties. Each school year at any age is marked by a certain percentage of failures among students who, according to usual criteria, are not expected to encounter difficulty.

This entire group, from kindergarten through college, who encounter difficulties without manifesting gross signs of disorder, are also progressively acquiring a designation as learners with "special learning disabilities".

The period from kindergarten through high school must be filled with activities. Each activity must in some manner contribute to achievement of society's goals for its learners. The systematic sequence of activities leading to that goal is a **curriculum**. The typical curriculum of the community school system is based upon the premise that certain proficiencies in skills and knowledges have already been established by the time a child enrolls in kindergarten, and therefore the program of activity can be organized to **advance** a child. Not only is the curriculum designed to move forward from an "expected level of proficiency" but from a different perspective it is also defined well in advance of the present child's entry. Curriculum designers must be "in tune with the times". As each social, technological, scientific, economic and industrial advance takes place in an accelerated world, it must be incorporated into the school program. Each theorem, fact, piece of equipment or belief which has become obsolete must be deleted and appropriately replaced. A curriculum must be dynamic—in a constant state of remodeling—a current reflection of the changing times. This mandate for a dynamic curriculum places a heavy burden upon curriculum designers. If the goal of a curriculum is to ensure a progression of achievements leading to a competency for an unknown future, then the rapidity with which the world of man and his Universe is changing must indeed require a "crystal ball". What kind of world will there be and what kind of a citizen will the kindergartner of today face and be some twenty years hence? However the historians may eventually characterize this era, there is little current doubt that the curriculum of today must reflect a Space Age. Despite the magnificence of atomic energy and the hydrogen bomb, it is the penetration of the frontiers of space that will receive historical priority. The curriculum, therefore, must not only reflect the Space Age in bringing knowledge of space explorations into the classroom, but it is the contention of this book that the basic set of concepts which have led scientists to achieve orbital flight must become the core set of principles to be applied in the true understanding of the dynamic human learner.

The casualty rate in elementary, secondary and collegiate levels, as well as the casualty rate in Special Education, clearly demand some alternative strategies. The strategies thus far have been tagential and proliferated and lacking in cohesive force. Some form of strategy unification seems imperative to optimize the educational survival of all future terranauts.

THE ADULT PERIOD

We can next turn to the third terrain in the development of the earth-bound space traveler—adulthood space.

A portrait of the spatially sophisticated American leaves much to be desired. If we mount all of the evidence, we must indeed be concerned with the fact that the promise of the Basic Design somehow becomes distorted with the passage of years.

What forces are at work from infancy onward to yield the staggering statistic from authorities in posture stating that 75-85% of the adolescent population of this nation has a significant postural deviation (Lowman and Young, 1960). Apparently, 15% of the total population walk and move with the grace and ease intended by anatomical design. In twelve short years some group of factors influence a healthy organized infant who achieves erect locomotive balance to distort that balance into a postural deviation.

A President's Commission on Physical Fitness expressed a national concern for the lack of fitness among our youth and our adults. In typical American tradition billboards, posters and magazine spreads are now attempting to achieve a national awareness of the need for physical fitness much in the same manner as we are led to believe that one detergent makes clothes whiter than the next one. Advertising campaigns now direct the attention of the nation to the fact that children require special attention to their fitness.

Much of this concern was generated by a series of comparative studies testing the achievement on tests of minimum muscular fitness between American school children and those in Switzerland, Austria and Italy. The studies of Kraus and Hirschland (1954) in the eastern part of the United States, Phillips, et al, (1955) in Indiana, Fox and Atwood (1955) in Iowa, and Kirchner and Glines (1957) in Oregon, all revealed an inferiority among American children.

From these two notes, the American child already seems destined on two counts at least, to have a postural problem and to be physically unfit. A casual observation on a busy street where many people are walking will reveal the slouched shoulders, protruding stomachs, pronated ankles, sloping shoulders and tilted pelvises which bear witness to the postural problems.

The litany of adult perceptual motor efficiencies is lengthy. Few adults are skilled athletes. The weekend duffer and the 125 average bowler are common sights. Basic training instructors in all of the Armed Services will attest to the large number of enlistees who must be painstakingly taught to crawl, roll, walk, stand, run, jump, and balance in order to insure their own battlefield survival.

Dented fenders, confused parking placements, and high accident rates are continual evidence of modern man's inability to properly judge spatial distance.

Modern man is a sitting-being comfortable in his easy chair content to be an audience and only mildly interested in being a performer. His society invested thousands upon thousands of dollars to make him a skilled reader and this investment in adult life has paid the minimal dividends of reading the daily newspaper and countless advertisements. The love for reading for pleasure and information carefully nurtured by dedicated teachers during his elementary years dwindles to what might be called the "survival level" of reading—just enough to stay alive. An occasional magazine and perhaps an occasional book keep alive the reading pattern—but for the most part, reading of books is regarded as something that was associated with formal schooling—and once the demand is removed, there is little incentive to continue.

His society invested thousands upon thousands of dollars to assist him in attaining mathematical competency, but his adult life is spent in a continual apology for the fact that he was "never much good with numbers".

Personnel managers complain of poor spelling, poor handwriting, poor arithmetic, and poor reading and frequently urge educators to emphasize such training to a greater degree. The complaints are registered not regarding the retarded, the disturbed or the handicapped, but refer to high school graduates of average intelligence and often to the college graduate with above-average intelligence.

The inventive genius of man continues to supply modern man with more and more time and labor saving devices to provide more and more free time and less need to move. The achievement of man's sedentation is nearly complete. He sits through approximately 80% of his school life engaged in the near-point visual task. The vast majority of the jobs in the nation are sedentary jobs, so he probably spends 80% of his vocational life sitting. His household chores which used to offer a possibility for movement become more and more automatized so he has more time to sit and watch television. Any distance over two blocks requires him to sit and ride in his car. He sits to watch sporting events and complains if he must park his car more than a hundred yards from the gate. A future of sedentation seems assured.

The spatial confusion of many average adults who admit to a poor sense of direction suggests that the "ugly American" and the "fat American" can be joined by the "lost American".

Almost at every turn there is evidence of adult inefficiency. Postural problems, accident proneness, dietary limitations, spectatoritis, increasing numbers of traffic fatalities, job failures, uncertainties and anxieties; poor listeners and inaccurate observers abound. Incoordination is a majority finding. Errors in communication are abundantly evident. The political world is in constant turmoil. Mental illness continues to increase in incidence. Everywhere the inefficiency of man is evident, and yet the science of human understanding and the understanding of the universe has progressed more rapidly during the past twenty-five years than it has during the past several centuries. "Obsolescence" has become a key word in the culture of today.

Three critical periods have been reviewed. The infant terranaut initiates his exploration in earth space under the guidance of parents who all seem to "wish they knew more about children", and for the most part, are eager to be more efficient. A set of constructs which could form the basis for a child-rearing curriculum in a Space Age might serve to improve parental efficiency. The school terranaut is in need of a curriculum which will reflect his own explorer identity and the Space Age in which he lives. A critical appraisal of the typical school curriculum will reveal that there is no real need to declare the curriculum obsolete. The major portions of most curricula are excellent. Rather than remodel or change the curriculum, it seems wiser to find methods to bring the learner to a higher state of learning efficiency. Changes in curricular content have a way of taking care of themselves in the due course of social change, but changes in a conceptualization of the human learner require an intensive inspection and analysis of the human terranaut as a learner. There is a need for a unified approach to curriculum at all points. Some scheme must be devised to unify curriculum concepts in both general and special education. The luxury of multiple theories and multiple curricula is uneconomical in an era of synthesis on so many other fronts. It must be possible to define a common set of practical constructs to guide the disparate elements in Special Education to a point of fusion and at the same time establish a second point of fusion with general education.

If both of these objectives, improved parental efficiency and the optimization of learning efficiency for **all** learners, could be achieved, we might produce a more efficient generation of adults. Also, if a set of constructs related to human performance efficiency could be conceived, it might serve to unify evaluative considerations at all levels of living. Perhaps a thread of efficiency must be woven into the fabric of human behavior to bind it tight at all ages.

Parental inefficiency, learner inefficiency, and adult inefficiency in a Space Age seem to provide a core of elements which might be converted into a meaningful synthesis if the negative were changed to a positive note, and the weaving of a theory were begun with the thread of EFFICIENCY. This triad of inefficiencies has become the first impulse towards a theory. The theory is called **Movigenics**.

2

BASIC CONSTRUCTS OF MOVIGENICS

Movigenics is a theory of movement as it relates to learning. The name resulted from combining two Latin words, **movere**—"to move"—and **genesis**—"origin and development". It is, therefore, the study of the origin and development of patterns of movement in man and the relationship of those movements to his learning efficiency. Its constructs and assumptions have application to the understanding of human behavior at all ages and in all circumstances. It is our conviction that these constructs are helpful not only in comprehending the pathological and deviant, but also the multitude of performances which may come under the heading of normal. It is, above all, a theory for education.

A theory starts as a system of explanations which seem to bear some relationship and offers a logical organization to some thoughts about behavior. It may emerge from a well-defined set of data, or it may be entirely provisional and temporary. It is only a method for establishing order among guesses, speculations, surmises, hunches, conflicting and at times contradictory data, clinical experience and established laws of behavior. It is, in its earliest form, a system of conceptualizations. Only time and much experience can truly test its merit. Any organization of thought about behavior must meet the criterion of practicality. If the conceptualizations cannot be implemented into day-by-day practice to benefit mankind, the theory has been an interesting intellectual exercise but little more. If, on the other hand, it prompts a restructuring or reformulation of present practice, then its value must be judged in terms of greater or lesser utility in the resolution of problems which confront our society.

Movigenic theory is a relatively new conceptualization. Extensive reliance is placed upon past and present research from many fields, "stretching" an interpretation here and there where it seems advantageous to do so. The theory itself is in an embryonic stage and is therefore not yet mature enough to support itself independently upon its own data although the quantity of data is accumulating. Perhaps, at this point in time its major value may be said to lie within its provocative nature.

Although we are convinced that the constructs have an exceptionally wide range of applicability, the principal focus of this book is centered on the developing child and his problems in achieving a mature adult status. Since the course of his developmental momentum is in large measure guided by the opportunities for learning which are devised and made available by countless adults interested in his welfare, some reference must be made to the problems within adults, as well.

No claim is made for the origination of these basic postulates—only to the formulation, organization and practical application of these principles into a "meaningful package" for those concerned with the optimal performance of the human organism at any age and in all degrees of health. Movigenics is an effort to view man as a totality in everything he does and to account for all components of that totality in any of his performances. It is not presented as a synthesis of **all** theories, although the statements and concepts of many theories have been brought together under one banner. It is also not presented as a "fait accompli" since it continues to be revised as critical comment demands further clarification. It shrinks and expands in a flexible manner as experience dictates its adaptation. It is offered as a way of viewing, analyzing and explaining human behavior.

The ground of human development has been covered many times before by others. The fascinating complexity of the human organism intrigues many travelers and insures that the ground will be covered again and again—with each coverage revealing some points of interest that were neglected by previous tourists.

Movigenics introduces a new language to label performance. Some concepts which are strikingly familiar may appear different because they have been dressed in a new term. These concepts, however, have not lost their identity because they have received a "nickname". Terms have been invented whenever it was expeditious to do so. New labels have been substituted for old when a Movigenic label was felt to contribute to the clarification of a concept.

Where only "blue sky" exists, we have projected concepts to fill that open space. We have taken liberties with the opinions of many authorities and investigators in interpreting a compatibility to Movigenics from their conclusions by casting their thoughts in Movigenic terms. This has not been a license, but a respectfully employed "translation".

Movigenics was born in clinical practice and developed in the laboratory of clinical confrontation with hundreds of children who presented one perplexing dilemna after another which could not easily be resolved by simple recourse to existing concepts in the field of child development. It evolved from a rather selective cognitive process of attempting to find ways to improve the learning efficiency of children. It is a deliberate attempt to cover a wide terrain.

The theory has been set forth to suggest a curriculum. It begins with a set of ten constructs on human behavior which are intended to establish the foundation stones upon which a curriculum can be erected. The specific dimensions of curriculum emerged from these basic premises and are discussed in subsequent chapters. Two abiding orientations are both implicit and explicit throughout the presentation. First, that Man is a magnificent product of the Great Architect and is therefore a mysterious unity of design. Within the obscured depths of that design lies the path to understanding. Second, that it is possible to pose a single question about existing research on the nature of Man and his Universe i.e. — **What information does it contain to clarify the spatial proficiency of Man?**

We can now turn attention to the ten basic constructs of **Movigenic** theory as the first stage in exploring the world of the terranaut.

Construct One: **The fundamental principle underlying the design of the human organism is movement efficiency.**

Man is designed to move. The totality of his being is organized into a harmony of interrelated anatomical, neurologic, chemical, physiologic, organic, glandular, and psychological segments and elements in a magnificent unity. This unity, in final analysis, appears to be directed toward a single goal — to permit the corporate structure to move in space. The basic biologic organization of the human system is directed toward movement.

The first manifestation of movement efficiency occurs at the moment of conception when the egg-sperm unity results from a pattern of cellular movement. Once the unity has been achieved a nine month itinerary of movement is activated to speed the organism to its first biological destination — delivery. This earliest patterning process of cellular movement of cell division, protein structuring and so on can be termed **biologic motility.**

Biologic motility provides the momentum to propel the organism into birth. Once externalized he enters his next phase of mobility — that of INDEPENDENT TRANSPORT MOBILITY. In this phase he must breathe independently, process nourishment and identify himself as a member of the human species by achieving a pattern of erect locomotion in space. Again the design for movement is superbly conceived in construction and timing.

Above all else the human being is designed to move — and if the development of the original design proceeds in its execution without interference — it is designed to move with efficiency. Muscle pairings, bone relationships, circulatory processes, neural circuiting, and chemical balances are all architecturally organized to promote efficiency of movement. Man is a constant mover. The most relaxed state may be recorded as one of least movement but not devoid of motion. Movement is a constant.

Internally, movement is continuous. Externally, the movement is directed by the situation. Anatomically, man is designed to walk, run, kneel, roll, crawl, bend, jump, retreat, advance, defend and attack. His skeletal frame and his musculature assure this freedom. His daily encounters determine which movement may be selected from his repertoire.

Rotation and revolution are the two basic forms of movement. Rotation on an axis and revolution around another body may be traced as the principal forms of movement **throughout the universe.** The order of the planetary system is based upon rotation and revolution. Patterns of circular movement define the order of the Universe. Man's concept of time, the tropism of plants, the momentum of a rolling object and many other phenomena of physical reality confirm this. As the earth rotates on an axis so does man rotate on an axis. Rotation and revolution become the core of movement. Any physical movement of man occurs as an arc. Were it not for the counterbalancing mechanics of antagonistic muscles every movement would follow a full rotation around some axis if its force of projection would be followed.

Threads of reference to the signifance of movement and of man's potential for movement have been woven through the fabric of all literary reference to man. Man cannot be discussed or described without including reference to movement. Man has moved to conquer, to build, to destroy, to pillage and to pray. He has moved to find food, shelter and clothing. He has moved to hunt and he has moved to tend the sheep. He has traveled from place to place. He has painted, sculpted, molded and shaped objects to his intent. He has developed tools and he has used his own hands. He has revolted and submitted. He has explored each new frontier.

Without movement atrophy occurs. Without movement stagnation sets in. Without movement no change takes place. Man moves to change something. As a dynamic being man is constantly on the move to change. His nature demands it and his design defines it. Life is movement. Without movement there is death. To understand himself man must come to an understanding of movement.

The movement he must come to understand is not limited to muscular movement. Physiologic, social, psychological, neurologic, and chemical movement must also be recognized as components of a movement totality.

He moves to higher levels of cognitive endeavor when he is positively stimulated and regresses to lower levels of cognition when he is threatened. He moves to take up a political or social cause. He moves to argue for his beliefs. He "moves" to enact a resolution. He makes progress in psychotherapy when he begins to "move." He moves from one social strata to another. He contains "mobility strivings" according to sociologists. He is moved to sympathy, moved to grief, moved to tears. He moves people with his ideas. He moves to understand. The essence of Man is movement and he is designed to move with efficiency.

Whether or not he achieves the efficiency in movement promised by his design will be determined by many factors—impairment, circumstance, opportunity, stimulation, experience and many more.

The important point here is that movement is the key to life—not only the movement of muscles and bones in a physical manner—but also in a social, psychological and cognitive sense. Each advance that scientific man has made in understanding his own nature has been recorded in movement terms. Connections, routes, paths, reciprocal influences have been the primary results of scientific evaluations. Man cannot scientifically describe himself without reliance upon words which connote movement in space.

Movement efficiency is the cornerstone of Movigenics. This first construct of Movement Efficiency therefore becomes the starting point for achieving a Space Age perspective on the human learner. Physical and cognitive movements are inseparable. Movigenics is not a theory of physical education—it is a theory of education—or learning wherever, whenever and however man learns. It is concerned with reading as well as walking, with speech as well as jumping, with language as well as running, with thought as well as push-ups. Man is not a motor. He is designed to "think on his feet" and to move in relation to those thoughts. He is not a machine. He is not a computer. He is described as such only because of the analogic limitations of the men doing the describing. He moves. He learns. He learns to move. He moves to learn. As he moves he advances himself in stature AND wisdom. To find ways to help each individual move with the greatest possible efficiency constitutes the principal challenge for those who wish to optimize the development of all children and adults.

Construct Two: **The primary objective of Movement Efficiency is to economically promote the survival of the organism.**

As the aerospace scientist of today proceeds with the planning for depositing earthmen on other planets for exploratory periods of time the questions concerning human survival in an unknown world must be uppermost in his mind. The terrifying destructive potential of the nuclear bomb has returned the word "survival" to the everyday conversational vocabulary of the entire world. Time was when "survival" was a term used primarily in the study of primitive tribes, ship-wrecked sailors, and deplaned aviators floating on an open sea. "Survival" is now a reality word holding daily significance.

The history of man has been a story of survival. Man was intended by design to survive. In his physiologic construction he is equipped with a wide variety of protective devices—emergency reacting forces which defend against annihilation.

Man has remained alive in the face of dire adversity only as he has been able to move to defend his life. He has learned progressively more complex systems to protect himself from the cold and heat and the possible devastations from excesses of both forces. He has learned to insure himself against flood and famine although these still continue to be major sources of threat for large percentages of the world. He has become progressively more complex in his techniques for defending himself against attack. A great deal of man's energy from the beginning of time has been devoted to finding means to economically promote his survival. This is every man's purpose—to survive—to continue. He acts to survive. However he may uniquely perceive a threat to his survival he acts to remove that threat. To build survival strength the human must learn from his experience, must obtain information and utilize this information for his own advancement.

To physiologically survive his respiratory system must process atmospheric information to supply adequate oxygen to the body tissues, the circulatory system must process information in the form of blood flow to all regions of the body and so on. Each system is receiving and dispensing information to all other systems in a vast communicative undertaking to maintain life.

Psychological survival requires the development of an appropriate system of defense patterns to maintain a comfortable state of psychological balance. He must learn to psychologically survive as well as physiologically.

Since he lives in a social world of interpersonal relationships he must learn to survive in the social context of his family, his relatives, his neighborhood, his community, his state, his nation and his world. He is a member of a society. He must survive in that society if he is to gain full measure of its development. Survival vulnerability is heightened by improper organization, lack of control and poor development of physiologic, psychologic and socialogic processes. When the survival integrities are not achieved physical, mental and social deviation results. The cancer victim, the penitentiary inmate, psychotic, and so on are survival failures.

A survival concept may be applied to other situational demands as well. The child who enters kindergarten is expected to survive in the world of academics. Failure to survive the customary demands for achieving competence in reading, arithmetic, spelling and writing requires removal from the mainstream of education and placement in some dependent environment such as a special class. Many of the children who seem to be surviving in the academic world are truly survival vulnerable because they have not properly achieved an academic integrity.

Patterns of behavior expressed by the individual always bear some trace of survival orientation. In the complexity of human performance, the survival orientation may be difficult to perceive, dimmed and obscured by countless social and psychological variables but always man is dedicated to his survival.

Each individual space world in the vast composite space world has its own standards for insuring vitality. Each has its criteria for success or failure. Family, school, play, job, and community worlds each contain methods for evaluating "life" in that respective world. Man must survive in many more ways than the physiologic.

He promotes and insures his survival by moving. He survives according to the competency he can bring to the world of demand. He can psychologically drown in a sea of anxieties. He can socially starve as an outcast. He can plummet into obscurity. He can lose his place in the world. He can wander aimlessly. He can thrive, succeed and advance. He can make it or not make it.

The greater the efficiency the individual brings to a given space world the greater the chances for survival. The inefficient student is academically vulnerable. The inefficient worker is vocationally vulnerable. The inefficient budgeter is economically vulnerable. The inefficient eater may become physiologically vulnerable. Inefficiency makes one vulnerable wherever and whenever it exists. Since man is a moving organism the efficiency of his movement becomes the measurement of his survival potential. The more efficient are his defense mechanisms the greater is his psychological survival potential. The more efficiently he moves in social relationships the greater is his social survival potential. The more efficiently he performs his vocational duties the greater is his vocational survival potential. His survival at any stage in life — young or old — simple or complex — is always a question of the efficiency he brings to the task.

Each individual is, by design, dedicated to the promotion of his own survival. He acts as his unique perceptions dictate to economically promote that survival. Every action or thought has "survival value" to the organism. Everything he does or says in some manner is tallied as a negative or positive contribution to his survival. The greater his physical and cognitive efficiency become the higher is his survivability. The lower his efficiency is — the more vulnerable does he become. Whatever he does has "value to him." While the values may not be readily or immediately apparent to others, each response is **valued** by the individual as a survival contribution to his own cause. Education must operate on the premise that a learner's life depends on the efficiency of his learning — for in fact it does.

Construct Three: **Movement Efficiency is derived from the information the organism is able to process from an energy surround.**

The process of birth deposits the infant into an energy filled physical world which has existed for millions of years before his arrival. With the sound of the birth cry announcing his entry he becomes a part of the vastness of the Universe. Having survived the gestational confinement he is now thrust into his next area of combat to "struggle for survival" in terrestrial space as have all of his counterparts since Man began.

The initial set of adversaries for him are the same adversaries that confronted Viking infants, Cromagnon infants, Babylonian infants—all previous and all future infants. The physical realities of the world have not changed. He is thrust into "booming, buzzing confusion." A world of radiant energy awaits him and he must progressively achieve mastery of its gradients to give form, contour and color to his world. A world of sound challenges him to define, discriminate, differentiate and localize. A world of heat and cold must be mastered to his advantage. The force of gravity will inflict many minor defeats upon him before he brings it under his muscular control.

He is surrounded by energy forms dynamically in motion. He interrupts the path of their motion with his corporeal reality. He is an absorber and assimilator of energy. The physical world is a constant. It is an ordered system of vectors. These vectors will challenge the organism for a lifetime. From the birth cry to the last gasp, these energy forms will be his constant companions. They will surround him wherever he may be. At times they will exceed his management and at other times he will eagerly seek to increase their power. Each may vary from moment to moment but they never disappear. Man must "make his living" in an energy surround. He must survive in an energy surround.

Under this constant state of bombardment from vectors of light, heat, sound, and electromagnetics the human organism is committed to a single course of action—to obtain information to economically support his survival. From this vectoral siege he must achieve an internal and external organization of interpreted data which has meaning and value to him. This organizational structure of valued information must progressively accumulate and expand in congruence with his developmental momentum projecting him irresistibly toward maturity. Therefore it is not only a question of obtaining information but rather a question of obtaining progressively more information from the same surround. His development is intended to constantly expand his information-getting process. If we could postulate an identical sustaining energy surround and allow the individual to grow in that identical surround it is expected that while the information potential of the surround remained the same, the organism would progressively process more and more of the available data as he developed.

The human organism is designed to thrive on information. Man is a constant seeker of data. His survival depends on it. It is essential to life.

Walter (1953) has referred to the brain as always "hunting" for information. He felt that the rhythms in the brain are in "perpetual quest." Thousands of potential signals are in constant exposure and these must be sorted into "patterns of significance." The brain is constantly speculative and expectant. Barnett (1958) and Glanzer (1958) described the organism as being in constant need of information to process. When there is not enough information it will actively seek it—when there is too much it will filter out what it needs. In order for the organism to remain vigilant, the nervous system would seem to require moderate traffic over its sensory channels. (Rosenblith, 1961)

This state of readiness to respond has been described by investigators in various ways. Malmo (1965) speaks of a "tonic" background as being a part of the whole physiologic activity seemingly required for sustaining a relatively even level of attention. Jasper (1958) refers to the "tonus corticale" as a background in the reticular system producing a readiness to respond. Lindsley (1958) offered the concept of **alpha excitability cycles** to account for the alternation which seems necessary to permit shifts of attention accompanying survival data. Harmon (1958) talks of a "tonus of attention." Pavlov (1927) described a "what is it? reflex" indicating bodily manifestations showing that the organism is ready to react to some portion of his environment. Other authors have talked about the Orienting Reflex. Luria and Vinogradova (1959), Razran (1961), Sokolov (1960), Maltzman and Raskin (1965).

Ever since Morruzzi and Magoun (1949) described their beliefs about the reticular activating system investigators have been increasingly busy in the study of how the organism is aroused to action. Lindsley (1958) has described three stages of alerting: (1) **general arousal** characterizing the general awakening of the organism from sleep, followed by (2) **general alerting** which transforms the organism from merely being awake to a status of attention, and finally (3) **specific alerting** which defines the alerting action toward a specific sensory stimulation.

The principle of economy is served by the design element which holds the organism in a constant state of motion and a constant state of readiness to respond, as a background phenomenon. It is a neurologic, physiologic, psychologic and cognitive background holding some form of temporality. Embedded among countless vectors of energy, forcefully impinging upon its receptor systems, the organism must have some controlling system to differentiate the survival import of this constant impact. It would be uneconomic to respond equally and with identical intensity to every energy form that entered the organism. It would also be uneconomic if a system did not have millisecond potential for response. Survival concepts dictate that the organism must be in a constant low key state of activity with readiness to alter, modify and redirect that activity as necessary. This constancy is a background of maintenance for action, however it may be labeled by different investigators. Secondly the organism must have an immediate response potential which can be activated to preserve its vitality. Lying in between the background and a survival response must be varying states of alertness. The state of alertness may be elevated or lowered by the condition of the surround. When in "dangerous territory" the alert must be greater than when moving in "benign" territory.

Energy forms enter the organism as raw data through channels of sensitivity usually referred to as senses. The next construct will discuss these channels in greater detail but for the moment we are concerned only with the fact that paths of entry are defined for energy forms. Regardless of entry point the energy forms pass along transmission lines called nerves, eventually ending in the brain where they are converted into information. Rushton (1961) stated, "Clearly the flow of information is limited not by the transmission lines but by the coding or decoding of messages transmitted."

The human organism is designed to process information. Raw data from energy forms must be translated into meaning to inform the organism of its own position and the position of everything else in the surround. To pursue a modern analogy the human organism is a computer island surrounded by an open sea of raw data constantly pounding against its shores demanding interpretation.

Wherever the focus may be, it is clear that the organism is designed to emerge victorious from the daily battle with energy vectors — not only victorious but also with the spoils of that battle — **information**. In some unknown way the brain converts light rays, vibrations, waves, clicks, impulses, temperatures, textures and the varying effects of gravitational pull into **information**. The organism does not collect information simply as though it were a data magnet, it seeks out significant information. It searches, scans and selects. The arousal value of a stimulus is not necessarily related to its intensity but rather to the significance it holds for the individual. (Fischgold, 1954 cited by Jasper, 1958). Every stimulus entering is acted upon by the brain according to the manner in which it affects the ongoing activity. (Jasper, 1958) A nerve impulse interrupts an existing dynamic state — it must be differentiated from a background in order to alert the organism to action. The net effect of an energy bombardment upon an already dynamic organism is to demand movement in response to that bombardment. The organism moves to acquire information. It maintains a vigilance in a field of constant forces. The vigilance is a rhythmic organization in the reticular formation and the cortex standing ready to step aside for significant entrants and to immediately resume its vigilance for further significants. The existing state of organization influences determination of the significance of the intrusion and once intruded the new bit must automatically influence the existing state. The excitations must always be integrated with the basic regulatory processes.

In summary, this construct defines the organism as a dynamic being capable of converting raw data from energy forces into information. The major purpose of collecting information is to economically promote its survival. The organism must therefore selectively seek pertinent data for its task.

Construct Four: **The human mechanism for transducing energy forms into information is the percepto-cognitive system.**

The human organism is stimulable and therefore responsive to the steady stream of energy forms which bombards it. Energy forms must be converted into information.

To accomplish this conversion task the human organism is equipped with six channels for carrying the data through the transduction process. These six channels are usually designated as senses of taste, touch, feeling, smell, sight, and hearing, but we view these standard incorporations from a slightly different perspective. As a unit these six senses seem to us to be more appropriately designated as **systems of sensitivity**. To call them senses as though they performed some activity other than mere transmission has attributed dynamic function of perception to a prebrain process. We are aware that the usual connotation of "senses" incorporates the perceptual process but the treatment of the senses as separate entities and perception as a separate entity has long been the practice among investigators. Investigators who have studied the senses separately or collectively have included the perceiving process in their consideration and perception researchers have generally taken the senses for granted.

We view the senses as avenues of access for information. Each sense in its mechanical organization contains some form of receiving surface or landing strip, a mechanism for transmitting the arrival to appropriate headquarters within the cortex and some form of protective device to preserve its own safety. In the eye the retina is the landing field, in the ear the cochlea, in touch the epidermal layer and so on. Remarkable as each sense may be in the complexity of its organizational structure the primary value of the senses is a service function to the brain. No interpretation takes place in the sense organs—they serve only as channels to pass stimuli along the route. Consequently, we feel more comfortable with the term **sensitivity system** to identify the sensing, the alerting, the arousing, the activating, energizing, transmitting, channeling, initiating, and collecting functions which they seem intended by design to perform. They carry stimulation to other parts of the brain. It is in the other parts of the brain that the stimuli are converted to information.

Man's movements will be directed by his perceptions. If he perceives pleasure he will advance—if he perceives danger he will retreat. His perceptions will always be related to survival in some manner. Hence we view the sensitivity system of man as a prologue or introduction to perception and the process of cognition. His perceptocognitive system is critical to his survival. Impairment to sensory mechanisms may reduce the amount of stimuli which can be carried or distort the quality of the stimuli but man's survival will be based upon the quality of information he can derive from the reduction of distortion. He must have information at all costs. If the transmission system is faulty he still derives information and acts upon that information.

By design the six channels of the percepto-cognitive system were intended to be fully operative in man toward his use in gaining the necessary information to efficiently promote his survival in an energy surround. To transform the senses into dynamic processing systems leading to perception requires a terminological change from sensory to perceptual words. Sight is the physiologic process of light gradients, lens, cornea, retina, fovea, optic nerve, striate cortex and so on operating with functional efficiency to form light into patterns for transmission to a perceiving stage. When the organism acts upon the light pattern and assigns it form, color, texture, detail, contour, edging, etc. he has converted the mechanics of sight into the dynamics of vision. Vision is the perceptual term. The constancy of this transformation of mechanical sight into dynamic vision we designate as the **visual mode** for processing information. The mechanical process of receiving and transmitting acoustic energy and arranging patterns in preparation for perception is the sense of hearing. To convert those acoustic gradients into meaningful sound the individual relies upon the perceptual procedure called audition. Hearing is the term applied to the mechanics of sound transmission while audition refers to the transduction of acoustic energy into information having value to the organism. The constancy of the audition process on a receptive and expressive level is designated as the **auditory mode**. The contraction and expansion sequence in muscles as they move has been designated as the sense of feeling but the interpretation of muscle movement into meaningful patterns of information regarding position and balance is best designated by the perceptual term, kinesthesia. Proprioception may define the mechanics of feeling but kinesthesia denotes the information process. This is defined as the **kinesthetic mode**. The sense of touch refers to the mechanical process of exciting layers of the skin and transmitting this excitation to brain centers. The perceptual product of this excitation is tactuality. The perceptual channel available for constant use is the **tactual mode**. The sense of smell is mechanically a function of bulbs and passage through an olfactory sensitivity system. Conversion to perception is olfaction and the constancy of availability is called the **olfactory mode**. The sense of taste is mechanically related to the function of buds, tubes, canals and so on but the discriminative process of obtaining information can be expanded to incorporate the total sensitivity potential in the tongue, buccal cavity, palate and the full digestive system in an incorporative perceptual term—gustation. The continuity of this perceiving process is designated as the **gustatory mode.**

The six modes—gustatory, olfactory, tactual, kinesthetic, auditory, and visual—comprise the percepto-cognitive system. These were designed as interrelated and interdependent systems temporally regulated in a sequence of development to emerge in ascending orders of efficiency. All modes are part of the action potential of the mature individual at all times. Each modality is initially manifest as a sense, with experience serving as the tool to shape it into a perceptual mode. In rank order the infant passes through an apprenticeship in each mode before advancing to the development of efficiency in the next mode.

Each of the six channels for processing information is derived from the constant experiential energy demands placed upon the individual seeking his optimal survival. Working as a harmonious unit of interrelatedness each remains available to him throughout his life, not to operate simultaneously as a single unit but rather to stand in readiness to function in whatever degree of emphasis or extent of interchange may be required to resolve each next encounter. Once organized the individual uses them as a repertoire to meet the variable demands of his daily life. When the demand is visual his visual modal efficiency determines the effectiveness of his response. When the demand is auditory he must rely upon his auditory efficiency.

In the mills of experiential emphasis each is woven into his fabric of function. If the weaving of the pattern has been guided on a loom of proper experience and emphasis for each mode in its proper time the result is an ideal efficiency with each mode functioning exactly as intended.

By design each is intended to support the next mode and to gain from the previous while continuing to advance itself. Like a repertory theater group each may be the star, a supporting player, a stage hand or a prompter. The moment by moment action of life will determine which mode must step forward to lead.

The efficiency with which each encounter is resolved will be determined by whether the intermodal efficiency of the individual is equal to the demand. In any given situation the individual must rely upon the efficiency of the percepto-cognitive system for his processing success.

In our conceptualization man employs a **cognition sequence** to discriminate, distribute, classify and organize the raw material of stimulation. The **cognition sequence** has four stages of activity. First the receiving surfaces of one or more of the six modal channels are sensitized or energized. This brings in raw material. Perception converts it into meaning. To economically record experience perceptions must be transformed into symbols as tools for sorting and classifying. To reduce the symbolic complexity concepts must be formed. This is the four stage process of cognition—sensitizing, perceiving, symbolizing and conceiving.

The dynamic cognition sequence is a constant in man. In early infancy each stage is separately developed in discrete stages which appear in clear perspective, emerging from within one another but by the time a child has reached the age of two years the cognition sequence is fully operative.

From the moment of its first operation as a sequence the course of life experiences serves to expand it by increasing the number of perceptions, symbols and concepts. This sequence is constantly operational. We may classify it as inefficient when it does not achieve expected complexity but it remains operational even if only minimal knowledge is acquired. No matter how extensive or limited an individual's knowledge may be it was acquired in this four stage process. It serves the mongoloid, disturbed, spastic, arthritic, engineer, physician, poet, artist and the linguist. It is a human characteristic. It may be more or less efficient but is nonetheless present.

The cognitive sequence is the vehicle by which man economically expands his knowledge of himself and the world in which he lives. It is designed to yield an immediate answer — even if such answer is imprecise. A threat to survival may be immediate or delayed — converting information into useful knowledge to react to threat may demand a millisecond process. The cognitive sequence is designed to meet such criteria. Whether or not it is sufficiently developed and enriched to serve man in his emergencies is determined by the net efficiency of the percepto-cognitive system.

Construct Five: **The terrain of movement is space.**

Man as a moving being expresses his survival orientation by moving. His movements from one locus to another occur in the abstract terrain of space. This is man's milieu of function — space. The first chapter in the story of survival is enacted in uterine space. All subsequent chapters in his survival text are enacted in one type of spatial surround or another. Space is everywhere. Man occupies a locus in space and all that surrounds him can be designated by some form of spatial attribute.

Space is filled with energy forms, masses called objects or bodies, and most importantly, an inferring, mobile, dynamic organism called man. Since man must move in space we can refer to space as the terrain on which man must evolve his survival strategies and develop his movement efficiency.

The natural timetable of his development is calculated to provide him with greater and greater sophistication as a space traveler.

Each infant becomes a geometrician when he begins his transport in space. He must manage the vertical to stand erect, move both sides around that vertical axis to propel himself forward, backward and to the sides and acquire an appreciation of depth.

Economy of movement is served by directional alignment. He lines himself up according to targets in his world. He centers himself for performance. He pursues his transport "head on" lining up his set of coordinates with a set of external coordinates which he imposes upon the outside world. In this manner he comes to proper alignment with his task.

He must learn to move in cognitive space as well as physical space. The same exploratory adventuring which marks his relationship to his physical world will also characterize his journey into cognitive space. He will anticipate and plan. He will scheme and plot. He will dream and be awake. He will engage in phantasy and distinguish it from the world of reality. He will ponder, contemplate, peruse, consider, probe, develop, judge, analyze, deduce, induce, and reduce. He will elaborate and expand. He will criticize and praise. His mental gymnastics from early childhood to adulthood will progressively become more complex. At times he will "jump" to a conclusion or "stumble" upon a solution. He will impulsively "swing" from idea to idea. He will be conservative or radical, patient or impatient, tolerant or intolerant, wise or foolish, naive or sophisticated. All of these will be a part of his exploration of cognitive space.

When physical space and cognitive space expand for him in a reciprocally interweaving, hand upon hand fashion as his exploring actions bring success, his physical and cognitive movements will become more and more efficient and more and more economical in the promotion of his survival.

Construct Six: **Developmental momentum provides a constant forward thrust toward maturity and demands an equilibrium to maintain direction.**

Man is designed as a forward moving organism. He can move with efficiency and certainty in the forward plane but is significantly less efficient in backward movement. This discrepancy in efficiency suggests that man was not intended to retreat but rather to push forward. The compelling force that "rushes" man through his childhood in a few short years toward an adulthood of sixty to seventy years we designate as **developmental momentum**. In the language of missiles it is a continuing thrust projecting man into a progressively more complex world of space. Momentum across space requires some technique for maintaining direction — some stabilizing and balancing mechanism. In the human design homeostasis or homeokinesis serve that purpose. This is man's technique for balancing and stabilizing the momentum so as to sustain proper course.

Developmental momentum is a continuous force extending throughout life. The cephalocaudad and proximal-distal directional principle is equally applicable in the learning of refined motor skills in adolescence and adulthood. The head-end of man gives direction throughout his life and becomes a lifelong principle for balance. Movement from a core to an extremity is a point of analysis for human motion at any age. Reciprocal interweaving is a constancy of thrusting and counter-thrusting in a bilateral organism from infancy to old age. Efficiency in movement requires the interweaving of sides.

Developmental momentum is a powerful thrusting force inevitably projected along a line from simplicity to complexity, from infancy to maturity in every system defined in the human organism. Death provides the only escape from this compelling momentum rushing the infant towards his adulthood.

Developmental momentum is a thrust of ascent. The path of the momentum is upward and onward to full maturity. When full maturity has been reached the thrust reaches its peak and the descent or decline begins. The trajectory of developmental momentum can be represented as a triangle.

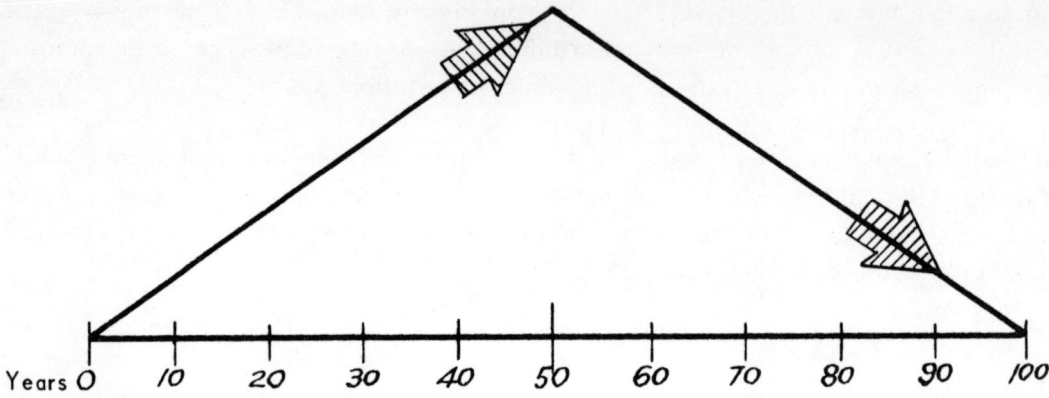

FIGURE 1   Trajectory of developmental momentum based upon a hundred year cycle.

From the point of conception enlargement, refinement, expansion and increasing complexity are the dominating characteristics of that ascent towards a peak of maturity. Once having reached the peak of maturity a gradual breakdown begins to take place eventually terminating in death. The span of life is marked by the ascent-descent arc in whatever organismic site we may choose to study. The aging process is one of decline in total organismic functioning.

Construct Seven: **Movement Efficiency is developed in a climate of stress.**

Surrounded by a constant bombardment from energy vectors, struggling against the incessant pull of gravity, aimed toward adulthood, propelled by momentum with a constant demand for balance the infant terranaut is accompanied by yet another constant companion called **stress**. He lives in a climate of stress. Each moment of life some stimulus is testing his yield tolerance. Forces are constantly attempting to model his development in a specific direction. He must yield to some forces and resist others. His tolerance level for stress must be equal to the demand placed upon him if he is to maintain an invariant true trajectory into ideal adult complexity. We may speak of two forms of stress. One may be defined as **necessary** stress referring to the establishment of required tones of tension in muscle patterns to maintain erect stance, arm and leg movement, etc. This becomes a learned process of "just right" stress or accent to be placed upon a muscle to hold position or support movement. Necessary stress must also be present to exert force to push, pull, lift and carry. There is also the consideration of necessary stress in the elimination of unessential behaviors, in holding one's attention to a goal, in forsaking tangential pleasures, in "fighting for a cause", in "keeping one's shoulder to the wheel" and in moderating an appetite. The general thought, however, is that there is a resistance set up against those stimuli which might deviate the performer from his course. Necessary stress is felt to be a positive, economizing and an efficiency laden concept and generally has not captured the particular attention of researchers.

It is the concept of **adverse** stress which in recent years has become a frequent topic in the experimental literature. Adverse stress by implication is a negative concept and likely to have some detrimental effect upon the organism. Adverse stress is always a threat to survival and places some form of demand upon the organism. It is perhaps more accurate to regard it as a by-product or the intervening differential between the capability composite of an organism and the demand for performance. If the demand exceeds the capability, stress is an inevitable component of the action. If capability is equal to demand comfort negates the possibility for stress to appear.

A great deal of research has now accumulated to suggest that each individual has a tolerance threshold for stress and that this varies according to the type of demand confronting the person.

Stress is everywhere. It appears in the form of a nagging mother, a final exam in history, a surprise quiz in biology, a sagging college gradepoint, a possible fraternity rejection, a mounting stack of bills, a slippery runway, a narrow bridge, a deadline, a request to perform in an area of inefficiency, an unfaithful husband, a court summons, an argumentative neighbor, a quota, a run for a departing bus, a pregnancy, a busy schedule — anywhere and everywhere. It is always variant according to the individual. There must be the element of threat and there must be the perception of some degree of inability to easily resolve the demand. Some individuals tolerate more stress than others. Stress does not obtain only in the "big emergencies" of life. It is a constant contender in the minor pursuits. If we continue to study the phenomenon in major proportions we will fail to see its day by day relevancy in shaping the adaptive patterning required by a dynamic organism in the minute, prosaic aspects of life.

Adverse stress may result from improper lighting on a school desk, unclear print, poorly designed chairs, auditory clutter, ambiguity, ill-fitting shoes, excess weight — anything which discomforts the individual in his attempt to achieve efficiency. Under stress an individual has but two courses of action. He may quit the task and relieve stress by escape or he may adapt and in this manner avoid one stress by inducing another more subtle stress. Shutting off the vision of one eye to avoid visual confusion is but one example of this adaptation process. The momentary relief within a series of tasks constitutes a visual adaptation which relieves a current stress but unwittingly invites another more subtle stress to dictate development. Harmon's (1958) statement that a "child grows along a line of stress to avoid a stress" captures the exact thought we are trying to convey. As an adapting dynamic organism the human terranaut will find a way to be successful but his immediate success may require him to choose a course of action which inflicts long term consequences.

Reaction to stress is always in some manner physiologic. The emergency reactor system is internal. The defense system in final analysis is internal. The penalty must be paid in physiologic coin.

Selye's (1956) comment on the "wear and tear of life" brings every human performer to the status of a battle-scarred veteran in his constant encounters with stress.

Each individual then may be considered to have a **stress threshold** which can be exceeded by a definite quotient of stress and become the "breaking point" to bring the organism to a state of panic, disorganization and helplessness. Before a stress threshold is reached there are many warning signals along the way. The spatial distance from a state of comfortable stress-resolution to the exceeding of the threshold we call the **stress tolerance** of a given individual. This space is the operational range, the degrees of freedom available, the countless positions under which the individual has some capacity for resolution. This is the range within which he can absorb, assimilate and adapt to stress and maintain his survival.

This concept of adverse stress operating as a constant in the life of every individual does not lend itself to neatly packaged units of experimental documentation. Where psychological stress has been studied, artificial laboratory situations preconceived as analogues of human experience have been used. These always leave the question open as to whether the **cognitive appraisal** of survival threat can truly be established in a population recruited to take part in an experiment located in a fine brick building which they know they will leave soon after the test.

The term **cognitive appraisal** used by Lazarus (1964) to define the discriminative judgmental or interpretative role of the perceiver in determining whether or not stress is present may be employed in this context. **The perceiver decides whether it is threatening.**

Stress may be studied in a laboratory setting by artifically contriving a stress situation or by fortuitous observations in life when emergencies arise, but whichever system has been employed there seems to have been a disregard for the concept that stress is an integral component of an energy surround and omnipresent in one form or another according to the vulnerability of each individual.

If adverse stress is a constant adversary the adaptation of the individual becomes critical. The less efficient the performer is in all areas of life the more constant will be the adverse stress as resultant of his efforts. The more efficient he becomes the more comfort will he find thereby reducing the possibility of adverse stress. While we cannot guarantee any terranaut immunization against adverse stress by insuring his movement efficiency we can at least reduce the possible incidence of detrimental effect. He must acquire his efficiency in a stress laden environment. He must constantly adapt. Setting the structures of living to ensure continuity for perception seems a significant first step. Any circumstance, event or environmental form which tends to destructure or place the organism in survival jeopardy must be analyzed and improved.

Construct Eight: **The adequacy of the feedback system is critical in the development of movement efficiency.**

In the face of constant bombardment from an energy surround containing vectors of varying intensity the organism must hold some system for equalizing the forces and maintaining some sort of balance from moment to moment. Not only must all of the outside forces be equalized but this balancing action must reciprocally interweave the internal vectors as well if the organism is to remain alert for the next threat of survival. The concept of physiologic homeostasis described by Cannon (1939) is an attempt to define this action in the organism. Cofer and Apley (1964) explained that physiological homeostasis conceives of the organism as an open biological system in contact with its external environment but maintaining relatively stable states of material and process within its own environment. Richter (1942-1943) regarded homeostasis as "one of the most universal and powerful of all behavior urges or drives." Smith (1962) prefers the term "homeokinesis" to indicate this equilibrating action placing the emphasis on the patterns of motion that take place to achieve it. The concept of a dynamic homeostasis representing not only a constant physical environment by reducing the variability and disturbing effects of the external stimulation and restoring prior equilibrium but rather as a process to establish an increasingly more complex and comprehensive equilibrium was held by Stagner (1951, 1954). Several other investigators, including Stagner, extended the concept of homeostasis into the area of psychological behavior.

Marten (1945) regards the organism as an action system receiving, organizing and distributing energy in a "patterned interaction of the personality and its environment." Freeman (1948) talked of the energetics of human behavior and believed that "all behavior is an attempt to preserve organismic integrity by homeostatic restorations of equilibrium." Psychological homeostatic disturbance as a concept in emotional disturbance has been described by Lindner (1945), Van Vorst (1947), and Rosenzweig (1955) among others. There is agreement among investigators on the general concept that the human organism must contain some equilibrating potential to hold a relatively steady state but each investigator varies the theme slightly as he presents his own interpretation.

The general concept of Cybernetics which has significantly influenced thinking about the organism in regard to equilibration exemplifies a current viewpoint on this question. Ashby (1956) has shown how the organism and its environment form an "absolute" system such that changes in one affect the other and vice versa. This reciprocal interweaving and constant reciprocating change achieve the temporary balances. The balancing must always be of temporary nature in a dynamic organism which is under a constant state of siege from its environment. The organism relies upon a monitoring system to "feedback" correcting information and maintain thereby some form of steady state.

The entire sequence of motor and sensory development in children is designed to build into the organism a feedback efficiency. The thousands of instances of inaccuracy in movement and sensing which are a normal part of the young child's experiments in motion and transport become an experience curriculum to progressively diminish the inaccuracies and replace the errors with more and more precise performance. Each move teaches a spatial lesson to the child helping him moment after moment to coordinate his muscular patterns with his sensory input.

The feedback phenomenon has intrigued many investigators during the past twenty five years. For our purposes only three citations appear to be necessary. The cybernetic model of behavior introduced by Wiener (1948) and his associates must perhaps be credited with initial focus during this period.

The work of Smith (1962) in behavioral cybernetics and Held and his colleagues (1963) are most representative of the thinking we wish to convey in building the model for Movigenics.

Held (1965) has said, ". . .only an organism that can take account of the output signals of its own musculature is in a position to detect and factor out the decorrelating effects of both moving objects and externally imposed body movement." The motor-sensory feedback loop requires an ordered arrangement of information. At any moment that the information through the looping is delayed or perturbed in some manner performance becomes imprecise. Held and Friedman (1963) stated:

> ". . .any condition that tends to disorder and decorrelate the information entailed in the relation that normally exists between motor output and contingent sensory input will increase the range of values of some constants and yield the degrading effect shown experimentally."

The significance of the motor-sensory looping in development has been noted by Held (1963) in his comment:

> "The feedback loop allows the sensorimotor system to set (as in development) and to reset (as in adaptation to rearrangement) its response characteristics as a consequence of its own past actions."

Almost all of the experimental work in the study of feedback processes has been laboratory oriented with the net result that the phenomenon tends to be regarded as some process uniquely related to the experiments instead of its rather prosaic position as an integral component of everyday living in a dynamic organism. Every individual has a feedback system. For some the informational exchange required occurs with a high degree of efficiency and they are able to maintain a directional course towards performance proficiency. For others the feedback system is less efficient and the reduction of performance errors is difficult to achieve. Some people benefit from experience in living and become more sophisticated while others seem to continue making mistake after mistake seeming to become no wiser on second and third tries than they were on the first trial.

The learner who demonstrates an increasing proficiency and complexity through time is utilizing the feedback mechanism at a high degree of efficiency while the poor learner has an inefficient feedback system. All learners err. More efficient learners improve after early errors. Inefficient learners continue to make the same kinds of errors over a period of time as though they were perpetuating their inefficiencies. A sharp learner benefits quickly from his mistakes. A dull learner is frequently unaware that an inefficient pattern has any real possibility for change.

All experimental work confirms the belief that any delay in feedback of decorrelation between the motor and sensory systems results in some degree of performance breakdown. Even though the experimental work has shown that the performer "adapts" to the variation in feedback and simply "builds a feedback correlation" necessary to adapt to the perturbation we suspect that the ease and speed with which such adaptation takes place is contingent upon the general feedback sophistication of the performer prior to the perturbation. In other words, it would seem logical that a sophisticated performer adapts more readily than a feedback-naive performer. When the developmental learning of feedback correlations is disturbed from infancy onward by cerebral palsy, neurologic impairment, congenital anomalies, sensory deprivation or emotional trauma decorrelation may be a constant interfering with the development of an adequate feedback process. The extensive experimental evidence in feedback suggests that a hypothesis of feedback perturbation being a primary agent in developmental disorder is a tenable one.

Construct Nine: **Development of Movement Efficiency occurs in segments of sequential expansion.**

Development proceeds in orderly sequential progressions. The documentation to substantiate such a statement has now become so voluminous that a state of common agreement exists.

The fundamental law of development is recorded as one of increasing differentiation and hierarchic integration. The force of developmental momentum propels the living organism along this course. Each unit of behavior, each organ of the body, each system within the structure proceeds from a simple form to a more refined and articulated form fitting itself progressively into a proper relationship with all other units in its appropriate echelon in the table of structural organization. Each unit expands to an appropriate degree of complexity, serving at one moment to support another structure and then again to serve alone. Each is dependent upon all others and each contributes to all others in some manner. The natural timetable of development insures the synchronization of complexity leveling. The hierarchy is intended by design. The hierarchy brings man to a state of performance far removed from all other creatures. The design of the hierarchy brings man to cognition, memory, invention, creativity, synthesis, conation, and the full utilization of intelligence.

This process of increasing differentiation can be defined in terms of a schematic diagram. The totality of the organism may be represented as a massive wheel composed of literally thousands of radii marking the wheel into segments of behavior. Behavior here is used to denote all developmental behaviors including the behavior of cells. This wheel has no rim, however, since by design there is truly no limit to the levels of complexity which might be achieved by man. The hub of the wheel signifies the initiation of life at its simplest level of existence. Each behavior has its simplest form which begins the cycle of development. As behavior complicates it expands to increase the range of performance and insure the progressive complexity necessary for maturity and survival. Each segment can be removed for cognitive microscopy. When removed from the matrix it would appear as diagrammed in Figure 2.

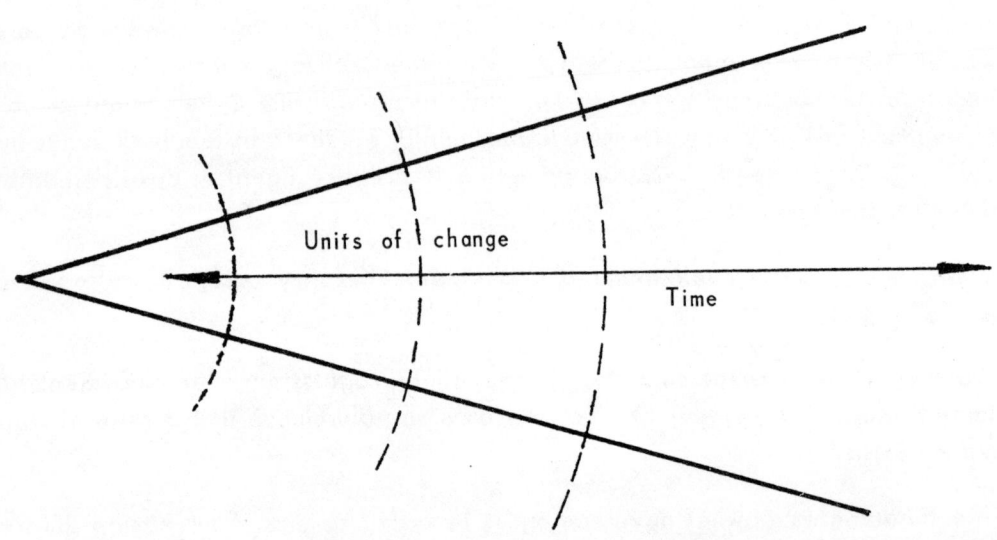

FIGURE 2   Developmental Expansion Segment.

Lines projecting into space as radii emanating from the "life hub" signify TIME through space. The circumscribed intersecting lines denote the complexity sequence for each behavior. Each increment in complexity can be described and defined as a "little bit better" than the previous stage. The intersecting lines are purposely extended beyond the radii to show that all functions are interrelated and interdependent for their advancement.

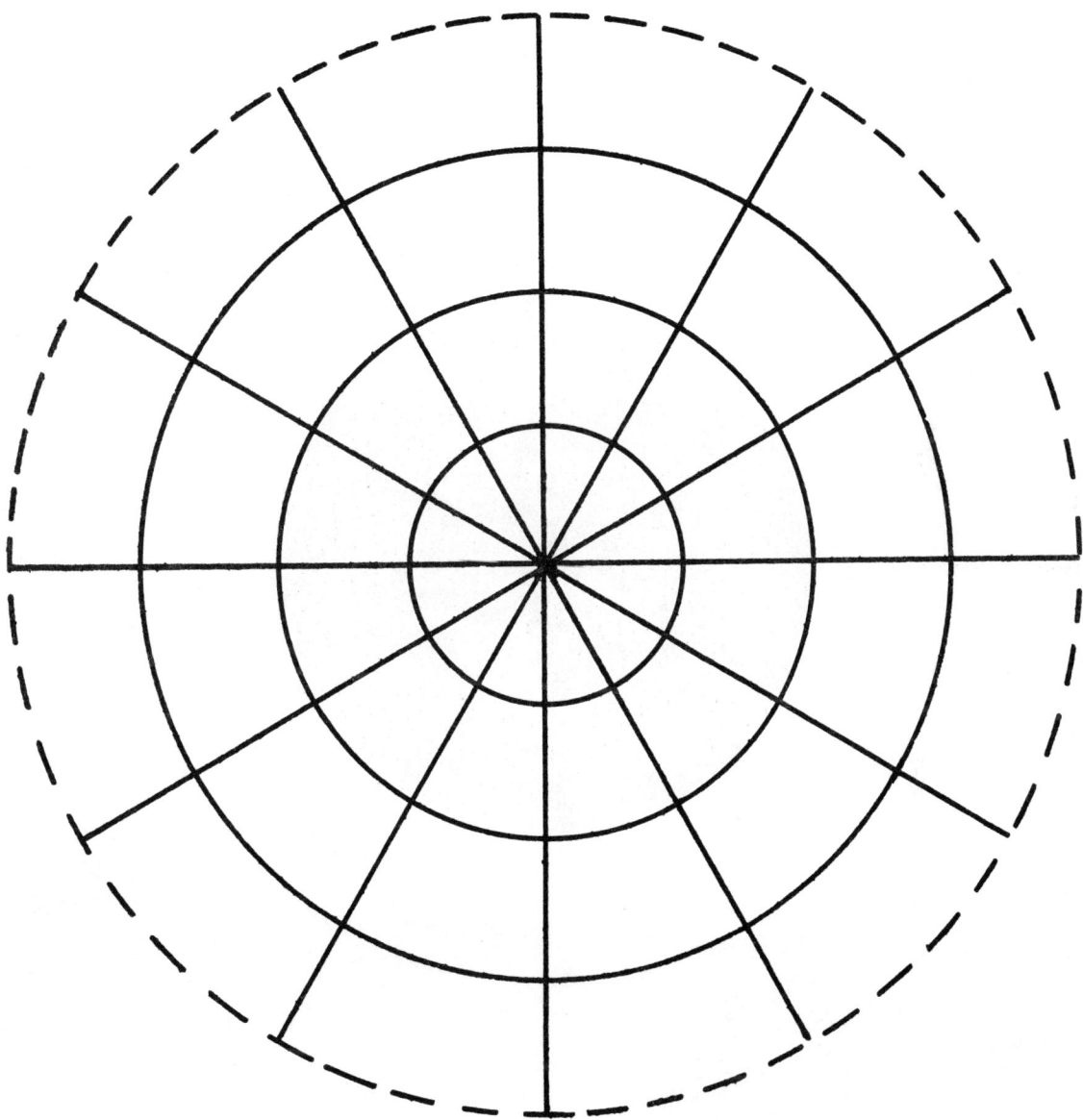

FIGURE 3   Schematic diagram of developmental expansion segments in a full life span.

The expansion not only accounts for an increase over a prior simplicity but also a widening of functional utility. As each trait or physical organ expands its functional utility the over-all range of the organism is enhanced. The range of capability expands. Finger dexterity, walking, tongue movements, visual memory, auditory discrimination, textural discrimination—any term which may be used to label the human organism can be placed on a segment of expansion and tracked through a series of changes from simple to complex function.

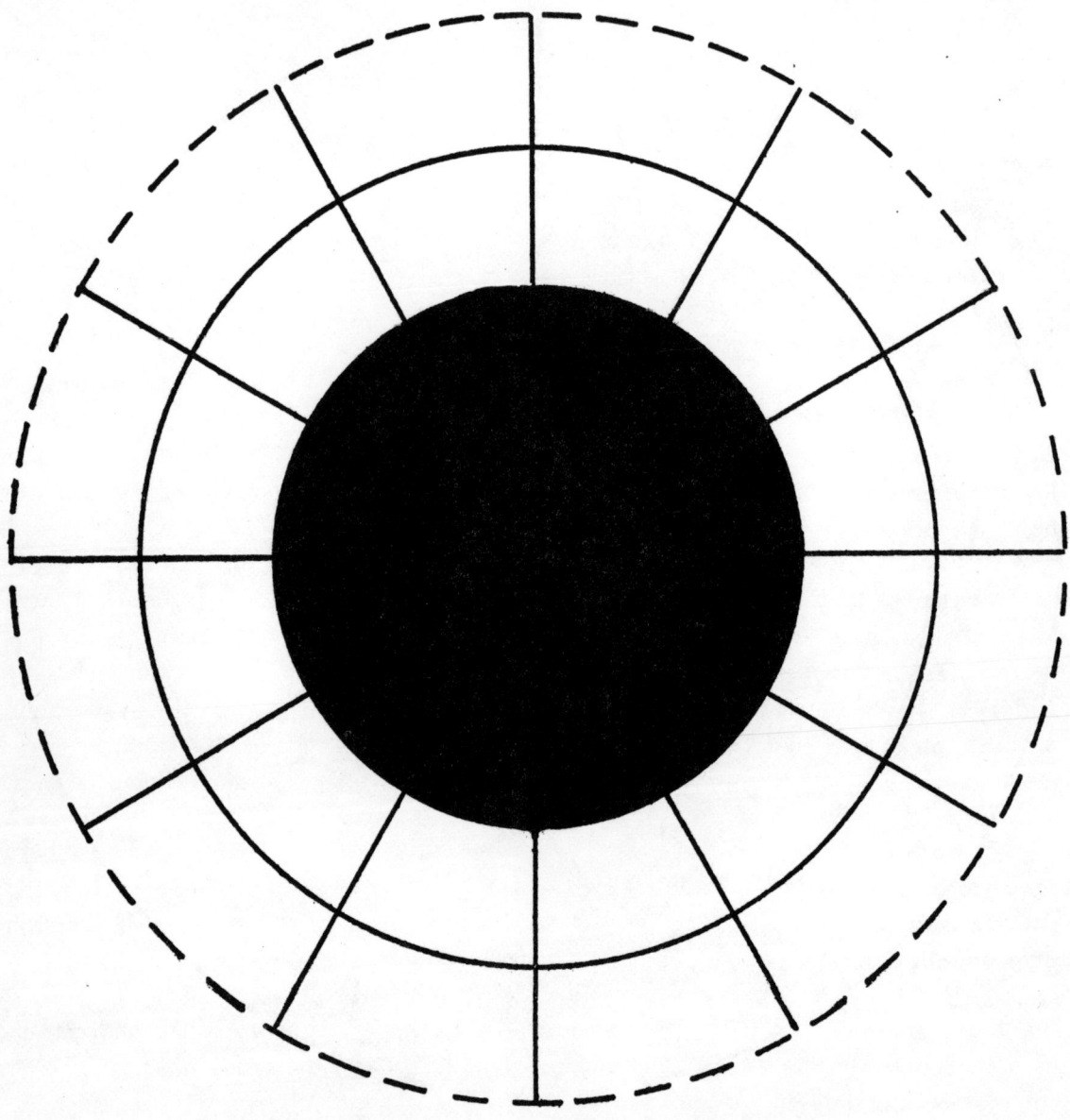

FIGURE 4   Schematic diagram of a balanced development.

The Developmental Expansion Segment is a schematic model for discussing the transport through a space continuum from simplicity to complexity, from naivete to sophistication, from birth to maturity. The number of segments which might be extracted for analysis is infinite. Every segment follows the same rules. It expands towards infinity. It is marked by intervals of increments in complexity. The intervals are concentric ripples defining all characteristics of the developing organism at a given point in time. The diagram in Figure 3 represents the full life of the organism. The number of segments are only representative—the true number is infinite.

Each concentric circle represents an interval of time. The intervals of time may be arbitrarily chosen to represent years, months, infancy-preschool-elementary-secondary-adult,—any temporal series one might care to define. As development is encircled by a time band the individual's functional achievements may be described as integrated, delayed or unintegrated. Figure 4 is an example of a development that is integrated. Each developmental space on each segment has been filled by achievement and the organism is stable and balanced for rotation and revolution.

This would signify that segments of function were proceeding properly on their course to complexity. If any segment were delayed in its transport to complexity as shown in Figure 5 the net effect of such a delay would be reflected as an imbalance in concentricity and would produce negative reverberations throughout the organism. Delay may be caused by illness, accident, deprivation, impairment, cogenital malformation, and lack of opportunity. The effect is upon the totality.

Movement Efficiency is derived from the optimal fulfillment of each segment in its sequential order. The plotting of development can be schematically defined on this model despite the difficulty of describing each human characteristic in sequential increments. The unity of the organism is maintained by concentric integrations. Simple function gives way to complex function. Every step in the sequence is both an increment over a previous existence and automatically an introduction to a subsequent step.

As each Developmental Expansion Segment fans out along its radial lines all others keep pace, on occasion biding time awaiting a signal to become emphatic—quickening pace to catch up—or taking larger steps to cover the same expansion terrain. Although differentially geared in varying segments the synchrony is maintained.

Macy and Kelly (1960) talk of a "basic progression and symmetry of life and growth in accordance with the individual's biologic time which links the many physical, chemical, metabolic and developmental processes into a functioning unit."

The history of mankind's development is re-enacted in the development of each child. The same ontogenetic principles may be traced in operation from birth to maturity in each human being and find equivalence in the developmental history of man. The progression from the primitive simplicity in adaptation of prehistoric man to the sophisticated complexity of modern man's adaptations can be charted in terms of developmental increments on an expansion segment along any continuum we might choose.

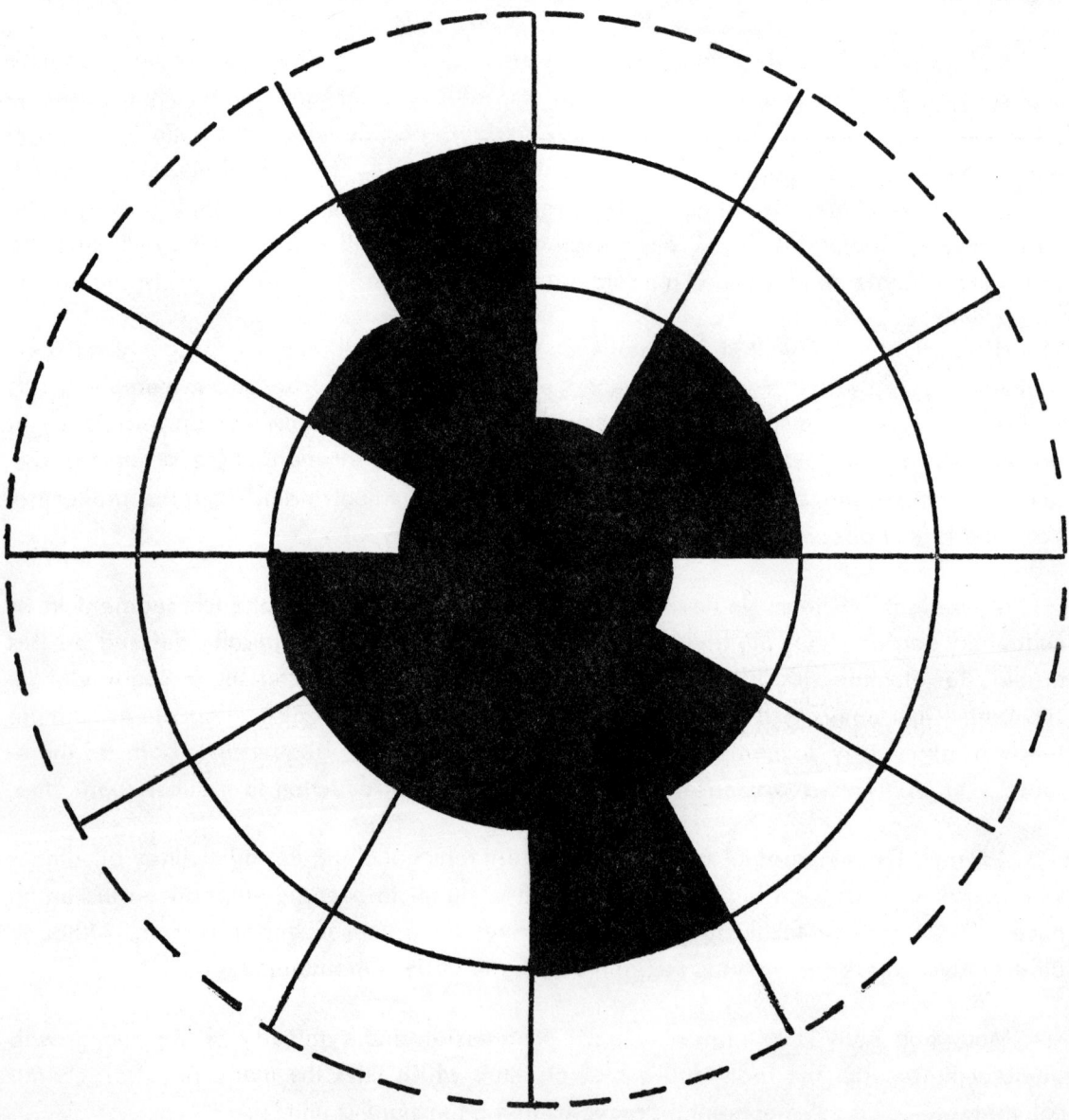

FIGURE 5   Schematic diagram of development which has vari - developed segments.

Each expansion in development occurs in a dynamic complex where many other functions are developing in simultaneity but at varying rates and degrees of complexity. Propelled by developmental momentum thrusting the total organism to convergent efficiency each function buds, matures and complicates in relationship to all other functions. No single phenomenon of development occurs in isolation. Development is continuous and temporally synchronized. The timetable was set by the Original Designer. Development has a rhythm. Development has a sequence. Each new stage or level of advancement is founded on a previous step. Each new step is an increment to the previous complexity. Each new step adds another element to the total complexity of the human organism. Each new step represents an advancement in mobility. All developmental change increases the child's equipment for dealing efficiently with movement demands. Developmental momentum carries the theme through to its finale. Throughout man's lifetime the theme of developmental momentum is repeated over and over. A variety of instruments are employed in the orchestration of life and entrusted with the main theme at different time periods in the full passage of life. While one modality carries the theme at a given moment (such as gustatory) all others faithfully enrich the theme with background readiness of counterpoint.

The achievement of Movement Efficiency becomes a matter of carefully and securely integrating each sequential interval with all other sequential intervals in a compact unity. Any problem encountered in achieving this integration is manifest as an inefficiency in Movement. Total integration is a rare finding. Some degree of inefficiency is characteristic of the human terranaut. The world of demand is too complex to manage it all without at least some minor error.

Construct Ten: **Movement Efficiency is symbolically communicated through the visual-spatial phenomenon called language.**

A mobile organism bombarded by energy forms subjected to stress, struggling for survival and seeking to develop efficiencies in its patterns of movements—must find meaning in the total surround. Millions of stimuli will be encountered day after day and week after week. Experiencing the world, one stimulus at a time, and retaining the meaning of each stimulus for its referential value to reduce errors, increase complexity and build efficiency would be a hopelessly complicated task for the developing organism. The design of the organism is directed by a principle of economy in so many other aspects that such economy must also be present in regard to accounting for multiple stimulation. A system for ordering and organizing experience into economical units is required to preserve the unity and economy of the organism's movements. This system is manifest as a representative capability in man to invent and use symbols. Man can economically represent his experience to himself and others by employing symbols.

A symbol is a form used by man to "stand for", "stand in place of" or to represent an experience, event, circumstance, happening, etc. Its employment is always governed by a principle of economy. It is a quick way of recording and expressing many multiples of stimulation at one time. Many details are incorporated into a single signal. It is a shorthand system for recalling and representing experience.

As long as the child's world is limited to oneness and each object has singularity and can be directly touched, tasted, heard, seen, smelled and moved there is no real need for symbols. His world is "too small" to require economy. Only as his world expands does the task of accounting for himself and all things around him require the use of symbols. The more complex the world becomes the more reliance must be placed upon symbols to organize that complexity with some degree of economy.

This has been man's task from the beginning of time. Each new terranaut, however, is not required to invent his own symbol system. Many generations have preceded him and have been busy devising symbols. He automatically benefits from history. The world has already been sorted out and organized by his ancestors and they have bequeathed their symbol system to those who follow. The heritage of each terranaut includes symbol usage as a vital component. In historical progression the employment of symbols has steadily increased and expanded. Each generation adds its unique experiences to the accumulation of symbols which have preceded it. The dictionary becomes thicker with each new edition.

In the timetable of development, as soon as the infant begins to move himself with independence into space and his world therefore expands rapidly he must begin to acquire words. He soon discovers that for each sight he beholds, each sound he hears, each surface he touches, and each smell that comes, somebody has been there before to give it a name. He must learn those names from his parental tutors. He discovers "nounness" or "labels" even though he will not categorize them as such until he studies grammar eight or nine years later. As **he** moves and objects move he learns the specific labels of motion and existence. He enumerates his world at first as if he were simply taking an inventory and then joins his names to motions. He is initially a walking oral telegraph talking with utmost economy and conveying his thoughts with the barest number of symbols. In the truest sense of the words he learns this set of symbols step by step. As he takes each new step in exploratory locomotion, another symbol must be learned. Progressively he learns to qualify and modify his labels by adjectives and adverbs. He gives precision to localizations by prepositional phrases.

The oral system of symbols which serves his mother and father and older brothers and sisters must also become his. He must call things by the same names, describe his desires with the same modifiers and identify motion with the same verbs if he is to receive and convey information. He will associate sounds in combination which he receives from his tutors with specific objects and will attempt to reproduce them for his own use. Because his auditory reception system and his auditory expression system are not precisely synchronized his earliest efforts at reproduction are garbled and unclear. His tongue which already serves him quite well for drinking and eating has not reached a degree of sophistication which permits for clarity of enunciation. With practice as a listener-receiver and practice as an expressor the symbol system expands and increases. That oral symbol system taught to him in the space laboratory of his immediate family is the language of his culture or his "mother tongue." He learns to speak as his parents speak. He learns to label space as they label space. Units of sound which he takes in or gives out, called phonemes, organized into a particular syntax constitute his language. He adopts an existing system. He may expand upon it in later years but the first language he learns is the language of his parents. In general this language is the same as his parents learned from their parents but because his parents have had twenty or more years of experience in a world that is somewhat different than it was 20 years ago certain changes have been introduced to account for the expansion of the world. While his native language or mother tongue bears the same general characteristics of the symbol system used by his ancestral lineage — it is not identical. As man has become more sophisticated in his understanding of his Universe labels or symbols have had to be invented to account for these new understandings which were not a part of the experience of previous generations. Languages develop as man develops. Each new terranaut comes to his native tongue at a particular moment in the timetable of that language's development. He is expected not only to learn the language as it is currently employed but expected to add to it from his own experience. Initially, however, his task is to simply acquire a basic set of symbols to economically order his experience in a limited spatial surround. He needs as much language as he has experience as an explorer. The greater his range of exploration the more does he need an enlarged reservoir of symbols upon which to draw. He quickly learns that his symbol system is useful to him in obtaining services from people, in defining his wants and expressing his pleasures and dislikes. The symbol system has utility. He obtains and conveys information by using symbols. He organizes space by using symbols and designates his own relationship to that space with symbols. He shares experiences in a social world in interpersonal relationships and shares the symbol system to express that union. He communicates his spatial experience to others and they communicate their experiences to him. He speaks a language. It is a language of movement in space.

Everywhere in his surround he will be confronted with symbols which are intended to convey information. Miniatures will symbolize full sized objects, insignias and emblems will signify units and products, streaks of paint on a convas will signify man's search for tranquility, a new leaf will symbolize spring and a snow shovel will symbolize winter. Many of these symbols he will readily identify and many will never become a part of his symbolic background. He may learn to "read" music note by note but there are many who will never incorporate that particular symbol system into their composite body of symbols. The symbols of mathematics and the symbols of chemistry

The world of tools and wagons is a major spatial terrain to be explored by the young traveler in his quest for competency.

will convey vital and detailed information to some and not to others. The size and the richness of his symbol system will depend upon his experience. If his explorations have been limited his symbol composite will be limited. As he moves in space he catalogues and accounts for his experience.

Theoretically every word in the dictionary is available to man for his use to communicate with others. All these words are available to be organized into expressions, oral or written. Some men combine these words into classics of poetry and fiction — literary pieces to incite man to action, sadden man, terrorize him, exhilarate him and inspire him. Others have difficulty conveying an organized thought in coherent syntax. The same words are available to all. Some use them wisely — some do not. Some have many, many words to call upon — some have very few. The size of a symbol system is a reasonably reliable indicator of the size of an experience background.

As man moves to act he symbolizes his actions to economically record his experience. His language reflects his efficiency in movement. The concept of language as a visual-spatial phenomenon has been previously discussed. (Barsch 1965)

Language may be classified as efficient or inefficient. It may be classified as having or not having movement efficiency. Just as we currently accept the premise that the entire construction of astronautics requires a vocabulary unique to such experience to represent travel in "outer space" the language of the terranaut must be viewed as a special vocabulary to represent spatial proficiency for the earth-bound traveler.

The designed course of human development is initially activated as a basic training ground of extensive movement and limited cognitive efficiency. Progressively the situation is reversed. As the individual matures he moves less and achieves more on a cognitive level. What once during his early childhood could only be known by active touch or physical movement eventually can be appreciated within the graphic symbols on the printed page. Sitting in his armchair the individual can have visual, auditory, tactual, kinesthetic, olfactory and gustatory perceptual experiences on a vicarious basis from the visualizations he is able to attribute to the printed page.

The story of development is initially written in gross movement terms but progressively switches its emphasis to the cognitive level. As thought processes mature there is less need for physical movement.

Symbolic fluency thus becomes the ultimate criterion of Movement Efficiency. It is the final synthesizer of the previous nine constructs of Movigenics. Symbolic man expresses the uniqueness of his intelligence with economic representational signs. He acquires it under the tutelage of parents, advances it in the formality of school, and expands it in his adult civic-economic and social world. Symbolic fluency relies upon movement for its development. It is simultaneously a contribution to Movement Efficiency and a reflection of it. It is modern man's most powerful weapon against ignorance. It is the singular expression of his unique design.

These ten constructs constitute the foundation stones of **Movigenics**. There may be additional constructs which wiser minds could add or retrospective critical evaluation will eventually suggest for inclusion. For the moment, however, we have settled upon these ten.

Man is intended to achieve Movement Efficiency. He is designed to contend with an energy surround and seek and find information therein to economically promote his survival. Propelled by developmental momentum irresistibly toward maturity he relies upon his percepto-cognitive system to devise his adaptations. He learns as his feedback system serves him efficiently to adapt in a climate of adverse stress. He utilizes symbols to define his spatial experience. He follows an orderly sequential progression of expansion from spatial naivete to spatial sophistication. He is dynamic, adapting and bilaterally equating. He is an open energy mechanism composed of multistable systems which rely upon one another for balance and integration. Above all, he is a space oriented being. His terrestrial destination is maturity. He may travel toward his destination with efficiency or inefficiency and reach his goal comfortably or uncomfortably. He must learn to travel efficiently for optimal comfort. Finding methods to ensure his transportation comfort must be the dedicated purpose of those who are interested in his safety and welfare.

3

THE

CONCEPT

OF

SPACE

The development of a curriculum based upon a space premise must be initiated with a definition of SPACE. Although the word is commonly used and is accepted in the construction of a variety of psychological tests as the goal of the test, the definition of space is rarely undertaken in the educational and psychological literature. If it is intended as the basic unit of consideration it must be defined, analyzed, diagrammed, molarized and molecularized.

The dictionary states that space is "the unlimited or indefinitely great general receptacle of things commonly conceived as an expanse extending in all directions (or having three dimensions) in which, or occupying portions of which, all material objects are located." While this language defines the word it does not convey the dynamic concept of one of those "material objects"—MAN—engaged in a survival effort in that "great general receptacle". It is the definition of that "receptacle" as an inescapable ever-present surround which led Fuller (1966) to describe the earth as a massive space "capsule". In answer to the question which at one time or another has crossed everyone's mind concerning what it must "feel like" to be **soaring** in orbit Fuller said:

> "...What does it feel like—you are and always have been on a very small spaceship eight thousand miles in diameter. The nearest star SUN is ninety two million miles away and the next brightest Rigil Kentaurus is not even there. You are very much alone in your spaceship. And this spaceship is designed so superbly, all its passengers so skillfully provided for, that they have been on board playing the game of self-reproduction for two million years without even realizing that they are on board a spaceship."

According to Fuller's view the "great general receptacle" is actually a "space capsule" among other capsules in the universe. In universal perspective the notion of the earth as a spaceship is an interesting analogue.

The human organism, as we have come to understand it up to this century is an earth bound being and as such must contend with terrestrial forces and terra-space. It is the space within Fuller's space-capsule that must hold our attention.

As men have historically contemplated their Universe and their place within that universe a conceptualization of space has always been derived. The "great general receptacle" has held a variety of boundaries for contemplative man according to this time in history and his particular locus on the globe. In some manner man has always found a method for defining space.

When contemplative man set himself to the task of defining space in metric terms, geometry was originated. The geometric model for computing space is based on the premise that space exists in all directions and is everywhere constituted alike. To diagram that premise a system of ordinates operating as axes and joined at a fusional point became the first metric conception of space.

The simplest point in space is a dot. When that simple point in space **moves** in any direction a line is created and a second dimension occurs. The movement of a line creates a plane and the movement of the plane defines the third dimension. It is movement in space that produces dimensionality. Within terra-space the human learner can be thought of as a simple point in space. As he moves he creates lines, planes and dimensions.

'"Progressive motion and the possibility of orientation in any direction cause space to be regarded as identical in all places and all directions" according to Mach (1906). Space is defined dimensionally by movement. While the geometry of space may be regarded as fixed the unique dynamics of the individual traveler moving within geo-space cause space to be fashioned and constructed in a highly individualized manner.

We may consider two levels of abstraction in the study of space. One level refers to the "great general receptacle" as a global generic construct, an abstract volume-surround common to all men. Every man from the beginning of time, regardless of culture, primitive or civilized, eastern or western has been deposited in that volume surround. The Cro-magnon infant, the children of ancient Greece, the sons of the Vikings, and the sons of the astronauts — all children of all time — learned geometry on a dynamic personal "life" basis because of a common heritage of the volume surround.

The second level of abstraction is a measurable and scalable construct referring to space as the "inbetweenness" of two points. It is this level which must occupy our analytic attention.

Man is but one object in a world of objects of infinite variety and number. He is a point in space dynamically moving in a linear relationship to all other objects located on his particular segment of the terrain. General and specific space are simultaneously to be managed.

Being a dynamic point in space his mobility enables him to create a plane, move a plane and form a personal tridimensional world. If we are to measure the efficiency of his tridimensional construction we must begin with a referrent. His own body serves as his unique referrent for computing space and his relationship to it.

Every infant is a budding geometer busily occupied with the incorporation of the axes of coordination as his personal model for metric reference. His geometric identification is not a matter of choice. It is his human obligation to become a computer of space.

To provide a working model of spatial computation an operational definition of space can be adopted to guide the explication of the life challenge of the learner. Space is an **abstraction derived from the relative intervals between and among objects requiring always a referrent and a terminal point.**

The original and sustaining referrent for all spatial computation by the mobile organism is his own unique corporate image. The security of that referrent is therefore critical to his computational efficiency. The human infant is a primitive being. Not yet equipped with the enrichment of symbolic functioning he must operate within the limited scheme available to him as he struggles for spatial sophistication. His progress from naivete to sophistication in symbolic spatial abstractions constitutes the principal occupation of his existence.

For the infant internal and external space are one. Together these constitute what Werner (1948) referred to as "primordial space". There is no separation of his corporate structure from otherness. All is one. It is the primitive space of survival. His heritage of mobility forces a separation and a space of otherness becomes a constructional obligation. Space becomes meaningful to him only in terms of his own movements. As he moves he fashions **his** model. He builds it and sets its boundaries in a succession of moves.

Because it is **his space** and he is constructing his model there are often occasions in which he cannot recognize it because someone has introduced a minor modification. If he cannot follow his own blueprint of familiar successive moves an event or circumstance may appear foreign to him. Parents everywhere are well aware of the young child's insistence upon "following the same steps" while he is in the early stages of spatial construction. A familiar succession of movements is a basic criteria for spatial comfort at all ages. Change is always initially discomfiting. At any point in life the adaptation to change is related to the performer's spatial sophistication. Only as the repertory of successive movements multiplies in a magnitude of complexity offering a countless set of possibilities does "primordial" space give way to a sophisticated appreciation of otherness.

Space is always a place of action, concrete and egocentric for the naieve performer. It is the naievete of the performer which determines the egocentricity of space. This thought must be kept in mind in evaluating the efficiency of the learner. As sophistication occurs space expands. The spatial terrain becomes filled with more and more terminal points. Space moves from in to out in expanding ripples of sophistication as the mover becomes more efficient.

Initially the child must construct a geometric model and finally achieve a cognitive appreciation of computing those abstractions which will allow him to move thought into adaptive patterning.

His mobility becomes the constructional raw material for increasing sophistication. Three distinctive territories of movements can be defined to analyze the dynamics of the constructional process. Space is composed of domains, fields and zones. Each of these territories constitute a developmental imperative. The challenge is always the same — to achieve grace, comfort, ease and efficiency of movement in each territory.

Domains of Space

The conception of space cannot be limited to the study of physical terrestrial realities but must be broadened to include a number of other spatial parameters. Other constructional units deserve position in the model.

The designation of the human physiologic system as a spatial domain dates back more than a century to the work of Bernhard (Macy and Kelly 1960) who first described the **milieu interior**, the internal environment composed of millions of cells bathed by fluids. Neuroanatomists, physiologists and biochemists have been the principal explorers of physiologic space. Countless researchers during the past quarter century have produced a careful mapping of that internal terrain. The development of physiologic space has been termed "invisible growth" resulting from a sequence of biochemical and physiologic adjustments involving integrated chemical, metabolic and functional reactions. (Macy and Kelly 1960) Variations in that internal space have been reported to be disturbing to mental activity, logical thinking and the ability to concentrate by Barcroft (1934). Macy and Kelly (1960) commented that normal physiologic and intellectual development can only be expected in an organism that could preserve constant conditions of vitality in the internal environment. Duffy (1932) conducted a comprehensive review of studies pertaining to the relationship between physiological activity and the efficiency of performance and came to the general conclusion that the quality of performance is best when physiological activity is neither too high or too low but is at some optimal level for the task. These are but a few of the citations which might be offered to support the general notion that performance efficiency is dependent upon the general status of the internal environment. There are many other reports along the same general line (Hovland and Riesen 1940, Lazarus, Speisman and Mordkoff 1963, Schnore 1959 and Malmo 1959). Our concern here is to simply establish the concept that the development of efficiency of function in the domain of physiologic space is another parameter of consideration which must be taken into account in the study of the concept of movement in space.

It is our belief that the state of organization which the individual achieves in physiologic space has significant bearing on his attainment of efficiency on the physical terrain of readily observable performance. A more detailed discussion on this point will be included in a subsequent volume.

The second domain is the traditional and customary territory of **physical space**. This is the world of objects and events which appear in a never-ending stream of bombardment in the energy surround. Energy vectors traveling at varying rates of speed converge upon the traveler demanding transduction into meaningful information. There is an "everythingness" and an "everywhereness" in physical space. Everywhere is variation. Everywhere is form. Everywhere is substance. Everywhere is distance. Everywhere is direction. This is the true space of geometry. Metric systems are readily applicable. This concept will also be expanded upon in a subsequent discussion but is introduced here to complete this piece of the space model.

Milieu space is the third domain over which the young traveler must exercise some control to promote his optimal survival. Much of the psychological literature of the past fifty years which has dwelt upon the general concept of "role" as well as the extensive work of Lewin on the concept of "life space" can be subsumed under our concept of **milieu space**. It is a space of social identification. Each milieu defines a pattern of spatial living, a code of behavior and an achievement expectancy. At any given moment it is possible to define an individual's position in one or more milieu. He must abide by the rules of that milieu if he is to travel in comfort and ease within that particular context. There are terrains of social identification which are marked by temporal characteristics or behavioral models. Infancy, adolescence, adulthood, apprenticeships, interneships, imprisonments, athletics, engagements and fraternities are but a few examples of the terrains which come under the headings of milieu space. Again the important point to be made here is the extension of the constructional model of space to another parameter of consideration. In each milieu there is a demand for a particular set of movement patterns to insure the individual's comfortable and efficient transport on that respective terrain. It is another part of the puzzle of space.

Man reaches the fulfillment of his human design as he travels in **cognitive space**. This is the terrain of symbols, thoughts, ideas and conceptualizations. It is the territory of reading, writing, arithmetic, spelling and drawing. It is the domain in which self-concept, self-realization, self-actualization, personal image and the ego are formed.

It is the territorial imperative of the intellect. It is the locus of the "assumption world" of Ames (1951), Cantril (1948) and Ittelson (1951), the "hypothetic world" of Bruner (1950), the "dissonance and consonance" of Festinger (1962), the "core and context" of Titchener (1909), the "gestalten" of Koffka (1935), and the "cell assembly and phase sequence" of Hebb (1949). It is the domain for the cognitive structuring and styling which Gardner (1964) is studying and it is the area which Piaget (1937) has so painstakingly observed and recorded.

Cognitive space must be organized and developed. Experience becomes the critical tool in shaping this terrain to the advantage of the learner. As he explores the young child "comes to know." For the infant cognitive space is an uncharted, unexplored wide-open terrain. Symbols are the transport vehicles for travel in cognitive space.

These four domains of space must be regarded as interrelated and interdependent and should not be thought of as time-separated in any manner. All four are energized at conception but their substance emerges in more finite terms throughout development.

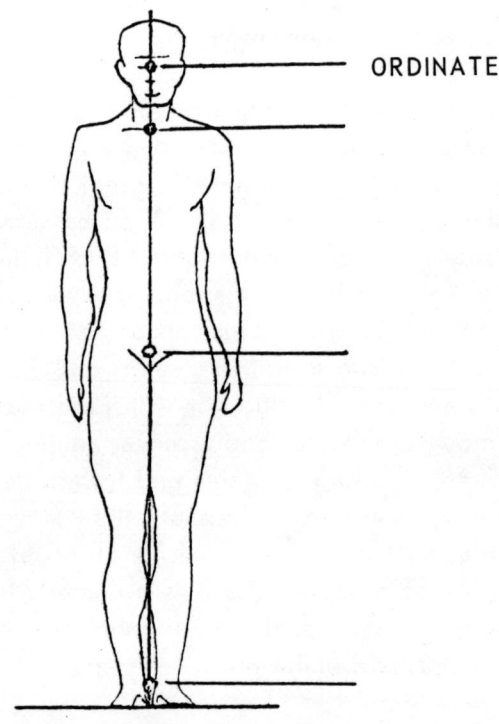

FIGURE 6

Presentation of the principal ordinates of vertical and horizontal space. (Based on a drawing which appeared in D.B. Harmon and G.N. Getman, PROPER CHALKBOARDS PROPERLY USED. Pamphlet of Weber - Costello Co. Chicago, Illinois.

They are each domains to be organized and maintained at a high level of efficiency to promote the highest possible achievement of the individual. Limitations in any of the four will have a reverberating effect upon the others and decrease the individual's efficiency in space.

Fields of Space

The coordinate system of the organism serves as the basic referrent for defining the division of space into six fields. In Figure 6 a vertical coordinate and a set of significant horizontal coordinates have been imposed upon a schematic drawing to illustrate the basic reference system.

The vertical ordinate divides Space into RIGHT and LEFT fields. The schematic drawing in Figure 6 illustrates the division for FRONT and BACK space. Any movement of the body behind that line is considered to occur in BACK space and any movement forward of the line is classified as a FRONT space movement. The line starts within the body and must be considered as extending laterally towards infinity on both sides of the midline.

The divisional organization of UP and DOWN space is also depicted in Figure 7. The dividing line is the natural line of sight when the body is at rest in the erect position. The line extends forward at a downward angle to a point in space approximately six meters ahead of the individual. Any stimulus occurring above that oblique line is considered to be in UP space while those occurring below the line are classified as being in DOWN space.

This spatial orientation scheme is embedded in the organism and projected outward as the individual moves himself in space. Wherever the individual may be and however he may be moving the coordinate system exists as a constant. The designations are a part of the organism and are not be be thought of as being fixed in space. They are always relative to the position of the individual. The projection of these coordinates onto space is a dynamic abstraction but it occurs as if the mover were projecting beams of light upon space to divide it into convenient segments for the purpose of his own orientation.

Theoretically the unimpaired individual is able to project a completely equated set of coordinates out into space and function with equal efficiency on all planes and in all segments of space to promote his optimal survival. Unfortunately, few individuals arrive at maturity with the theoretical efficiency in all planes.

The task of the traveler, however, is to seek efficiency of performance in each of the six fields. From infancy onward the performer must learn to locate objects, events and happenings in those respective fields. He must identify, differentiate and discriminate fields of experience and move in response to those experiences. From the perspective of survival it is reasonable to believe that the traveler must hold some degree of efficiency in responding to threat from **all** segments of his surround. Anything less than global efficiency renders him vulnerable from a survival standpoint. If danger threatens from LEFT-BACK-DOWN space and he computes information inefficiently from

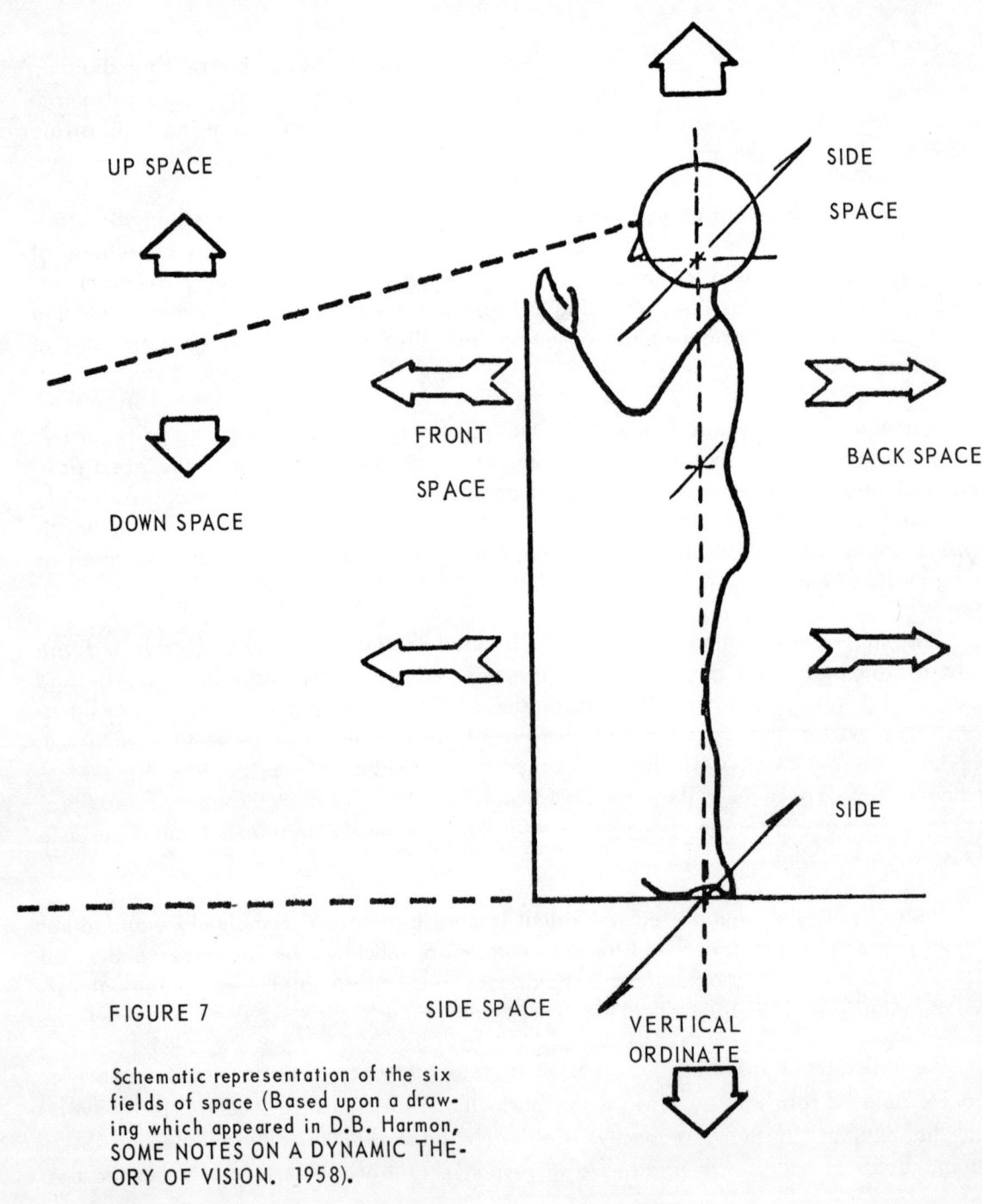

FIGURE 7

Schematic representation of the six fields of space (Based upon a drawing which appeared in D.B. Harmon, SOME NOTES ON A DYNAMIC THEORY OF VISION. 1958).

that field he will experience a reduction in potential to marshal an adequate response. Regarding the fields simply as territories laden with information it is imperative that the performer acquire an efficiency as a processor of information in order to expand and enlarge his store of knowledge about his world and its particular relationship to him.

The fields of space are geometric and based upon the concept of ordinates. As such they tend to be classified as a set of physical sites. For the full understanding of the dynamic construction of space which occupies the developing traveler these same fields must be given the dual perspective of cognitive operations as well as physical. At a cognitive level BACK space may be regarded as memory, FRONT space as the site of planning, projection and assumption, LEFT-RIGHT space as the territory of conviction, bias, prejudice, opinion and so on.

A tridimensional being operating in a tridimensional world is in the constant action of centering himself upon his task and holding some form of alignment in the face of a stimulation bombardment. The use of the six fields of space serves as a system for the assessment of the relative efficiencies and inefficiencies of the performer in an information laden world of happenings. The scheme of fields may be used to ascertain areas of weakness and strength in the ease of information processing. They can be used to critically evaluate the success of the effort to master the variants in the world.

Zones of Space

Space is always relative. The relatedness between a point of reference and a point of termination determines the spatial measure at any given moment. The change of position of either the referrent point or the terminal point will vary the measure. It is the referrent point, however, which is the primary and critical factor in the definition of space.

Space contains objects which have fixed positions and others which move. Since the human performer holds no fixed position in space "inbetweeness" becomes a constant variant. When man moves and objects move there is a constantly changing relationship in space unless the movements of both are temporally organized to preserve the distance.

The relativity of space must be symbolized by man as he moves in an object world in order to establish an economic system for judging the survival threat of any single object. The space closest to the performer holds the highest density of survival import. The greater the distance between man and danger the more deliberate and careful can be his defensive maneuvering.

From an ontogenetic viewpoint the spatial sophistication of the human infant becomes a matter of extending the distance between himself and the world of objects. Space develops first within his own circumference bounded by the length and reach of his own body. The boundaries of his own body determine the first and primary zone of operation in space. The extension of his spatial operation to distances farther and farther away from his own body referrent can be schematically defined as four zones of space.

The **near-space zone** can be diagrammed as a boundary extending two feet away from the corporate midline in all directions. This is the distance of reach, grasp and release and the performance area for manipulation. It is the distance of most school tasks, factory work, design and so on. It is the eating, dressing, reading and writing space. It is the zone of physical function and physical defense. It is also the zone for minute detail inspection. It is the basic zone of performance. It is close, immediate and primitively related to survival.

Developmental momentum propels the organism forward demanding that near space become organized to the highest possible level of efficiency in preparation for movement into distance zones extending beyond the body periphery. The second zone is classified as **mid-space**.

On a physical space measurement mid-space is considered to be a distance extending from two to sixteen feet in all directions. It approximates a general boundary within the spatial surround that can easily be managed by a few steps in any direction. Mid-space requires location or projection from the referrent but it also allows for immediate access to near-space. It is the zone in which the learner may venture into extension without fully deserting a primary base of near support.

The third zone of space has been designated as **far-space** and is measured as a distance of 17-30 feet. At a physical level of measurement this metric range was derived from the natural line of vision extending from the gravitational line to a point in space some twenty feet distant from the erect individual. A commitment to move into far-space takes the performer a considerable distance from a base of operation and requires a security and freedom which permits function without recourse to a base. It is a zone of extension.

Remote-space is the fourth zone of space and includes any distance beyond thirty feet extending into infinity. This zone lacks clarity and distinctiveness. Details are not sharply defined and global masses tend to serve as a general outline for differentiation. Remote-space is the terrain of perspective. It is the space of landscape, farmland, sky, horizon, "down the road", "in the next block", "next week", "when the time comes" and so on. It is the space of the neighborhood, community, the state, region and the nation. The absence of detail forces reliance upon generalities rather than specifics.

Once again it must be emphasized that the human learner is a cognitive processor of space and while metrics may be employed on a physical level to define zones of space there is always a cognitive counter-part to the model. From this standpoint each of the zones can be viewed as cognitive as well as physical.

Remote-space is the territory where goals reside, objectives exist, ambitions are pointed, efforts are directed and promises are kept. It is the distant past and the tomorrow of the future. Near-space is the immediate zone of detail, the here and now of thought, the reality of the moment and the "security blanket" of the performer. Midspace is the cognitive zone of compromise and mediation. It is a space for the unification of the security of the near, comfortable and familiar with the daring, questionable and possibly ambiguous urgings of far-space. **Far-space** is the cognitive zone of "what could be." It is more detailed than remote-space but often too far distant from near-space to be reality-oriented. It is a zone of planning for future achievement with sufficient relationship to **mid-near** zones to offer some potential for successful closure.

The natural developmental pattern sets a timetable of organization for each child to practice and develop some degree of competency in each of the four zones in successive order. By the time a child reaches the period of academics he has experienced all four zones and achieved some degree of efficiency in each one. The optimum in zonal efficiency calls for the individual to move freely within, between and among all zones with a high degree of efficiency. It is very likely however, that optimal efficiency is rarely achieved and the typical course of events is for each traveler to develop some form of hierarchy in the organization of the four zones.

A Spatial Perspective on Behavior

The definition of space as an "inbetweeness" and use of the corporate referrent as a model for construction of spatial efficiency is basic to the study of movement. The conceptualization of the domains, fields and zones of space as dynamic terrains upon which the mobile organism establishes his integrity for survival sketches in form and substance to the SPACE model.

A SPACE model for behavior permits one consistent frame of reference for studying the dynamics of human performance at any age, at any degree of illness or pathology, and in any circumstance. The entire body of knowledge which pertains to emotional behavior among human beings may be looked upon as a spatial terrain of repression, rejection, sublimation, defenses, sites of consciousness, introversion, extroversion and balance. The emotions of man may be charted in space terminology. The movement of children from the security of maternal space into the world of independent behavior may also be conceived as a spatial phenomenon. The learner's movements among peoples in his world and his social status at any given moment may be thought of as **sociologic** space. The historical study of culture patterns and the shifts within those patterns occasioned by new technology may be construed as **cultural** space. **Academic** space defines the terrain where the formal exercises of reading, writing and arithmetic take place.

The SPACE model continues to fit wherever it is tried on. Space is everywhere. The behavior of the organism is always spatial in some manner. The metrics of domain, fields and zones serve merely to organize a system for charting the efficiency of the traveler. Attention must next be turned to the components within the corporate structure of the individual which make specific contributions to the achievement of the movement efficiency of the terrestrial learner.

Components of Movement Efficiency

Three different groups of components have been defined as constituent parts of the composite entity which we have labeled Movement Efficiency. One cluster of components is related to the basic problem of moving in an energy surround and represents fundamental units required of a dynamic mobile organism.

Each learner must acquire sufficient MUSCULAR STRENGTH to support an erect pattern of movement in a gravitational field. Movement of muscles to support motion demands both static and DYNAMIC BALANCE. Strength and balance in patterns of motion give the mover BODY AWARENESS. Existence and movement in a tridimensional world requires SPATIAL AWARENESS. If movement is to be forceful, balanced, controlled and directed some degree of TEMPORAL AWARENESS will be necessary to synchronize such movement to the survival advantage of the individual. These five components are necessary for efficient transport and for building a posture.

We have assigned the classification of POSTURAL-TRANSPORT ORIENTATIONS to these five components because we hold them to be critical to the organization of motion. These five are fundamental to movement and set the foundation for all future motion. If each component is efficiently developed and contributes to the development of subsequent components in the developmental timetable the supporting foundation for comfortable and economic transport is assured.

Man moves to acquire information. Another cluster of components is therefore designated to represent that aspect of man's make-up. The information-getting modes, Gustatory, Olfactory, Tactual, Kinesthesia, Auditory and Visual have been grouped together as PERCEPTO-COGNITIVE MODES. These modes provide the channels from which the traveler derives information to organize his movements, direct his actions, control his behavior and attribute meaning to his surround. The PERCEPTO-COGNITIVE MODES are designed to implement the organization of the POSTURAL-TRANSPORT ORIENTATIONS by adding meaning to movement. The modes provide purposes, goals, objec-

A fine example of a right tilt in the drawing of a second grade child who has prolonged the vertical orientation in preference to the horizontal.

An example of a child who finds comfort in the vertical orientation and "ventures" in the horizontal with the smoke line.

Another second grade child whose drawing demonstrates not only the obvious problem with window placement but also a spatial problem with tilt variations in the vertical plane and in the horizontal plane.

A nine year old second grade boy reflects a number of spatial problems in his drawing of a house. Distinctive tilts in orientation are present in both the left and right fields. Window placement is distorted and there is evidence of a spatial problem in "down" space.

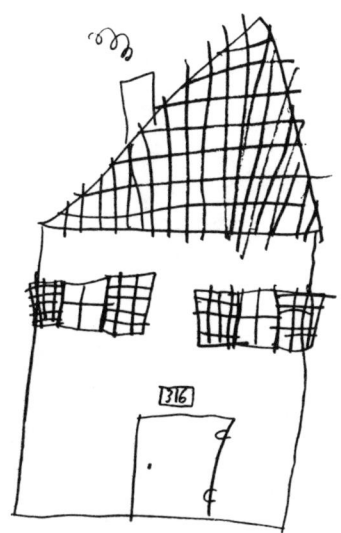

Spatial boundaries present a problem even when they are established as a part of one's own design. This fourth grade child shows the subtle signs of a spatial dilemma.

A seven year old child with a dominantly vertical orientation to his drawing who also gives evidence of visually shifting from left to right vertical planes in the tilt of his forms.

tives and definition for mobile man. They become the fashioning and modeling tools for shaping the POSTURAL-TRANSPORT ORIENTATIONS.

Finally we hold that four additional components may be identified to permit man to occupy the pinnacle of Creation. We have labeled this last cluster as DEGREES OF FREEDOM.

Under DEGREES OF FREEDOM we include the components of **bilaterality, rhythm, flexibility** and **motor planning**. These are designed to enhance and enrich the learner's performance and enable him to achieve range, amplitude and broadness within his behavior. They provide him with alternatives. They permit him to adapt. In final analysis they determine the epitome of man's performance—as a planning, critical, evaluating, executing and revising being.

These fifteen components have been selected on an a priori basis. They have not been derived from a statistical procedure of factor analysis but have emerged from an evaluation of cross-discipline literature. Common terms which have long been associated with defining the makeup of the human being may appear to have been ignored. It is a case of subsuming other terms under these fifteen headings rather than eliminating traditional terminology. Our principle question continues to be: "How does a learner become an efficient traveler in space?" To maintain a consistent viewpoint we must engage in some terminological remodeling to fit conceptualizations into a space model. Another consideration which has entered into the selection and labeling of these fifteen components has been that of curriculum development. Having once defined these components as critical to Movement Efficiency these headings automatically become the goals of a curriculum.

We would like to use the analogy of a symphonic orchestration to describe the manner in which the fifteen components are integrated in development to convey the idea of emphasis, shading, interweaving, intervals and so on but this falls somewhat short of conveying the concept we intend. In a symphonic presentation not all instruments are sounding at all times; there are rests, combinations, crescendoes and the like. While we recognize the variations in emphasis and shadings it is our belief that all fifteen components are constantly active, constantly changing and expanding and constantly contributing to one another to achieve an integration—Movement Efficiency. This appears a logical essential for a dynamic organism. Vectors of influence are in a constant state of dynamic flux directed by growth forces, the energy surround and an ever-present environmental stimulation. The human organism is never truly at rest when all movement ceases. It is rather a matter of greater or less states of movement. This continuity of a state of movement and the continuity of stimulation in a steady stream clearly suggest a constancy of input to feed all fifteen dimensions. This vital constancy is a well-established scientific fact. The simple extension of this concept of vitality to the incorporation of the constancy of components in movement is a short conceptual stride which can be made in comfort.

Despite our conviction regarding simultaneity and contributive constancy, the limitations of expressive language force an apparent contradiction at the outset. To explicate the Movigenic orientation in the fifteen components each one must be discussed singly as though it were isolate and separate. This is best considered a literary strategy and not a belief in separateness.

Two additional points must be made before proceeding to a detailed discussion of components. We must recognize two principles, **simultaneity** and **developmental synchronization**. All fifteen components are simultaneously active and developing from birth throughout life. The human performer is at all times a composite of relative efficiencies and inefficiencies of all components. Each component provides its own emphasis in contribution to the total in a hierarchial pattern from infancy. As they have been listed in order, we hold that order to be chronologic. The first to receive emphasis is MUSCULAR STRENGTH, and the last to be emphasized is MOTOR PLANNING. Each provides a foundation for the emergence of the subsequent components and each subsequent one continues to enhance and enrich those that have gone before. All are interrelated and interdependent. We view each component as containing a dual perspective. Not only do we look upon MUSCULAR STRENGTH as a physical phenomenon of muscle patterns, but we also stretch the conceptualization to include a cognitive strength such as "the strength of a conviction", "the firmness of a belief", and "dedication to a cause". DYNAMIC BALANCE is not only the physical process of maintaining balance in a gravitational field, but also a factor in psychological homeostasis. Each component is regarded from a physical viewpoint and a cognitive viewpoint. Rational man moving in space in dynamic adaptation requires this dual perspective.

4

MUSCULAR STRENGTH

The story of movement begins with the skelton. The skelton is a mechanical triumph. It is designed to move. Bones of varying shape and length are designed in an interrelationship to allow for direction of movement. How amazing that bone alone endures through centuries in fossilized states conveniently left behind for anthropologists to discover that they might chart the course of man's history. All else decays and vanishes but bone remains to enable modern man to reconstruct his image from thousands of years before. Bone is alive manufacturing blood cells. Bone is protective housing the brain, heart, lungs, viscera, spinal cord in various encasements. Bone is supportive to the weights of the body. Lines of force go through the bones of the skeleton and the feeling of motion is in them. As Todd (1937) said, "the living machine walks."

The skeleton is the prime substance of movement. Like steel, bone has the qualities of hardness, stiffness and elasticity so prized by the engineer. To make full use of the bony levers in the skeleton muscles, tendons, joints, ligaments and cartilage are added to provide a dynamic system for moving the skeleton. Four hundred pairs of muscles are located within the body. Some are large and some small. Each pair has been carefully located and named. Each movement involves a muscle or group of muscles.

Muscular strength is the first dimension of movement efficiency. It is fundamental to movement. When it is not developed in accord with the movement needs of the individual, some degree of survival vulnerability is present. Muscular strength develops as the individual moves.

We are concerned in this space-oriented approach with the development of muscles not for the sake of building hardened muscle tissue, but only as a "tonic background" for movement. Not only is an adequate degree of muscular strength necessary to move the bony levers of the skeleton in the desired directions, but the "push-pull-lift- and resist" demands encountered by the learner from infancy to maturity require a muscular strength adequate to the task.

Each infant must learn the "weight" of the world in relation to his own muscular strength. In the complex world of objects in space the child must learn what he can lift, push or pull with comfort, and that which is beyond his strength. He must learn which objects are movable through his own forces, and when he must call upon stronger muscles of others to do the moving for him. He must develop a personal scale for what is heavy and what is light. He must achieve what Helson (1947) calls an adaptation level for "the weight of the world".

Muscles are responsible for the thrust-counterthrust operation in a moving body carefully balancing each thrusting effort with a counter-balancing action to hold alignment and control.

In the supportive role of weight bearing, bones grow according to their usage. Some limits are placed upon the range of operational freedoms for bones. Design of bones and their structural relationships indicate that the greatest ease of movement is in the frontal plane propelling the body forward on the "Z" axis. Lateral movements are performed with less efficiency than forward moves. Backward moves are least efficient of all. Movements to the side always involve movement away from a central line of balance off the gravitational line and move the head-to-toe segmental alignment into a line of stress. Backward moves place the segments in the least favorable relationships to permit quick shifts and directional revisions. Forward movement is the skeleton's principal direction according to the design of all levers within the body.

The design therefore sets certain limits as to distance and range of movement possible for any segment. From this standpoint, we may talk of function being determined by form.

The organizational task of the neonate is truly a formidable one. Four hundred pairs of muscles must be organized into an efficient relationship to one another to permit all of them to serve the organism in his struggle for survival. In a very practical and real way, each infant must establish an order and organization among all muscles to support him in a field of gravity, resisting its pull in order to stand erect and move as he desires. They must be brought under his control to crawl, roll, jump, walk, twist, duck, spin, pivot, squat, stoop, hop, stretch, lift, push, pull, and squeeze. The demands that will be placed upon those muscles for varying degrees of force throughout a lifetime constitute a listing that seems endless. Unless some specific impairment is present, each infant starts life with a muscle supply measuring four hundred. As the neonate itself is ignorant and untutored so also is his entire muscular system. Under his control, it must "learn" how to function.

Gesell (1945) described the embryology of the trunk muscles in the 2-3 week old embryo as "ancient muscles in the history of the race, early muscles in the biography of the embryo. Even in the eight-week-old embryo the muscles which will someday pronate and flex the forearms...and the muscles which will flex the digits are already present".

Two-thirds of the neonate's basic set of equipment for movement are the skeleton and his muscular system. When we add the neurologic system to this trio the fundamental triad for movement is complete. LIFE stands before the neonate pointing a demanding finger and insists upon organization of all three parts of the trio to bring the infant to his human identification as an erect locomoting being. The ability of man to stand on his feet with balance and coordination prepared to move in space is a major part of the heritage of humanity. From the time of the birth cry to the time when the infant will walk independently towards a goal he chooses is a short span of space measured in terms of a lifetime, but a vast expanse of time to the neophyte traveler. What a tremendous task lies ahead of him. The major barrier to his achievement of erect stature moving confidently through space is the powerful force of gravity. Morton (1952) referred to gravity as the "major designing agent of structure".

The action system is an intricate balance machine. Every movement, no matter how slight or extensive, in some manner influences the equilibrium of the total machinery. The physiologic interrelations of these movement patterns are so complex that the resolution of the intricate interweavings is extended over more than twenty years of life. The gestational period is mere prologue to the life enactment against the forces of gravity. (Gesell, 1945)

Gravity will be the major adversary for the infant in his initial struggle to achieve efficiency in movement. Building the necessary muscle patterns to resist gravitational pull becomes the dedicated objective of the infant, and the design of his anatomy and his timetable of development are equal to the task if no type of impairment is present. The bones are the weight bearing parts of the body and gravity the primary force to which they are subjected.

The general timetable of movement which regulated the stages of preparation of the organism in sequential order of increasing complexity leading to the final stage of readiness for delivery is again in evidence to prepare the neophyte traveler for full transport. A sequence of complexity can again be delineated.

As a first stage the infant moves in random and diffuse thrashing, jerky forms. These are probably intended to sensitize the muscles and develop a certain degree of stretching and tension. This may be described as the earliest stage of muscular tonus. It is a "tuning up process" for what lies ahead.

The first definable pattern of muscular tension and alignment is the tonic-neck-reflex. The developmental roots of posture are probably localized within the dynamics of the TNR. It is present in the uterus and follows the infant into the free world. It is basic to movement.

Gesell (1938) found the TNR to be a dominating characteristic of normal infancy during the first three months of life. Gradually the TNR pattern is reduced in frequency as bilateral patterns emerge and eventually give way to unilateral patterns.

Gesell (1938) suggests a number of purposes for the TNR: (1) to help the fetus accommodate to the conformation of the uterine cavity;(2)to facilitate longitudinal presentation to the birth canal; (3) in the neonatal period, the TNR helps in posturing for suckling at the breast; (4) it promotes visual fixations on the extended hand, and (5) reduces the hazard of suffocation.

The TNR is the neonate's first pattern and perhaps, in final analysis, remains the significant fundamental to all future physical movement throughout his lifetime. The tonic-neck-reflex in children is replaced by an increasing equilibrium between ages 2-1/2 and 5-1/2 months. (Hellebrandt, Franceen, 1943)

Interest in the TNR pattern has not been limited to observations in infants. The work of Hellebrandt and her associates (Hellebrandt, Schade, and Carns, 1962; Hellebrandt et al., 1956) in studying the TNR in adult subjects has shown the continuity of this phenomenon throughout life. While the infant readily falls into the pattern, the adult requires a special rotation and body twist to evoke the TNR.

Hellebrandt, Schade, and Carns (1962) have studied this phenomenon quite extensively and have contributed a deeper understanding of the manner in which neck and labyrinthine mechanisms relate themselves to good body balance and orientation.

Although the TNR pattern is a foundation experience for a "motor future" the head must eventually disengage itself from the lateral turning if the head containing the eyes is to serve its major purpose of "steering the movement of the organism through space". The eyes must scan a field and direct the transport. To do this the design principle requires an inhibition of the head turn when arms and legs are moved in order that the higher purpose of vision may be served. In other words the head resists the TNR inclination and holds to a centering task to set a midline course. Thus is the infant able to move on to the more important steps in preparation for erect locomotion.

If the head cannot disengage itself from the TNR pattern this becomes a prognostic sign that the child will never walk. (Gesell, 1938) This disengaging process becomes critical in the development of children with cerebral palsy. The head must be disengaged from the TNR pattern to go on with its principal role as the key structure in building an erect posture. The head must be liberated to scan the space field and steer the organism. True to design the infant's emergence from the containment of the TNR enables him to roll from the supine to the prone position with his turned head leading the rest of his body as it rolls into the prone position. The muscles of the neck and the trunk now make this possible. It is interesting to note that the normal infant is a "one-turn roller". He does not roll through space in consecutive rolling turns. He rolls once. This single roll may have many implications for general metabolic processes but we view its purpose to be that of placing the body in a position where the neck muscles may now be stretched to support the elevation of the head against the pull of gravity. The head has been delegated as the first offensive force against gravity. We regard this delegation as holding major significance to the entire question of Movement Efficiency and intend more commentary on this singularity in the section on Dynamic Balance. For the time being let us simply underline a second time that the head end of man is entrusted with the first assignment against gravity. As it wins or loses or may even achieve a semi-victory it sets the pattern for all future battles with gravity. It must emerge in some state of victory if development toward erect locomotion is to proceed along the true line of developmental momentum. Since it has, in temporal terms, just recently been liberated from the TNR and not only assigned the formidable task of conquering gravity but also assigned as the initiator of posture the "weight of the future" rests upon its success. We also view this developmental stage as one which truly activates the nervous system to the cognitive controlled service of the infant. It is the head end of man which differentiates him from all other living creatures. It is logical that it should therefore receive the first cognitive-muscular assignments.

The infant does not easily achieve his head-end victory over gravity. His early efforts are marked by only brief successes. Gradually his neck muscles strengthen and he can sustain his head in elevation against gravity for longer and longer time spans. He is now capable of positioning himself in the prone position and elevating his head — but he is not high enough to scan space for movement exploration. He must take the next step and lift his upper torso on the support of his arms to raise the head still further to scan his world as he prepares to move.

Ames (1937) found a uniform sequence of prone behavior patterns in the normal human infant which proceeds in accordance with the directional law of cephalocaudad and proximal-distal progressions culminating in a well established quadrupedal creeping pattern by the end of the first year. She described 14 definite developmental stages occurring in a consistent order in the majority of infants, initiated during the sixth month of life and achieving completion by the twelfth month. Within that six month span the infant prepares himself for the quadrupedal journey into the world of space. Creeping is the logical end result of these progressive learnings of movement patterns. Here again is the logic of the basic training concept of preparation time to achieve movement efficiency for third dimensional transport.

Control proceeds downward to the shoulders and upper extremities through the lower trunk and concludes with the control of the muscles of the hips, legs and feet. (Shirley, 1931) There is a gradual fusion of new elements with those of previously established patterns so that there is an increasing ability to perform at more complex levels. (Deach, 1950)

His crawling pattern passes through three stages as he moves into the third dimension of space. In the first stage he moves his entire body as a unit pulling the weight of his pelvis and legs. He propels himself by the upper part of his body. The cephalocaudad progression has only reached his shoulders. His lower body has yet to learn its role in the gravitational battle. This crawling motion is **homologous**. Gradually the pelvis is arched and the leg is drawn under the pelvis to support body weight and he achieves a quadrupedal position. In that learning process the leg frequently does not achieve a full supportive position and the infant moves in frog-style. However, once in the quadruped position he moves forward by a **homolateral** pattern thrusting the leg and the arm of the same side forward followed by a similar thrust from the contralateral side. He is at once, one sided or the other. Gradually, again, he achieves the efficiency of **crossed-diagonal** patterning by thrusting the left leg forward in a simultaneous movement of the right arm and hand and vice versa. The **homologous** pattern is uneconomical and must be abandoned as soon as possible to serve his movement needs but cannot be given up until the progression of cephalocaudad development enables him to score another victory over gravity and permits the lower extremities to improve the economy of movement.

The **homolateral** pattern is also uneconomical because it induces a swaying and rocking motion as he crawls. This requires a continual correcting action if he is to hold himself on his target line. It is an indicator of less freedom to move. The most economical pattern is achieved when he can assay the crossed-diagonal move. His balance is now so well established that he can hold a two point contact (arms and legs) at a midline while opposite sides of his body are simultaneously thrusting forward. Now he can economically hold direction. Having achieved this efficiency crawling now becomes a skill to file in a library of movement patterns to be called upon as necessary in future life encounters but not to be relied upon as a locomotive mainstay. Developmental momentum is insisting upon a higher center of gravity and his design heeds the demand. Lowman and Young (1960) pointed out that a "baby that crawls will have a straighter spine and better balance when he assays walking". Crawling helps to exercise the big pelvic and trunk muscles. The pelvic girdle becomes the key mass in alignment linking the upper and lower portions of the body. When sufficient muscular strength has been achieved in crawling he lifts his body to an erect position supporting himself in that stance by holding on to some object. He stands — and soon he walks.

The infant period has been a fertile field for research. Since the early development of the child is so dominantly oriented in the direction of motor or movement achievements the reports have largely been focused upon defining the temporal schedules for each new achievement. The study of walking has been of special interest.

Shirley's (1931) study of the progression of movement patterns in infants showed that 50% of her study infants were able to elevate their head and chest above the examination table at the end of the second month of life; knee pushing movements were achieved by the majority between the fifth and sixth month; rolling over appeared within the sixth month and primitive walking movements appeared at a median age of nine months.

McGraw (1939) divided the first two years into four periods. The first period from birth to the fourth month is characterized by gradual reduction of subcortical control. The second period from the fourth to ninth month involves development of voluntary movements in the superior spinal region. The third period from the ninth through the fourteenth month shows increased bodily control in the inferior spinal region. The fourth period lasts approximately ten months and becomes a space of rapid development in the association centers. Gesell and Ames (1940) defined 23 separate steps in the progression of motor behavior leading to walking, carrying the timetable to the fourteenth month of life.

The toddler does not become an expert walker until nearly the end of his second year. Even though he has been walking erect for the better part of ten months his expertise is delayed by his naivete in battling gravity. He walks on the full soles of the feet with the legs spread wide apart. He toddles from side to side using each side of his body as a separate unit walking in a homolateral pattern. Only gradually does his walking pattern shift to a crossed diagonal driving of sides toward a midline. The lesson of leg convergence in alternation on the forward plane which will be his style for the remainder of his life takes about ten months to be deeply embedded into his full movement matrix. In the course of those ten months he falls forward, and backward, topples to one side or the other, dances on his toes, walks too quickly and entangles his feet, misjudges distances and literally charts a list of errors. Gradually his error score for locomotive transport becomes less and less because his feedback system gives corrective information to be integrated into the pattern. Usually by age two he has achieved a fair degree of expertise as a walker on **flat terrain**. Stairs and inclines and other terrain variations are yet to be learned.

Gesell (1949) described the 18 month old infant as being in the "dart and dash" phase of his visual-motor organization which results in multiple invasions of an expanding environment.

> "...He attends chiefly to the here and now. He wants everything he sees but his localization of far off objects is crude...He plunges uncritically into nooks and corners and by-ways and goes up and down stairs. By one device or another he carries a toy from place to place—abandons it, returns to it and resumes with postural twists and variations, making sudden rapid turns of 180 degrees or even walking backward. It is as though he were deliberately exploring and discovering new vectors of space. He is a rather bungling explorer because he functions in an episodic and one track manner."

Although the child is usually considered to be fairly expert in walking at age two he cannot be judged as an efficient walker since his repertoire is still quite limited according to the ease of terrain. It is critical for his locomotive future that his walking pattern achieves a crossed diagonal efficiency in which there is a smooth relaxed bilateral equation of stride with slight in-toeing to drive the body forward on the midline. If his early achievement does not reach that level of bilateral efficiency his walking pattern may already be classified as inefficient and forecasts a locomotive problem for the future. It is not merely a matter of resting the case simply because the toddler has achieved erect locomotion but consideration must be given to the efficiency of his walking. Poor patterns of walking may be analyzed in a two year old. The significance of an inadequate walking pattern may not be immediately noted—it may take many years before the full negative import will become noticeable. A widened base, a narrowed base, a scissored gait, and so on all point to future difficulties. The foundations of dynamic posture are built in those early encounters with gravity and the proper alignment of skeletal segments must be the initial outcome of the gravitational victory. Any other alignment than a properly balanced arrangement bodes for inefficiency in movement in future years.

Stair climbing is another early pattern which must be built into the movement repertoire of the preschooler. Three successive stages in stair climbing may be defined: (1) Two feet resting on each tread; (2) alternating feet with support and; finally (3) alternating feet without support. Wellman (1937) using a concept of motor age studied the stair climbing of preschoolers on a 3 step flight and an 11 step flight. Ascending the stairs in both flights was accomplished at the third level (alternate without support) a full 18 months before the same level could be obtained in descending the stairs. Approximately 7 months transpire from the two feet per tread pattern to alternating without support (24-31 months) before the ascending pattern is well established on the 3 step flight. The 11 step flight required a full year differential before the final level was achieved (29-41 months). Descending the 3 step flight requires a two year differential to achieve some efficiency (25-49 months) and nearly the same differential for the 11 step flight (34-55 months). The 11 step flight is a much more difficult task for all three methods used by children.

McGraw and Breeze (1941) charted the developmental course of the bilateral integration in walking in the infant.

The toddler takes approximately 170 steps per minute while the adult takes 140-145 steps per minute. The use of the foot as a rocker in receiving and supporting the body weight and the use of the foot as a source of power becomes progressively better integrated in the third and fourth year. By the end of the fourth year his walking pattern is equivalent to that of an adult. Gutteridge (1939) set the mean age for perfection in walking skills at 50 months.

McCaskill and Wellman (1938), in their study of preschool children, found that 50% of their group could heel-toe along a one inch line with no step off at 33 months of age. Walking a one inch circular path was not accomplished by their group until 45 months of age. Bayley's (1936) observations on walking patterns in toddlers set a mean age of 16.5 months for walking sideways and a mean age of 16.9 months for walking backwards. Walking tiptoed does not usually occur until after the thirtieth month. Galloping is not found in three year olds but seems to become a proficient skill for four and five year olds according to Breckenridge and Vincent (1955).

While investigators of infant movement-chronology have been busy recording various timetables, the study of walking as a human phenomenon has engaged the attention of many workers interested in adult locomotion. Walking is not a simple motor behavior, prosaic though it might be.

Wells (1955) stated, "The complexity of the movements in walking which appears to be simple have been shown to be exceedingly complex by kinesiologic analysis. The dovetailing of muscular acting and the synchronization of joint movements illustrate the team work present in all bodily movements."

Steindler's (1953) review of studies related to human gait credits Borelli with being the pathfinder in the 17th century with his fundamental concept of muscle action and the center of gravity. Despite what is now retrospectively viewed as an extremely important set of concepts nearly 200 years passed before investigators picked up the trail Borelli had set. Photographic recording was introduced in the latter part of the 19th century and Braune and Fischer completed their classic work of analyzing the essential factors in gait. Scherb of Zurich first defined the sequence of muscle action in the lower extremities during the early part of the 20th century. A few other investigators, Han von Baeyer, Schwartz and Inman are described as recent researchers but the topic has not intrigued the interest of a significant number of scientists.

Essentially one might conclude that walking man has been taken for granted. Although the length of stride, rotation of the foot, press of landing and so on have been carefully defined in numerical terms none of these studies accounted for the visual state of the subjects, only fleetingly described child-adult differences, ignored the postural state of the subjects and made little or no effort to account for variables of a psychological or physiologic nature which might be related to gait variations. In general, the studies seem to have assumed a homogeneity among walkers with the concentration given to the detailing of minute muscle relationships.

Variations in gait according to age, disease, postural warp, visual problem and many other variables which might influence walking remain obscured. The analysis of gait patterns in children cannot therefore rely upon the literature for translatable results — only for methodological leads. This leaves the issue wide open for a "blue sky" form of speculation as to the relative influence of the variables suggested above.

Kelly (1949) described the manner in which walking should be organized to ensure greatest efficiency:

> *"The feet should toe straight ahead or only very slightly outward with not more than a 15° angle between feet. The body weight should be carried slightly more on the outer borders than on the inner borders of the feet; with each step there should be a smooth transfer of weight from the heel along the outer border of the foot to all five toes, followed by a vigorous push-off; the footprints of the two feet should fall in two parallel lines, slightly separated from each other, not in one overlapping path; the legs swing straight forward and backward from the hips, not in a slightly circular movement around the supporting leg."*

Any variation from this ideal pattern can be expected to contribute to some state of inefficiency in walking.

Muscular Strength — Hands

The anatomical organization of the hand becomes of vital concern in the study of transport at the manipulative level. Turning again to Gesell (1945) a developmental progression has been recorded dating back to embryonic stages. At the eighth week of embryonic growth the hand is paddle-shaped with some ridges foretelling the fingers with all of the related muscles already present. By the twelfth week the fetus now has developed all moving parts of the hand. From the twelfth to sixteenth fetal week the fetus deploys hands in the medial plane, opens and closes hands, and moves the thumbs independently. There follows a practice period of gripping (an advance over fisting). After such hand practice the hands return to a fisted flexion (apparently having completed its fetal practice in preparation for its journey into physical space).

Having already engaged in a fetal rehearsal the hands seem to repeat their developmental progression on the open stage of neonatal life. His life performance starts tight fisted with incurled thumbs. For four months he grasps with the heel of the hand and drops the object readily because the digits do not contribute to the grasp. By the fourth month the infant grasps an object getting his thumb well out of the way but not using the thumb for a contribution to his grasp. Within the next three months he achieves a radial palmar grasp, can bring the object to his mouth, transfers from hand to hand and recovers what he dropped. It seems to take another three months before his fingers actually begin to direct and control his grasping efforts. It takes the infant a full year to get the thumb properly organized in relation to the palm and the other four digits. (Castner, 1932; McGraw, 1940) In six more months his fingers achieve a finesse for turning pages, building blocks, inserting pellets, scribbling with crayon and clutching a ball. All of the fundamental movement patterns of the hand have been established by approximately 18 months. Counting some fetal rehearsal we can regard hand development as a two year sequence proceeding from the palm to extended digits. The proximal-distal principle is again in evidence.

As Tabori (1962) has noted the marvel of the opposable thumb sets man apart from all other creatures. This is perhaps the real secret of man's technology — the thumb enables the hand to act as pliers, squeezer, holder and grasper.

From the moment of birth to death's dark finality we carry a masterpiece throughout life which no sculptor has ever equalled, a precision instrument which has never been surpassed by the most elaborate mechanical brain or the most delicate tool — the human hand. (Tabori, 1962)

The achievement of a full foundation range of hand skills coincides with the achievement of locomotion. In the near space world of the crib and play pen there is actually little need for hand skills but when the youngster begins to locomotively explore his world and to "take hold of it" with all of its complexity his hands will support a major share of his learning. As soon as the hands are no longer required for creeping they have been liberated for exploration and in perfect synchrony of development they have been progressively prepared for their exploratory work. They become the critical tools for the next important advance in space sophistication.

Once the hand has established its fundamental functional pattern the next three years serve as an advanced stage of preparation to eventually become sophisticated, refined, precise "learning hands". During those preschool years the hands will receive training in pressure application for grasping — not because anyone consciously plans a program of pressure training — but because typical life experiences will provide multiple opportunities for defining a relative adaptation level for applying pressure to grasp. He will learn to apply an adequate pressure to grip a crayon or a pencil if he wishes to direct a line of movement. Paper cups, ice cream cones, cookies, drinking fountain handles, doorknobs, window shade cords, light switches, pull toys, fork, spoon, glasses, cup handles, cabinet doors, faucets and thousands of other objects will be managed with success only as he manages a "just right" application of "finger and thumb" force. While he is developing this pressure proficiency there will be many experiences of failure in broken cones and cookies, spilled water, resistant handles, unopenable doors and cabinets and so on. Nearby parents will respond to his pleas but eventually he must manage on his own. He must achieve his personal proficiency for appropriate grasp, release and grasp.

During those preschool years he will also be required to become a tactual explorer of texture to build a reference system for tactual discrimination. Rough-smooth, soft-hard, thick-thin, round-square, narrow-wide, paper-wood, metal-plastic, liquid-solid, movable-immovable will be but a few of the opposites and differentials his hands will be required to organize. "Explore", "differentiate" and "discriminate" will be key words in the cutaneous and muscular organization of his hand. Those fingers, thumbs, and palms will each have to be organized into a smooth synchrony of movement to button, zip, pull on stockings, lace shoes, brush teeth, wash hands, shovel sand, point to desired objects, hold a sandwich, catch a ball, steer a bicycle and many more activities. All this must be accomplished before entry into school because school curricula are intended to build upon and advance beyond that basic learning.

In the school setting the proficiency of the hands will be expected to advance in refinement to manage a scissors, color, paste, draw and write. Craft projects, arithmetic workbooks, chalkboard activities and many other demands will successively require a finer and finer level of competency.

Hands become a major tool for executing one's perception. They help to give perceptions visible form. They are vital to movement. The assessment of manipulative efficiency has long been a prime area for determining overall ability. Many tests of visuo-motor perception rely upon executive movements of the hands to determine visual-motor adequacy.

A popular expression of manipulative awkwardness is to refer to someone as being "all thumbs" or "the left hand doesn't know what the right hand is doing". The manipulative proficiency of a skilled musician is highly regarded. The "touch of a master" exemplifies the concept of proficiency. On the one extreme we can consider the speedy, efficient fingers and hand movements of many skilled workers in a wide variety of fields and at the other extreme we may place the many deformed hands of the spastic, arthritic, rheumatic and other handicaps. In between those two extremes of exceptionally skilled and physically impaired reside many different degrees of manual efficiency.

The analysis of the movement efficiency of any individual at any age requires concentrated attention to manual efficiency as a major expression of movement. Hand analysis can be persued from a variety of approaches. Evaluation of methods of grasp and release can be studied by observing the manner in which the fingers and thumbs are used in relation to the palm when grasping an object.

It is not at all infrequent to observe an immaturity in hand development among elementary school children in the use of scissors, buttoning, pencil grasp and so on. The developmental viewpoint suggests an analysis of current hand usage according to the progression criteria which have been described above. Although some children seem to have clearly achieved thumb opposition for general purposes the fisted thumb may creep into their manipulative performances under periods of stress and fatigue. Others may rely more frequently upon a radial palmar grasp apparently operating more at the proximal end of the continuum than the distal and impress the evaluator as lacking in digital efficiency. Some children may be unable to move each finger independently from all others. Some may frequently drop objects because they have not properly organized their pressure adaptations. Often in puzzle and block-arranging the child's own fingers "get in the way" of his performance.

Introducing a demand for speed in hand tasks may cause the individual to lose efficiency as the synchrony of palm, fingers and thumb becomes progressively more de-rhythmic. In general conversation one often hears people say "I was never very good with my hands", as though this rationalizes some genetic factor. There is a popular belief that some people are more proficient at manipulation tasks than others and this observation is simply accepted at face value and attributed to the very nebulous and unhelpful concept of individual differences.

When there is no evidence of impairment to muscle tissue or neural innervation and for all practical purposes the anatomy of the hand contains all the necessary components we must assume an anatomical equality. The variations in proficiency among people must then stem from experience and the contributions of many other factors than muscles, bones, and tissue. Variation in proficiency is directly related to a general state of movement efficiency. Manual inefficiency stems from some form of immaturity in the developmental progression of hand usage. The observation of manipulative inefficiency is not an isolated finding. A similar inefficiency is notable throughout the movement patterning of the individual. Being a unified organism one motoric inefficiency will be replicated throughout the systems. Even though our present sensitivities in observation and measurement may not reflect such replication the design of the organism dictates the belief.

Here again a variety of tests are available to assess manipulative dexterity usually labeled as one or the other of those terms. The usual procedure is to expose the subject to the manipulative task, note his speed and accuracy, compare it to some standard and conclude that he is below, at or above average levels. In many industrial settings such tests are used to determine whether or not an individual has the manual qualifictions for a given job. It is interesting to note that the assessment of manipulative dexterity is primarily a vocational consideration and is rarely studied in children. When it becomes a question of job efficiency we focus upon the phenomenon but attach little import to it in the elementary school child unless he manifests a gross and obvious problem. The Lincoln-Osseretsky test (1954) includes several items which can be classified as tests of dexterity but the entire test has not been widely used in general clinical and educational practice.

Observations of infants have confirmed the plan and the pattern of the "Basic Design". The practice period to prepare for independent exploration has a quality of simultaneity about it but lacks the precision of everything developing at once. While the net effect may approach simultaneity the precise gains appear as units of skill taking turns in the spotlight, preceding one another with each complementing the advancement of all of the fellow players. No specific timetable can be plotted for hands, as an illustration, without there being a series of temporal intervals between "hand-landmarks". The intervals between these hand stages "unilateral reaching", "rotates wrist", "completes thumb opposition" have timetable insertions of "rolls from back to stomach" etc. The pattern is a single theme with temporal variations introduced at intervals each contributing its own counterpoint to building toward a crescendo and a climax of erect locomotion into space.

Within the first year of life the infant rises to the standing position and wins his victory over gravity as he moves his full body through space. His antigravity muscles hold his skeletal frame erect and by stretching and contracting enable the frame to move in desired directions. Without this muscular energy "our tower of bones set on elastic cushions and highly lubricated surfaces tends to collapse". (Rogers, 1938) Also within that first year the infant can extend his arm and hand in mid-air and resist the pull of gravity to manually explore his world. This dual victory over gravity liberates the space traveler to the freedom of exploration. Only the fundamentals of muscular strength have been achieved during this first year — learning has just begun.

He must develop muscular strength to run, jump and hop, to throw a ball, swing a bat, pull a wagon, pedal his tricycle uphill, lift his cup, punch a playmate, swing on playground equipment, kick a ball and thousands of other tasks where force will be a factor.

Man was designed to move in space. The most economic transport on his customary terrain is to become an erect locomotive being. To stand erect surveying his domain and to move in pursuit of selected goals is the first major challenge to the developmental timetable of the neonate.

The intensive study of movement patterns among infants has pointed up the developmental preoccupation with establishing the foundations to support later "mental" development. (Bayley, 1933, 1936) Developmental time is devoted primarily to preparing the body for locomotion, the hands and fingers for refined grasp and release, setting the righting reflexes, early exploration of gravity relationships and the organization of sides and top and bottom. Once this basic foundation has been set the organism is truly liberated to independently explore space to acquire a knowledge of the world in which he is to live.

In the general course of child development there is an implicit assumption that the natural activities of the preschool years will somehow automatically produce an adequate level of muscular strength to meet the typical demands of school and play. Scarcely anyone thinks of formal muscle-training activities for the preschool child. Our national concern for the physical fitness of children begins at age six. Yet it is within the first two to three years that the basic muscle patterns are established. Subsequent development is truly only a matter of expanding existing muscle fibers or correctively exercising particular groups in order to achieve some balance.

Muscles are used to produce force. Force may be used to resist, to move the full body or parts of the body and to react to an external force from some other source than one's own muscular exertion. Muscles throughout the body exert force by shortening and the resultant action is a pull. The exertion of force may be extensive and prolonged as with an "all-out" effort or may be minimal and brief for minor transports or resistances. The purpose of a movement determines the extent of force to be applied. The general course of behavior probably requires an intense concentration of force quotients located within the central tendency toward moderate force—with modest amounts of "all-out" force and modest amounts of minimal force requirements. It is very likely that we could employ the concept of the curve of normal distribution as a model for expressing the general prosaic muscular demands upon an average individual. Although each individual varies according to occupation and opportunity the general concept of balanced living suggests that each individual's muscular performance could very well be plotted on a 16% all-out segment, a 68% moderate or average effort and 16% minimal effort. Large amplitudes exist within the central range but it is very likely that each individual can be regarded as having an average output of muscular force to insure daily survival with potential to operate at either extreme as the daily demand may require.

The exertion of "just right" force becomes the critical factor in maintaining alignment for proper coordination. Undue tensions or poorly synchronized shortening of muscles may cause a steering wheel to be pushed or pulled too quickly, a putt to be missed, a batter to strike out, a tennis ball to be hit out of bounds, a free-throw to be missed, a line of writing to be distorted and so on.

Efficiency of movement at a muscular level is obtained when all of the forces that can contribute to the desired outcome are employed in appropriate intensity and sequence. The degree of relaxation must correspond to the degree of contraction. (Broer, 1960) Thrust must be accompanied by a countering process. If the reciprocal interweaving of the relaxation and contraction sequence is distorted in any manner, jerky, hesitant uncertain movements result. In muscular contraction sequentialness is an essential component for efficient movement. A disruption to the serial ordering in a muscular sequence produces a dysrhythmia in movement. Such dysrhythmia is most readily noted in the spastic, athetoid and ataxic individual but may also be noted in a general array of incoordinations among average individuals.

If a body is to move in rhythm employing appropriate amounts of force in order to accomplish a desired goal muscular strength appropriate to the task must be available. Muscular strength is the first vital component for movement efficiency at all times. Strength must not simply be regarded as muscle "hardness" and the capacity to exert great amounts of force but must be conceived as the capability for exerting variable and appropriate amounts of force to resolve a performance demand. Despite extremely "hardened" muscles acquired by stringent exercise of certain muscle groups an individual may still be deficient in coordination because the muscle groups have been "trained" for great force and may not respond fluidly to minimal delicate muscle patterns. Large hardened muscles may enable the individual to project himself into far space and exert great pressure but unless all degrees of contractional competency are achieved the precise minute movements in near space may be dysrhythmic.

Development of a wide range of contractional sequential competency requires consideration for multiple opportunities for all muscles in the body to "learn" their appropriate role relationship for each type of movement. A full repertoire of muscular efficiency requires that all muscles "learn" when to contribute and when to remain silent observers of the activity of their fellow members.

Muscles may be graded according to **tonus** classifications as hypotonic, hypertonic, atonic and adequate tone. Hypotonic muscles are lacking in appropriate tone and are therefore reduced in efficiency potential. Hypertonic muscles are prematurely and excessively toned and as a result reduced in the efficiency of their contribution to performance synchrony. Atonic muscles make no contribution. Maintaining proper muscle tone throughout life becomes a critical consideration in building Movement Efficiency.

Since all movement involves muscles there is a constant demand upon those muscles to perform in relation to one another. As the body walks, runs, skips, hops, pushes and pulls there is a constant demand for some degree of force.

Although a great deal of emphasis has recently been placed upon the development of vigorous programs of recreation and exercise for the elementary school child, the physical education programs of American education continue to offer major services at the secondary level.

Muscular strength is the first developmental dimension in building Movement Efficiency but basic and primary though it be, it must be interrelated and interwoven with all other dimensions if it is to serve its purpose. If muscles are pulled in a given vector of force without proper counterbalancing actions they serve to shift a skeletal alignment from its true segmental relationship.

The study of Movement Efficiency in the infant, preschooler, elementary, high schooler, adult, retarded or average, sick or well, sensory impaired or unimpaired begins with an analysis of Muscular Strength. Problems of muscle tone, inability to project appropriate amounts of force and variations in strength must be studied in relationship to the movement of the individual.

The curriculum consideration must be given to the provision of a vigorous program of activity to help the child explore his muscles and give him the opportunity to bring his total muscular system into appropriate relationships to serve his needs.

5

DYNAMIC

BALANCE

Balance is a state of stability produced by the equal distribution of weight on each side of a vertical axis. In the human organism the vertical axis is an imaginary midline dividing the body into its two sides. The skeletal frame cushioned by paired muscles, tendons, cartilage and so on stretched to its full height is designed to rotate organismic halves around that vertical axis as it moves through space. The entire scheme of the first year of life is one of preparing the infant to stand erect in a state of balance distributing its full body weight equally on either side of that axis. When the individual can align his body segments in such a way so as to be in a state of equilibrium with a minimum amount of energy and a minimum amount of fatigue upon any one particular muscle or muscle group we designate him as being in balance. (Lowman and Young, 1960)

The infant terranaut is not one solid structure but a jointed structure with many movable parts. As any part of the body moves the total body acquires a new shape and undergoes a different distribution of its weight. The center of gravity shifts with this new weight distribution in order to maintain the condition of having equal amounts of weight on both sides of it. (Broer, 1960; Metheny, 1951) The vertical axis which is necessary for the definition of balance may also be described as a line of gravity. Along this line of gravity passing through the body a center has been defined as the convergence center for vectors of force. This center of gravity is located within the region of the midpoint between the hips. The pelvic girdle is the massive segment of the body uniting the upper and lower halves.

For males this point represents about 56% of their height measured from the floor and for females the center is at 55% of the body height according to Wells (1960) and Morehouse and Cooper (1950). For children the gravity center is somewhat higher. We may talk of a body being balanced when its center of gravity is squarely over its supporting base. There are a number of principles of equilibrium described by Broer (1960) which have pertinence to this discussion:

1. The nearer to the center of the base the line of gravity falls the more stable the body.

2. The larger the base the more stable the body.

3. The base should be enlarged in the direction of the moving or opposing force.

4. Any widening of the base to give greater stability should be accomplished in such a way that movement in the joint is not restricted or strain put on any joint.

5. Any widening of the base must take into account the direction of the force which is exerted by the individual against the ground.

6. Whenever one body part moves away from the line of gravity in one direction the center of gravity shifts in that direction. If this shift puts the center of gravity beyond the base another body part must move in the opposite direction to bring the center of gravity back over the base or balance will be lost.

7. External weights added to the body become part of the total body weight and affect the location of the center of gravity displacing it in the direction of the added weight.

8. The lower the center of gravity the more stable the body.

9. Forward (or backward) rotating motion increases stability.

The base to which Broer refers is defined by the position of the feet in the erect body. If the vertical axis bisects the center of the base line drawn between the two feet at rest-stance the weight will be evenly distributed and we may refer to the individual as being in static balance. As an individual moves his legs in any direction to walk, lunge, dodge, avoid, escape or approach he shifts the line of gravity and must modify the base accordingly if he is to move in a state of dynamic balance. Since the body is never truly in a state of complete immobility some movement is a constancy. As a consequence it is not possible to truly speak of such a state as an automatic equilibrium. All the individual centers of gravity that are possible in various individual segments of the body cannot be brought within a common line of gravity. As the body maintains a constancy of movement the effect of the varying centers of gravity is to establish an active rotation. To maintain directional control it becomes necessary to have a system of counterbalances to hold alignment. The muscular system serves this purpose. (Steindler, 1955)

The skeletal frame is a weight bearing structure. The individual holds his body weight in a given position resisting the pull of gravity by appropriately tensing the larger muscles of the body. The feet become the weight bearing base and therefore become critical in the study of balance.

Morton (1952) described studies of the human foot and its support of body weight in terms of units of weight transmitted to each foot. Twenty-four units of weight represented total weight in his model. Thus, an individual weighing 168 pounds whould have a distribution of 7 pound units x 24. In his scheme, 12 units were assigned to each foot with 6 units on each foot given to the heel and 6 units given to the forepart of each foot. To carry this distribution to its full analysis, half of the body weight is given to the heels and half given to the forepart of the two feet. If body weight is evenly distributed, the feet, according to this model, carry one half the body weight on each foot. According to Morton, if weight is unevenly distributed, the demand on each foot will be disproportionate and lead to structural deformity.

The sequential organization of progressively passing movement ease from the head down to the feet appears to be a calculated design to achieve this equalized distribution once the erect stance has been attained. As homologous patterning gives way to homolateral or one-sided patterning the equality of the sides is being established for its eventual utility in balance. The infant patterns homolaterally to become aware of its two-sidedness. As the crawling youngster achieves a cross diagonal patterning he is already establishing the reciprocal interweaving of the two sides across the midline which will serve him again in his walking. Crawling is also a pattern requiring a dynamic balancing around a midline with the center of gravity lowered and the base established at the knee tucked under the pelvis. A balanced crawl becomes an equalized distribution of body weights on both sides of a midline subject to the same linear scaling as occurs in walking. Having achieved a cross diagonal patterning in his crawling the young toddler must again go through the same three stages as he assays walking. His first walking pattern is homologous with his full body moving forward as a unit one step at a time. He moves himself forward in one step but dares not try the next until he has firmly brought the whole body to a position of static balance. This is a necessary initial procedure in learning weight distribution in the erect positioning. This is followed by a homolateral type of walking in which he shifts his weight from side to side, toddling as he goes with a wide pedal base. Gradually as he learns the lesson of shifting weight this walking pattern smooths out in the crossed diagonal pattern reciprocally weaving the midline. We suspect that the speed with which the neophyte walker passes through these three walking stages is determined by his crawling achievements. If he passed through the crawling stages successfully coming to a state of relative efficiency in each, the three stages in walking are quickly managed. If the crawling patterns were not managed efficiently or omitted from his developmental repertoire some degree of inadequacy accompanies his walking pattern. It is possible to identify a toddle-type of walk, a homolateral pattern among older children and adults who never quite achieved a comfortable, smooth pattern of equalizing the weight distribution for optimum dynamic balance. The quadrupedal progression is a practice period for dynamic balance. Children who omit this progression have denied themselves the practice period intended by the Designer of the mobile organism.

Broer (1960) listed as one of the principles of body equilibrium, "Whenever one body part moves away from the line of gravity in one direction, the center of gravity shifts in that direction. If this shift puts the center of gravity beyond the base, another body part must move in the opposite direction to bring the center of gravity over the base or balance will be lost." The various body parts are constantly moving causing the center of gravity to continually shift. This shifting procedure requires a constancy of opposing forces to maintain stability. Thrusting and counterthrusting become the major components of dynamic balance. A large share of the infant's time is spent in learning the valuable lessons of thrusting and counterthrusting. If he is to maintain any degree of accuracy in direction as he moves through space regardless of the direction in which he chooses to move he will be fighting against gravitational pull, shifting centers of gravity in a constant demand for balance. His success will be determined by the ease with which he manages his thrusting and counterthrusting actions. The early efforts of the neophyte traveler are marked by stumbles, hesitations, pratfalls, toppling and many other behaviors indicating that the counterthrusting actions have not yet been learned to the advantage of the mover. After much experimentation he acquires the knack of counterthrusting and achieves a confidence in moving. Every shift is a tonic shift and he must respond to it. Every shift is an angular stress upon the principal axes and must be managed in order to hold a balance.

The question of how the organism acquires a knowledge of direction in the organization of his movement patterns has been answered by Harmon (1958).

"Any tonic shifts induced by environmental demands in motor systems affected by reflex actions toward gravitational balance become angular stresses on the principal axes and planes of the frame of reference of the body set up by the myotatic reflexes. From the differences between changes in muscle actions to satisfy environmental need over the basic supporting muscle action for gravitational balance — differences representing angular stresses or changes in relation to the principal axes and planes — comes the organism's 'knowledge' of direction of movement. Whether the differences are from tonic shifts or overt action they both represent transformations or movements referrable to the body's basic frame of reference, and both 'feedback' to postural control centers (through proprioception or kinesthesia) a signal pattern representing the degree and direction of the movement or shift as compared to the tonic actions for gravitational support."

A moving organism traveling in a terrestrial field of gravity must be constantly devoted to the task of maintaining balance. The infant geometer expresses his devotion to this cause by seeking a continuing bilateral equation. The equations must occur on all three axes. Since balance is achieved in a gravitational field the organism, by design, must be equipped with the potential to achieve this goal.

The cerebellum of the brain and the semi-circular canals have historically been granted the principal focus in any discussion of balance and continue to hold the primary locus but many other components must contribute to the organization and maintenance of balance. The development of an appropriate organization of anti-gravity muscles is a significant component of balance but again this system is only a contributor and not the singular element in balance. The eyes are organs of balance, the ears are organs of balance—in fact all sensory channels are intricately linked with the organism's effort to gain and hold balance. We cannot speak of balance without examining the manner and degree of contribution which is made by multiple components.

Balance is a many-splendored phenomenon. It is a composite derived from many sources. Since many sources contribute their respective measures to balance the efficiency of balancing for any individual becomes a matter of defining whether each source is making its appropriate contribution.

If the cerebellum or the semi-circular canals are in some manner impaired balance is in jeopardy. If muscular organization has not been achieved at sufficient levels of strength and tension balance is a problem. If the individual does not properly "steer" his body in visual space because of some degree of deviation in visual efficiency balance will be a problem. If he cannot properly orient in an auditory surround to localize and define sound, balance will be affected. If he has difficulty in tactualizing his foot or hand placement on base terrain balance will be impaired. If proprioception offers any kind of difficulty balance will be negatively influenced. Only as all of these sources make adequate contributions can we be assured that the organism is well balanced.

Only a small percentage of the population fails to achieve erect locomotion because of significant damage to the nervous system or other body parts. All those who move through space independently have achieved balance. Since balance is a bilateral equation, however, it may be achieved in many ways less than ideal. Perfect balance requires perfect alignment of all body segments, bilaterally equalized. The percentage who achieve such perfect alignment is relatively small. The fact seems to be that each individual achieves the best possible alignment that he can and pays whatever segmental price is necessary to secure balance for himself.

Building a postural warp is a relatively easy matter. All that is required is to disturb the alignment of body parts so that one or several body segments are not properly centered over their supporting bases. Each body segment has its own line of gravity which is a vertical extension of the gravity line from the part below to the part above. When one segment is moved out of line the center of gravity shifts to that direction. To hold some reasonable measure of balance another segment of the body above or below must be displaced in the opposite direction to bring the center of gravity back over the supporting base.

Whatever may be the precipitant cause of the malalignment the mechanics of dynamic shifting to hold balance remain the same. The individual, to find some measure of comfort has two alternatives. He may counterbalance by shifting another bodily segment and thereby restore his gravitational line in sort of a zig-zag fashion or he may change his base of support by shifting his feet to a wider and wider stance. Whichever alternative is selected reduces his movement efficiency.

Anatomic architecture calls for a balanced muscular process on a bilateral basis with each segment appropriately aligned on a gravity center above and below one another. Even in a so-called static standing position some degree of freedom was designed into the pattern to maintain this alignment without undue stress. This is the "sway phenomenon" which is involuntary but necessary to return venous blood and ensure the adequate circulation in the brain. (Hellebrandt, 1938a, 1938b, 1940)

His destiny is to move. The most economic system of transport is walking. By the end of his first year he is actively identified as an erect being. His developmental momentum directs him toward that status. He spends a year in basic developmental training to prepare himself for locomotion. All of his movement patterns from birth to his triumphant "walk" in space are designed to systematically prepare him for his "human" identification. By design he is a "forward" moving being finding his greatest efficiency in that plane.

As he thrusts and counterthrusts to move himself forward he builds his characteristic posture. If, in order to balance he must shift his center of gravity slightly to the left or the right he does so and becomes comfortable in that positioning. If he must curve his spine inward or outward he does so. A dynamic organism **builds** his postural balance in a gravitational field. His developmental momentum forces the construction of that balancing in the "best possible way he can manage under the circumstances of his particular life". If any of the component parts such as cerebellum, canals, proprioception, muscular strength, vision, audition, tactuality, kinesthesia and so on have in some manner been less contributory than they should be—he still manages to come to balance. His need for balance is primary. He pays whatever cost he must to achieve it.

Consequently the posturing of the individual is at once a reflection of his characteristic way of "coming to balance". As a geometer of space he will define the three princiapl axes of his movement patterning and construct bilateral equations in whatever combination of plus and minuses may be advantageous to him at the moment.

A variety of literary voices have sought to call attention to the multiple factors in balance. Cohen (1961) pointed out that proprioception in the neck is equally as important as the vestibular organs in maintaining balance and assuring the coordination of the full body in action. Howorth (1960) urged that the full study of the foot was vital to analysis of dynamic balance. Harmon (1965) has described the significance of vision in postural balance:

> *The labyrinths, extraoculars, muscles of the neck and balancing muscles of the trunk are potentially tied together so that each can directly or indirectly influence the other in gravitational balance and visually centered performance. Malfunctioning in any segment can affect function in any other segment and further add to the malfunction of the first segment....*
>
> *At minimum tonus the body functions as if it were made up of a number of semi-independent horizontal segments, with a side of one segment responding to the opposite side of that segment only as stretch reflexes called for the functioning of the two sides. In such a hypotonic state vision has only the 'universals' of past experience to draw on for orientation and localization in current space. A naive child in this situation would have distortions in visual space. Good vertical alignment and an adequate gravitational axis on which to build sound coordinates of visual space is derived from the upward signals of the righting reflexes which tie the actions of body segments together in a unitary trainable system.*

Postural variations induced by different positions of head balance have been studied by Jones and associates (Jones and O'Connell, 1958; Jones and Narve, 1955) pointing out that the balance of the head determined the efficiency and speed of movement and was of critical import in analyzing movement efficiency.

The position of the head is of vital significance in all movement patterns. The head is the final point of gravitational centering. The line of gravity passing through the body bisects the frontal plane of the face symmetrically. To properly align the body for comfortable and easy performance the head must contribute its coordinates in proper conformity to the supporting base.

From the earliest period of neonatal life the position of the head is significant. The infant must elevate his head from a prone position and establish its posture as a scanning, guiding and directing tower in order to properly progress to the crawling state. Riding a tricycle, walking on a slope, climbing stairs, sitting at a table all require proper head position to set the eyes into proper alignment with the space surround. In diving, boxing, golfing, hockey, basketball, baseball, in fact in **all** sporting activities the eyes must bring the head into proper alignment with the rest of the body in order to sustain balance comfortably. Thousands of golfers can attest to the fact that the slightest disturbance to the positioning of the head can cause a "duffer" shot. The position of the head is equally important in the skill of writing, drawing, lining, etc. for the same phenomenon that happens in golf can occur in the graphic process when the eyes are turned from the task. The child can "duff" the position of puzzle pieces, letters, dots and so on by simply lifting his eyes from the task while the hand is performing.

Gesell (Carmichael, 1954) discusses the principle of reciprocal interweaving which accounts for the process whereby man develops an orderly interrelation of his paired organs. The child, in order to have effective motion, must develop control over opposing muscles so that when one set is in excitation, the other is reacting in an inhibitory fashion. From the neurological viewpoint, this implies that an intricate cross-interweaving takes place in neural control mechanisms.

In all degrees of movement, balance is an important factor. The human organism represents a balance of forces. Seashore (1947) defines the dynamics of balance as follows:

> *Physically, dynamic balance refers to the case of a body whose weight is so distributed that the resultant of the forces is varying from moment to moment. Neuromuscularly, dynamic balance refers to the maintenance of an organized postural orientation under conditions in which the activity pattern of the muscles is continually changing so as to disturb the gross postural orientation and require further muscular activity to re-establish the orientation. Psychologically, dynamic balance refers to the postural orientation of the body when the organism is performing a specified motor activity which involves relatively large motions of all or parts of the body which act to disturb the gross orientation of the organism (p. 247).*

Harmon (1958) points out that mechanisms for postural centering to balance are determinants of the organism's orientation in the space world. The body operates in unison, starting before birth, making a coordinated and integrated functioning organism. Bodily growth is directed toward a balanced bisymmetric process. "From birth to maturity, the child—from a dynamic point of view—is a totality which is constantly undergoing alteration to maintain an equilibrium of parts which are in many and various stages of completeness. Any distortion of any of these parts distorts or limits the growth of the whole"(p. A-17).

We can draw our discussion of dynamic balance to a close by turning again to the words of Huxley (1954):

> *Most biologists do not seem to realize the extent to which functional modification occurs in the normal vertebrate body. It appears to be true, not only that the size of every muscle in the body depends upon function but the size, direction and structure of every tendon and bone; the detailed configuration of the blood system depends largely or perhaps wholly on hydrodynamic considerations; the size of every gland is regulated by its function and even the nervous system does not escape. It is only in the earliest development that structure precedes function; later structure is the resultant of function.*

Dynamic balance is a significant companion component to muscular strength in the construction of movement efficiency. It requires a lifelong effort to maintain. Once achieved, it is not fixed. The organism is a bilaterally equating and dynamic being and as such may modify his posture according to the stresses he must resolve. Posture from infancy periods may improve or worsen.

The achievement of dynamic balance is not only a physical goal but a physiologic one as well. The total physiologic system must achieve its own homeostasis for complete comfort. Any disturbance to the physiologic balancing of the organism will inevitably reverberate to the physical balancing problems. To complete the picture of balance we must incorporate the concept of psychological balance.

The space worlds of men have always contained some expression of belief in the concept of two fundamental contending and opposite forces—one good and one evil—existing in the universe. The concept of these two forces probably stems from a day and night—light and dark—difference which has been a universal experience for Man from the beginning of time. Darkness has always been associated with mystery, intrigue and danger. When Man cannot see clearly he experiences a feeling of threat to his security. The opposites of God and the Devil have been associated with light and darkness. Perhaps the clearest and most widespread expression of dualism is to be found in the "Yang and Yin" beliefs of the Near East. "Yang" was designated as aggressive, masculine, forceful, driven by self-interest and consumptive. "Yin" represented the feminine, passive, receptive, compassionate, creative nurturing and creative force. In the Confucian interpretation of these polarized forces it was held that there was benefit only when there was reciprocity, complementation and cooperation between the two poles. This reciprocity and balancing of influence was necessary to maintain a stability of goodness. The belief was and is that imbalance or preponderance of one principle over another, the universe itself and the moral and social orders were subject to disintegration and catastrophe. This version of balance between these two forces have permeated Man's religious, social, moral and political beliefs for many centuries. In some manner the individual space world incorporates this fundamental concept. Its major form of expression appears in the religious segment of the individual space world. An incorporation of an attitude and belief of "rightness" and "wrongness" however defined becomes an integral part of each space world. The thinking of any individual may imbalance these polar opposites too far in either direction and encounter thereby much difficulty in his life space.

The concept of the "balanced personality" has long been a vital model for psychological theorists. The balanced point between extroversion and introversion, between passivity and open aggression, between emotional lability and dampening excessive controls has been an important consideration in mental health. We frequently read of the need for balance between play and work, eating and exercise. Everywhere someone is advocating balance. The theme of the bilateral equation runs through the life of man, physically, physiologically and psychologically. Balance is a vital factor in the movement of mankind.

Our principal concern in emphasizing it as a significant component in Movement Efficiency is to delineate balance as a derivative of experience constructed in a span of gravitational encounters. It is built by a dynamic moving being. The result of that building helps each learner to answer more clearly the question of "who am I?" Regardless of the perspective from which we view the concept—physically, physiologically, socially, universally, astronomically, intellectually or emotionally—balance becomes a contribution to identity.

When this component is considered in curricular terms the teacher must continuously be aware of the balance of the student—physically and cognitively. Activities must be scheduled in the cognitive realm to help the learner develop "a balanced viewpoint", "to see both sides of a controversy" and so on. As a complement to Muscular Strength children must be given multiple opportunities to explore balance in various physical ways. Equipment which helps the child explore balance on a physical basis should be used to establish an alignment. Holding balance for lengthy periods of time provides no real learning increment to the performer. Only as the learner comes to a cognitive appreciation of "coming to balance" in order to properly support each subsequent move will "balancing projects" have any real value.

Those who are concerned with the optimal development of children must consciously strive to make observations of child performance in terms of balance. A failing effort of a child can often be converted to a successful one by simply noting an inadequate base or a position of imbalance and correcting it by "immediate suggestion".

Both Muscular Strength and Dynamic Balance must be regarded as making a contribution to personal identity bringing the individual to a state of awareness of his own body.

6

BODY AWARENESS

Since the introduction of the body image concept into the field of psychology many efforts have been made to devise ways of measuring the integrity of the image in both normal and pathological populations. In general two forms of measurement have been favored. One system has relied upon the drawing of the human figure and the other upon some form of verbal response to labeling body parts.

The drawing of the human figure has been quantified as a measure of intelligence by Goodenough (1949) with scoring based upon the number of details included. It has been used to assess various states of psychological behavior by Machover (1961) and as a complement to the study of organic pathology by Schilder (1950), Bender and Silver (1948) and many others.

Distortions of details, omission of parts, variations in size, difference in emphases, planes of drawing, perspective and so on have been the criteria for inferring that such distrubances were a reflection of an internal state of confusion in the image the drawer held of his own body. Fisher and Cleveland (1958) have regarded the technique as "controversial" and open to much question and Levy (1950) stated "the technique of analyzing drawings is without experimental validation and rarely yields unequivocal information". Despite its controversial nature the technique of analyzing body awareness through the use of human figure drawings continues to be a relatively popular clinical procedure.

The technique of assessing body image by requesting the subject to name body parts or identify by pointing is the second most widely used procedure. Schontz (1956), MacDonald (1960), Kephart (1960) and others have described such techniques. Ayers (1961) reported testing knowledge of fingers by touch. Neilsen and Sult (1939) requested patients to state the relative position of body parts. Fisher and Cleveland (1958) in their review described the Adams-Caldwell technique of using ten wooden balls in a **Somatic Apperception Test**, the Katcher-Levin technique using triads of schematic body parts in three sizes to represent father, mother and self and many other approaches.

Inaccuracies in labeling or localizing are attributed to disturbances of the body schema in such approaches.

The schema of the body serves as a primitive model for the development of number concepts. Werner (1948) discussed the manner in which primitive tribes used a body orientation for quantifying events in their world and saw in it the origination of our present numbering system. He referred to the body as a "numerical gestalt" containing built-in units of twoness, fiveness and tenness. Strauss and Lehtinen (1947) and Kephart (1960) have also emphasized the factor of body awareness in building a system of spatial relationships related to the visual space of arithmetic. Strauss and Werner (1938) and Benton (1951) studied finger agnosia in relation to arithmetic functioning among subnormal boys. Neilsen (1938) studied finger naming in adults. Kephart (1960) suggested that balance training should be combined with arithmetic training in the young child so that he can be "aided to a fuller understanding of quantitative concepts by the use of the total body in their demonstration".

Many studies of the relationship of right-left orientation difficulties to reading problems have been conducted. Money (1962) concluded that the findings of most studies suggest that such a relationship exists but that the extent and significance of such a relationship remains debatable.

Benton (1959) refers to three elements which are necessary to the formation of body awareness beginning in early infancy; integration of sensory information, learning and symbolic representation. Impairment in any of these three can be expected to produce a lag in the development of body awareness.

Cruickshank (1963) expressed the belief that unless a child has a coordinated and coherent understanding of the body image, learning to read and process numbers either does not take place or is extremely retarded. From his studies on body image among achieving and non-achieving children he concluded, "Until the child realizes that his total body functions in a coordinated way, that there is meaning and reason to the relationship of the several parts and that each part has its separate and appropriate functions in relation to the total, learning of a socially acceptable nature apparently cannot take place. As these concepts enter the conscious understanding of the child achievement may be observed to take place in the abstract areas of reading and arithmetic."

The investigations in the area of body image have been many and varied in the past 30 years. There can be little question of the general acceptance of the concept. Each individual does develop an "image" of his body. How the reflection of this "image" may be measured with certainty and accuracy remains in the realm of controversy with various investigators expressing a high level of confidence in the approach they use and others expressing doubt. Even though methodologies may be criticized, the extensiveness of interpretations questioned and the techniques of reflection remain controversial

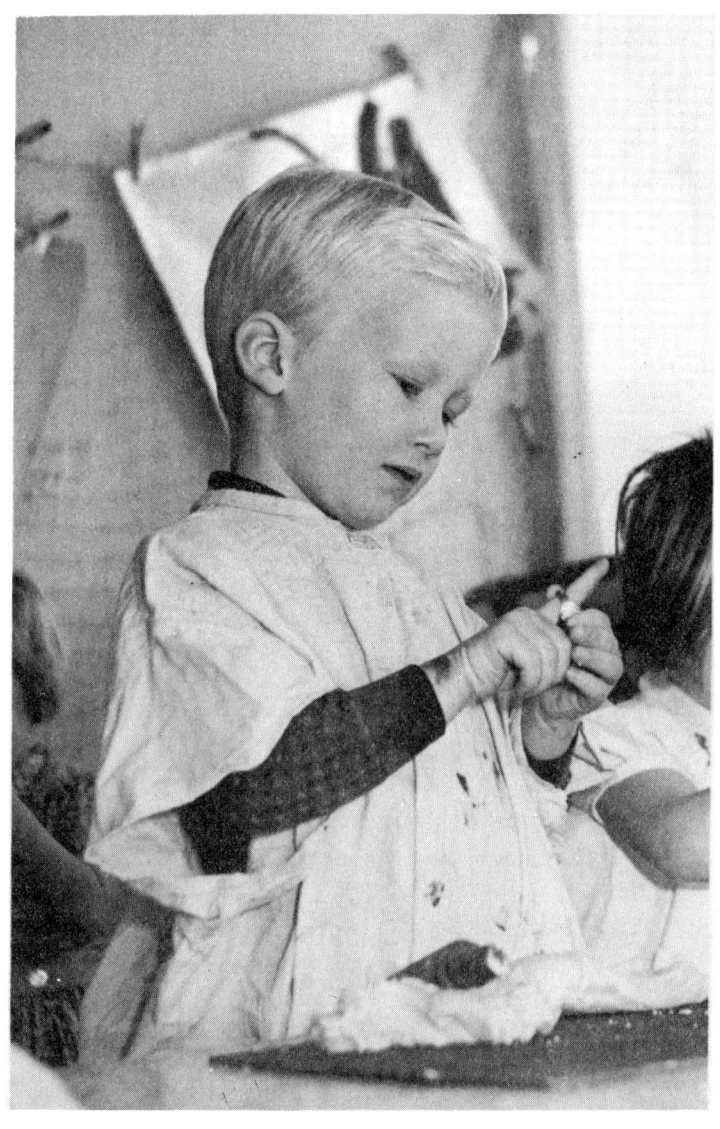

A clay do-nut ring offers an opportunity to add another small bit of information to the expanding composite of Body Awareness. A brief moment of personal discovery during a developmental period when discovery is so vital to expansion of the space world.

the existence of "body image" as a vital component of behavioral organization is no longer doubted. Everybody has a "body image", everyone has "body awareness"—in varying degrees of complexity.

Despite the emphasis upon distortion of that image in the literature, the image although "fractured", "disturbed", "confused" exists in some form. Each individual, normal, brain-injured, emotionally disturbed, deaf, blind, physically handicapped and culturally disadvantaged has some composite awareness of his body.

Body Awareness becomes the final member of the trio of dimensions required to provide the individual with the primitive foundation for answering the question, "Who am I?". The literature as well as logic support the contention that Body Awareness is related to the movement of the individual to advanced stages of more complicated behavior. As a foundation block, there is need to be properly cognizant of this awareness in providing opportunities for learning in the young child.

Any individual manifesting a disturbance to Body Awareness must encounter difficulty in answering the question "Who am I?". Any degree of uncertainty and vagueness in this dimension tends to produce some degree of malalignment and maladaptation in the earliest stages of formation for Movement Efficiency. Any disturbance to the natural acquisition of Body Awareness will tend to diminish its supporting value to the previous dimensions and create a state of imbalance for the complexity buildup which must follow.

Any effort to assess the Movement Efficiency of the individual must incorporate some technique of judging the adequacy of Body Awareness. A disturbance in this component, major or minor, is a significant lead to analyzing the relative state of efficiency. Any individual lacking an adequate identity can be expected to manifest a negative reverberation throughout the total component system. His synthesis for efficiency will show some degree of deviation from an optimal line. The individual who experiences any difficulty in acquiring a satisfying and adequate image of himself can be expected to be uncertain in space transport. The individual with an inadequate identity becomes "lost in space". Having not yet found himself he can scarcely be expected to find anything else. Since he does not know "who" he is he must lack direction and purpose for any form of transport. His quest must be a preoccupation with the basic question of identity—any other questing becomes superfluous and non-contributory. Identity as we have already suggested is a constantly emerging process varying with age and life situation. It is therefore never static but always shaping with experience. Thus "who am I?" is not a question to be answered once and thereafter ignored. It is a perpetual question for the learner. The ease with which he answers the question from day to day, year to year and place to place is always determined by the ease with which he answered the question the first time it was posed.

Each time he must answer the question he relies upon his previous successes. If the answers have been adequate previously his identity potential is increased for the next encounter. If the answers have not been adequate each subsequent need for defining identity becomes more vague and the individual becomes "more and more lost in life space". When the problem of adjustment at any age is defined as an "identity dilemma" some degree of ignorance in body awareness is the obscure culprit.

Body awareness has unfortunately fallen into a scheme of polar opposites. There is at the one extreme the pathological manifestation of inadequate body schema in gross terms as described in the reports on organic and psychotic populations and at the other extreme the "normal" subjects judged to have an adequate body schema. The position taken here is that the many shades of gray along the continuum must be considered as representing the vast majority of our population. It is our contention that relatively few people may be classified as having a high degree of body awareness.

Physiologic space is not well understood. Physicians can attest to the ignorance of most people in regard to where things are in their body and the difficulty that most patients encounter in trying to spatially localize and define their symptoms. Teachers of the dance will attest to the difficulties among their students in acquiring awareness of muscle groups and the voluntary control which must be exercised for appropriate movements. Once the average person has completed his required courses in high school biology he tends to take his body for granted.

The literature on body image is unfortunately emphatically in the direction of the pathologic. The studies of "normal body scheme" are in the minority. The developing characteristics of a body schema have largely been detailed in terms of human figure drawings tending to present a very narrow consideration for the full concept. We can only speculate at this point on the manner in which a child goes about organizing a body scheme. Our first speculation is that he probably follows a cephalocaudad line acquiring an awareness of head, shoulders, torso, pelvis, legs and finally feet. The developmental sequence for movement suggests that he must become aware of each of these body parts in the sequence in which he must incorporate their use in building his movement patterns. Secondly, this awareness probably also follows a proximal-distal rule with awareness of sources coming before awareness of end members. Our third speculation and perhaps most important relates to cognition. Unless awareness is brought to a cognitive level no schema can emerge. Among pathologic populations of children and adults, clinicians will often encounter patients who walk, run, sit, stand, climb, etc. having no awareness that they are doing so. Often brain-injured and emotionally disturbed children will seem to move about with a certain degree of agility but with no

Floor space can become a quiet terrain of learning immobility.

Quadrupedal movements help establish an awareness of the body in motion.

A simple exercise for developing the eye hand point of convergence.

real awareness of what they are doing.

Body awareness may be scaled along a line of progressive complexity consonant with the general advancement on all fronts. We expect a four year old to be more aware than a two year old. There is a progressive expectation of greater awareness with advancing age. Even though we have no careful cataloguing of the characteristics of body awareness at age 6 or 9 or 12 or 40 there is an assumption of greater complexity. We seem to assume that as long as everything else about the individual advances in complexity so also will his awareness of his body. This form of conventional wisdom is generally accepted but it has never been adequately documented.

These considerations hold some significant concepts for therapy with inefficient movement patterns at whatever age they may be found. The clinician, the movement therapist, the teacher, the parent—whoever is seeking to improve the functioning level of the individual must regard Body Awareness training as an essential part of the therapy program. Emphasis upon training for Body Awareness is not a new concept, it has been underlined in the literature for over 200 years but usually employed only when there is ample evidence of body image distortion. Our concern here is that it is an essential component in Movement Efficiency for all people—those with small problems as well as big problems—and therefore must be part and parcel of a training program in movement for young children, high-schoolers, college students, executives and those wishing to correct a slice tendency in their golf shots.

The simple verbal labeling of body parts does not constitute a cognitive awareness of a composite schema. Cognitive direction of movement and appropriate utilization of parts in producing efficient movement are the main ingredients of a body schema. It is learned by the infant as he moves. Thousands of gross and fine movements in the exploration of his environment become bits of information to be fed into the human computer to yield an "image". A body schema is derived from movement and the feedback from such movement.

As the "skeleton walks" aided by muscles, seeking a balance it comes to a cognitive appreciation of its own identity. Dynamically operating in an energy surround, traveling in domains, fields and zones of space it formulates an "image". It answers the question, "Who am I?".

7

SPATIAL

AWARENESS

The first three components establish the initial awareness of identity as a unit of existence apart from otherness and serve as a cognitive terrain on which the child builds his answer to the question, "Who am I?" His answer to the question is far from complete—only a vague and sketchy outline of a composition yet to be clarified but the buds of the self-concept have begun to swell. A great deal more searching will occur before the question is satisfactorily answered, but each passing year and a succession of countless experiences will help to shade in contour, color and form on the initial vague self-image. The answer will become clearer in time. His identity may be clearly established by the time he is a third-grader or he may search a lifetime for identity. The supporting foundation for identity is established by his erect locomotion.

Having scarcely been oriented to the first vital question of life, he is immediately confronted with the next serious question, "Where am I?". He must promptly define the parameters of the "whereness" of his world and relate himself in a significant manner to the objects and people "other" than self. This places him squarely in the field of the fourth component in movement—Spatial Awareness.

Within the dynamics of this component, he acquires the metrics of space. In order to define space he must develop **within himself** a reference system for delineating the metrics of his movement. His reference system is a set of coordinates. He moves on and around the vertical, horizontal and depth planes as he transports himself in space. These three axes serve as a basic reference system for promoting space sophistication. Since he moves in a surround of space, he must acquire a sophisticated awareness of the over-allness of that space. He must become aware of **up** space and **down** space, **front** space and **back** space, **left** space and **right** space.

His developmental progression of movements activates his muscular system to move his bony framework into a position of balance, and through such pulling and thrusting he achieves body awareness. Were his development to stop there, he would be a static being, poised in balance and aware of himself but "having no place to go". To move in space he must become aware of it. He must estimate space, measure, organize and live within space—efficiently or inefficiently—according to the degree of spatial awareness he is able to achieve.

The three coordinates are established in a gravitational field and are evolved by each individual from his experiences with movement against the pull of gravity. In the course of building the triordinate system within himself, the individual must relate himself to a triordinate system imposed on the outside world. All space and objects occupying space may be plotted on the lines of the three axes. Any object in space can be assigned a vertical, and horizontal and a depth axis. Alignment, then, becomes a matter of a dynamic equation between an internal set of triordinates and an externally imposed set of triordinates. The "field dependent and independent" perceptual characteristics defined by Witkin and his associates (1954) have bearing on this point. In Movigenic translation, the field dependent people lack a well-defined set of internalized triordinates and as a consequence frequently experience a mismatch between the internal and external. Their course of adaptation must be to modify their internal triordinates under the influence of the external. The field independent people hold a reasonably secure set of internal coordinates and direct their effort to realigning the external triordinates to match their own. The field dependent person may conform his body alignment to the slant of pictures improperly positioned on walls, deviated verticals and horizontals at any position in his world. With environmental distortion present, the field dependent person warps in conformity to the perceived distortion or remains in a bewildered state of immobility.

The field independent person observes the triordinate distortion in his environment and relies upon his own triordinates for balance using his internalized alignment to rectify the object world if this is possible. If this is not possible, he finds stability in the face of distortion within the security of his own alignment. He holds balance within himself despite the imbalance of his surround. While the research of Witkin and others seems to show a relatively clear-cut split into two categories, we believe the dynamic answer lines somewhere in between.

In developmental terms, the building of the triordinate system into an adequate internal alignment requires a reciprocal interweaving action between the external and the internal. Both sets of triordinates are built through movement. Any perceived external distortion is relayed to the construction process in building the internals. The misalignment of internals is subsequently imposed upon the externals. Both act upon one another.

It is possible to relate some of the findings of field dependency with distorted rooms, inverted lenses, trapezoidal windows, and so on, to the earliest stages of locomotive alignment in the young child. When alignment is built by the reciprocal interweaving of a tridimensional organism moving in a tridimensional world of triordinates, internal and external have early equivalence.

The child relies upon the dimensions of his surround to "get his bearing" for economic transport. It is entirely possible that the architecture of his physical world may have direct pertinence to each child in building his alignment. Slanted ceilings, wainscotings, arches, draperies, gooseneeked lamps, frilly curtains, and many other objects in his day-by-day world may in some manner interfere with a secure system of visual verticals and horizontals as he moves through space. While the decor and the general architecture may be pleasing to the adults who have already learned to maintain their verticality in the face of distortions, the young child may experience considerable difficulty in establishing his alignment in a criss-cross pattern of alignment cues. At first glance this consideration may appear to suggest a great to-do over trivia, but the results of the adult reactions to physical environmental distortion suggest that postural alignment realies upon visual cueing from environmental verticals. If the modification in postural response can be noted in adults, there is reason to suspect that the earliest period of development may be particularly sensitive to distortion and relate itself to that distortion in the building of the triordinate internals.

The Vertical Coordinate

The vertical coordinate is the most important of the three coordinates. The fundamental dignity of man comes from an erect stance with head held high, locomoting in erect posture, moving through space in an upright position. The horizontal and depth coordinates are secondary to the achievement of that erect stance. The two other coordinates emerge from the development of the vertical. If the vertical coordinate develops with some degree of deviation from a true midline, both the horizontal and the depth coordinates will suffer a proportionate amount of deviation from true line.

The vertical coordinate begins its development at birth. The infant in a supine position is a diffuse responsive being activating both sides of his body simultaneously in random movement, but this random movement is bilaterally contributing to the building of the vertical. Each time the infant is lifted for feeding or dressing, a contribution is made to the midline. Parents bending over the supine infant, dangling objects in front of him, pulling him to a sitting or standing position with both hands, placing suspended objects in his crib for manual exploration—all offer some contribution to the development of the vertical. As the infant achieves a roll-over to the prone position, he must rotate on the vertical axis. Rolling over requires a vertical line of rotating the full body-half on the axis and bringing it to a position of rest on the stomach. While the infant is in the first stages of acquiring an adequate roll-over pattern, the vertical line is likely to be distorted so that the final result is a twisted version in which the full vertical is not managed. The arm and hand are not properly extricated in the roll-over, and consequently the infant is in an uncomfortable position. Eventually, however, he manages the roll-over with relative ease and another contribution is made to his vertical orientation. Tonic-neck-reflex posturing is also a necessary contribution to the vertical alignment moving each lateral half into position in relation to a midline. Once the infant is able to assume a prone position, he is ready for the next step in building his vertical alignment, that of lifting his head and his upper torso. In rapid succession he follows that move with further development down the vertical line of his body in cephalocaudad direction to bring himself to the crawling position. He crawls as directly and accurately towards desired objects or persons as the equality of contributions from each side converge upon a midline and allow him to hold a straight line of movement with visual guidance. This movement is in the depth plane, but its contribution is made to the vertical, for it becomes another stepping stone in the achievement of a vertical orientation. As the infant comes to the erect stance and takes the first faltering independent steps into space, the vertical alignment is receiving its first vital test. Although his TNR, head lift, rolling, crawling and all other movements have involved the horizontal and the depth planes and his vision, audition and tactuality have operated in the other planes as well—all of these experiences were supplementary to and secondary to the major goal of erect locomotion.

His first major conquest over gravity has been achieved, and he is then ready to explore other aspects of his vertical world. Once moving in the erect position, the entire world must appear different to him. In the vertical stance his sighting of objects, localization of sounds, touch of furniture, feel of muscle movement—in fact, everything about him appears somewhat modified. Having learned something of the world of space from a prone and a crawling or sitting position, he must now organize it again at the vertical level in relationship to his own verticality. In achieving walking, he has identified himself with the other humans in his world and has truly joined the ranks of Man. Once again his vision must guide his vertical moves. He must look where he is going. He must direct his forward momentum visually. He must center himself on targets of approach. He must move directly to that which he wants. He must learn to circumvent obstacles when they spatially block his path. At all times, however, he must maintain a visual guidance of his direction of movement. Very often the neophyte walker neglects this important aspect and finds himself fallen, bumped, bruised and defeated. Even though he has achieved erect locomotion, he has not yet achieved the sophistication in vertical orientation which will serve him for a lifetime. He needs to add to his erect locomotion the visual guidance to judge distance, height, accessability, etc. Once having achieved his full height in vertical orientation, he must integrate all of his other learnings into that vertical plane to become an efficient mover. He must take all that he has learned to do with his eyes, ears, hands, feet and body, and bring his state of knowledge to a point of integration to serve his vertical orientation. The time period during which erect locomotion is achieved probably represents the first major synthesis of the human organism as a mobile unit. During this period he practices his new orientation. He tries walking sideways, backwards, on tiptoe and countless other variations. These are not cognitively oriented but simply represent explorations of the newly discovered vertical in a practical space of activity. Gesell (1949) spoke of the 18-month-old as showing a "predilection for vertical sectors". He builds towers, draws vertical lines, climbs stairs and spends much time in exploring the vertical from the initiation of walking until well into the sixth year of life.

The first five years of development appear to be primarily devoted to the full acquisition of a vertical orientation. While developmental observations have indicated that a child has many experiences in all three dimensions of space, the multiples of experience seem to be clearly weighted in the direction of the vertical. Other forms of space exploration are made in preparation for the time when the horizontal and the depth planes will become the most vital. In this sense they serve as an introductory background, but their major purpose seems to be in service to the vertical orientation.

In addition to the many investigators who have carefully catalogued the development of the infant and young child, there have been many investigators in the field of physical education who have been interested in the motor development of the preschool child. While their purpose in conducting investigations was expressly intended to evaluate and describe differences in motor capabilities, it is possible to regard them as investigations of vertical orientation from the standpoint of the type of activities which were studied.

McCaskell and Wellman (1937) observed differences in ladder climbing proficiency in their preschool population as a part of their general study of motor performance. They used a small ladder having rungs spaced six inches apart and a large one having rungs spaced twelve inches apart. They checked ascent and descent on both ladders again using the classification of marking time (2 feet on a rung before proceeding) and alternation of feet as levels of differentiation in advancement, adding to their classification the comment as to whether the child proceeded cautiously or with comfort and facility. The criteria of 50% passing the test was used to determine motor age levels. By age 38 months, the ascent of the small ladder was managed with facility in alternation, but another nine months passed before the same proficiency occurred on the large ladder. Descending the ladders posed a more complex problem to the children. Descent of the small ladder was not managed with facility until 53 months, and the large ladder was not managed until 63 months. Nearly a full year difference was noted between the simple and more complex descents, and a fifteen-month difference existed between facile ascent and descent on the small ladder. A nine-month difference was found between facile ascent and descent on the large ladder. Again there were wide differences in climbing proficiency, and using a criteria of 50% passage to set the motor age leaves a sizable percentage of failures among the group in each category.

Although a number of questions might be raised about methodology, criteria and so on, if one wishes to pursue a course of precision, the general information from this study has developmental merit and has value despite its shortcomings. The ladder study, in our terminology, represents an exploration of vertical space for the child and is a further verification of our contention that a full five-year span is devoted to the acquisition of a comfortable and proficient vertical coordinate. The study also suggests that "upness" is organized before "downness" and that the visual guidance available in ascent contributes to ease, whereas the spatial organization of dropping the foot downward relies upon kinesthetic judgment and must therefore be a less efficient system.

Another form of climbing for children occurs in the use of playground equipment and walking on varying forms of inclined planes. Gutteridge (1939) found that 50% of her study group were reasonably proficient at age 3 in climbing on jungle gyms, packing boxes, inclined planks and other similar equipment. By the age of 6 the percentage of those who were proficient in such skills was increased to 90%. Ten per cent of her group did not achieve success at age 6 and presumably could be classified as having some form of movement problem, at least in relation to the tasks which Gutteridge used. It is of interest to note that even those children who could be classified as "good" climbers relied upon a crawling approach to ascend an inclined plank when they felt that an erect ascent would be too difficult for them. The study showed wide differences in climbing ability at every age.

Exploration of vertical space also takes place in a child's adventures in jumping. Jumping from a perch of varying heights can be classified as a downward expression of the vertical, even though the "Z" axis is involved to some degree and can be evaluated from two points of focus, the lift-off and the landing. McCaskell and Wellman included a jumping series in their preschool study and expressed their findings in motor ages based on a criterion of 50% of the group being successful. Their findings indicate that most children can jump from an 8" perch and land with both feet together at 33 months, but when an additional 20 inches are introduced to the elevation, successful two-foot landing does not occur until 46 months. Whatever the developmental factors might be that contribute to this difference, the 20-inch increase in vertical space poses enough of a problem to the child that 13 months of additional developmental experience seem to be required before the increase can be managed. Gutteridge (1939) also confirmed that 80% of her group had attained reasonably proficient jumping skills by age five.

Another favored investigation among physical educators has been the standing broad jump. One such study was conducted by Kane and Meredith (1952) with 560 elementary school children. Results indicated that performance improved with age and that boys showed greater rates of improvement than girls. Average jumpers at age seven performed as well as poor eleven-year-old jumpers, and skilled nine-year-olds performed better than average eleven-year-old jumpers. Again there was a finding of a wide range of variability in each age group.

When the child does not have to contend with gravity in moving himself through space, he moves with ease at an early age. Supported on the balanced tripod of three wheels and the seat of his tricycle, his balance is reasonably assured. Pumping his legs and visually guiding the handlebars, the child achieves tricycle competency at age 4. This is a transport competency which is achieved long before he is as secure in covering the same terrain on his own erect locomotion. This competency acquisition will be repeated many more times in his journey to maturity. Throughout his lifetime, whenever he can assign the gravity problem and balance to some sort of device, typically in the seated position, he will move more swiftly and accurately through space.

Another type of performance on the vertical axis is the bouncing of the ball. The downward thrust with the expectant rebound return to the hand is a difficult task for children. In a study of ball bouncing in a population of 2-7 year olds, Gutteridge (1939) reported that none of the children could demonstrate any proficiency until the age of four, and even at six and one-half years of age only 61% of the group could manage this. The usual form of error is for the child to thrust the ball downward at a forward angle which causes the rebound to return far out of the child's reach. The rebound must be on the vertical axis if the child is to catch the ball without moving from the base of the initial thrust.

In none of these studies was the vertical alignment of the child questioned. A general assumption seems to have been made that each child was somehow adequately organized in vertical space and whatever differences were found among children were likely to be attributed to maturational differences rather than to any possibility of deviations in the vertical alignment. It seems reasonable to assume that a child's sophistication in the vertical space of upness and downness will bear some relationship to the degree of accuracy he has achieved in aligning himself on the vertical plane in the general course of his experience. If, for any reason, the midline within him is deviated from a true vertical line, some degree of malalignment is present requiring some form of counterbalancing from one of the sides in order to hold balance. In the process of synthesizing his vision with his walking, his hearing with his walking, and his tactual and kinesthetic processes with his walking, some form of error was introduced to the detriment of his vertical. It must be remembered that the developmental process demands the synthesis of literally thousands of details into an organization adequate to support the next advancement. The sheer complexity of this demand for synthesis at various points in development suggests the possibility for mild errors to enter into the

The drawing of a second grader reflecting a pronounced vertical tilt to the right in a right handed child. To achieve such a production a considerable amount of postural deviation is required in the sitting position.

Sometimes a spatial organization becomes so confusing that it is abandoned in a half-finished state.

synthesizing process, which may take many years before the full impact of the miscalculation may be noted in the performance of the individual.

The errors in synthesis may be occasioned by illness, disease, accident, lack of opportunity, deprivation or any number of other causes. Since developmental momentum is rushing the organism to its completion—it continues relentlessly unable to wait until all elements are in a complete state of readiness. The synthesis occurs with whatever contributions are available at the developmental moment. The possibility for varying states of unreadiness has been accounted for in the general pattern of development, for there are various lulls in development which seem to serve as a collecting period for the individual to bring together all of his existing knowledge into some form of unity before proceeding onward to the next level. The possibility that the various ingredients necessary for an adequate integration may not have achieved the proper state of readiness at the time they are required to contribute their appropriate share toward the synthesis may well thrust the individual on to the next plateau of development not quite as well-prepared as he should be.

The adequacy of the synthesis for vertical alignment becomes critical for all future performance. Any difficulties in dynamic balance, visual deviations, mislocalizations in audition, inequalities in bone structure or muscle organization must have some impact upon the vertical organization.

It is entirely possible that the variations noted in vertical performance skills among preschool children might be accounted for on the basis of some deviations in the vertical orientations of the children and not simply be attributed to variations in maturation.

The Horizontal Coordination

Although the young traveler has experienced all three dimensions and all planes within those dimensions almost from the date of his birth, it is our contention that the movements on the horizontal and depth axes bear only a minor significance relative to efficiency on those two planes. We view those movements, rather as a multiplex of spatial experiences intended to specifically refine the vertical orientation of the organism. Out of his early lateral experiences and forward and backward movements, the individual draws the necessary feedback to stabilize the vertical. Despite the fact that there is a considerable body of evidence from observation and experiment that the infant is more active on these two axes than he has previously been credited, we wish to persist in our contention that such experiencing is intended to benefit the vertical.

Having devoted five years plus or minus to the building of the vertical, his spatial development then seems to shift its emphasis to the building of the efficiency in the horizontal plane. Developmental momentum apparently projects the youngster into the period of lateralization regardless of the state of his vertical efficiency. At this point, his vertical efficiency, at whatever level it may be established, serves as a reference point for building the horizontal. Once again, while he continues to experience both the vertical and the depth axes the encounters are now directed toward contributing to the horizontal. The horizontal emerges from the vertical and already has a pre-destined quality about it, according to the degree of efficiency achieved in the vertical. Any significant deviation in the vertical organization of the individual presages some form of difficulty with the horizontals.

The general body of literature in child development does not reflect a focus upon the lateral development of children as a coordinate axis. The emphasis has rather been placed upon such questions as handedness, mixed dominance, inaccurate labeling systems, and so on.

Developmental studies in form perception, drawing, academic performance and right-left discriminations in idenitifcations and reading have consistently pointed to the six to eight-year-old span as the critical period for the development of the oblique line of direction and the bilateral coordinate. This period seems to be crucial to the development of the horizontal plane.

Gesell (1949) referred to the three and a half year old as being in a period of transition when higher forms of behavior must be imposed upon lower forms and he must be made ready for the full impact of the symbolic process. The task of development is to bring opposites (near-far, up-down, etc.) into effective counterpoint (p. 159). The major period of decision on these opposites seems to occur in the four- to six-year-old time span. This age period seems to be a critical one for sides to become confused in the acquisition of the horizontal coordinate. This developmental time is laying the foundation for fusion. In some respects this period may be regarded as the key moment for the development of visual problems, particularly strabismus because of difficulties in achieving an adequate and efficient horizontal in visual space.

Studies of right-left discrimination skills in children have shown that those who show systematic reversals in designating right and left are typically retarded in language functions. (Benton, 1959)

Problems in right-left discrimination have also been shown by children with reading disability. Benton (1959) and Kephart (1960) have discussed the problems of lateral organization in great detail.

A study of 150 retarded readers nine and ten years of age from Aberdeen, Scotland, revealing a significant incidence of inability to identify right and left on their own bodies as well as in things in the environment, has been reported by Birch and Belmont (1965).

Passey and Guedry (1949) tested pilots in a trainer device subjecting them to inclinations on four planes deviated from the gravitational vertical. They found that adjustments in the lateral plane are made with greater accuracy than either medial or left and right obliques

A further differentiation of the body scheme occurring during the fifth and sixth year in the form of a **right-left gradient** has been postulated by Benton (1959) after his extensive study of the area of right-left discrimination in children. Children consiously become aware of a "felt difference" in the two sides at that point in their lives. The gradient is sensory-postural in nature and verbal concepts of right and left do not enter into the development of the gradient. The gradient represents a particular type of "topographic configuration" and implies that these elements are organized in **space**.

One example of stages in the development of spatial relations, that of "left and right", has been discussed by Werner (1948). The first stage was described as purely a space of action and spatial qualities of action in which the young child relates spatial thinking only in terms of his own movements. Approximately five years pass before an individual achieves an identification of left and right on his own body as the second stage in the sequence. Drawing upon the work of Piaget, Werner points out that another two years pass before the child can mirror the left and right on his own body to assign these terms on a contralateral basis to the bodies of others. Another three years seem to be needed before the child can attribute a rightness and leftness to chairs, tables, boxes, books and signs.

This sequence suggests an eleven-year span from a primitive to a sophisticated conceptualization. There are probably many children who achieve such sophistication earlier, as well as a number who require more than eleven years. Even when this sequence is regarded as merely suggestive rather than a rigorous timetable, it is clear that a considerable length of time is required to bring the child to a concept of leftness and rightness. It is probably no exaggeration to consider that the average child experiences thousands of confrontations of leftness and rightness during his preschool years, and certainly his orientation to the academic world involves thousands more of such confrontations. What cognitive processes finally come to a stabilization after all those confrontations to yield an integration of leftness and rightness as abstractions? What factors are operative in those children who acquire this conceptualization earlier? What factors are inoperative among adults who continue to experience uncertainty when left and right identifications are demanded in prosaic daily experiences? The answers to these questions rest in the understanding of how overall spatial proficiency is acquired by each individual.

In none of the literature on left-right orientations have we been able to note a discussion of the vertical orientation of the performer as being of significant bearing upon the problems which may be encountered by the child. The span of eleven years which Werner and Piaget report before the child actually has fully internalized the horizontal coordinate and can cross match and impose his own coordinates upon the physical and cognitive world suggests that, by design, an equal number of years seem to be devoted to both the vertical and the horizontal.

The number of adults who continue to be plagued throughout a lifetime by lateral uncertainty may well be an indication that such lateral efficiency is not an automatic achievement of a bilateral organism. It must be evolved by experience. Secure knowledge of sidedness may be more intricately related to the vertical than students of human efficiency have ever considered. To move with efficiency both the vertical and horizontal coordinates must be synchronized. They are interrelated and interdependent.

The Depth Coordinate

Mobile man is a forward moving organism. Developmental momentum thrusts him into the third dimension. By design he is a convergent being. His eyes are designed to converge, his auditory system is designed to converge, and his hands join at a convergent midline point to center tasks before his eyes to match his visual convergence. As a bilateral organism, man must be a balanced converging machine to move with directional accuracy. The depth coordinate in his system of principal axes can be considered as the most important one of the three in determining his movement efficiency. His movement on the Z axis advances him. His developmental momentum demands a forward movement. He may retreat or advance by choice and by circumstances, but his destiny is definitely in the forward plane. If we are correct in assigning a primary value to the Z axis, there must be evidence of careful design to verify its primacy.

Movement on the depth plane is an emergent from the vertical and horizontal and must therefore rely upon the efficiency of the first two for the determination of its own vitality. It is to be expected, therefore, that any distortion in the vertical or the horizontal coordinates will have a significant negative impact upon the acquisition of an efficient convergence for movement on the Z axis—and so it is. The hemiplegic, laterally imbalanced by a paralyzed side, must make special postural accomodations in his gait pattern if he is to move forward with any degree of smoothness in his walking transport through space. Gesell (1949) in his developmental study of vision describes the negative impact upon convergence efficiency when binocularity is lost. Convergence is an emergent from movement experience in a gravitational field. Therefore, it is not immediately present for the infant. It develops in varying degrees as the infant explores his world, but since it is dependent upon the vertical and the horizontal, it does not reach a level of maturity until the work of the upright and laterals has been completed. The infant practices convergence as he bimanually explores toys and objects held in front of him at his midline. His tonic-neck-reflex posturing has been the training ground for defining the distance of proximal-distal extension, and when he finally brings his two hands together at midline his eyes enter their training program in convergence. His eyes and his hand have practiced their lessons in laterality and once they have completed their unilateral training they advance to a convergence harmony for efficient performance. Exploring hands are the drill sergeants for vision. The infant continues to move to investigate depth. He rolls, crawls, toddles and walks. He explores his world frontally in many ways. For a long time, we suspect, there is no **back** space for the infant. He knows only **front** space. Whatever may transpire behind him cannot be appreciated unless he rotates himself to set the event on a frontal plane. He moves forward because developmental momentum compels him. It is a method for building an efficient vertical and a horizontal — and these have early priority over the Z axis. Experiences in the depth plane are for the purpose of acquiring a fundamental orientation to a three-dimensional world — the efforts directed toward building an **efficiency** in the third dimension are concentrated at a later age.

Other than the definitive work on vision by Gesell, the developmentalists have not held an orientation towards the convergence phenomena in human behavior.

The general body of literature in psychology and education is relatively silent on the question of the Z axis in the development of the child. Only as physical educators attempted to define various kinds of motor norms did the literature blossom with reports on the depth performance of the growing child.

Ball throwing may be regarded as an exploration of forward space and give some indication of a child's proficiency in projecting into the third dimension. Gutteridge (1939) found that proficiency in throwing did not occur until age six, and then only 80% of her group could be judged as proficient at that time, leaving one in five children who were not proficient by that time. Wild's (1938) study of throwing behavior in a group of 2 to 7 year olds offers a somewhat more precise delineation of developmental patterns. Children 2-3 years old throw with the arm alone involving no shift of body weight or trunk rotation. Between 3-1/2 and 5 years, children begin to shift weight and rotate the trunk when they throw but maintain both feet in contact with the ground. In the next year, the child apparently acquires the forward glide of one foot in the delivery, usually gliding forward with the same foot as the throwing arm. By the time boys have reached 6-1/2 years, they have generally mastered the cross-diagonal process, gliding forward on the foot opposite to the throwing arm. Subsequent to this the pattern gains only in refinement and accuracy of projection. Girls tend to retain a homolateral throwing stance well beyond seven years of age. The explanation for this delay is obscured.

Throwing development, as recounted in these two studies, can be regarded as sequentially passing through a homologous, homolateral and crossed-diagonal pattern. The homologous pattern identified as a static body position with only arm movement, the homolateral as same side arm and foot, and finally the crossed-diagonal of the opposing foot glide. The most comfortable, economic and efficient pattern in terms of body mechanics for grace and accuracy is the crossed-diagonal pattern. From the standpoint of the Z axis for movement, the retention of the vertical stance until age six before the body is thrust into the forward plane is further evidence for our contention about the primacy of the vertical.

The investigation of hopping in young children is another example of behavior in the third dimension. The homologous pattern of hopping on two feet on a forward plane occurs with some degree of proficiency before a child is ready to entrust his forward momentum to hopping on a single foot. Even as he is willing to entrust his balance in hopping to a single foot, he is usually more successful on one foot than the other. Hopping is a movement combination on two planes. To hop the child must move first in the vertical and then with momentum move himself along the Z axis. Single foot hopping coincides temporally with the development of the Y axis of movement at approximately six to seven years. Some children are proficient before age six and others do not acquire proficiency until later. We feel that such proficiency bears a direct relationship to the overall climate of laterality for the child at a given point in his development. Hopping on one foot is but one of many manifestations that laterality is emerging. If the child is still struggling with the establishment of the vertical ordinate, he is more likely to rely upon two-footed hopping to transport himself through space. Rotating his sides around the vertical axis and along the convergence axis is not yet incorporated into his system of sustaining dynamic balance, and as a consequence he will prefer the more secure process of two-footed simultaneity. Cognitive employment of laterals in sustaining dynamic balance is the agent of proficiency. Although it seems obvious that the spotlight must be placed on his immaturity in lateral awareness, it is more likely that a careful investigation of his techniques for holding dynamic balance will be more revealing.

Another form of transport on the Z axis has long occupied a favored diagnostic position in the minds of American educators—skipping. The kindergarten child's failure to skip with some degree of proficiency has frequently been classified as a signal of motor immaturity and a sign of developmental lag. Here again we can observe the child's developing sophistication with the laterals. Most children evolve some version of a skip in the midst of running. To shift gears while running and signal the legs to alter the pattern of movement, the child usually starts with some form of hop or jump woven into the running pattern in an awkward manner. It is as though his repertoire consists of walking, running, hopping and jumping, and he systematically explores that repertoire to determine which combination will produce the required pattern. In the same manner as he has done on so many previous occasions since his birth, his skipping is monolateral at first, then bilateral and finally a bilateral interweaving. One leg learns skipping, then the other leg learns, and finally in triumph the legs reciprocate in a reasonably proficient pattern. Even though most children have achieved this pattern by age six, the range of gracefulness in execution is very wide. The most poised and graceful have the firmest grip on the convergence point of the three directional axes.

Another phenomenon of convergence is experienced in attempting to catch a ball thrown on a trajectory. Gutteridge (1939) noted that only 63% of the six-year-old boys and girls in her study were able to do this. With increasing age the percentage of successful catchers increased. A small percentage of children could manage this at age four. Catching a ball requires the child to center himself on the glide path of the ball following it visually into his outstretched arms. Children with convergence problems cannot accurately judge trajectory on the Z axis and usually duck away from the flight path. Throwing the ball directly to their chest or stomach may allow them to clutch at the ball upon contact, but if the flight path is not visually guided they are unable to accommodate their body position to center on the ball. A ball thrown to their left or right, up or down, lacking a visual-somatic accommodation, goes past them or strikes their body without awareness until contact has been made.

The development of movement on the Z axis takes on another refinement during the 5th to 7th years when the child synchronizes the position of his arm and its forward thrust with a step forward in throwing a ball (Wild, 1938). Boys seem to develop this movement sooner than girls and usually demonstrate reasonably good form during their 7th year. Gutteridge (1939) reported an essentially similar finding noting a wide range of proficiency at all ages.

The development of visual fusion is coincided to this 5- to 7-year span (Gesell, 1949). When many other aspects are developing to aid the organism in its appreciation of the third dimension, vision is the coagulating agent or the synthesizer of the efficiency potential. Many things come together in an integrated pattern. This appears to be the critical span of years for the child to achieve fusion in all parts of his anatomy. It is within this period that he advances from the plateau of convergence to a higher plateau of fusion. He now fuses visually, auditorially, kinesthetically and tactually. He no longer simply looks **at** something but now looks **into** things. He is now better prepared to understand the howness and whyness of his world. He has an appreciation of depth and can efficiently employ it in both his physical and cognitive explorations. A dimension has been added to his world and with it has come a deeper significance. All this follows as a direct outcome of the organismic design. He is developing as he was intended to develop. His fusion on a kinesthetic level contributes to a coordinative efficiency which makes a graceful performer. His tactual fusion now gives him a **deeper** and profound comprehension of texture and quality. His auditory fusion makes him an efficient listener capable of comprehending the probing questions and directives which he encounters. His visual fusion allows him to perceive the profundity of graphic symbols. Having now reached the fusional point with all three axes organized to his advantage his geometric training period for space is finished. His future can now be dedicated to expanding upon those basic efficiencies in acquiring wider and wider ranges of skills, refinements and precision in movement — the pursuit of knowledge can now become his full-time occupation.

If he carries with him any inefficiencies in vertical, horizontal or depth orientations, his dedication to knowledge is not quite as comfortable a pursuit as it might have been. Since developmental evidence points to the fact that the efficiency of the horizontal coordinate is dependent upon the efficiency of the vertical, and that the depth coordinate derives its efficiency from the other two, then it logically follows that any inefficiencies in supporting axial orientations will effect the total efficiency. Some penalty must be paid. The penalties take the form of discomforts, incoordinations, limitations and narrowing the amplitude of performance. The terranaut travels in physical and cognitive terrestrial space burdened or comforted by the composite of his early efforts to build a vertical, horizontal and depth coordinate. His awareness of front-back, up-down, left and right will be proportionate to his efficiencies. The geometer lives with his equations. There is no choice as to whether he can avoid building the coordinates — he **must** if he is to move with **any** degree of success. The only variation possible occurs in terms of spatial efficiencies and inefficiencies.

The Axes of Cognition

The three axes of coordination must also be organized in cognitive space in order for the individual to move with efficiency in his thought processes. The vertical may be regarded as a height of intellectual achievement in a given area, the horizontal as the broadness of achievement, and the depth axis as the profundity of achievement. An individual may accumulate knowledge in a vertical piling stacking one bit atop another, in a tower of information. He may also build laterally, broadening and enriching his information on a given topic or series of topics. In addition, he may choose to do a probing and penetrating analysis. The well-coordinated mentality can move with efficiency on all three axes, acquiring the tower, broadening the scope, and investigating the depth. Concentration on the vertical axis results in a collector of facts in a given area, but reflects a lack of pertinent and related information and a probable absence of critical evaluation of significance. "Spreading one's self too thin" is a verbalization of excessive concentration on the horizontal coordinate. The appreciation of both sides of an argument with a resolution of the opposing views by reference to compromise becomes a matter of reciprocal interweaving around a cognitive midline. Only as an individual can converge his intellectual energies upon a given topic can we anticipate a profundity of thought. Many more examples could be listed to illustrate the point of an axis of cognition.

The individual's awareness in cognitive space becomes an equally significant consideration in appraising the over-all character of his Movement Efficiency. Although we are unable to define a specific set of measures to precisely identify an acceptable numerical correlation, we believe that the postural and movement inefficiencies which may be noted in the physical performance of an individual are highly correlated or replicated in the cognitive performance of the mover. The deviation of the postural vertical is reflected in the inability to mount facts. The laterality problem in sidedness is reflected in bias, prejudice, specific attitude, uncompromising position, refusal to negotiate, being opinionated, etc. The fusional problem physically is replicated cognitively as a shallowness and superficiality.

The Scope of Coordination

The scheme of the axes of coordination has a wide range of applicability. Emotional space may be analyzed in terms of coordinate planes. Social space can be defined by the coordinates. Historical space also lends itself to such analysis. Any time a space can be designated, the coordinates can be applied. Movement occurs on and around a set of planes whether it be physical, cognitive, emotional, social or organizational.

All space must come within the cognitive awareness of the mover. The performer must utilize that awareness to continue to define the **whereness** of his world.

The observations of Piaget (1937) represent the most extensive efforts to describe the manner in which the notion of space develops in the child. He described three types of spatial notions or stages which occur for the child. During the first two years of life, usually defined as the sensory-motor period, events occur in space which have relatively minor perceptual value to the infant but serve the primary purpose of developing a stimulation surround to alert and activate his touch, kinesthesia, vision, audition, smell and taste. In the initial stage which Piaget terms "practical space", there is a one-to-one relationship to objects such as one object—one look, one sound—one alert, one touch—one effort. Any object out of reach is spatially "gone". This is followed by searching, groping efforts to "follow" an object out of reach with hands initially undirected by eyes but eventually coming under visual control. This second stage is a trial-and-error or "empirical space" in which any form of hiding still causes the object to disappear from the infant's space world. The curiosity here gradually brings the infant to the "container period" of putting in and taking out. By the end of the first two years, he has acquired the primitive fundamentals of the "objective" world of space and is catching on to spatial relations of up, down, in, out, in front of, etc., pulling toys, pushing, moving toys from place to place.

Those first two years furnish a basic training for the three spatial notions that will become the foundation for all of his future space travels. The complete naivete gives way to some effort to cope with space and the objects in it, even though this is frequently unsuccessful, and finally things come to "have a place" in relation to himself. Those first two years can be considered as the primitive first plateau in spatial sophistication. The second plateau is achieved from two to five years. The acquisition of varying levels of sophistication coincides with the progressive refinement and improvement of his vision, audition, tactuality and kinesthesia. As vision improves, distance and clarity are refined and spatial expansion takes place. As each channel of sensitivity becomes more perceptual in processing information from space, greater and greater objectivity develops. As he refines his processing tools his world expands.

Piaget (1937) felt that a notion of space was derived from the comprehension of spatial relations between objects and comprehension of the individual's own shifts of position. Meyer (1940) devised a study along Piagetian lines for children from 1-1/2 to 5 years using problem-solving situations to observe variations in space relationships. She set up five situations involving the comprehension of spatial relationships: (1) nested boxes; (2) performance box involving dowel-form insertion; (3) variation of number 2; (4) objects hidden behind a fence; and (5) a rotating board containing a chip at one end. The results were essentially the same in all five tests. The children from 1-1/2 to 2-1/2 showed no comprehension of forms, sizes or spatial dilemna and gave inappropriate responses. From 2-1/2 to 3-1/2, they tended to grasp a part of the problem and attempted solutions on a trial-and-error basis, sometimes being successful. At age 4 to 5, children showed complete comprehension and systematically solved the problems. In another set of experiments she evaluated the child's spatial comprehension when a shift in his own position was required to resolve the problem—he had to make detours of various kinds. For some tasks the two-year-olds managed well, while in others tasks success was not obtained until four years. The tasks were not equatable so no real ranking could be made. A number of conclusions were drawn from both sets of experiments which are in agreement with Piaget's descriptions. Up to the age of 2-1/2, the child relates objects to himself as the center of space, and he comprehends little of the relationship **between** objects. Between 3 and 4 years he moves im "empirical" space. He transfers patterns, tries new ways and experiments, but still remains the center of his spatial universe orienting objects directly to himself. At age 4 he begins to move in "objective" space. He adapts his patterns to the objects instead of trying to adapt the objects to his pattern. He now knows that **he** is one object among many objects, and he is attaining a better grasp of the "betweenness" of objects as well as the specific nature of their relationships to one another. In this critical period from 2-1/2 to 4 years when he is acquiring an identification of himself from many sources, the first budding answers to the question of "Who am I?" give him the freedom to knowledgeably come to grips with his next big question of "Where am I?", and he is then ready to devote his first real attention to the "whereness" of his world.

The three levels of spatial sophistication described by Piaget form a developmental progression indicating advancing comprehension of a surround and the individual's unique relationship to that surround. Practical, empirical, and objective space may be viewed as steps in a dynamic progression for any individual in any situation at any time. The critical factor of personal orientation within a given space can be used to determine which level of sophistication characterizes the individual's adaptation at any given moment.

At any time that the individual operates within a given surround as though he is the privileged center of that particular universe relating objects only to himself and his use of those objects without regard for the relations of otherness in that surround, he may be characterized as operating in "practical space" at the same level of naivete as Piaget described for the very young child. The hyperactive brain-damaged child or the disorganized emotionally disturbed child who touches simply for the sake of touching, kicks for the sake of kicking, throws for the sake of throwing, is "in action" in that space for the sake of activity and not for the purpose of meaningfully relating himself to that space. He lives in a primitive "space of action" as defined by Werner (1948).

There is no element of discovery and no element of perceptual organization. His relationship to space is unorganized and defined only in terms of "action". He is in "practical space"—engaged in meaningless action whether he is two years of age or twelve. The autistic child remains in "practical space". For the autistic child objects are present only to satisfy activity. The objects bear no relationship to one another. Each is there only for the autistic child to act upon them without concern for the inter-relatedness which exists.

It is also possible to conceive of an organized individual operating in "practical space". A child's impulsive reaction to physically try each toy in the toy department with no consideration of the propriety of such actions is governed by the need to "try it". At that particular moment, his "touchingness" and action place him in "practical space". Within the same period the same space may become "empirical" space as he is reminded of certain restrictions by his mother and limits his explorations to experimenting with specific features of the toy, and he may switch to "objective" space in a moment when he notes the relationship among objects.

In the "empirical space" the individual makes some generalizations but tends to use **his** system of response in a form of rigidity regardless of whether "it fits". With only a little effort at experimenting, the individual quits if his initial efforts do not bring results. He generally has no real plan of action. The total scheme of orientation remains with the self and the otherness of the surround is of no real concern. There is trial-and-error activity in "empirical" space, but little evidence of generalizing one learned form of behavior to other situations.

In "objective space" the individual adjusts and adapts to the objects in his world. Patterns are constantly differentiated and reorganized in conformity to demand. There is an awareness of otherness and specifically an awareness of that otherness to the self for orientation purposes. "He acts among things and not only upon them." There is a recognition of the relatedness among objects which specifically influences behavioral response.

Presumably by age five a child has acquired a position in "objective space", but this must be regarded as attained only insofar that relatedness has been achieved commensurate with a general level of over-all sophistication. Under the stress of adapting to novel situations, any one of the three forms of space reactions may be demonstrated.

Entering a new school, a new building, a new group of children, a new store, a birthday party, a circus or any one of hundreds of different "spaces" which are somewhat like or quite unlike "spaces" previously experienced, there is an immediate need for the child to organize that new space objectively determining the objects in that space, the relationship of those objects to him and his relationship to them. Each new space may be reacted to in the disorganized fashion of "practical space", in the rigid, minimal exploration of "empirical space" or in the adaptive and adjustive response of "objective space". Which form of space world occurs for the child will be determined by the level of integration he has achieved in spatial awareness.

The three different levels described by Piaget to account for varying stages in the spatial development of children has descriptive utility at all ages for characterizing the reactions of people within space. Anytime an individual enters a novel space situation for which he has no ready experiential referrent, he is thrust back into practical or empirical space often relying upon rigid or stereotyped efforts to find some degree of comfort in the new situation. In a short space of time he may process the new space through all these levels in his spatial behavior, or if sufficiently threatened by the novelty of the space may remain in an empirical stage as Piaget defines it. Such spatial processing may occur in visiting the boss's home, starting a new job, entering a strange building, and so on. There is good reason to suggest that the behavioral descriptions of subjects suffering stress in various sensory deprivation experiments might readily fit these three space classification schemes.

Man moves in a constant spatial surround persistently required to be aware of the all-sidedness of that space. Spatial awareness is therefore extremely critical to man's adaptation.

The individual moves in a surround. Orientational adequacy rests upon his awareness of all segments of that surround. Wherever he is, there is some expanse of space extending to his two sides, his back, his front, above him and below him. He is at all times a center of a spatial universe. As we have already pointed out, space is originally a near boundary expanding to mid, far, and remote boundaries as the organism acquires a more complex level of sophistication. To fully promote his physical, social, psychological, academic, and economic survival, he must acquire an awareness of his own position in each space circumstance and attribute meaning to the relative position of all objects which fill the spatial expanse around him. He must acquire an awareness of the physical realities of space, distances between objects, characteristic properties of objects and their relationship to him as near or far, above or below, in front or back of, to the left and to the right. He must become fully aware of symbols in spatial configurations to promote his academic survival. He must eventually achieve an awareness of social forces and their relation to him. The psychological space of attitudes, prejudices and bias must come to a state of awareness. All these vectors of spatial force must be accounted for, organized into meaningful patterns, and contribute to an enlarging spatial awareness.

The Acquisition of Front, Back, Up, Down, Side, Side

The task of acquiring an efficiency in spatial awareness is a monumental one which challenges the human organism persistently from infancy to maturity. The six fields of space introduced in Chapter III serve as the schematic framework within which the individual must achieve his awareness. The question, "Where am I?" is posed not only to the infant in the early stages of acquiring a transport orientation, but is a question to be answered continuously as the individual's range of movement in space expands. The infant may be categorized as existing almost entirely in FRONT space. His world of experience lies mainly in the forward plane. Eating, dressing, bathing and parental play are frontally oriented. Although some infants crawl backward in the early stages of locomotion, the general force of developmental momentum keeps them in the forward plane. It is the front vertical which is first organized as the center of gravity is progressively elevated to the erect locomotive position. It is the front vertical which occupies the infant's major attention as he begins to move among objects in his world. Chairs and tables in front of him become vertical supports to bring him to a standing position. Vertical bars of the playpen help him to rise. Cabinet doors intrigue him. Bit by bit he organizes front space, setting targets to move toward, becoming aware of that which is reachable and that which is out of reach. Some objects and people rise high above him, others are at his eye level, and still others are shorter than he. Every experience with the front space vertical makes its contribution to his expanding state of awareness and from his experiences he organizes a schema of front space. He uses his eyes, hands and feet and his mouth to confirm space. As his feedback becomes progressively better correlated with his experience, awareness grows.

The side space of left and right presents a greater challenge, for the initial world of the infant does not contain sidedness. This must also emerge from experience. The greatest lesson to be learned for side space is that he himself has two sides and that all objects in his world have sides. The lesson takes a long time to master, as the work of Piaget has indicated. Approximately 11 years of experience take place before he has achieved some certainty about the leftness and rightness of objects in his world. His own left and rightness is achieved after only 6 years of effort, but an additional 5 years seem to be necessary before he can contralaterally attribute the same concepts to the space world which surrounds him.

His first task in defining side space becomes a matter of achieving a hand preference. Some authorities believe he has no choice in this matter — his preferential side has been genetically predetermined. Other authorities feel that his preferred side is trained by parental treatment. Still others believe that it emerges from his personal experiences. Whichever may eventually prove to be the true cause of preference it must nonetheless be achieved for efficiency. His earliest efforts at manipulating his world are bilateral and from this initial bilaterality one side becomes the leader and one side becomes the follower. One hand will become the preferred tool for handling toast, cookies, crackers, spoons, building blocks, pulling toys and so on. Some children acquire this preference very early but others are delayed in finding a leader hand. Some children have not yet acquired a preference at age five. So great a delay usually requires considerable investigation by therapists, clinicians and physicians to determine a preference and establish suitable training procedures to achieve leader status. During those first five years he will explore walking sideways, pushing toys to one side or another, relating to people from either side and literally have thousands of experiences with left and right space. It is possible that his developmental timetable is so firmly scheduled to acquiring a vertical orientation that all of his lateral experiences play only a secondary role of preparation for the time when the timetable will emphasize the cognitive awareness of left and right space.

Even though 11 years appear to be an average for acquiring a full self-other awareness of left and right, there are many people who do not achieve this awareness with any degree of certainty in a full lifetime. Many adults require a hesitation for processing before committing themselves to a course of right-left action. They must "think twice" before moving left or right. They are uncertain in driving, finding locations, looking for room numbers—in fact any time a decision of "move right—move left" confronts them they experience difficulty. If one were to judge from the number of adults who have problems in efficiently managing left-right space orientations, the acquisition of competency in lateral space is far more difficult than it has been considered to be. Some children have been seen in clinical practice who were quite secure in the identification of right and left hand but readily confused by the right-left identification of eyes, ears, legs, feet, knees and so on. Often it seems that laterality awareness is judged to be achieved when hands are appropriately identified without a check of full-sided awareness.

There are those who feel that general cultural patterns are so exclusively organized for the right handed person that the left hander is at a disadvantage throughout his lifetime. The left handed individual may be thought of as having a LEFT SPACE orientation to the world confronted by a relatively constant need to adjust his pattern of performance against the design of furniture, equipment, sporting goods and so on.

DOWN space is probably tentatively organized at the early levels of development when the child spends so much time in that spatial area. Once he becomes an erect locomotive mover, however, UP space and the development of his upper extremities for skill acquisition become so demanding that awareness of down space is relegated to incidental status. Down space is important when the individual must travel on variable terrain, when steps must be descended or ascended, when an ankle or leg is injured, when learning dance steps, etc. Down space is important to the soldier crawling through the underbrush of the jungle. Various occupations require efficiency in down space awareness. As a general rule, however, down space tends to become habituated and ignored in the usual course of daily transport. The principle of cephalocaudad direction in development suggests that UP space is probably considerably better developed than DOWN space skills. The emphasis in the typical elementary and secondary school program can be characterized as predominantly oriented to developing a greater and greater level of sophistication in UP space.

A sophisticated awareness of BACK space is probably the last of the segments to become organized. The propulsion of forward momentum in development is so emphatically frontally oriented that BACK space is ignored in the haste for maturity. BACK space awareness (1) allows the child and adult to localize stimuli with accuracy which occur behind him, (2) permits him to evaluate events occurring in back of him without the need to forsake the task with which he is occupied in front space, (3) permits the individual to estimate his position in a surround by attributing dimensions to back space from his judgments of front space, (4) permits him to sustain a consciousness of a world behind him without the need for constant checking.

All six **fields** of space must be cognitively experienced and related for space sophistication to occur. All **four** zones of space must be explored, organized and brought to a state of persistent awareness. All four **domains** of space, the physiologic, physical, milieu and cognitive must be brought to a level of awareness consonant with daily demand. These three spatial organizations serve one basic purpose for the organism—to define the "whereness" of his own person and all objects in space. Only as he can achieve a high degree of sophistication in spatial awareness can the individual continue to satisfactorily answer the following persistent questions: "Where am I?", "Where is it?", "What is it?", "Where is it happening?", "What relationship does it have to me?", "Where is here?", "Where is there?", "Is it moving away, toward, left, right, above, below?", "Is it stable or changeable", "Is it fixed or moving?". Literally thousands of other questions of "whereness" are posed day by day, situation after situation, experience upon experience. The ease with which the individual answers all of those questions individually and collectively is dependent upon his awareness of space.

There is no question of whether or not spatial awareness is a significant component for transport orientation—it is an essential factor in human orientation to an energy surround. The development of spatial awareness occupies a great deal of the young child's waking life. Our knowledge of how the world of space comes to have progressive meaning for the child is poorly documented but there can be little doubt of its importance for the child's future. Perhaps the space-consciousness which is increasing throughout the population may yet extend itself to the researchers in child development. Regardless of how limited our understanding of space development might be, the importance of spatial sophistication is logically a significant fiber in the warp and woof of transport orientations and a significant strand in the building of Movement Efficiency.

8

TEMPORAL AWARENESS

The progression of development must incorporate one more component to complete the Postural-Transport orientations and insure the substructure for Movement Efficiency. The young traveler must develop an orientation to Time. In this stage of his orientation he must become acquainted with the "whenness" of his world. Past present and future must become another set of cognitive terrains to enrich his movement. He must find his answers to "When is it?" to add to his growing volume of awareness. Time is a dimension of transport, not a dimension to be separated from space by a bridging hyphen — it is but an extension of space. Time is the distance between two points in space. Time is a space interval. Time **is** the "betweenness of space".

Time is **movement between two points in space**. Energy forms move through space bombarding the human organism from all sides varying in intensity and velocity according to source distance from the individual. The individual's position in space in relation to the emanating source determines the quantity of each energy form with which he must contend in a given second.

In the daily traffic of community life, the range of temporal efficiencies among people is great. There are people who can be classified as "forever late" apparently persistently unable to regulate and order their own behaviors to conform to appointed time. College students characteristically delay the composition of term papers until the "last moment" and then frantically rush to meet a deadline. There are also those who are deliberately punctual and have an exaggerated concern with time. Most of the civilized world lives on a relatively routinized schedule of time for at least five days per week. Some form of temporal deadline confronts the human performer during most of his life. Time is regarded as a blessing in overcoming disappointment and sadness, and a curse when the performance demanded cannot be comfortably managed within the time limit. Time determines the youngster's entry into kindergarten, the length of his school day and year, the privilege of voting, his daily working hours, the length of an engagement, the duration of an illness — on and on. Everywhere is TIME. Some people come to manage TIME comfortably and economically. Others spend a lifetime of discomfort and inefficiency because TIME has never come to a comfort level of meaning.

This fifth component in the Postural-Transport group we have designated as Temporal Awareness. This label is given to the composite behavior of the performer as it relates to his awareness of time. It is regarded as a dynamic component of a mobile being transporting himself in space. Reaction time, so long an honorable variable in psychological experimentation is a part of the composite. Processing time to mount an appropriate response to a posed demand is another part of the composite. Temporal labeling and estimation are also part of the composite dynamic we have called Temporal Awareness.

There are many forms of time. In this study of time, le Lionnais (1960) spoke of "the jungle of time". Different concepts of time are used in mathematics, physics, in the theory of relativity and the quantum theory. There are differences in biological time, psychological time, social, historical time, aesthetic time and so on. In its simplest definition time is the measured or measurable period during which an action or a process or condition exists or continues. Many efforts have been made to explore Time as a concept in the hope of establishing a clear understanding but most authors would probably agree with the concluding comment made by Way and Green (1951) in their book:

> ....perhaps it is just as well to bring this little book to an end with an admission that, having started to write about Time and its Reckoning we really do not know a thing about the main subject. Our sole consolation must be that nobody else does either.

This expression of futility is not shared by all investigators however, since the study of time has been and continues to be a lively topic of investigation. Despite the many difficulties encountered in the attempt to clearly define and understand time the curiosity of many researchers leads to a continuation of effort.

Time studies have usually taken the form of estimations of lapsed time, responses to questions concerning time and the effect of time upon performance. Other than the developmental studies already cited the general literature on time study is a collection of assorted studies which defy any kind of continuity in concept. A few may be cited as representative.

The rhythm of life, expressed in the activities which fill it, is the basis of our experience with time. One period of time is distinguished from another by the movements and the events which occur within a given span. The nature of those events may influence the estimate of duration. Activities which are painful or difficult may be temporally overestimated while play or pleasure events may seem shorter. (Hurlock, 1956)

Most time concepts are learned through verbal expressions of the timing of events.

Richardson (1962) felt that the manner in which a child used time words in his expressions would serve as a fairly accurate indicator of his temporal development. He also suggested that children with language development delays and those with auditory deficiencies will manifest delay in the development of time concepts because the temporal labeling system will not coincide with their experiences.

Primitive notions of time have been discussed by Werner (1948). The Arunda of western Australia have 25 different words to indicate 25 divisions of the day starting with the first streaks of light from the east. The ebb and flow of the tide mark the divisions of the Eskimo's day. Uganda peoples have "milking time", "watering time", and "homecoming time for the cattle". Timereha Indians have 10 months to a year believing that two months of the year do not count. The same primitivation characterizes the time development of the child. "Winter" means snow and "spring" means flowers. Children may believe that tearing pages from a calendar "makes" time. Katz (cited by Werner 1948) told of children differentiating Sunday from the other six days because the calendar date was printed in red compared to the black dates. Children divide the day into breakfast, lunch, nap, dinner and bedtime and divide years into birthday, Easter and Christmas.

Farrell (1953) administered a questionnaire to five, six and seven year old children of superior intelligence to ascertain their understanding of time relationships. Questions which involved the immediate, repetitions and the personal were answered more accurately than those involving remote, non-personal and complex time periods. Time understanding was more clearly differentiated between five and six year olds. McCauley (1961) studied second grade children and found an opposite result. Barndt and Johnson (1955) found delinquent boys to have shorter time spans than non-delinquents. Boag and Neild (1962) found that high school students improved their standings on test scores when time limits were removed and Knapp (1960) found a similar gain in studying Mexican and American subjects on a group intelligence test. Other studies have followed along these same lines but offer virtually no contribution to the development of our concept of temporal awareness.

Oakden and Stuart (1902) asked 4-10 year old children two questions: "What time is it for your mother at home now?" and "What time of the day is it in x (neighboring town)?". Only 50% of their four year olds could answer the first question accurately and only 14% of the four year olds answered the second question. Accuracy increased with age, showing 100% accuracy among ten year olds on the first question but 14% of their ten year olds were unable to accurately answer the second question.

College students were only 15-18% more accurate than fifth graders at estimating time intervals. (Hurlock, 1956) Delayed development of temporal concepts has been correlated with predelinquent behavior in Brock's (1963) study on stealing behavior among children of lower socio-economic groups and Davids' (1962) story completion study of boy and girl delinquents.

The variability in time estimation is related to the amount of tension produced by the need to complete the task. High motivation states produce underestimations. (Rosenzweig, 1954)

Standard time concepts seem to stabilize for children at about age 8. Children at this age and older show considerable accuracy in estimating seconds especially if kinesthetic cues are available. (Goldstone, Boardman and Lohamon, 1958)

Gilliland **et al**. (1946) stated that the significance of time intervals is interpreted in terms of body tensions and rhythms. As the child becomes more complex in his behavior he learns more about evaluating how much activity can occur at a given time. Ames (1946) spoke of an underlying plan of growth, a patterning process in the development of time concepts and felt that the time concepts were maturationally related.

The most extensive discussion of the early development of time concepts in children, is found in the works of Piaget (1962). Six stages of temporal development have been described by Piaget, with four of the six stages occurring before the age of one year. At stage one, the child organizes his movements in a primitive temporal sequence, such as opening the mouth before sucking. The second stage, a sequence of movement, is associated with sound localization. On hearing a noise, the head is turned as a scanning mechanism. These two stages are primitive temporal ordering not perceived or cognited but holding a form of sequence. Duration, here, is the span covered by the sequence of the movements. The third stage involves a "memory phase" in which the child can return to a previous activity after it has been interrupted. In the fourth stage, the child shows some comprehension of time as applied to events external to himself and can retain a series of events in which he plays no role. Stage five reveals time as the "continuous and systematic link which unites the events of the external world with one another". At stage six, the child deals with time as a representative series. He can mentally reconstruct events from a more and more extensive past.

A compilation of observations and investigations from three sources (Gesell and Ilg, 1946; Hurlock, 1956; and Stone and Church, 1957) suggests a normative sequence of temporal awareness. The cataloguing of time behavior starts at 18 months when time is the immediate present for the child and he finds it difficult to wait. Within 3 months his chief time word is "now" but he is beginning to anticipate events in the near future. Next he acquires some concept of delay (24 months) and uses phrases like "in a minute", "gonna" and understands simple time sequences when one event closely follows another.

He next acquires words to denote past, present and future (2-1/2 years). At three he can wait for things and adds many new time words to his vocabulary. At 3-1/2 years he can express habitual action such as "on Fridays". At four he begins to use words like "month", "next summer", "next year". He knows morning from afternoon and knows the days of the week. At five he becomes vitally interested in calendars and clocks. He knows what day it is and how old he will be on his next birthday. At six he shows interest in distant past events and in coming holidays and special events. At seven he is interested in the details of sequences of time and can tell time in hours and minutes. He knows the seasons and is aware of the passage of time from month to month. From this age upward time continues to be a more and more elaborate concept for him.

The estimation of time intervals has attracted the attention of many investigators who have studied this phenomena in various modal patterns such as judgment of light flicker intervals or beep tone intervals and so on in laboratory settings. A recent study by Treisman (1963) using light stimuli is a typical example. The subject is expected to reproduce the interval established by an examiner. Treisman reported the classical findings that short intervals are overestimated and long intervals are underestimated. **The development of a motoric rhythmic pattern was found to improve estimates.** When no motor patterns were demanded as part of the procedure, subvocal counting, slight head movements or some non-instrumental movements were used at suitable intervals to aid in making judgments. Treisman went on to present a model of the time keeping mechanism in the human organism consisting of a pacemaker, counter, store and comparator (decision mechanism). Pulses are counted, stored and compared for relevance. The "internal clock" of Treisman is a recent effort to account for a timing mechanism. More than 30 years ago Hoaglund (1933) introduced his concept of the "chemical clock" within the human organism. Abbe (1936) investigated the effect of increasing the amount of physical space upon time perception. Two blinking lights were used to delimit the time interval. The distance between these lights were varied but the time between their flashes were left constant. Subjects reported greater time intervals with greater space. In related experiments, he also found converse to be true—if space intervals were given in a longer interval of time, the space between the lights was judged as being longer than when given in a shorter time.

White and Cheatham (1952, 1953, 1963) conducted a series of studies of temporal numerosity in the human perceiver, i.e., the perception of sequences of pulses in all the major sense areas and concluded that there is some temporal process in the central nervous system that limits and orders the perceptual events of the major sense modalities. Sweet (1953) investigated the ability of the human eye to discriminate between two flashing lights temporally spaced and found the perception of movement to be more precisely differentiated in the periphery than at the fovea.

Another version of time study is to be found in investigations concerning various physiologic rates such as heart rate, pulse, blood pressure, breathing rate and brain rhythms. Shafer and Gilliland (1938) found that none of these physiologic rates bore any relationship to the individual's ability to estimate time suggesting that the perception of a time interval is not affected by the various rates or rhythms occurring within the organism. Murphree (1954), however, found a significant relationship between the ability to perceive form in rapid successive spatial perceptions and the alpha rhythm of the brain.

Researchers have indeed been busy in the study of time. Man is a temporal machine. The organism contains a variety of rates which have been studied and defined. These multiple rates are synchronized into a harmonious pattern. Next, man is a time perceiving machine capable of estimating and judging time. The development of time concepts has been documented from early childhood to adulthood. It is paradoxical that while a great deal is known, very little is known.

Domains of Time

The four domains of space and the zones of space which have been discussed in Chapter III may also be considered as domains of **time**.

Physiologic time is internal time and defines the variegated rates occurring within the individual's corporeal systems. In the metabolic system there is the rate of processing nutrients. In the glandular system there is the rate of performance of the glands on a regular sustaining basis versus the emergency rate excited during periods of stress. A heart rate, pulse rate, a skin conductance rate all occur in physiological time. Each rate in physiologic time occurs in developmental perspective changing to some extent as the individual matures. Perhaps the most intriguing internal time occurs in the brain. A developmental perspective on the rhythms of the brain has been described by Walter (1953).

Up to age of one month the neonate's brain possesses practically no measurable electrical activity but gradually the pattern of waves becomes definable. Theta waves usually associated with affective constructs are dominant in the child from 2-5 years of age and between the ages of 3-4 the alpha wave makes its appearance. From then until early adolescence the alpha and theta rhythms vacillate in the growing child. Walter (1953) has speculated that early presence of the theta rhythm and its association with pleasure and pain suggests that adjustment and disappointment form the firmest foundation for personality. The work of Walter in relating EEG patterns to personality states indicates that the brain reaction to tension and anxiety is to speed up its rate. Adults with aggressive behavior tendencies, flash tempers, selfishness, impatience, childish intolerance and suspicion tend to show a high incidence of theta waves.

Internal time consists of many different rates with changes in rate occasioned by stress, threat, desire—generally stable but variable under certain conditions. Consequently we can talk of a stable synchronization of internal time referring to the integration of the various body rates into harmonious stability insuring the day by day preservation of vitality. A respiratory rate is meshed with a heart rate. A brain wave-rate is meshed with an endocrine performance rate and so on. Various rates, like a complex machine consisting of dozens of gears driven at different speeds but meshing in synchronization to provide a stable over-all tempo and rhythm, form the characteristic time pattern in physiologic space. The entire scheme is so interlocking that a rate interference in any of the various components serves to dyssynchronize the entire system. By design the entire internal system is geared to a sympathetic temporal balancing when one component is under attack and must change rate. However, the persistence of a state of emergency requiring acceleration in any degree of regularity tends to imbalance the internal temporal system. This aspect of temporal dyssnychrony is considered by Selye (1956) in his concept of the physiologic effects of stress. Establishing a stable internal rhythm with the interlocking of all body rates frequently poses a formidable challenge to the physician dealing with the child with cerebral palsy who has an altered respiratory pattern, the polio case, the asthmatic, the allergy ridden child, the hypertension case and the epileptic. Whenever one rate is disturbed the therapeutic course must consider the other rates and their synchrony.

In our concern for clarifying the broad concept of Movement Efficiency the temporal synchrony in physiologic space is an essential consideration. Any disturbance to internal body rhythm must be viewed as a movement disorder which in some manner must manifest itself in the visible behavior of the individual as he performs. The allergic child during special seasonal periods may be in desperate straits to maintain any temporal internal balance in the face of disruptive allergens and as a result may become unusually active or unusually quiet, may be extremely irritable, anxious and upset and be unusually variable in his performance. The seizure-prone child before and after seizures may evidence marked changes in behavior which are not characteristic of his "usual" response. The asthmatic child before, during and after attacks may show great variations in behavior. It would appear logical to assume that any individual suffering from a temporal imbalance in internal states will manifest some reduction in external efficiency. When internal coordination is affected, a variety of external incoordinations can also be anticipated. Perhaps the most obvious impact of internal temporal problems is upon the temporal tolerance threshold for performance. When timing is internally upset the tolerance for time in the physical world must be affected in some manner. Sustaining time through a performance becomes a critical problem. Sustained effort is frequently not possible under those conditions. A stable rhythm in physiologic time is therefore a critical variable in the achievement of Movement Efficiency.

Physical time is marked by the traditionally defined units. The first component of awareness of physical time is related to the sequence of night and day. Seconds, minutes, hours, days, weeks, months and years become units of physical time. Seasons of the year, eras, eons, ages are other units of time. Most of the research has been devoted to the study of physical time. In general we may refer to physical time as "clock time" or "calendar time". It is a learned time — a system defined by man to label duration. The child must achieve an awareness of time and once having achieved an awareness he must perceive duration. His perceptions of duration must then be brought into conformity with the symbol system employed by his culture to denote time. From the interweaving of awareness, perception and a set of symbols he progressively builds a concept of Time which can serve his continuing adaptation to his world.

As the research has pointed out, his first stage of awareness is to day and night difference. He next marks time by personally related events. His own actions become his first standard for time estimations. Gradually he learns to call the units of duration by their accepted names and incorporates into his vocabulary "tomorrow, yesterday, next week, on Friday, in a few minutes, not now, three o'clock, time for supper" and hundreds of other labels. As he progressively advances in "stature and wisdom" in his space world he continues to increase and expand his symbol system for denoting time. His adult concept of time and his state of efficiency in regard to time are dependent upon whether or not he has efficiently managed the developmental progression. If there have been misperceptions or symbolic confusions regarding time during his childhood period which have not been corrected, these same confusions will plague him throughout a lifetime and often serve to embarass him during his adult travels. Time exists for each individual as an immediate present. It is a forward momentum phenomenon. Duration ticks forward from Now. This moment can never occur again except in symbolic form as memory.

Man moves in physical time. As he moves in space between and among objects variations in duration occur. Spatial judgments of near and far are basically calculated on a premise of "How long would it take me to get there?". Distance is perceived in terms of duration. Space which can be spanned quickly becomes "near" and space which cannot be spanned quickly becomes "far". The distance between "here" and "there" is a duration space. "Fast" and "slow" are physical time constructs attributed to duration from point to point in space. The speed of interval between two points determines a relative judgment of "fast" and "slow". As a child moves between two points in space he acquires a symbol to characterize his rate of movement. He hears adults refer to his moves as "fast" or "slow" and learns to match these words to his performance. Gradually he learns that "faster" requires less interval between thrusts of his hands, legs, eyes and so on — less time in between movements speeds up performance and earns the label "faster".

A greater interval between thrusts—more duration before the next move — reduces the speed and increases the span and earns for him the label "slower". Progressively he incorporates the labels as governing symbols to direct his own actions. He learns that the same span of space can be covered quickly by running or moving his hands more rapidly or less quickly by moving legs and arms at a slower pace. The spatial span remains the same, it is the duration of movement from point to point which may be varied by the speed of transport. His concept of time must include the shifting potential of his own movements to accelerate or decelerate as the situation may demand. Temporal awareness in transport becomes a matter of personally regulating the speed of movement in keeping with the perceived need for variation.

Another perspective in physical time is the synchrony of motion. Each movement of the body has a source and a termination and the span between source and terminus is a time span. Muscular movements are sequenced. Each movement may be defined in terms of serial order steps which must follow one another in sequence to complete the action. The cycle of motion in picking up an object, throwing a ball, thrusting a sabre, hitting a golf ball, climbing a fence and so on may be analyzed in terms of discrete steps which must follow one another in rapid sequence for the act to occur smoothly. An individual may be very rhythmic in his movements in which case the sequences of movement in various body segments are synchronously integrated. He may be dysrhythmic, in which case sequences become temporally confused and result in awkwardness. He may also be arhythmic in which case the sequence necessary may not be established. Many variations may occur in sequencing movements into smooth patterns but all of these represent a temporal awareness of muscle timing. The perception of kinesthesia is the cognitive counterpart of time in movement. Many sprains and strains occur in athletics because of a momentary dysrhythmia in which the temporal sequencing became dys-phasic. Many household accidents occur because one part of the body was in a different motion cycle from another part and the time lag distorted balance.

Physical time is physical movement. As such it is essential to movement efficiency. Physical time is awareness of duration and the regulation of movement speed. Physical time is symbolized by standard referrents. All of these are combined to evolve a concept of time.

Milieu time defines a person's experiences during a specified period. Milieu time includes six basic periods within the life of the individual. There are the time periods of infancy, preschool, school, adolescence, adulthood and old age. Each period is composed of multiple experiences associated with the needs of the individual at each life space. The milieu time of infancy is marked by an initial period of awake-asleep alternations, a crawling period, a toddling period, a vocalizing period, and so on. The milieu time of the preschool period is marked by breakfast, play, lunch, nap, play, dinner and bedtime interspersed with visits, shopping, taking a ride and so on. The school years are marked by semesters, grades, vacations, the Friday spelling test, the Cub Scout meeting, the music lesson, two weeks at summer camp, religious instructions, dental visits, holidays, and so on. The adolescent years are marked by the pubertal change, the weekly games, the next dance, semesters, final examinations, dates, club meetings and so on. In early adulthood there is a practicum, internship and apprenticeship along one continuum and courtship, engagement and marriage on another continuum. Pregnancy, delivery, wash day, bridge club, Sunday church, garden show, holiday dinners and so on constitute another type of continuum. In old age the milieu time is made up of retirement, visits, holidays, and so on. Milieu time marks off significant periods in the life span. Milieu time is one of constant anticipation—always some event approaching, arriving and passing. Milieu time is usually lengthy covering weeks and months and years.

For each individual milieu time is spanned differently despite the similarity in physical time. In each of the six stages of milieu time there may be accelerations, delays, retardations, and punctuality. Awareness of milieu time is necessary in committing one's self to a course of action. Choosing to go to college involves a four year commitment. Joining a Cub Scout troop becomes a commitment to regular meetings and passing through the stages. Often people negate their commitments because they had no original conception of the time span involved. Once engaged in a commitment they come to realize that it involves a great deal more time than they estimated and must therefore be terminated.

The child has little choice in making decisions about milieu time. He is committed to an apprenticeship through the circumstances of age and social patterns. However, the general efficiency he achieves in his early years in temporal awareness becomes a significant determinant of the manner in which he manages milieu time when the opportunity of decision is his. His developmental problems with temporal orientation, tolerance, sustenance, and estimation which may be more or less efficiently organized become the foundation for his time sense as an adult. Milieu time in adulthood is also subject to analysis in terms of orientation, tolerance, sustenance and so on. Problems of temporal inefficiency may be noted in milieu time at any age.

Cognitive time is probably the most complex of the four domains. The most general term to be applied to cognitive time is that of "processing". Processing is the span from receipt of stimulation to the terminal conversion into meaning. This is the amount of time it takes for the individual to convert energy forms into useful information. A wide variety of psychological investigations have been undertaken to study **reaction time** fall under the heading of cognitive time. In cognitive time the individual formulates sentences, thoughts, ideas and attitudes.

Cognitive time is the span required for **recognition**. The "re" prefix on "cognition" defines the act as dependent upon previous experience. In recognition the individual is defining the "here and now" in terms of criteria originally formulated at some previous time in his life. Recognition requires a drawing upon a cognitive deposit for matching purposes.

It is cognitive time which permits a past, present and future. Time does not stand still. It moves relentlessly forward. Only as Man is able to conceptualize can he come to an understanding of the past and an anticipation of the future. What has happened in the past can never truly occur again—that moment in time has passed—but the mind of man can recall events, objects and circumstances in relatively clear detail and cause them to mentally occur again. What may have taken hours or days to achieve in physical time in the past can be returned by memory in a millisecond for man's use in his present. Man always exists in the present, but the quality and character of his present behavior is inextricably interwoven with his past experience. Man is constantly relying upon experiences of the past to direct his behavior in the "here and now". He is continuously trusting his previous successes and failures to formulate his current response patterns. On the one hand he repeats courses of action which have successfully resolved problems encountered in the past, and on the other hand he deliberately avoids repeating responses which have been unsuccessful in the past. There is a widespread belief among behavioral scientists that man's current behavior is always subject to analysis in terms of antecedents. Actually, it is probably a fair statement to say that man's behavior is always governed by past time. All of his antecedent behavior becomes a determinant of his present response in some degree. We seek to analyze his early development for possible clues and seek to define characteristic patterns of behavior which have been sustained through time. This form of investigation is undertaken in the hopes of understanding his present behavior and to enable the setting of predictions of his future responses under certain conditions. One form of psychotherapy seeks to have the patient recall events, circumstances and relationships of his past in order that he may analyze them from the changed perspective of his present status and "reperceive" them in the light of his adult sophistication. It is felt that the difference in perspective will bring about a re-evaluation of significance and contribute to a positive modification of his ongoing behavior.

Cognitive time has a dimension not shared by the other three time zones. Physiologic time has no memory. It moves in a constant forwardness. There is no way to recall a heartbeat or a brain wave. Once occurred, there is only the next beat or wave. Physical time does not allow for turning back the clock or the calendar. Each second passes never to pass again. The next second is followed by the next second. There is no turning back. In milieu space no segment of the milieu is repeatable. An internship moves only forward in time. It is only in the **memory** of man that time can be repeated.

In a very precise reading of time, Man is constantly dependent upon his immediate past. Even as an action is started in the present "right now", a millisecond or more occurs and as an action progresses towards completion, each "present" step depends upon an immediate past. In staging a movement, responding to a stimulus, choosing a course of action, and so on, there is always some interval of measurement between each of the many discrete steps. By the time an individual moves a leg to cast a stride, seconds have passed and the original impulse is past history but a vital contributor to whatever is going on in the "right now". Time moves forward in milliseconds. In a strict sense the present is only measured by the millisecond clock. As soon as the next click occurs the previous one has entered the past. In another sense, we can say that all of man's actions are directed toward a future time. As man moves, he spans time. Each move is oriented to a future time. It takes time to complete a space between two points. The time honored S-R bonds which Thorndike originally postulated and which have been the focus of tremendous amounts of research ever since, serve as an interesting illustration of that point. The small hyphen which traditionally separates the S from the R is probably best interpreted as a Time phenomenon. That particular time phenomenon has generated much research to account for the events that transpire between the original Stimulus and the terminal Response. The general concept of man's every action being future-oriented in a strict physical time sense is congruent with the concept of developmental momentum.

To return to processing terms, we can say that man's information processing is future oriented. He processes information to increase, advance and expand his future behavior. Man processes information at varying rates of speed. Simple information which can speedily be related to past experience is quickly processed. Complex information which requires more probing for association with the past may involve a lengthy time span. It was Guthrie who suggested that we truly learn to swim during the winter and ski during the summer. In our terms, he was referring to the processing of the actions in cognitive time.

It is cognitive time which becomes the critical determinant of man's actions. From the time a question is posed until the response is given, the individual is toiling in cognitive time. We refer to people as being "slow on the uptake, square, thick-headed" and many other slang expressions to indicate that they "process" slowly. The bewildered look on the pupil's face when the teacher asks a question as he "mentally searches" for an answer is an example of cognitive time in action. Riddles, the "point of a joke", the meaning of a remark, often occasion an obvious effort in cognitive time. In children and many times in adults it is possible to observe a "processing pause" as the individual attempts to make all of the necessary connections and associations before giving a response. The response may indicate a "processing failure" if an error occurs. Some people arrive at accurate solutions quickly. Some arrive at accurate solutions slowly, but none the less accurate. The difference in speed is attributable to variations in cognitive time.

Another illustration of cognitive time is the listening process. To gain information the listener must take in individual phonemes in a series, interpret each independently as received, store the series, attach meaning to the full series of words, sentences or paragraphs, continuing the intake as if uninterrupted by his own processing action and simultaneously or nearly so organize a possible response. This is a good example of what might be called a simultaneity of past, present and future in cognitive time. In most instances, this process in cognitive time moves swiftly in its course with no breakdown in pattern.

If during the flow of listening the speaker mispronounces or introduces a word which is foreign to the listener, some impairment in processing is likely to occur. The listener must then struggle to identify the strange word either as an independent processing action or from whatever context clues may be present from immediately previous words, those which follow, or the entire situation. In this case it may be necessary to suspend that word in cognitive time "pending further information".

Since physical, physiologic and milieu time are always positive, i.e., forward-moving, it is possible to conceive of cognitive time operating on a minus **and** positive time basis. Minus time is a reversal of the forward momentum of time allowing for "back time" with no interference with positive time. Other times continue to go forward. The processing time necessary to formulate a response cannot operate as a countermeasure against the forwardness of time. This would essentially produce a mechanical stutter effect of pulling in two directions, bringing time either to a standstill or some type of stumbling or temporal asynchrony. However, if we postulate a minus or negative time, it could operate independently of positive time formulating thoughts and ideas and re-entering the positive time cycle when "ready" to do so. This would explain man's ability to dwell upon the past, recall the past, use "memory" without disturbing the forward momentum of the time cycle throughout his body and his physical world. Minus time would allow for storage and retrieval—fitting words and thoughts into the ongoing time cycle as necessary to the situation. Minus time would account for a form of time suspension—holding events, names, experiences in a state of suspension—available as a reservoir to re-enter the time cycle as required for modification of man's next response.

The concept of regression is still another version of what might be called **negative** or **minus time**. Man contains the capability of returning to earlier stages of behavior under the duress of organic injury, illness and extreme environmental stress. Even though his regressed behavior is far from being identical to what it was at that earlier time, we nonetheless speak of his return to an earlier type of behavior as a regression. This "going backwards" occurs without significant disruption to the ongoing time cycle in physical, physiological and milieu space.

People may "lose" time having no recall of certain time periods. They may "confuse" time by connecting events in a temporal linkage which did not occur in the temporal order they now recall; they may "collapse" time and recall an event as being brief which actually spanned considerable time. Many pathologic subjects "lose" time and "confuse" time. Temporal disorientation is a common characteristic of neurologic impairment or psychotic breakdown.

The memory deficits which are associated with mental retardation may also be viewed as the inability to suspend time. The problem of some organic adults having clear recall of distant events and little or no recall of immediate past events is another example of a problem in cognitive time.

Cognitive time thus becomes a very critical determinant of the efficiency of the individual's temporal orientation. All four zones of time are essential to the adequacy of postural-transport efficiency.

In his awareness of time, the learner finds the early answers to the "whenness" of his world. With temporal awareness his movements in space take on additional meaning and refinement. He progressively learns to attribute a time quality to his movements, and this enables him to produce some temporal regulation into his behavior. Events occur in time. He can exert more or less muscular effort to move quickly or slowly. With temporal orientation he can recall previous movements. He can place events, objects and people in space with greater accuracy when he can also attribute a "whenness" to them. The child must not only learn to walk, run and sit, and how to reach, grasp and release, but he must also learn **when** to do each. There is a time to move swiftly and a time to move slowly. He must learn to speak and when to remain quiet. He must learn when to drink and when to eat. The "whenness" in his world is a vital component. He must incorporate this cognition of "whenness" into his orientation for movement if his survival potential is to be enhanced and his movement efficiency is to improve. He must acquire a timing for movement. "When to move" is often a critical point in success. Effort extended too soon may produce an error as well as effort extended too late. He must progressively become more accurate in estimating distance. His referrent for space estimation will initially at least be his own movement potential. "Far" will be defined in terms of the duration of his own movements. Time can be an ally or a foe.

Performance efficiency must be **sustained** through time. The inability to sustain a high level of efficiency over a span of time becomes a significant indicator of the true efficiency of a performance. If a child's performance quality in the beginning of a task reflects a high efficiency but his accuracy and quality deteriorate as the task wears on, the original efficiency is perhaps available **only when tasks are brief**. It is therefore not a well-integrated skill. When efficiency cannot be sustained through time, a reduction in accuracy and quality is the inevitable consequence.

Often one can find children who perform at high levels during the early stages of a task and then progressively worsen as the task extends through time. Analysis of performance on writing, arithmetic and spelling tasks may reveal an increasing number of errors in later stages of the task, even though the general level of complexity from start to finish is relatively constant. Simple continuation of the same activity over a period of time may reveal a gradual diminution of behavioral control—the child's voice may rise to a higher register, speech rate may quicken, articulation errors may increase, restlessness may be more noticeable, distractibility may become pronounced, poking and shoving may appear, tangential talking may occur—some evidence of **threshold for time** becomes manifest to a sensitive observer in a changed tempo of behavior. The signs of such behavioral change should be considered as possible indicators of the fact that the temporal tolerance level of the children is nearing its outer limits. In the face of such signs, a discontinuation of the activity and a diversion may prevent a more serious behavioral disruption.

It is generally accepted that children will be able to sustain a performance through time in progressively larger spans as they mature. The attention span and performance of the two-year-old is accepted as brief and variable. By the time he is four, attention and maintenance are expected to be lengthened over his two-year-old span. With each passing year he is expected to span greater lengths of time in his performance. The greater length is expected within the **same** performance. While his first grade reading will be brief, by the time he is in the fourth or fifth grade he is expected to sustain his reading efficiency over a three to four hour span. How the child or adult is able to sustain an efficiency through time becomes a critical indicator of whether the various components of Movement Efficiency have been well integrated. It is the concept of sustaining efficiency through time which constitutes the major portion of Temporal Awareness. Estimating and labeling time can be regarded as a mechanical relationship to Time. The child may be able to mechanically recite the symbols of time and have an appropriate estimation of time but unless he can utilize these mechanical achievements in the temporal dynamics of his own daily performance these mechanics have little value to him. To be aware of time the performer must utilize time to his own advantage. Time is personal. It gains value as it is personalized. Yesterday, today and tomorrow must have personal significance if temporal awareness is established.

The performer must be aware of time in reference to his own behavior. He must be able to accelerate or decelerate his own actions according to the demands of his environment. He must learn from personal experience the meaning of punctuality, tardiness, "saving for the future", travel time from place to place and thousands of varying relationships where **time** is a factor. Temporal awareness adds the rhythm of synchronization to his transport and introduces grace and poise into his postural orientations.

SUMMARY

The five components, Muscular Strength, Dynamic Balance, Body Awareness, Spatial Awareness and Temporal Awareness possess a characteristic hierarchy. Each of these components appears to have been design-intended to follow in rank order of development with each subsequent component serving as an expansion of what has gone on before. Each in turn is derived from and emerges from the predecessors. Each has its own period of emphasis for setting a foundation and each steps back into the developmental chorus to improve and refine itself in concurrent effort while another is in a major state.

There is a concert of postural-transport development played in crescendoes and descrescendoes, andante and largo, pianissimo and forte———unified and organized to prepare the learner for independent transport in grace. The theme of economy and efficiency is constantly in evidence.

Those who wish to serve as "conductors" of this concert as teachers must come to recognize the subtle interactions of these five components and provide ample opportunities to the developing learner to explore each component, separately and in combination, in order that each may come to make its proper contribution to the personal composite of efficiency.

9

THE PERCEPTO-COGNITIVE MODES

The key to every man is his thought. Sturdy and defying though he look, he has a helm which he obeys which is the idea after which all his facts are classified. Emerson

The learner must process information to survive. He must convert a bombardment of energy into directive information to guide his adaptation, to seek and provide nourishment, to protect and defend, to selectively approach, avoid, escape, encounter, attack and engage. He must be able to sort variations in illumination into shadows, contours, edges, shapes and details; convert vibrations into identified and organized sounds; interpret contact with his body surface and discriminate and differentiate ordors and oral substances. He is engaged in a perpetual task of differentiation and discrimination.

The system by which the learner converts energy forms into meaning to promote his survival has usually been labelled, perception. The consideration of perception as a survival system has not, however, been the usual perspective among theorists and investigators. The general body of literature in the study of perception is massive but the variations in viewpoints among theorists requires the student of perception to make a choice between a search for synthesis as an independent scholarly effort among the many and varied theories or to adopt a single favored theory and rely upon it in attempting to understand the dynamics of perception in a mobile being.

The answer to the question, "What is perception?" must therefore be answered only with reservations and qualifications. It is also possible to seek the answer by taking a route of synthesis.

Theorists have addressed themselves to all sides of the perceptual elephant. Titchener (1909, 1914, 1915) defined perception as an interrelationship of a core and context of sensations to derive meaning. Werthermer, Koffka and Koehler (Helson, 1933) produced the many propositions of Gestalt theory. Lewin (1935, 1936, 1951) placed perception in a social perspective and introduced motivation as a factor. Hebb (1949) conceptualized a neurologic model of perception with his cell assemblies and phase sequences. Werner and Wapner (1952) showed the role of motor factors in spatial perception. Freeman (1948) related the physiology of energic set to the field of perception and pointed out the universality of tonic states and proprioceptive feedbacks in determining how the world appears to the perceiver. The manner in which needs, tensions, values, defenses and emotions contribute to the perceptual process became the focus of Bruner (1947), Krech (1951), and others. The basic concepts of "pooling" and "weighting" to establish relativities in perception came from Helson (1947). The view that perception is a transaction between the organism and its environment and based upon the confirmation or negation of assumptions was offered by the group at Hanover. (Ames, 1951; Cantrell, 1948; Ittelson, 1951a, 1951b, 1952). Brunswick (1936, 1943, 1939) emphasized an investigation of the manner in which the individual achieved perceptual constancy. The concepts of cybernetics cast perception in an analogue model and emphasized feedback, open, closed systems and scanning. (Wiener, 1948) Allport (1955) critically reviewed the theories cited above and evolved his own concept of structure to explain perception. He concluded that the perceptual act is really a dynamic operating **structure**:

> *It appears as a structure that is closely knit yet not isolated from surrounding happenings, that it is built up of the events of ongoing and interacting elements — events that have assembled as it were through space and time, a structure that can endure, that is flexible and yet ordered and resistent to disruption, that has both a non-quantitative and a quantitative aspect, that pools or averages its energies, that "gears in" with some adjacent structures and opposes or reduces others and that operates as self-closing or self-renewing cycles.*

More recently, Festinger (1962) introduced cognitive dissonance and consonance to explain the perceptual process and Smith (1962) proposed a neurogeometric theory based upon behavioral cybernetics.

Literally thousands have prospected across the rugged terrain of Perception. Some have turned over an investigative shovel or two and moved on to other fields. Others have worked a vein of ore for a lifetime uncovering varying lodes of perceptual riches. The terrain continues to attract new prospectors year after year. The elusive mother lode is yet obscured.

The study of perception has run along two main tracks. Some investigators have concentrated upon the perceptual process and outcome in groups of non-impaired children and adults seeking to identify "normal aspects" of the process. Others have centered their investigation upon the definition of deviational characteristics in perception among populations containing some form of physical, social, emotional, neurologic, or intellectual problem. Frequently, the investigators working with "problem" groups have compared their deviant groups to the so-called "normal control group" to ascertain the extent of perceptual deviation in the problem group and to draw inferences from these findings to increase the general understanding of the "problem group".

From this second type of concentration a vast body of literature has emerged to describe the multiple variations in perception which might be categorically subsumed under the heading of "perceptual disturbance". The general publication list has tended to equate "perceptual disturbance" with some pathological state and has usually been applied to populations with organic lesions or significant emotional disorders.

This dual tracking has tended to divide the field of perception into the broad categories of normal and disturbed as though these were the only categorical possibilities.

Much of the literature on "perceptual disturbances" has resulted from the study of single performances or even a series of performances resulting in a conclusion that the individual subject suffered from a generalized perceptual inefficiency. Unfortunately this type of investigation has led to wholesale generalizations about the individual's perception. Failures in visual perception in no way permit a generalization about the totality of an individual's perceptual efficiency. Similarly, failures on any given perceptual task do not warrant summary conclusions about his total performance.

There have been many ingenious laboratory experiments devised to study perception but the translation to practical application of these findings into considerations to be given by a classroom teacher or a parent seeking to optimize a child's development have been the exception rather than the rule. The professional world has a long road to travel to bring the benefits of experimental data to the practical level of application to enhance child learning.

The effect of a perceptual disturbance on the total life functioning of an individual has not been detailed. For example, a child's failure to reproduce an adequate copy of a geometric form may be taken as a sign of a perceptual deviation but the manner in which such a perceptual problem might manifest itself in his daily living in tasks of dressing, eating, talking, playing and so on has not been a typical extension of perception research. The impact of a perceptual disturbance upon the totality of performances in an individual's daily experience represents a void in the story of man and his perception. The student of human behavior is left to his own resources to fill in the blanks. Witkin (1954) and his associates have perhaps come nearest to this form of extension in relating perceptual performance to personality attributes in their study of the perception of verticality but did not extend their considerations to the manner in which their subjects might perceive verticality on a daily basis in the hundreds of confrontations they might experience. We regard the human organism as an essentially consistent being whose discrete performances are always representations of his totality. It would follow, therefore, that any daily perceptual demand which invoked the same efficiency components which formal testing had already defined as deviant, would be subjected to the same difficulty as manifest in the test. If lined geometric forms were confused in a formal test then all elements in the visual world requiring a discrimination of form difference should be equally confused. If a child cannot discriminate circle, square and triangle forms on a purely abstract basis but manages such discrimination when the circle becomes a colored ball on the page and the square a colored block or box and the triangle an Indian tepee then the question of the components of perception in the two instances must be carefully differentiated for respective values to daily living.

The general body of literature on perceptual disturbance contains a wide assortment of competent investigations on various aspects of perception. The general collection of diagnostic categories which are represented in the field of Special Education have fared well in regard to interest in examples of perceptual inadequacies or distortions. Hospital populations of various sorts have also fared well in this respect. The delineation of marked perceptual aberrations in a pathologic population has been comparatively easy. Pin-pointing an explanation for such aberrations has not come so easily.

What is usually meant by the term "perceptual disturbance" is the gross tendency of the performer to perceive in other ways than he was expected to perceive. He distorted what he saw, heard, drew, tasted and smelled. He perceived **something**—but not what was expected. It is very likely that every pathological subject does a great deal of accurate perceiving during the course of a day and every normal subject does a certain amount of misperceiving every day.

We have made quick generalizations of perceptual disturbance without recognition that we are only assaying a small portion of the total perceptual activity of the individual. When he fails to properly close the diamond form we say "perceptual disturbance" but fail to recognize that he does perceive a fork, dresses himself, does not fall down stairs, crosses streets, asks for a cookie, etc.

To classify an individual as perceptually handicapped has little significance unless such a statement is accompanied by a description of the types and classes of events and categories which are characteristically misperceived by the individual. Usually this label results from a series of scattered test performances in one modality.

Man is an information seeking mobile being. Distorted or clear, sharp or dull, fast or slow—perception takes place. It is the scheme by which man gives meaning to himself and his world. The effort to understand this phenomenon must continue if we are to comprehend the movement potential of man.

Basically perception has been investigated as a sense-oriented phenomenon with studies divided into compartments called visual perception, auditory perception and so on. On a purely quantitative basis the study of visual perception has been the overwhelming favorite. The investigations of auditory perception run a very poor quantitative second to visual perception. The quantitative disparity increases on a geometric ratio as one seeks for references on tactual, kinesthetic, olfactory and gustatory perception. Few theorists would disagree that the other perceptual modes exist in man but their investigative efforts have not been significantly directed to the other modes. On the basis of sheer quantity alone one would have to assume that visual perception has been a favored subject while the other modes have suffered the fate of rejected children. There is agreement that they exist but there is little true concern for their developmental welfare. Such neglect of the other perceptual systems suggests that the understanding of the perceptual process in man is incomplete.

If it is initially accepted for the sake of argument that all perception investigators did in fact contribute significant perspectives to the understanding of the phenomenon then each investigator should be obligated to account for the various elements in his own study population. If "feedback" is significant as a perceptual element it should be accounted for by all investigators. If "set" is a significant factor all theories should incorporate the concept. If the learner "pools and weights" to establish perceptions it must be a constant in any perceptual process. In each perception experiment the contributions of all previous work must either be incorporated or purposefully excluded. This is a rare occurrence. The usual approach has been to stress a particular concept of individual belief, incorporate some previous concepts on a selective basis, indicate disagreement on one or two other points and to rest the case on the experimental data of a given study.

The study of perception among non-impaired children is a curious collection of miscellany providing little guidance for the consideration of a natural progression of perceptual efficiency from infancy to adolescence.

Gibson and Olum (1960) reviewed experimental studies and methods of studying perception in children. In their concluding discussion they noted two major areas of weakness in the general study of perception in children: (1) rarely have any investigators utilized a developmental approach to the study of child perception, and (2) a significant absence of programmatic research in this field. They commented that many of the studies appear to have been opportunistic—because children were conveniently at hand. Few studies reflected a long range plan for a series of investigations with one study developing from a previous one and building to a comprehensive body of knowledge. An overview of the status of perceptual investigation in children is a disappointing one. The description of perceptual development in children has not enjoyed the same careful attention to detailing the developmental differences in successive ages as may be found in the area of vision or motor patterns. Most perceptual theorists have concentrated their efforts upon adult populations with an occasional effort to apply the same techniques to children in an attempt to give some developmental perspective to their constructs. Once the student of child perception gets beyond the work of Piaget and one or two other investigators he finds rough going on the trail with only scattered poorly defined landmarks to guide him in building an integrated picture of perception. For the most part he must rely upon adult-oriented theories and infer the probable reference downward to the child level.

Perception and cognition have been generally regarded as two separate performance entities in human behavior with bodies of literature representing each. In our thinking these two phenomena are not so readily separable. When semantic or even conceptual dilemmas arise one can seek to resolve the dilemma by diligent reference to pertinent literature to seek a clarification but years of contact with the literature have failed to produce a comfortable clarification. While it is true that the literature reflects a separate treatment of the two the justification for that separation is not clearly established—at least for us. Lacking such clarification from professional literature one can take an entymological approach and take recourse in a standard dictionary where the simple definition of words without beneficial or deterrent explanatory clauses must be the guiding rule and where the author has no particular investment in a given word. The dictionary indicates that perception is cognition and cognition is perception. Both convey a meaning of "coming to know". Both describe the end product of an information process. For several years we have sought a word which would convey a synthesis of these two so as to properly label our thoughts on this matter but as yet have not been able to find an appropriate term among existing words or even to coin one. Consequently we have employed the hyphenated term percepto-cognitive to label our conceptualization with the hurried explanation that we consider the process to be a simultaneous fusion of the two. If they must be separated such separation perhaps occurs in a millisecond interval between perception and cognition. It is analogous to a walking gait in which two feet are necessary in a reciprocal pattern of fusion to yield a "walk". It should be understood that in all subsequent discussion of Movigenics the use of the terms **perception** or **cognition** separately is mainly a matter of writing style but each separately is intended to imply this fusional belief.

We regard this percepto-cognitive fusion to be the ignition system for movement which provides the combustible force to energize man's motor systems for the purposeful movements of adaptation. If this fusional process does not take place whatever movement may occur is not truly under the control of the mover.

For survival reasons the learner must be a constant perceiver. He is perceiving at all times. He is designed to scan, appraise, evaluate, select and act. He may develop a very wide range of perceptual acuity or a very narrow range. He may perceive physical objects more readily than language symbols or he may perceive sound more efficiently than he does texture. He may be more or less directed by his values, prejudices, attitudes and emotional tensions. He may be field dependent or independent. The variations in perceptual efficiency from one individual to another may be legion but by design he is continuously active as a perceiver.

The human performer is by design a full-time perceiver, always perceiving **something**. What he perceives may not be appropriate to the situation in which he is performing—he may miss the point, ignore a detail, fail to attain closure, and so on—but he continues to perceive if there is any mark of human-beingness in his behavior. There is no choice for him. If he is to move with any degree of purpose and direction he must perceive. Tart (1962) and others have shown that the human is capable of perceiving even while asleep.

At any given moment in time and space there are two quanta of percepto-cognitive potentials which are operative for the perceiver. One potential consists of the total number of details which exist in the surround. These are fixed and would be identical for any perceiver in the same circumstance. Color, form, light, heat, sound, etc. are the details fixed in a given time and space circumstance.

If we take a college textbook and open it at random in a given setting of illumination and sound and prop it on a desk we can define this as a fixed situation. Light, heat, sound, furniture and so on can be measured. We can then assemble a mongoloid child, a two year old, an engineer, a physician, a bookkeeper, a high-schooler, etc. and set each in turn to the task of processing information from the opened page. This is an obvious illustration of variance in return. The physical setting is identical for each so no real variance can come from this source but each will sit at the task with a varying amount of capability to meet the perceptual demand.

It is possible to view a situation and make a listing of all perceptions which could be transacted. Any situation would produce a lengthy list. This is the fixed perception potential of that situation regardless of the character of the perceiver. The second quantum of percepto-cognitive potential resides within the individual perceiver. At an optimal level the percepto-cognitive potential of the perceiver will match the fixed potential of the surround so that whatever is possible to perceive in that situation is within the capability of the individual. Placing a dynamic perceiver with a percepto-cognitive efficiency equal to the fixed quantum of perception potential in the surround would require only the introduction of a demand into the setting to initiate and guarantee successful performance. The demand enables the optimal perceiver to select from the multiple perceptual surround those cognitive elements necessary to resolve the demand. In any situation the perception potential always exceeds the performance demand. Even though a perception experiment is defined, for example, as a test of capability for perceiving reduced time exposures of geometric forms, the instructional or perceptual set must be employed to selectively diminish the perceptual surround for the subject. Within the setting the subject **could** perceive the size and texture of the projection screen, the heat of the room, the feel of his body on the chair and countless other elements within the situation. These are extraneous to the demand but are available in the event that the performance demands were to change.

Consequently, three elements are necessary for a perception: (1) a surround consisting of a multiplicity of percepto-cognitive possibilities; (2) a dynamic perceiver within that surround who brings to the surround a certain level of perceptual sophistication, and (3) a performance or perceptual demand which enables the perceiver to select from the surround those details which require processing to resolve the demand.

At any moment that the perceptual efficiency of the individual is unequal to the demand the individual perceiver must fail in the resolution. He cannot resolve the demand with optimal success because his efficiency level is less than adequate for that particular situation. Many explanations may be offered for a given perceptual failure but the dynamic process of failure is always the same. The failure may occur because of neurologic impairment, cultural bias, emotional disturbance, mental retardation, language disorder or any other causative factor usually associated with perceptual disturbance. It may also occur in a non-impaired or non-involved individual whose experiential background has not provided him with a sufficiently enriched perceptual background to equip him with a perceptual facility equal to the confronting demand. Many normal adults confronted with a complex mathematical problem suffer a perceiving failure. Attempting to comprehend the meaning of a foreign language spoken fluently by a native can produce a perceiving failure in those unacquainted with the language. Perceptual failure is a universal possibility among men. When successful performance depends upon a certain level of percepto-cognitive efficiency and the perceiver cannot produce the necessary efficiency the result is a failure. This is not to say that some other form of perception does not take place. Being a constant perceiver the dynamic individual simply perceives something else in the situation than that which is necessary for efficient resolution. Confronted with a dilemma his flagging perceptual efficiency recognizes a survival emergency and perceives **something** to remain perceptually alive.

Consequently, the question to be asked after any perceptual failure in anyone is the same — "Since he did not resolve the perceptual task efficiently what other perceptions occurred on a survival basis?" If the so-called average man is handed a part from a piece of equipment from a beauty parlor and asked to identify it he is confronted with a perceptual dilemma. The only optimal percepto-cognitive result would be an exact naming. Unable to accurately define it he may resort to calling it a "thing", "a gadget", "a whatchamacallit". He may also resort to labeling its texture, weight, color, substance or any of its other characteristics. He does perceive **something** even though not accurately. Many children and adults are inefficient listeners and often respond to "what they think they heard" and may be surprised to discover they have erred. General observation has led us to believe that perceptual failure is also a constant among mankind. All that is required to produce perceptual failure is to present a demand which exceeds the percepto-cognitive efficiency of the confronted perceiver. This can occur to physicians, statesmen, waitresses, teachers, sales clerks, bus drivers, first graders, infants, scientists — to anyone. It is always a question of capability and demand.

A light gradient, a sound wave, a texture, a thermal gradient, a muscle stretch — these are the raw materials of percepto-cognitive action. Perception occurs in an energy surround.

The energy form must be transduced into programmed information and made ready for perception to take place. Perception converts the energy form into meaning by sorting out the intake, assigning it a discriminative differential and identifying in some manner its difference or similarity to all previous transductions. Once perceived it has little value to the organism unless it is assigned a symbol to provide for proper use, storage and retrieval availability. By labeling the perception the individual can economically compare it to previous experience and decide upon a hierarchical value. If it is perceived and labeled directly it may be a **universal**. Under the heading of universals are those percepts which can be suffixed with "ness" such as "chairness, writingness, etc." Once having attacked a symbol to the perception the next step becomes an economy transaction. Since perception is dynamic, continuous and multiple it becomes an impossible task to label each perception with a separate name. The economy system devised by human intellect is **conceptualization** which can briefly be a computer-massing of percepts into meaningful classifications for the retrieval process.

In order to tabulate, discriminate, differentiate, and organize his perceived information, man converted his perceptions into symbols. He represented his previous perceptions with some sign to determine similarity and difference. Whatever form these symbols may have had, they were an inevitable result of the selective process in perception which logically required some organized system to record the perceptions.

This processing sequence is an ongoing dynamic for the individual during all of his waking hours. While we may separate each stage for ontogenic study, the purpose is artificial and primarily to show each derivation and early childhood emphasis. In truth it is almost impossible to define a perceptual stage that is totally devoid of symbolization or conceptualization or even abstraction. A little of each is present at all times during early development and remains available throughout one's lifetime.

The sequence of processing starts with **sensitization,** which is an alerting of one or more of the six channels to a receptive state. This is followed by a **percepto-cognitive transduction** of the incoming data. This, in turn, is **symbolized** by the perceiver and sorted among existing **concepts**. From the concepts, **abstractions** are derived. The entire sequence is vital to what is generally called perception. The more efficient the perceiver becomes, the more readily can he bring each perception to the level of abstraction.

The perceptual world of each perceiver—the totality of the millions of perceptions he has experienced up to the moment of confrontation with the next perception—brings him to each new perception more sensitized and ready to perceive, symbolize, conceptualize and abstract with speed and accuracy in an immediacy, or less sensitized and therefore less ready to perceive with a groping search for symbols and a perplexing seeking for accurate classification and categorization. For this reduced sensitization we perceive an immediate closure, and when the symbolic stage cannot readily be managed, we rely upon "feels like, looks like, sounds like, could be, sort of, similar to" and many other related expressions which represent a search for symbolization and conceptualization.

The five stages are in constant operation in a dynamic being. As the individual is confronted with novelty in his world, the working of the five stages may occur with less speed, usually because he must grope for an appropriate symbol, but it must nonetheless occur if the experience is to have meaning and value.

As a continuous perceiver he functions as a totality. All of him is perceiving at any given time. We cannot truly say in any given situation that only his eyes perceive or only his hands or only his ears. While it may appear that the primary intake is visual or auditory, his perceptual efficiency is dependent upon his totality. As an integrated being, he cannot function in an isolated-part manner. By design he has been developmentally programmed to acquire in sequence gustatory, olfactory, tactual, kinesthetic, auditory and visual perceptiveness. Proceeding from the more primitive to the more sophisticated levels, his perceptual range constantly increases. Each in turn organizes in a period of emphasis and retains its identity as it gives over the developmental spotlight to the next mode. Each subsequent perceiving mode enriches the previous one, and each in turn prepares the road for the following mode while simultaneously insuring its own facility. The perceptual efficiency of each mode is literally dependent upon the efficiencies of all others according to design. As a consequence of this interdependency and interrelatedness, which will be discussed in more detail later, his total percepto-cognitive efficiency is the product of his intermodal acuity. To his intermodal product must be added values, attitudes, tensions, and so on. This is the totality of the perceiver which confronts the perceptual task. This aggregate, with all of its weaknesses, strengths, shadings and nuances, constitutes his perception potential and becomes the critical factor in his success-failure ratio in meeting each and every perceptual experience. It is the perceptual "know-how" which enables him to function in varying degrees of perceptual comfort.

He contains all of the elements that have been defined by perception theorists — and more. The detailed analysis of his perceptual complexity is only at the drawing board stage with many more diligent hours and years of laboratory experimentation lying ahead.

The development of these six modalities proceeds along a hierachical scheme with each having its period of dominance in organization. While each modality is continuously in the process of receiving stimulation to enrich its development, there appears to be a "biding time" phenomenon. While one is in center stage occupying the developmental spotlight, other modalities are being stimulated in lesser degrees as if they were awaiting their turns for assuming the starring role. Development is a symphonic arrangement with a dominant theme of enlargement, enrichment and refinement. All six instrumental modalities will be accorded their solo passages in the harmonic lines of the theme, while others recede into the background to maintain the general course of the melody. As if in crescendo toward optimal efficiency, the gustatory gives way to the olfactory which in turn recedes in favor of the tactual. When the tactual sensitivities are reasonably well established, the proprioceptive organizations to prepare for purposeful movement begin to emerge. Then as if to indicate that all is in readiness for the climax, the auditory becomes ascendant, and finally in triumphant build-up the visual comes in with purpose and meaning to complete the perceptual theme. Each successive mode has been holding its place in the harmonic arrangement building its unique contribution step by step until it reaches a peak of readiness and assumes its rightful place in the developmental hierarchy. When the instrumental modalities have learned their passages well, they can be called upon individually or collectively by the human conductor to respond in necessary emphasis to play out a rich rhapsody of daily adaptation.

The sequence of development of these six modalities may also be considered a survival sequence. The first major survival obstacle to maintain life is the problem of food intake to nourish for maintenance and for growth.

10

THE

GUSTATORY

MODE

A mobile chemical organism requires energy to support its transport explorations. Man must nourish the tissues and organs of his body if he is to move with efficiency and comfort toward survival. The terrestial space traveler, young or old, is a processor of nutrient information—a vital information for tissues, muscles, bones, glands—leading to growth of the skeletal frame and the sustenance of movement potential. The gustatory mode is a primitive allegiance to physical and cognitive development. The concept of gustatory processing as the initial mode in the percepto-cognitive system embraces a number of factors in addition to the usual sense of taste. The mechanical functioning of the tongue, the digestive system, food preferences, and chewing must all be considered in developing the full story of how the organism processes nutritional information.

The Gustatory Mode is a channel for obtaining information. At the most primitive level, nutrient information is conveyed to physiologic space in the form of proteins, carbohydrates and fats. When the balance of intake is disturbed or not achieved, the traveler may experience a wide variety of disorders. In physical space the infant must learn the differences between the edible and inedible. He will select according to preference certain types of food. In **milieu** space, his information from the gustatory mode will vary. The infancy milieu will be marked by a progression from liquids to foods with greater and greater substance. An athlete in training will eat a special diet, the patient in an "illness milieu" will partake of a special food regimen, and so on.

The oral cavity with its tongue tool becomes the first organ of perception for the infant. His search for meaning begins in this area.

The survival oriented sucking reflex becomes a necessity for life. If this basic pattern is impaired in any manner, the infant's life is jeopardized. Whatever the reason may be, a sucking reflex failure must be considered as a survival threat. Such a problem creates a need for a differing form of feeding.

The infant who requires an experimental procedure to find an appropriate level of formula experiences a gustatory processing problem. Even though a suitable balance is achieved with some substitute substance, the fact remains that the infant has failed to adapt and conform to the expectancy of breast-feeding or standard formula. Generally the dilemma is resolved with little upset and loss of time. Once a diet has been established and the child's nourishment is no longer questioned, the concern for the possible long-range effects of this initial failure have rarely been studied. Allergists have perhaps been the most concerned about the food allergy problem at all ages.

The infant who is unable to process liquids within the oral cavity is already at a survival disadvantage since the primary mechanics of establishing a progressive refinement in oral processing leading to independent feeding is absent. The foundation blocks for independence are not in place, and the promotion of self-management is limited. This situation usually calls for gavage feeding, i.e., relying upon gravitational force to lower the food down the alimentary tract. The severely involved child with cerebral palsy is the most pressing illustration of this need.

Tongue movement facility is vital to the control of saliva. The human infant drools until he learns proper control of tongue musculature in processing salivation. Any person lacking tongue mobility will tend to drool. The mongoloid child, the organically damaged child, the child with cerebral palsy, the severely retarded child, may all experience difficulty in managing the tongue. They do not have the problem **because** they are mongoloid, retarded, organic or palsied but because they lack tongue mobility. This problem is not a characteristic of their diagnosis, but rather is a characteristic of anyone lacking tongue facility. The majority of cases in these diagnostic categories do learn to manage the tongue and consequently give little evidence of drooling.

This facility must not only be learned but integrated into a habituated pattern. When it has not been fully integrated, lapses in saliva control may occur when the individual is deeply engrossed in a task. For some the lapse may occur when they are deeply engrossed in some manipulative task; for others when listening intently, and for still others when they are intent visually. Clinical observation of this behavior suggests that it is a regressive phenomenon more likely to occur when the concentration is upon a modality process which is not in itself well-organized.

If hand usage is not precise and well-organized, the demand of a manipulative task requires a massing of concentration on the pressing mode, and the stress of this attention disinhibits other habituated responses. Inefficient listeners or viewers may drool when concentrated listening or looking is demanded. It has been noted in many clinical children that if drooling is periodic and usually under control, regression occurs not as a general characteristic but only when the learner is experiencing difficulty. A regressive drooler with some visual and auditory efficiency may show no liquid signs until his manipulative inefficiency is exposed. When demand for efficiency is made upon feebly organized modes, the drooling is more likely to be noted. A further observation may be recorded related to tolerance levels in any given mode. While regressive drooling may not be observed under ordinary circumstances of viewing, listening and manipulating, it may appear at those times when the learner is required to process difficult information in any mode, i.e., it becomes a symptom of stress, signaling that the demand has exceeded or is at least pressing the limits of efficiency in a given mode.

Gustation is an ever present processing system for man. While it remains vital for the intake of food and drink, it also serves as a supportive agent in the development of perceptual-cognitive efficiency in the five other modes. Since it is first born in the family of processing modes it serves as a big brother or sister in enhancing and enriching the development of younger modes progressively introduced for family integration as development proceeds.

The study of gustatory sensitivity in infants has generally been conducted by placing standard stimuli on the tongue such as sweet, sour, salt and bitter substances and observing reactions. In one such study Pratt, Nelson and Sun (1930) found citric acid and quinine to be equally effective in raising the activity level while sugar and salt produced an increase in sucking movements. Jensen (1932) used five concentrations of salt solution for determining differential reactions compared with milk. All of his infants discriminated the 0.900 per cent solution but could not discriminate at lesser percentages. Very young children and animals were found to accept solutions having a sweet taste in preference to distilled water in a study by Richter and Campbell (1940). Bornstein (1940-1941) established a set of limits for the strength of solutions to detect taste impairments in man with inference for cortical involvements.

Increased activity or withdrawal has been noted for solutions which might generally be classified as unpleasant while increased sucking action has been the characteristic response to pleasant taste in infants. In other subjects, the verbal judgments of the subjects have been used to define some limits of taste tolerance-intolerance. Taste can be impaired by cortical interference. The general tendency in the research has been to study differentials in response for various solutions.

Another form of research in the gustatory area is related to thermal reactions in the mouth. In 1932 Jensen reported on threshold values for newborn infants for hot and for cold in the mouth. Riesen (1960) reviewed the meager literature on touch and pressure and cited the work of Fitzgerald and Windle (1942) and Hooker (1952) in concluding that the "only firm conclusion is that the region about the mouth is one of the earliest to develop sensitivity (compared to other skin surfaces) and retains priority thereafter as one of the more sensitive areas".

Some 40 years ago Scheck (1925) studied the involuntary movements of the tongue under varying forms of stimulation. Using a pneumograph and a small balloon held in the mouth he recorded the involuntary respiratory and tongue movements of subjects as they sat at rest, wrote under dictation, as they read silently and while varying types of music were played on a phonograph. He concluded that involuntary tongue movements were "very common if not always present" and that these varied in accordance with the stimulus situation. Gesell (1949) referred to the "mouthing" behavior of infants as a form of tactual-spatial exploitation which contributes a nucleus to the visual perception of form and substance.

Many cases of gustatory primitivation have been observed among neurologically impaired and emotionally disturbed children. Some organic children have been seen who appear to need to "taste" their world in order to know it and as a consequence will put toys, blocks, puzzle parts, paper, crayons, etc. in their mouths to inspect them before attempting to use them properly. In the emotionally disturbed child this is frequently identified as a primitive arrest at the "oral stage". The mouthing of the objects appears to have value for perceptual reinforcement.

In moments of insecurity the characteristic thumb in mouth position will be assumed by many young children. While for many children this may appear an almost constant position, for others it may appear only sporadically as they feel threatened in a given situation. The regressive thumb in mouth may serve as an indicator of the severity of the perceived threat. If it has not been noted in a child for some time the return of such behavior becomes a clue to a state of disturbance within the child's ongoing reaction to his world.

The gustatory has been related to emotional states throughout history. Man seeks out food to exhibit his jubilation and avoids food when he is depressed. "Loss of appetite" has long been associated with emotional upset. Consider the many cultures where the loss of a loved one is marked by mourners bringing food to the home of the bereaved to make the "passing" bearable. From another perspective psychiatry has extensively described the compensatory eater and portrayed him or her as satisfying needs through overeating which are not being met in the usual course of daily living.

American society might be considered as holding an abiding gustatory orientation to life. A large percentage of the society has been accused of "eating too much". At the opposite extreme are those who are "eating too little". A dietary consciousness has permeated at least the middle and upper class strata of our nation. The consciousness is not emerging as a wise understanding of the balanced diet but rather as a caloric model for intake—the diet to reduce weight. Food preferences and food fads may be psychologically determined by tensions and anxieties. Parsons **et al.** (1962) stated, "...by now it is psychological commonplace that in certain individuals an aroused gregariousness or an aroused fear drive may also express themselves in the hunger need. Individuals so affected will be observed to overeat in loneliness or stress".

Gustatory processing is a constant for man. There are always new foods and new drinks to be tasted, discriminated and accepted or rejected. There are always occasions to detect the spoiled or distasteful and to reject such before swallowing.

Tastes vary in food largely based upon learned patterns of eating. Culturally determined patterns are identified with various ethnic groups and many restauranteers capitalize upon appealing to the public with specialty dishes associated with a particular group. The public learns to eat Italian, French, Chinese, Mexican, Hawaiian, German, Danish, etc. dishes which may never have been a part of their food experiences in their own homes.

Digestive upsets occur under conditions of tension as a prosaic event in American life and the use of post-eating alkalizers is a rather standard practice for many. When tensions are sufficiently intense and not readily resolved the development of an ulcer is a frequent outcome.

It is an obvious fact that man is a lifelong processor of foods and that the gustatory mode is a constant information channel. Foods may be selected wisely or unwisely. Balanced or imbalanced diets might be taken. Eating may be a comfort or a penance.

Developmental scaling for the Gustatory Mode has only been described in very general terms. The infant will pass through a food consistency sequence from liquids to solids as his dentition takes place. Progressively more chewing is demanded. A synchronized scheme is again in evidence requiring the interaction of teeth, tongue, jaw musculature, lips, oral cavity, etc. The child who experiences difficulty in passing through the food consistency sequence and arrives at age three or four unable to chew solid foods has failed to achieve an adequate organization of the gustatory mode. Since such failure suggests an inefficiency in the primary survival mode all other perceiving modes are consequently inefficient. If the designed sequence is not achieved the total perceptual system must pay a toll for such lack. The mastication of food is but a first step in organizing the gustatory mode. The food must be passed on through the digestive system for appropriate cellular distribution of nutrient energy. Consequently, the next organizational element to be integrated into the gustatory mode is the digestive process. Any form of infantile difficulty with the digestive process produces discomfort and requires special consideration of dietary modification. This is a lifelong possibility. The digestive element in the gustatory mode may be the site of a problem at any age. There is a constant demand upon a mobile organism to take in food in quality and amount to maintain a level of comfort. Those youngsters who are beset with food allergies during infancy or later have failed to follow the expected route in digestion and distribution. Food specialization required because of physiologic imbalance is a negative feature in gustatory development. Even though the special diet serves to achieve a physiologic balance the infant, child or adult must be classified as having a gustatory problem. A limitation has been defined. Failure to attend the special diet results in negative physiologic consequences and digestive balance therefore, has a limited range of freedom.

For many years nutritionists have sought to educate the national population to understand the need for a balanced diet. It has probably been a standard piece of rote learning for every American school child during the past 50 years. Unfortunately, the learning has not been integrated for large masses of our national population. To move the body requires energy. Energy is derived from food and drink. When the energy source is not properly presented, the loss must be manifest in some reduction in mobility.

Lacking in degrees of energy because of inadequate nutrient distribution, there must be a corresponding inefficiency in movement. The stark dramatic cases of malnutrition which have been publicized reveal emaciated unenergized bodies moving in continual discomfort. We have learned from year to year new and startling lessons in the field of biochemistry related to nutrient energy. Our point of concern here is not with the dramatic results of dietary lack but with the possible implications of dietary imbalance for the development of Movement Efficiency. Physiologic balance requires a balanced intake. The organism who is physiologically balanced has a higher potential for comfortable and economic movement. It therefore becomes developmentally critical that balanced intake in early infancy and childhood in keeping with the gustatory design sequence serves as a foundation source for movement. Any type of problem in this area threatens the adequate development of a movement foundation.

On a general developmental basis throughout life it is likely that behavioral response in any situation is inextricably related to nutrient supply of the performer. Learning can be enhanced or deterred by gustatory events. Overeating and hunger both contribute to a reduction in perception, cognition and comprehension. As a performer is nutritionally balanced so will his performance be efficient. The study of learning efficiency in correlation with nutritional balance has not been undertaken but we suspect that it might someday be possible to correlate poor performance in a single spelling lesson with a temporary metabolic difficulty.

The Tongue

The tongue occupies a unique role in the acquisition of movement efficiency.

The tongue has been the focus of investigation by professionals only when some pathology is present or suspected. If a tongue is diseased it warrants attention. If dysarthria is present the tongue is of vital concern to the speech therapist. In some types of speech disorders an apraxia of the tongue may be suspected. Feeding and sucking difficulties in an infant may occasion a diagnosis for the tongue. In general, however, if an individual speaks clearly and gives no open evidence of difficulties in eating there is an automatic assumption that the tongue is well organized, facile and of no specific relation to other movement patterns within the body.

The concept of the tongue as a primitive initiator of basic survival patterns has caused us to pursue a course of investigation of the tongue in all cases of children and adults with learning problems. The investigation has taken the form of clinical assessment, primarily in relation to movement patterns, as a means of collecting observations which may yield a series of testable hypotheses.

The tongue operates on the triordinate system in its patterns of movements. The tongue moves on the vertical, horizontal and depth axes and manages a full rotation. Most speech therapists carefully assess the movement facility of the tongue to determine whether the tongue musculature is sufficiently fluid to place the tongue in appropriate position for various sounds. Muscular inadequacy may be identified as dysarthria if spasticity is suspected. Almost all articulation disorders are caused by some degree of incoordination of the tongue. Inefficiency on the lateral plane produces a lisp. Inefficiency on the depth axis caused problems with sounds formed by the tip of the tongue.

Our interest in the tongue as a vital tool in processing information has led us into a line of investigation which is at this moment strictly clinical in its orientation but our work with both children and adults during the past five years has produced some interesting findings. We were first intrigued by the observations of "tongue steering" in people who were deeply engrossed in minute nearpoint visual tasks, such as threading a needle, doing a puzzle, hunting for words in a dictionary or fitting some small part into a machine. Next we began to note that many children in classrooms seemed to be using their tongues to "steer" their writing or drawing. When we became sensitive to tongue observations we were amazed at the number of instances in which tongue steering seemed to play a part in the performance of a task. Intense concentration in the face of difficulty seemed to be the critical combination for bringing the tongue into steering position.

Guided by a belief that the tongue can serve a supportive role in directing performance, we began urging children to point their tongues at their work as they performed. As they attempted to balance standing on one foot we noted that children who had difficulty managing to sustain such balance showed a marked improvement when they thrust their tongues outward. As they experienced difficulty in joining objects, balancing on a fulcrum, walking a beam or throwing a ball or a dart there was a noticeable improvement when they thrust the tongue forward. Three adult cerebral palsied discovered that they could lengthen the extension of their spastic arms or legs if they simultaneously steered the reach by tongue. They were also able to reach and grasp more accurately when the simultaneity of tongue thrust was included in their effort.

A number of incoordinated children pointed their tongues to the opposite side of their mouths from the side on which they were performing a task, as though the tongue was serving as a counterthrusting mechanism in balance. We suspect that people who frequently sweep their tongues in a rotary motion over their lips, are using the tongue to come to visual balance.

For several years we have tested the ocular motilities of children by means of a small cat bell suspended from a short string. (This technique for determining whether the eyes teamed in horizontal, vertical and rotary pursuits was first used by G.N. Getman in his work at the Yale Child Study Clinic while studying children's vision.) (Gesell, 1949) When children showed some difficulties in tracking, they were asked to follow the bell with their outstretched finger. Often the involvement of the hand improved the pursuits. In addition to the hand, we asked the children to "follow the bell" with their tongue and also noted that tracking patterns improved. In some manner the tongue brought the eyes into a better motoric patterning. While some children revealed a dramatic improvement in ocular motilities, the same improvement was not noted in all of the children with whom we tried this technique. As a second step in making a preliminary assessment of the child's eye-motor patterns, we placed the children on the floor in a supine position and suspended a ball (white plastic) on a string about 12"-14" above them. The ball could be swung in the horizontal, vertical and rotary planes in the same manner as the cat bell previously described and the tracking ability of the child could be noted. In this position, the request to "follow the ball with your tongue" also brought improvement to visual tracking. As we have observed this particular tongue phenomenon in approximately 90-95 children (ages 4-15) there are a number of suggestive findings.

1. Eye movements improved for some in a sitting position when the tongue was introduced as a "follower". If this did not produce improvement, the same child in a supine position when asked to "follow with his tongue" **did** show improvement.

2. In some children the eye follow was observed to "shift" at the midline, i.e., the eyes teamed while following the moving target in the right field and as the pursuit crossed the midline into the left field the eyes seemed to "shift" gears at the midline. A similar phenomenon in other peformances has been described by Kephard (1960) and

Getman (1962). When the tongue was introduced into the "follow pattern" one of two things happened: (1) the eyes did not "shift" but held a true course, or (2) the tongue showed the same "shift" pattern in the horizontal plane.

3. If the eye follow lagged on one side or the other and could be called unequal the tongue followed the same pattern or the eyes equalized with the help of the tongue. In some children with an obvious internal or external strabismus, the tongue also exhibited what in gross terms might be called a similar lateral suppression. A number of these strabismic children also manifested a lateral lisp in their speech pattern.

4. The tongue seems to contribute most toward improving the ocular motilities in the supine position.

5. This had led us to devise a tentative scheme for evaluating the severity of a problem in visual tracking. If the introduction of the pointing finger improves the eye tracking while sitting, this seems to represent the best prognosis for good quick results in tracking exercise. One step lower than this but still on the highly positive side, is the improvement gained by tongue-follow in the sitting position. This also suggests relatively rapid improvement in visual tracking from simple exercise. If neither the tongue or hand improve eye-follow during the examination, the severity of the problem is intensifed. The next step in the scale is to make a similar set of observations in the supine position. If the pointing finger improves the tracking, this remains positive. Also, if we move to the next lower step and introduce the tongue to achieve improvement, we remain on the plus side. However, if neither the tongue nor the finger produce tracking improvement, experience has shown that repeated exercises to improve tracking tend to show poor results. If the visual tracking does not improve under the supportive reinforcement of either the hand or the more primitive tongue the inadequacy of the ocular patterning is quite severe.

The tongue is frequently used by people as an aid to convergence. When the visual system is operating under stress and convergence breaks they sweep their tongue across their lips and project it outward. As a result of this process they probably return themselves to convergence and visual alignment. The frequency of this occurrence is based upon the incidence of fusion-break. Instead of simply attributing such behavior to some category of tension release or neurotic manifestation the value of such behavior to the organism must be considered. We now consider such tongue action to be a system employed by the individual to come to balance.

The vast majority of consonant sounds are based upon tongue facility on the Z axis. Well articulated speech, however, will be dependent upon tongue mobility on all three coordinates. Any problem with the horizontal coordinate (lateral muscles) will produce some form of lisping. Inefficiency on the vertical or depth axes will result in difficulties with certain consonant sounds. It is not unusual for children to approach their kindergarten year with a variety of consonant sounds which are not clearly articulated, thus, causing some manner of "sound substitutions" in their speech pattern. For many children the articulation pattern seems to clear up with the passage of time. The incidence of clarification is of such proportion that this phenomenon is considered by many speech authorities to be a maturational lag which does not require corrective exercise. An interesting temporal coincidence exists at this time. This same time span places the child at the peak of visual convergence when he is being placed in a near point visual environment for sustained work. He is also placed in a controlled setting where listening becomes a more critical need than it may ever have been before. All of him "converges" upon the vital survival task of academic learning. Perhaps it is the developmental convergence at this time that contributes to the directional refinement of the tongue as well. Some limited observations have suggested that if the visual convergence phenomenon does not take place the "maturational lag" in articulation persists well beyond the expected time and requires the intervention of corrective exercises. In line with the general constructs of this book, it is held that persistent articulation errors are accompanied by convergence insufficiency in vision.

People who have been exposed to prism lenses as a technique in visual training, have expressed two types of comment pertinent to our consideration here. Some have complained of becoming very thirsty after a session with prisms and indicated that the thirst remains for several hours. Others have commented on a "tingling sensation" in the tongue and the roof of the mouth "almost like the feeling of novocaine" which also lasts for several hours. Our interest here is not in precise neurologic explanation but rather to offer a thought on the concept of psychological stress as a causative agent for the gustatory referrent. A prism lens severely alters the world of space and forces the wearer to call upon other clue systems to confirm spatial judgment. The lens causes objects to appear curved and as the hand or foot may search for contact—the object or surface is not quite where it was "expected to be". This disturbance to spatial computing may be so threatening to the individual that more primitive survival mechanisms are activated—hence the gustatory reaction to indicate survival threat. In some instances, the patient has temporarily acquired a lisp or slurring to his speech due to the tongue lag. While this reaction may not be universal in anyone exposed to prisms, it may well serve to indicate the degree of spatial disturbance in a given individual—those who regressively experience a gustatory response, may be more upset by the spatial confusion than those who do not. Clinical experience bears out the belief that those people who are tightly bound in space as a general characteristic are more likely to react in this manner than those who have a relatively free flexible space world.

As a general observation of clinical reactions to specific visual training activities aimed at achieving a differential in spatial computing most people feel quite hungry after a training session. While this must be treated as a casual passing comment, it is nonetheless an interesting point to be considered in this particular context. Perhaps any form of effort on the part of the individual to define and reorganize his space world is accompanied by some form of gustatory component. Historically, man has thirsted and hungered after battle and the waging of a battle for spatial reorganization may be more wearying than first reading may suggest.

Although we have not been able to locate specific experimental citations on this point, we are inclined to believe that the lateral preference of the individual is also expressed in a favored side for chewing foods and we wonder whether right handed people are likely to experience a higher incidence of dental caries on the right side of the teeth rows and vice versa.

The gustatory mode has also been incorporated into the cognitive domain with various symbols employed in a cognitive duality to represent certain forms of experience. We refer to ideas or notions as being "palatable", to certain behaviors as being "in good taste" or "poor taste". Choice of color combinations in clothing and furniture are also evaluated as being in "good or poor taste". Appreciation of painting and sculpture, selection of books, choice of automobile—all may be considered as representative of the "taste" of the individual. Thoughts may be expressed "with tongue in cheek". We may "digest" an idea, be "nauseated" by a notion, find a particular comment "hard to swallow" and "regurgitate" facts in a collegiate quiz. As man has developed language to symbolize his experiences, his personal function and structure have provided a source of dual representation. Again, using his own experiencing as a referrent, he has elevated the physical terminology to the cognitive terrain to be intellectually useful in his mental explorations.

The gustatory mode has essentially been taken for granted in the human performer but we conceive it to have primary significance in the development of the percepto-cognitive system. It is the first mode available to the infant for meaningful information. Discrimination and differentiation in the oral cavity and the digestive tract are critical to survival. The structures of the gustatory system are designed to preserve integrity and protections and safeguards are built into the anatomic processes to insure the integrity.

Our conceptualization of the gustatory mode extends well beyond the boundaries of the physical structures which are involved. We wish to emphasize the perceptual implications, but seek in vain for the literary clarity necessary to convey the concept. Perhaps the following discussion of some speculations on this topic may offer a nuance of clarity.

Parents of young children might do well to make a special point of devising games and activities for tongue facility in the child using movement on the coordinate system as a guideline. Since there seems to be a natural tendency to tongue-steer in motor activities, parents, teachers and therapists may find some value in specifically suggesting such steering when a child is experiencing difficulty with a particular act of coordination. In our own experience in working with children, we continue to be impressed by the gains in accuracy which are achieved by some children when they are encouraged to tongue-steer. Although there may be some negative social implications for tongue steering as a general practice, the suggestion here is to explore the use of this technique as an aid to efficiency in movement. As with many other actions, tongue-steering may be exaggerated in the early stages and progressively refined to more subtle use as the individual becomes more adept.

If a learner, adult or child, manifests a tendency to tongue-steer, we regard this as a sign of reduced efficiency since reliance is being placed upon a primitive modality. Evidence of such steering, however, may have initial value in developing activities to improve coordination. The use of the tongue as a steering device is an indication that it has value to the learner. His own system can, therefore, initially be exploited in an activity program and gradually be reduced as visual steering becomes more effective.

Our interest in the gustatory mode has led to a clinical exploration of gum chewing as an asset in a learning situation. At the moment, our adventures are purely empirical and probably best classified as a search for an hypothesis which will lend itself to a critical experimental design. Even though our efforts might be considered as "blue sky" venturing at this time a listing of these will contribute to the general exposition of the conceptualization we have of the gustatory mode.

There are a number of observations from clinical practice with children with learning problems which generated our interest in this area. Occasionally, a very talkative child appears on the scene who is a "conversational waterfall" setting forth a constant stream of words much to his detriment in a situation where quiet visual control is necessary to learn the task set before him. Requiring the child to chew bubble gum during his lesson brought about a dramatic reduction in verbalization. It was as though his tongue became preoccupied with the gum and words became secondary. In other situations, we have found that some children seem to learn gross movement coordinations more readily if they chew gum while they are performing. We have additionally found that some children perform more rapidly and accurately on drawings, puzzle activities, designs and so on if they chew gum as they are working.

Several college students agreed to experiment with a gum chewing approach in the study of subject matter which posed special difficulties for them. Each time they sat down to study the difficult subject, they chewed gum during the study time. Upon completion of the study period they gave up the gum. They chewed gum during each lecture period of that subject and chewed gum during the quiz sessions and the final examination. As a part of this program, they abstained from gum chewing at all other times. Gum chewing was associated with a particular school subject. The reasoning process followed along these lines: the student facing his difficult subject introduced adverse muscular tensions into his study because he entered the task with a feeling of stress. Under this stress the chewing of gum provided a muscular release and produced a reduction in discomfort. The salivary conditioning occurred in relation to a given topic. The gustatory reinforcement became a memory stimulant. Vigorous chewing during examinations kinesthetically served to recall cognitive associations built during the practice periods of study. Each of the students successfully achieved in a subject which initially was regarded by them as very difficult. A variety of other explanations might also be offered to account for their success. At this stage in our explorations, we are reluctant to award credit to the gum chewing procedure as the critical variable in their success but on the other hand, we look upon this experience as a promising one. Admittedly, this venture was a very loose form of experiementation, but it has suggested a wide range of possibilities for further questioning.

Tensions produced by fear may elevate or reduce the PH count and produce a parching. Gum chewing may serve to balance this procedure. Perhaps chewing during learning may, in some manner, bear a relation to comprehension. The mid-morning snack, "the coffee break", the tidbit which have so much become a part of the American scene and in one form or another, have historically been a part of man's pattern are not only energy retrieval mechanisms, but actually essential to man's cognitive achievements. The well fed performer may be equal to or surpass the creative achievement of the starving performer. Perhaps the consideration of a gustatory component in developing a therapeutic approach for children with learning disabilities may have merit. Those clinicians and educators who advocate a reinforcement approach to learning find food rewards a valuable reinforcing agent. Food rewards content children and tend to make them more receptive to directions. When one considers the wide range of circumstances in which food or drink is traditionally regarded as valuable to clear thought, comprehension, decision making, and so on, the relevance of gustatory conditioning for improvement in learning seems clearly worthy of further exploration on a rigorously controlled basis.

Imaginative teachers may find many ways to enhance the learning task with a gustatory emphasis. The numerous expressions involving gustatory terminology which have been a part of man's language systems may well be an intuitive recognition of a physiologic correlate between learning and gustation.

The gustatory mode is a cognitive element in the building of movement efficiency. It may be the foundation upon which the information getting system in man is built. The range of its relationship to the total percepto-cognitive efficiency of a mobile organism must at this time, be regarded as uncharted. Not only is it the initial system of cognition for the infant, but it is a persistent informational mechanism for the life traveler at all times. We regard it a relatively unexplored terrain in the field of learning and hope that the discussion offered here may generate some further thought in this direction.

11

THE
OLFACTORY
MODE

The development of olfaction as a method for securing information from an energy surround is the second mode to become organized in the Percepto-Cognitive system. It must be acknowledged at the outset that there is practically no evidence available to support this contention. The designation of olfaction as a second position mode in the cognitive hierarchy is frankly a matter of theoretical "blue sky" maneuvering. The general literature is not kind in providing a set of experiments which would offer any degree of comfortable support to our hierarchial contention except for some isolated comment regarding the primitive nature of olfaction and its relationship to survival.

Those clinicians, teachers and parents who have experienced the behavior of certain types of seriously disorganized children have undoubtedly encountered emotionally disturbed, neurologically impaired or mentally retarded children who must characteristically sniff crayons, pencils, toys, clothing, and so on, before attempting to deal with the objects. We view this as a perceptual primitivation reflecting an inability to deal with material at a higher mode of perceiving. It is indicative of a severe degree of perceptual-cognitive impairment. The child is relying upon a primitive mode to acquire information. Where vision, audition or tactuality would be more economical and effective, his performance is encumbered by a need which should long before have been relegated to a secondary status ready for use as needed in specific situations but not as a steady information mode.

On a positive note, workers in the field of the blind will attest to the utility of olfaction in assisting the young child to acquire a spatial orientation. The body smell of the father, the perfume of the mother and the specific smells of objects become valuable elements in building a world of identity for the young blind child. For this population, the exploitation of the olfactory mode with deliberate aromatic stimulation may prove a highly beneficial therapeutic tool. For the blind, the survival significance of olfaction is accepted. Even though the mode is primitive, it serves as an exceptionally valuable clue system.

The recent work of Wright (1954) contains a valuable synthesis of the current status of research in smell, as well as a discussion of some notations and theoretical constructs which he has pursued. It is the most extensive coverage on the subject of smell which we have been able to find, and consequently our documentary discussion on the olfactory mode must rely heavily upon citations from this work.

Wright commented on the sensitivity of the nose:

> ...*The sensitivity of the human nose is by no means contemptible. Of course if it is treated with contempt, if it is ignored and its power wasted or if it is embalmed with smoke or anaesthetized with gasoline fumes or corroded with chemicals, it will not amount to much. A professional smeller can do some wonderful things whether he is a perfumer or a food taster or an aboriginal savage who finds his nose nearly as useful as his eyes in tracking down his game.*

The primacy of the olfactory mode has been cited by Clark (1956, 1957) who felt that from an evolutionary point of view, the cerebral hemispheres in the vertebrate series were developed in relation to the olfactory bulb. Fay (1955), in discussing the evolution of the cranial nerves, also commented on the importance of olfaction:

> *The importance of these individual pairs of cranial nerves has increased and diminished in dominant perceptive and expressive function from era to era and from species to species; but the first pair have always concerned themselves with smell and psychoemotional reactions dependent upon odors, integrated with the awareness of food, friends and foe.*

Wright (1964) also holds an opinion about this primitive primacy:

> *If the function of the brain is to regulate the activities of the organism on the basis of "information received" it almost looks as though intelligence had its beginnings as an apparatus for handling olfactory signals from the chemicals that bathed our first progenators in the primeval ooze. If this is so, then Descartes'* **Cogito ergo sum** *(I can think, therefore I am) must yield priority to* **olfacio ergo cogito** *(I can smell and therefore I can think).*

The olfactory process is basically a chemical one with complex absorption and diffusion gradients along with receptor specificity, which accounts for the discriminatory responses to odors. (Pieron, 1952)

Smelling takes place at a molecular level, and all of the structures within the nose are scaled down accordingly. The tiny size and the fact that the molecular surfaces are too close to the brain have tended to discourage anatomical researchers from penetrating investigations of this area in the human. The informational capacity of our sense of smell suggests that the smelling organ has more than 13 or 14 kinds of end organs, and that each responds to a different kind of elementary odor. Certain smells may be perceived by some animals which are not perceivable by man. It would seem that the smelling mechanism is survival-related with each species capable of smelling what it must in order to economically promote its survival.

The human nose is responsive to an enormous number of smells, and the concentration of these smells can vary over an enormous range. We are not efficient as perceiving small differences in the strength of two odors as we are at perceiving small differences in its quality. The average person is believed to be capable of distinguishing several thousand odors (Wright, 1964). Even with so extensive a range the human nose is not an accurate instrument for quantitative work, but seems to be a superb device for qualitative work. Smell is a non-directional sense that can produce a directed response. Wright suggested that individual variations in the ability to smell some odors and not others which contemporaries may smell is probably due to hereditary factors.

To perceive a smell odorized air must be drawn into the nose and actively sniffed. Recently de Vries and Stuiver (1961) concluded that eight individual molecules on a single nerve ending in the nose will trigger an impulse and that about 40 nerve endings have to cooperate before some form of perception takes place. Wright (1964) reported that the capability to perceive odors varies according to physical state, differing in certain illnesses, pregnancy, anticipation, anxiety, and so on. Children have different capabilities than adults. Briggs and Duncan (1961, 1962) in Australia reported an experiment in which 50 cases out of 56 who were classified as anosmic (inability to smell even though the olfactory apparatus is intact) recovered their power of olfaction when given large doses of vitamin A.

Smell is the mechanical product of the sensory apparatus, while olfaction is the dynamic process of gaining information from odors which has directive value to the organism. In its most primitive form, olfaction is a crude differentiation between the noxious and the pleasant. At a survival level there must be an alerting response to potentially dangerous odors to prepare the organism for flight. The odor of escaping gas and the aroma of smoke must still be identified by the highly sophisticated man of the present as survival-related. It is also necessary to detect spoiled food in order to prevent poisoning.

Modern advertising exploits the avoidance of negative odors as a necessity for the sophisticate calling attention to body odors as social negatives, special sprays to eliminate germ-caused odors in sinks, pails, and so on. Cooking odors are quickly eliminated by household fan vents. Cosmetics, perfumes, soaps and anti-perspirants are advocated for optimal social adjustment.

Very little seems to be known about the development of olfaction in children. What little has been done in this area has centered around a withdrawal or toleration response but not on a perceiving level of identification. The principal subjects for smell research have been rabbits, dogs and fish. As Wright pointed out, the study of olfaction is "one of the most neglected fields of scientific inquiry". A search for investigations on a child population is a singularly unrewarding pursuit.

A century ago Seguin (1866) described the gustatory and olfactory behavior of "idiots":

> *Rarely do we see them have a taste for non-alimentary substances or an exclusive appetite for one kind of food. Some of them, without swallowing, chew beads, suck pieces of broken china, etc. with apparent relish. The smell may take possession of the same articles and scent them for hours or delight in the fragrance of two pieces of silex, stricken one against the other; or, this sense may substitute itself for any other, as a means of discrimination and knowledge; or, on the contrary, be dead-like to all intent and appearance. But the difference between the errors of function of these two senses is, that taste is oftener depraved and the smell is more frequently exalted. (p.59)*

Few developmental studies exist in the area of olfactory sensitivity. Riesen (1960), in his review of studies of receptor functions, stated, "Methods applicable specifically to infants and children are sparse and depend exclusively upon signs of aversion, irritation or pleasure...Lack of adequate methods has produced contradictory statements by different investigators ..." Disher (1934), Pratt, Nelson and Sun (1930), and Stirnimann (1936) were several of the investigators who have attempted studies in this area.

The developmental aspects of olfaction are unknown. Yet there can be no question concerning the fact that the human organism is a perceiver of odors and a differentiator of smells. In some manner this mode must also comply with general principles of development. Olfaction must proceed from a very simple discriminating process to differentiate gross differences and progressively become a more complex information gathering mode as the organism becomes more complicated by experience and maturity. The adult has a vastly expanded range of sensitivity because his identification processes are more numerous. Whatever the developmental stages may eventually turn out to be when investigators turn attention to this mode the belief in the existence of such stages is certainly warranted by our current understanding of the basic design of the human organism. In the absence of documentation, we must proceed at the clinical level of observation to suggest the relevance of olfaction to Movement Efficiency.

The work of Briggs and Duncan (1961) has pointed to an olfactory inefficiency (anosmia) as related to a vitamin deficiency. Perhaps minor problems of vitamin insufficiencies or a wide variety of chemical difficulties which are so frequently being linked with performance breakdown in modern man also serve to reduce the efficiency of the olfactory system. It seems reasonable to entertain the notion of a partial or even a temporary anosmia due to a variety of dietary factors in the light of the vitamin A findings. Following along this line, it is possible to conceive of relative, temporary, periodic, spasmodic and variable states of olfactory efficiency in the growing child under varying forms of stress, dietary changes, increased metabolic rates and so on. While the human organism must be viewed as a dynamic olfactory being constantly utilizing the olfactory mode in some manner to gain information for survival, it is likely that we can speak of him as efficient or inefficient in this area as well as in others.

In the absence of systematic studies in olfaction among children, the area of information processing through the olfactory mode becomes another "blue sky" zone in which speculations must be the main vehicle of transport. When olfaction becomes cognitively useful to the infant is not known but we suspect that it has relatively little utility during the first year. It may operate in some manner on an aversion basis to noxious odors but we have little evidence of its operation in the positive attracting sense. It is possible to consider that children with higher olfactory sensitivity may become bowel-trained at an earlier age than those with lower sensitivity because of aversion to excremental odors.

A lifetime of odors stretches before each infant. Flowers, perfume, foods, dampness, decay, and countless other smells are yet to come. Each must be perceived, labeled and categorized. As his cognitive efficiency expands in other areas, so also will his olfactory efficiency increase. Since it is a primitive mode—other modes are likely to be more economical and efficient and the role of olfaction is obscured in the general dynamics of living. Only as an emotionally ill or neurologically impaired child or adult seems to exaggerate his reliance upon scent as an information medium are we likely to consider its relevance to the total picture of the individual's processing of information.

In spite of the absence of supporting evidence to substantiate our belief that the olfactory mode is in second place on the percepto-cognitive hierarchy, we continue to hold this hypothesis. The citations on the primitive primacy of the olfactory system and the clinical observations of disorganized children clearly suggest an important survival implication. As we follow along those lines, the possibility of enhancing the movement efficiency of an individual by heightening the olfactory sensitivity is an intriguing concept. If the olfactory is vital to man's survival—it is vital to his learning and should be reinforceable. It is certainly stimulable. Scented learning aids may prove very profitable to the learner. Aromatic environments may enhance or detract from one's efficiency in that setting. This is an area of investigation which might provide some exciting leads for imaginative educators.

12

THE
TACTUAL
MODE

The third mode in the chronology of the Percepto-Cognitive system is **tactuality**. As the mobile organism moves in space to economically promote its survival and enhance the body of knowledge required to intelligently construct satisfying answers to basic questions confronting the developing traveler, there is a constancy of touching and being touched. From touch the learner derives information. An extensive cutaneous envelope encasing the skeleton and internal milieu holds varying degrees of sensitivity to stimulation. Touch is variable. What is to be touched and what may touch varies according to the unique day by day experiences of the individual. Whatever the variability may be, the principal value resides in the accumulation of information.

The literature on the topic of tactuality is by no means extensive. While the general bibliography certainly outnumbers the references in gustatory and olfactory investigations, the study of the skin as an information receiving mechanism has not attracted the interests of researchers in the past hundred years except for a few notable reports.

More than a century ago Weber (cited in Mach, 1906) studied the space sense of the skin by using two points of a pair of dividers placed against the skin in varying locations asking his subjects to identify the distances between the two points. The tongue proved to be the most discrete sensor of all parts of the body. In the early 1920's and 1930's a number of investigators became interested in the possibility of substituting cutaneous stimulation to serve man communicatively if the tympanic membrane failed in some manner. This turned out to be a relatively unrewarding effort from the standpoint of finding an adequate substitute but rewarding in the sense that it provided the information that the "skin does not hear well". Although the search did not provide the "hoped for" answer, it nonetheless provided a significant negative answer which often can have as much significance for future research and understanding as a positive finding.

The skin can be used as a receiving surface for communication of words with a coded system of vibratory signals. Geldard's (1957) "vibratese language" based upon translating vowels, letters, numbers and words into vibratory intensities, durations and loci using a typewriter system to generate a distant set of vibrators attached to the receiver's body is an example. Morse code reception of 30 words per minute on a sustained basis is a rare achievement but the subjects in Geldard's study were able to receive 38 words per minute with the vibratese language system with a probable ceiling of achievement estimated at 67 words per minute.

In Geldard's work the spacing between contactors on the skin surface became the critical variable in achieving unmistakable localization of vibratory bursts. Even the spacing, however, does not insure against localization errors if the frequency of the vibratory bursts is varied according to the ingenious experiments of von Bekesy (1956) who demonstrated that the skin has elastic properties which cause vibrations to become traveling waves having flat maxima changing their location as frequency is altered.

Bender and his associates (1951) found normal, schizophrenic and organic adult and child subjects localized the touch on their face more often than identifying both hand and face when both were touched simultaneously. The simultaneous touch of the hand was either obscured or reported as a second touch on the face. The only departure from these results occurred among the organic adults who seemed persistently unaware of two points of touch.

The study of touch in cognition has largely centered upon investigations among blind populations. Merry and Merry (1933) studied the ability of blind children to recognize embossed pictures by touch and concluded that it would be unwise to extend any teaching effort toward tactual recognition of three-dimensional objects by the embossed method. Lowenfeld (1955) commented that "almost no research is available concerning the psychological and educational problems of touch observation". The most extensive study, however, comes from the work on touch reading where Burklen (1924), Heller (1895), Fertsch (1947) and others have made contributions. However, even in a field where interest in tactuality might be considered to be greater than elsewhere the study of touch perception has been relatively neglected.

In 1883, Rousseau described a child as wanting to touch and handle everything. He felt this to be a necessary part of a child's training: "It is by looking, fingering and hearing and above all, by comparing sight and touch that he learns to feel the heat and cold, the hardness and softness, the heaviness and lightness of bodies and to judge of their size and form and all of their physical properties". Pereire (Boyd 1914) felt that the sense of touch was basic to all other learning and that all sensations were in some manner a modification of the tactual. Nearly 70 years ago Bain (1899) referred to touch as the "fundamental and generic sense...the combined power of soft contact and warmth amounts to a considerable pitch of massive pleasure".

A number of authors have expressed opinions on the importance of tactual stimulation during infancy. Montague (1953) suggested that persons who received insufficient tactual stimulation during infancy are likely to be shallow breathers and be more susceptible to gastrointestinal and respiratory disorders. Frank (1957) felt that the tactual stimulation given in infancy is related to the individual's eventual verbal abilities and all of his interactions with the outside world. Escalona (1953) quoted Mirsky as saying, "In the earliest stages an infant's security is a matter of skin contact and of the kinesthetic sensations of being held and supported". Escalona also commented that "very early in life the senses of the skin are dominant". Ourth and Brown (1961) made a comment after their study on extra handling at feeding time which although difficult to experimentally validate is interesting, "adequate mothering of the newborns consists of continuing the patterns of stimulation that normally occur intrauterinely especially mild pressure and rhythmically changing cutaneous stimulation."

Recently, Casler (1965) arranged a ten week period of extra tactile stimulation for institutionalized infants having "handlers" stroke exposed areas of skin for ten minutes each morning and afternoon. Gesell Developmental Scales employed on a pre- and post-testing basis reflected significant improvements in functional behavior. White (1962) also reported beneficial results from extra handling of institutionalized infants during the first five weeks. Solomons and Solomons (1964) found that first born children are more extensively handled than subsequent siblings which appears to account for what has been described as advanced motor development.

The study of tactual space perception in children has not intrigued child development investigators to any significant extent. Few studies can be found in this area. Renshaw (1930) studied tactual localization in children 8-11 years of age and adults by marking 30 spots in a square on the hand or forearm, blindfolding the subject then stimulating one of the spots and asking the S to localize the stimulated spot with a small pointed stick. The findings showed the children to be superior to adults on this task. Renshaw with Wherry and Newlin (1930) tried the same experiment on congenitally blind children and adults and found improved localizations with increasing age.

Benton and Schultz (1949) reported a study on tactual form perception among 3, 4 and 5 year old children requesting the children to identify simple objects by touch. By age 5 such identification was nearly perfect for the objects used in the study.

A number of studies have been reported comparing the relative sensitivity of body parts. Franz (1933) found the arm to be more sensitive than the thigh. Major (1898) and Zigler and Barrett (1927) reported the palm to be more sensitive than the forearm and the thumb and fingertip to be more sensitive than the palm. Shewchuk and Zubek (1960) using an air pressure flicker technique concluded that the more mobile areas of the body such as lips, tongue, thumb and fingertip were discriminatively superior to arms, neck and cheek. Some information on the question of comparative sensitivity between the dominant and non-dominant hands has been reported by Ghent (1961). She found the left hand to be more sensitive to pressure in a right handed population of adults. This was especially true of the left thumb. When she turned her attention to children, she found that girls tended to show greater sensitivity on the dominant side until age six when the pattern shifted to the non-dominant hands. Boys maintained a greater sensitivity on the dominant hand until age 11. Sensitivity of the thumb became the critical indicator of the shift from the dominant to non-dominant hand.

There seems to be a general agreement among investigators (Weber, 1906; Woodworth, 1938) that the tongue is the **most** sensitive and accurate area for tactual discrimination and that fingertips may be assigned second ranking.

Tactual perception of form outlines by indentation or embossed processes has been found to be easier than the perception of solid geometric forms. (Major, 1898; Zigler and Barrett, 1927) The opportunity to move the fingers is the most effective method for tactile discrimination. (Austin and Sleight, 1952) Sigler and Northrup (1926) pressed geometric forms into the palm and the under surface of the forearm and concluded that a dimension of 12-15 mm was necessary before discrimination could be expected to be accurate. Zigler and Barrett (1927) showed that individuals depend upon visual imagery to perceive tactual pressures.

Bartley (1953) felt that if visual imagery was important to perception when only tactual and kinesthetic clues were available, square blocks placed near the performer would be perceived as being larger than the same blocks located further away. His findings supported his belief. Fisher (1965) has recently followed along the lines of Piaget's topological-primacy hypothesis in studying tactile perception in young children. Tactual recognition prior to thirty months is a matter of accident for the child since there is no tactual searching with the hand. Approximately seven more years of tactual experiencing and practice are necessary before the child can tactually search according to a Euclidean coordinate system in seeking to accurately identify.

Exact point localization of touch is a difficult task. While a subject can generally note the area of touch, the exact point may not be accurately identified. It is apparently not even possible to predict or plot a consistent pattern of errors for a given subject. (Franz, 1916)

Swanson (1957) compared mentally retarded and normal children on a task of perceiving simultaneous tactual stimulation. When the groups were controlled for the factor of mental age the retardates showed a better response pattern. Satter and Cassel

(1954) found brain damaged mentally retarded boys to be more erratic in localizing touched areas of the body than psychogenic mentally retarded and a familial group. Tactual perception of form and figure and background is characteristically poor in a population of subjects with cerebral palsy. (Dolphin and Cruickshank, 1952; Cruickshank **et al.**, 1957) Tactual discrimination of incomplete forms with progressive increments towards completeness was studied by Ross (1954) in a normal and a brain-injured population indicating that the brain-injured subjects required significantly greater completion of the form before recognition took place. The tactile sense in a population of spastic cerebral palsy cases has been studied by Hohman, Baker and Reed (1958) leading to the conclusion that the most frequent loss is in form discrimination followed by errors in two point discrimination and loss of position sense.

Speed and accuracy of tactual discrimination have been found to be unrelated to sex, handedness, number of fingers used and pressure exerted by the fingers. (Austin and Sleight, 1952). The implication here is that an accurate and speedy tactual perceiver may be boy or girl, left or right handed and require no specific tactile searching pattern.

Cratty (1964) cited a study by Hunt in which brain damaged children, inhibited in their movements were placed together in a little "house" requiring that they maintain contact with each others bodies. Under these conditions of "constant contact" they became more willing to move, verbal and social behavior improved and they achieved a heightened awareness of various parts of their own bodies. The experience contributed to a clearer body image freeing them to move and explore space.

Two paragraphs from Eisenson's (1955) observations are pertinent here:

> *Some children with delayed speech isolate themselves as far as the physical situation permits from others in the room. They will spend periods of up to an hour or more "playing" with a single toy object, or just sitting off to one side apparently doing nothing.*

> *Some delayed speech children appear to enjoy close physical contact with older persons and with inanimate objects. They may be seen to rub their bodies along the walls as they move from place to place. They rub their faces against their toys. Occasionally and very impulsively they will grab hold of another child or a clinician and cling with great force for a moment before releasing the person. Apparently there is a need for sensuous contact which the child obtains from accepting individuals or unsuspecting objects.*

Teuber (1959) found that patients with a right parietal lesion could report a single contact on either their left or right hand but when simultaneously stimulated on both hands could only report the right hand to have been touched. Teuber also noted that sensory impairment of one hand impaired the ability to discriminate objects held in both hands.

The distribution of tactual sensitivity depends upon the postural status of the organism and changes occur as postural shifts occur. McFarland **et al**. (1962) found that sensitivity of the right palm was increased when subjects were tilted to the left and that the straight-ahead directional line was shifted to the right. A similar reverse effect was noted when the body was tilted to the left. As a result of this study, the authors postulated an inner relationship between these two types of shift — "distribution of sensitivity" and the organization of space.

Three sources can be cited where the analysis of the tactual process was the major intent of the investigators. Lowenfeld (1955) cited the work of Heller (1895) and Steinberg (1920) in the field of the blind. Heller distinguished two types of touch, **synthetic** and **analytic**. Synthetic touch, according to Heller, occurred when a single hand or both could enfold over an object and determine identification as a unit. Analytic touch referred to successive impressions gained by the hands as they moved over larger objects tactually observing parts as they went along and unifying these multiple impressions into a gestalt of the object. Steinberg referred to a mental process under Gestalt principles by which the blind "expand tactual space".

The more recent work of Gibson (1962) in differentiating active from passive touch has probably produced the clearest description of the tactual process.

> *Passive touch involves only the excitation of receptors in the skin and its underlying tissue, although the patterns may be elaborate. But active touch involves the concomitant excitation of the receptors in the joints and tendons along with new and changing patterns in the skin. Moreover, when the hand is feeling an object, the movement or angle of each joint from the first phalanx of each finger up to the shoulder and background makes its contribution. And these inputs occur relative to a continuous input from the vestibular organs along with the cutaneous input from contact with the ground. Presumably, the feeling of an object by the hand involves the feeling of the position of the fingers, hand, arm, body and even the head relative to gravity, all being integrated in some hierarchy of positional information. In short, the so-called sense of touch as it is most often employed by using the hands involves the play of inputs coming from the whole skeleto-muscular system.*

These comments by Gibson are perhaps ideally suited to the general constructs of Movigenics since they reveal the integration of touch with a total system of inputs and relate touch to a total movement pattern. A statement by Tabori (1962) is also pertinent here: "Touch means movement, not only because the fingers have to move to examine larger objects but because it is movement that seems to permit form to emerge".

In another part of his discussion on active and passive touch Gibson, commenting on the incidence of investigations dealing with tactile form perception, stated:

> *It might be that the skin does not have as its primary function the registering of form as this has usually been conceived. Impressions of form and location relative to the skin might be quite separate from and incidental to the use of the extremities as sense organs. The informative stimuli might well be incorporated in the seemingly complex motions and transformations of the skin. There must exist relations of separation and proportion which remain invariant over time and which are specific to the object. They do not represent the shape of the object but they specify it. The solution to the problem of object perception in touch would then be that continuous change in the proximal stimulation is accompanied by non-change—that is, the set of invariant relations. The former is not noticed; the latter is separated out and attended to.*
>
> *The role of exploratory finger movements in active touch would then be to isolate the invariants, that is to discover the extereospecific component in the flux of stimulation. Only thus could the paradox be resolved.*

Gibson (1963) discussed a number of useful dimensions for tactuality. Objects held in the hand despite the multiplicity of cutaneous impressions retain a spatial **unity**. The **rigidity** of an object is perceived actively by cutaneous yielding against the rigid object and less accurately but similarly the yielding-rigid ratio holds for passive touching as well. An object is perceived as **stable** when the hand moves over a surface accumulating in motion a variety of sensations. **Weight** is relatively defined by lifting or holding and more accurately perceived if the object can be shifted back and forth from one hand to another. Passive touching is less accurate for weight perception. The cutaneous surface of a hand has a **form** sense detecting slant of surface, concavity or convexity, edges and corners, junction of two surfaces and separation of edges.

A set of exploring hands encounters a variety of pressure patterns accumulating textural data for conversion to objective shape. A multitude of tactual inputs must be synthesized to yield tactual form.

Nearly a half century ago Head (1920) wrote of two types of tactual systems, one designed to serve for primary survival, warning the organism against impending danger and two, a tactual system to convey information about the surrounding world of his cognitive development. We might think of the first as reflexive acting in defensive status for immediate withdrawal, primitive in its neglect of evaluation of all possible factors. The second system could afford itself the temporal luxury of perceptual scanning and evaluation. The terms "protective" and "discriminative" might also be used. The first system is designed to "save" the organism while the second is designed to enrich the organism's knowledge of his surround. By design, it would appear that the reflexive protective tactual system is organized and operative at birth while the second system emerges in the developmental sequence in its proper time and place finding its proper rank and its relative contribution to total efficiency.

The literature has answered many questions on touch but has left more questions unanswered. The hands have essentially been the main focus for tactuality but in recent years the entire integument has been considered. Passive and active touch have been differentiated. Two systems of touch have been defined.

There seems to be little doubt that tactuality is a vital component in human behavior and that it is of prime import during early infancy. Insufficient tactile stimulation serves as a sensory deprivation with presumed deleterious consequences to the individual's cognitive and psychological future. Extra tactile stimulation has been consistently beneficial to institutionalized infants. Stimulation has been regarded as a "booster" for perceptual functioning in other modes. Somewhere within these notions lies the meaning of tactuality for the developing child in a world of space and energy. Winnowing and sifting appear to be required to filter out the meaning of "what is tactuality?".

While the literature is quite clear on the possible detrimental effects of insufficient tactile stimulation and the beneficial effects of extra stimulation there has been virtually no discussion of what constitutes a "just right" amount of tactual stimulation. It is apparently presumed that under "ordinary" circumstances an interested, warm, devoted mother automatically provides a sufficient amount of tactual stimulation to her baby in the natural course of feeding, carrying, dressing, bathing and so on. Unless there is good reason to hold a mother suspect of rejection, neglect, apathy or some other negative an assumption of sufficiency is made. Interest in other variables obscures further attention to tactuality.

The manner in which tactuality develops to progressively more complex levels of sophistication as the child matures has not been documented. Unfortunately, no investigator has turned his attention to cataloguing the extent of difference in tactuality to be found in the one year old, two year old and so on as Gesell (1949) has done for children's vision. Despite the research findings in infancy, the authoritative beliefs in the primacy of tactuality and the accepted belief that tactuality is a lifelong attribute of a cutaneous organism, the clinical seeking to clarify a diagnostic dilemma in a problem child is at an extreme loss when it comes to the clear investigation of a child's tactual development. Assessing a current state of tactuality in a child is an embarrassingly difficult task because instrumentation is lacking as well as a sound line of developmental reasoning which would allow a clinician to find the strand of tactuality in the warp of the problem and trace it back to a rating of sufficiency, insufficiency, or extra sufficiency.

Lacking a clear line of research in this area, the story of tactuality must be told on the basis of remnants, beliefs, conjectures, surmises and narrow threads which must be stretched far beyond their intended span to link points in the story. Tactuality is in some measure an integral part of an action-perception system and enters into the efficiency makeup of the individual. The nature of its contribution to efficiency is obvious in a blind child's approach to knowledge but quite obscure in the non-blind child. When a situation clearly demands tactual proficiency, the contribution of tactuality can be assumed but in the general day by day steady stream of experiencing, it is quite difficult to determine where tactuality makes its contribution in the midst of all the other modes. On such hazy terrain there is a tendency to proceed very cautiously lest some misstep occur but there is also latitude for cognitive exploration since the terrain must be considered relatively uncharted. With the foregoing considerations in mind, we can explore a hypothetical construction of tactuality as a processing mode from the framework of **Movigenics**.

Tactuality may be defined as a system for gaining information from the cutaneous surfaces of the body by means of active or passive contact. The cutaneous surface of the body receives various energy forms channeling the data to higher control centers for information processing. We prefer the term **tactuality** to touch to convey the composite idea of a reception, transmission, tranduction into percepts, cognition and feedback-correlation and to convey the idea of a processing entity in a constant state of energization.

Tactuality develops in an orderly sequence. It is probably initiated in the uterus by the friction of transport during the gestational period and continued in the neonatal period through the general regimen of infant care. This first stage may be classified as the **sensitivity buildup**. The purpose of this stimulation period may be viewed as preparation of the cutaneous surface for information processing. It activates and alerts the body and leads into the second stage of tactual **awareness** during which some form of cognitive linking begins to form in preparation for the stage of **perception** during which the individual attaches specific meaning to variations in tactual pressures cognitively identifying a source and a type as differentiated from whatever state of contact existed before the new touch. As stimulation leads to awareness and then to perception in a multiplicity of experiencing in constant flow on both the active and passive level, the organization of tactuality begins and expands through time and multiple variations resulting in a composite level of sophistication for obtaining information from tactual sources.

This same sequence is constantly operative thoughout life. Each contact, passive or active, is initially a stimulation to awareness alerting the percepto-cognitive system to action to identify and give meaning to the touch in relation to previous experience. A given touch may be observed, recorded and ignored as irrelevant. It may be perceived as noxious or threatening and thus, induce some form of withdrawal behavior. It may be perceived as pleasurable and attracting and appropriate behavior initiated to sustain it or repeat it. The organism must constantly make decisions about touch — his survival depends upon those decisions. Decisions are percepto-cognitive phenomena. They govern the initiation of a response pattern. The individual makes his next move according to the perception he attributes to the touch. He may persist, withdraw, release, attack, repeat and so on. His decision-making is dependent upon the state of integration he has achieved in the perceptual organization of tactuality. If touch has meaning for him, he obtains significant information from it and utilizes it to expand his knowledge. If he has not achieved tactual integration, touching is a mysterious stimulation which confuses and bewilders him.

Myklebust (1954) has described a clinical technique of touching a child's back while he is engaged in activity to determine whether he is aware of the touch, can identify its source and attach a meaning to it. Failure to respond is regarded as a deficiency in tactual integration. In our own experience with neurologically impaired and emotionally disturbed children, we have often encountered children who were bewildered by passive touch or seemed impervious to it. One dramatic illustration will serve our point. A 5 year old boy with minimal brain damage persistently became upset if anyone placed their hands upon him in a gesture of affection such as patting his head, his shoulder, arms or back. He would show a momentary panic expression and then cry out, "Take it off, take it off". It was not only a matter of removing one's hand but rather of removing the "touch" that had been left there after the hand was removed. Brushing off the "touch" with a sweeping gesture of the hand calmed him and he was able to return to his task. Many times he sat and whimpered helplessly pleading for the touch to be removed — as if he were in real pain. Often he made strenuous attempts to "brush off" the touch with his own hands. It was very clear that he could not localize the touch, being aware only that he had been touched. He could not integrate the touch into any organized perceptual structure and thus any touch was threatening. The same behavior was elicited by any form of touch such as a ruler tapped on his back or shoulder, paper placed over his hands and so on. Even when the action was fully visible to him his request to remove the touch was nonetheless present. This same child was also terrified of water on his skin either in the bath or in a swimming pool and had a variety of bizarre behaviors in relation to clothing rubbing against his skin.

Among populations of deviant children there are countless ways in which the primitivation of tactuality may be manifested. The fact that the child can use his hand to reach, grasp and release objects does not indicate that he is tactually aware. (Barsch 1965) The child may be unaware of differences in texture, substance and shape. He may give no indication of tactual scanning for information even though he tries to touch everything in sight. The critical consideration is whether or not touch serves him as an information source. He may touch but not be consciously aware that he is touching. He may be touched and be either unaware that such touch has taken place or being aware, be unable to interpret the touch. Autistic children frequently lack such awareness. In pathologic populations, the manifestations of deficiencies in tactual integration are multivariant but are probably present to some degree, as an integral part of a general state of disorganization.

Tactile stimulation during infancy probably serves to initiate body awareness and thus holds a major role in the achievement of identity. The deleterious effects of insufficient tactile stimulation during infancy, find their eventual expression in a disturbance to the individual's search for identity. Infant stimulation is, therefore, critical in the formation of a lifelong identity making its foremost early impact upon the dimension of body awareness. The handling, rubbing, patting, sponging and stroking which serve as the techniques of tactile stimulation contribute in a variety of ways to the development of his self-ness and the world of "otherness". If the quantity of such stimulation is adequate, the cutaneous surfaces are in a steady stream of bombardment from different contact sources providing an abundant supply of data from which a program of body awareness and tactuality can develop. If the quantity of such stimulation is less than desirable, the reduction can be expected to take its toll upon the individual's self-identification and a diminished appreciation of the textures in his world.

To prepare the organism for a lifetime of gaining information from touching, design and experience must contribute in some manner to this gradual acquisition of tactual sophistication. The totality of the gestational period serves as the first training ground for tactuality through the cutaneous variations in uterine transport. Carmichael (1954) noted tactual sensitivity in the fetus at 20 weeks. The nine month period prepares the dermal layers for their eventual independent relationship to free air. Gesell and Amatruda (1947) have pointed out that the infant is responsive to cutaneous stimulation at birth. Whether the tactual needs of the neonate represent a need for continuing the intrauterine pressures and cutaneous variations in a "tapering off" process as suggested by Ourth and Brown (1961) or whether these needs simply represent the next stage in a chronological sequence of tactual prepration, the actual facts are that the infant is a tactile being requiring tactual ministrations from a mothering figure. In the natural course of infant ministration in our culture, the infant is covered with soft cloth, held in feeding positions, rubbed with oils, powdered, bathed gently in warm water, carried from place to place, from lap to lap in a succession of tactile stimulations. This matrix of tactility is but another step in preparing the cutaneous surface to become an astute processor of information. It is not a perceived experience of differentiation but serves to activate the body surfaces to a condition of awareness from which perceptions will emerge.

The matrix of tactile stimulation which is inherent in the typical day by day life of the neonate is a passive application of touch and requires an administrator. If the mother finds personal satisfaction from a constancy of contact, she probably spends a significantly greater amount of time touching, caressing and patting the infant than the mother who finds no general personal satisfaction in contact and therefore ministers tactilely only as is necessary for proper child care. This speculation places no value judgment on the quality of love held by the two mothers but refers rather to the tactual organization of the mother. One feels comfortable in tactual ministration as a result of her own modality preference organization while the other may find other ways of expressing herself toward her infant. We use this illustration to introduce our concept that the tactuality of the mother may well be a critical determinant of the amount and quality of tactile stimulation given to the infant—not only the quality of love. Some mothers mechanically perform the necessary acts of touching while others enjoy, prolong, and seek these acts as a part of their own self-expression in interaction with their infants. Our intent is to introduce this nuance into the consideration of how tactuality becomes organized for the infant.

Touch is also subject to the principles of figure-ground. There is a background of touch operating as a constant which becomes habituated and generally irrelevant to performance. The substrates for movement become tactually habituated, clothing rubbing on the body, air on the exposed surfaces, the feel of common objects such as cups, spoons, pencils and so on all become a part of a touching background which is habituated. The individual no longer is aware of the contact phenomenon involved but is more concerned with performance. Contact becomes irrelevant to the individual at a cutaneous level and thus is relegated to background status. However, at any given moment, these same phenomena may require immediate attention and be brought to a foreground by the individual such as occurs when variations in terrain occur, or we become conscious of the texture of a familiar object, or difficulty of some sort is encountered. Tactuality, thus, has an ebb and flow quality per situation—at times operating as a background and at times as a foreground. A flexibility in shifting from figure to ground as a circumstance demands is a necessary attribute in a dynamic cutaneous being.

Thermal dynamics enter into tactuality in the individual's need to build a perceptual differentiation between hot and cold and to become aware of changes in air temperature, cooling breezes, hot winds and so on. He must learn to differentiate dry from wet by touch. A large series of polar opposites and the relative variations among these must achieve an adaptation level for the individual such as soft-hard, smooth-rough, firm-yielding, and so on. Substance can be defined by touch such as wood, iron, metal, plastic, rubber, paper and so on. Thick-thin, narrow-wide, and round-square among other opposites are all measurable by touch. The perceptual organization of all these opposites and all the ranges of variation existing between the extremes must be a part of the gradually expanding tactual world of the young child. These must be adequately defined and organized into an increasingly complex matrix to serve the individual through a lifetime of processing tactual information.

Touch does not become perceptual for the infant until awareness of difference becomes a part of his ongoing behavior. He must come to know that he is being touched or is touching. We have tended to regard a change in behavior as an indication of awareness of difference. Thus, if the infant cries and the mother attends him by holding, stroking and patting and this action quiets him some degree of awareness is thought to be present. We are inclined to regard this as a state of awareness leading eventually to perception but not to be regarded as such in the early infant period.

The term Tactual Dynamics is used to designate the component which encompasses the multiple ways in which both active and passive touch contribute to the enhancement of an individual's Movement Efficiency. We are concerned not only with the traditional concepts of touch as a sensing process but more specifically with the percepto-cognitive aspect of bringing sensation to a state of meaning having value to the organism. A dynamic being moving in an energy surround is in a field of "constant touch" since some force is persistently activating the cutaneous surface. Since the individual cannot suspend himself in midair free of contact for any significant amount of time, he is always in contact with something. There is always a substrate for the feet or the body while moving or at rest.

The neophyte toucher lying in the crib has a lifetime of "touchingness" stretching before him, above and beyond the ministrations of his mother and others who will handle him during his infancy. Still to come is the difference in texture among carpeting, linoleum, cement, wood, grass and gravel as he crawls and walks. Still to come is the difference between the silk shirt, the woolen sweater, the muffler on his face, gloves on his hands, and cap on his head. Sitting on cold cement, walking on sand, running sand through his fingers, melting chocolate in his hand, jelly on his chin, his tongue licking the ice cream in the cone, the feel of fur, the elusiveness of jello as he tries to pick it up, the touch of a cracker—all these are in his future. Later, the handle of his coaster, the touch of the pedals on his bike, the feel of a flower, a fork, spoon, a wax

The world of texture in process of exploration with bilateral use of hands and intensity of visual concentration. Another small part of the tactual world to be fit into place.

crayon, chalk, the handle of a bat, the grip on a golf club, a casting rod, skis gliding over snow, the prickly feel of a shower, will all become a part of his tactual organization. He will feel tears run down his cheeks and the bruise on his knee. He will feel the punishing slap of his parents when he errs. Raindrops will fall on his face and arms, perspiration will ooze from his pores, cold winds will chill his skin, and he will feel the shove from a playmate. His hands will feel paint, clay, glue, pencil, paper mache and water. Mud will squish through his fingers. He will caress and be caressed. He will kiss and be kissed. He will pet the fur of animals, feel the roughness of sandpaper and fondle a turtle in his hand. A lifetime of touching and being touched, bit by bit, builds a body of tactual information. He adds to his organization touch by touch — if all goes well — and each touch has meaning for him. If he does not derive information from his touching the development of his Movement Efficiency does not proceed to his advantage.

Our conceptualization of tactuality is not limited to the physical cutaneous expression of active and passive touch but extends into the realm of psychological experiencing as well. The primary factor in touch is contact. It is but a short conceptual stride to reach a point of relating contact in the physical sense to contact in the psychological sense. The behaviors involved in the psychologically honored concept of approach-avoidance reactions is a matter of willingness or desire to contact or avoid contact. We speak of attachments, cathexis, belongingness, fixations and many other descriptive terms, all of which convey an idea of contact. In some manner, not yet experimentally validated, the efficiency of tactual learning in the physical sense bears a significant relationship to an individual's positive rapport with others in his world as a contactual efficiency. George Eliot once wrote, "In a man whose childhood has known caresses, there is always a fibre of memory that can be touched to gentle issues".

Tactuality is both physical and psychological. For efficiency the young traveler must become sophisticated in scanning, searching and identifying what touches him and what he touches. He will be more or less sensitive on various parts of his body surface. In some manner he is a constant tactualizer. He may be touched to tears, touched to sympathy, touched to charity. He may be "in touch" or "out of touch" with his world but touch will be a vital part of his makeup.

In the general chronology of the Percepto-Cognitive modes the gustatory, the olfactory and the tactual have now been founded and according to the quality and quantity of organization which have been established in each of these primitive modes, the traveler is more or less prepared for purposeful independent physical movement. Even though the emphasis in this chapter appears to be clearly placed upon the infant, it must be noted that tactual efficiency can be observed at all ages and must be a consideration in helping learners at all ages. From his tactual learning the traveler must next proceed to the kinesthetic mode.

13

THE KINESTHETIC MODE

Kinesthesia is referred to by different authors as "deep sensibility" (Geldard, 1953), "position sense" (Wells, 1955), and "muscle sense". Bell has been credited with discovery of the muscular or kinesthetic sense but it was Bastian in 1880 who originated the term **kinesthesis** — literally "feeling of motion". (Smith, 1962) The organs of sensing for kinesthesis are located in the muscles, tendons, and joints receiving a continuous supply of information about the movements made by the individual and the pressures or tensions produced in various parts of the body from all centers. Schilling (1955) said, "a unique feature of kinesthesis...is the fact that the stimulation comes from within the organism itself rather than from some external stimuli". In the Handbook of Physiology of the American Physiologic Society kinesthetic stimuli are described as:

> ...pressing upon or displacing without injury the connective tissue underneath the skin, periosteum, bones, sheaths of the joints leading to sensations often referred to as a deep sensibility. Under physiological conditions, of course, it is the contraction of muscles which act as a major kinesthetic stimulus.

Kinesthetic feedback is based upon previous experience. There is a remembering process which is a vital component of kinesthesia. Milne and Milne (1962) have pointed out that in making habitual movements such as we do when using any of our limbs, we are relying on muscular movement in rapid succession following patterns memorized after practice and "etched into barely conscious parts of the nervous system".

Kinesthesia has been described and defined by many authorities and apparently placed in the category of an automatic human birthright to a muscular system to be used forever more as an adjective or a noun but not to be regarded as a dynamic scientific variable in behavior to be treated as a variable and studied under varying experimental conditions. It is the contention here that the concept is not well understood despite its widespread incorporation into behavioral literature and its acceptance as a natural phenomenon of human behavior. As a term, it is frequently regarded as a cousin to proprioception, a partner of tactuality in a "haptic" union and as a stepsister to kinetics. The perceptual component in kinesthesis has been referred to many times in the descriptive literature but this too has been regarded as an automatic human "given". The perception of human motion has enjoyed little favor among investigators. It has not been completely ignored however. Smith (1962) has recently focused a bright spotlight on the topic and his findings are bringing a third dimension into the understanding of the relationship between kinesthesia and perception which has been long overdue.

Wells (1955) viewed kinesthesia as an important factor in learning new skills.

In learning any given skill the memory of the former sensations and the consciousness of the present ones in the performance of the skill, help us to judge the correctness of our movements.

Schilling (1955) regarded it as "our primary source of information about movement and position" providing impulses to produce coordination of all body parts for complex acts. Geldard (1953) also viewed it as an "information" sense giving the human machine data concerning the relative position of its parts, one to another.

In 1820 Brown stated that "our muscular frame forms a distinct organ of sense which enables perceptions of spatial extensions to take place." (cited by Boring, 1942) The relationship of kinesthesia to space efficiency has been cited many times in the literature. Thurstone (1950) and Roff (1953) in factorial study have shown a kinesthetic factor to be important in forming accurate and rapid judgments about spatial configurations. Bartley (1953) demonstrated that factors operative in visual judgment of size and distance are also present when only tactual and kinesthetic clues are present. Thurstone (1950) and Guilford (1947) considered the cognitive process of kinesthetic imagery to be an important factor in "mentally manipulating" seen objects. Kinesthetic sensitivity has been another concept for investigators. Slocum (1953) found that fatigue did not significantly alter such sensitivity and Leuba (1909) found that fatigue was dependent upon duration of the task, rate of performance and work-load but that sensitivity remained high if it was basically high in the performer.

Another perspective is that of relative Kinesthetic sensitivity in body parts. Hip and shoulder joints have been found to be most sensitive to movement. (Laidlow and Hamilton, 1937; and Goldscheider, 1889) Cleghorn and Darcus (1952) found the elbow joint to be more sensitive to movement when extended than it is when flexed. Since hip, shoulder and arm extensions are so vital to postural transport and man's adaptation as a moving organism in a variable world, these findings appear to be logical outcomes of the basic design of the organism.

The most accurate movements in manipulation are made toward the frontal plane of the body and slightly below shoulder level. Fetts and Crammell (1950) found the most common errors to be those of reaching too low in a target touching task. Erect man moving forward in a position of performance is at his best when his hands converge on a task in line with the downward gaze of his vision. (Harmon, 1958)

Another perspective on kinesthesia was initiated by Gibson's (1933) work on kinesthetic after-image. Kohler and Dinnerstein (1947), Wertheimer and Leventhal (1958), Bakan and Weiler (1963), and Corah (1961) have all contributed experimental evidence for the importance of kinesthetic after-image. Cratty and Hutton (1964) had subjects travel sharply curved pathways while blindfolded and produced after-effects. Purkinje in 1820 was the first to discover that an after-effect occurred in the opposite direction when a rotation in an original direction was suddenly stopped (cited in Baker, 1960).

Kinesthesia has been studied from many vantage points and yet we are impressed with a lack of synthesis. There is no question about the existence of the modality. There is a pervading quality of "taking for grantedness" in the literature but we, for one, have a feeling that the literature is unclear. We concur with the literature about its importance and we find each result to be convincing but we are uneasy about the apparent explanation of the nature of kinesthesia. This feeling of restlessness prompts us to attempt a clarification.

In **Movigenics** we regard kinesthesia as a **cognitive emergent** resulting from feedback. It is an awareness of movement bringing purpose and direction to muscular contraction for effort. When movement is perceived by the performer kinesthesia is the technical label of the product of such perception. Only when the young infant purposefully moves a body part and **cognitively** directs that movement can we properly assume that kinesthesia is present. The cognitive component is essential to kinesthesia; without it there is no kinesthesia. One cannot refer to kinesthesia as "position sense", "deep sensibility", "memory of movement" and the many other terms which have been employed without full recognition of the cognitive fundamental inherent in those terms. The young infant may engage in much random and diffuse moving but such movements are not kinesthetic. They may be preparatory and facilitative to eventual kinesthesia but they lack the critical component of cognition. Kinesthesia is the cognitive employment of position and patterned muscular effort to resolve a task. While we may talk of a kinesthetic component in the behavioral composite of every human, we cannot regard it as an automatic associate with every movement of the individual.

During the early stages of walking we talk of a kinesthetic component being present in the effort, but once a resonably adequate stride and gait have been achieved and walking has become automatic, there is no kinesthesis. There is muscular contraction and proprioception in automatic walking, but since the cognitive component is no longer needed the term kinesthesia is descriptively inappropriate. At any given moment that cognition is returned to the act of walking such as required on uneven terrain, rail walking, dimly lit grounds, variable stair treads, kicking a football, accelerating or decelerating gait—kinesthesia is a product. When the individual must become consciously aware of the positioning of his body, modifying rate or in any manner departs from a habituated pattern the K process is activated. Consequently K is not an automatic accompaniment to movement. Some mental effort related to modification of movement must be present. A child may become a good stair climber and automatize the foot lift and positioning. In the initial process of becoming a stair climber, K was active but automation ignores cognition. He must be required at a given moment to think about his movement and initiate action according to his thoughts in order to qualify as kinesthetic in that instance. The individual must be consciously aware that he is changing something in his movement. The introduction of novelty into an habituated performance, will generate the K component to action.

The standing individual is kinesthetic only at the moment that he purposely changes his stance in order to achieve better alignment with a task or shifts his position to obtain comfort. He must be aware of why he is changing stance and must have directed his change for a reason.

When we press a little harder on a knife because we realize that we have not cut the tissue of the meat; when we press harder on a pencil in order to mark through a carbon onto a copy paper; when we regulate the pressure on a paper cup because we already spilled water because we pressed too hard on the first attempt—when some form of modification is cognitively introduced the K is present. The mere act of writing is only kinesthetic when you are first learning; when a novel writing surface is used; when a novel set of symbols are employed; when a writing tool is novel—when thought must be directed to the mechanics of execution. Speech is kinesthetic only when a conscious effort is made to be enunciatively precise or when strange words are being practiced.

Kinesthesia must be an available variable to enable the individual to process movement information and be **directed** by the information he processes. It is essentially cognitive modification. It is the product of feedback.

Perhaps there is a feeling that we belabor a semantic point and have an insistence upon a hair-splitting issue but we do so with good cause. We are concerned with defining the dynamics of the percepto-cognitive system as a totality and with the highest degree of conceptual precision we can manage in defining the six components of that system. Kinesthesia must therefore attain its unique identity in the composite and be clearly differentiated from the others. We are well aware of the frequency with which kinesthesia and tactuality are companions in performance but their companionship should not obscure their individual identities as internal and external phenomena. Describing this companionship as "haptic" tends to convey an equality of contribution in a given performance when no such equality is possible according to our view. The term "haptic" also implies a simultaneity which we do not believe is possible. One may tactually perceive and immediately kinesthicize (perceive) and tactually perceive again and kinesthicize in some reciprocal interweaving process which is entirely believable to us. This reciprocal interweaving of a bimodal cognitive process will then rely upon the synchrony and efficiency of each member of the pair. The performance must then be differentiated in terms of that reciprocal interweaving with the relative contribution of each and the chronologic order becoming a significant set of considerations.

We also view kinesthesia as being dependent upon the perceiver. The individual's total efficiency as a perceiver becomes the determining factor of the extent or prevalence of kinesthesia. Kinesthesia does not just happen. The perceiver must make it happen. According to this view, a teacher, parent or therapist can only provide muscular opportunities which may lead to a kinesthetic experience only if the performer perceives it thus. Despite the teacher's careful plan to give the child a kinesthetic learning experience the essential ingredient in the situation is the cognitive processing of the student converting the action process into kinesthesia. The provision of kinesthetic reading exercises has value only if the child kinesthicizes. We suspect that the reason this approach has failed with some delinquent readers is entirely due to the kinesthetic naivete of the subject and not to the method. The perceiver must make an action kinesthetic. It is recognizably kinesthetic when appropriate modifications are introduced by the subject, when corrections take place and when some form of kinesthetic generalization takes place in relation to similar tasks and similar movement patterns.

A kinesthetic sophisticate is a constant perceiver of his own motion and thrives upon processing information through his muscular system. It is a favored way of learning about his world. The muscles become the tools of adaptation. The kinesthetic pauper on the other hand, finds himself wanting time after time. His muscular system acts as though it were perceptually retarded. His learning efficiency must be referred to other modes.

The performer may repeat an action many times before he kinesthicizes it. He may repeatedly err because he cannot "get the hang of it". We have often seen both child and adult performers bumbling and bungling in some movement pattern suddenly become synchronous, smooth and efficient in the same task because they finally kinesthicized it. We have seen many others quit tasks in frustration and rage because they could not kinesthicize the muscular pattern.

Whether or not a child can benefit from a so-called "kinesthetic approach" to anything depends upon his level of kinesthetic sophistication. For some such an approach becomes a magic formula to learning, while to others, it becomes a psychologically depressing experience laden with errors. The performer is the critical variable not the approach.

Kinesthetic opportunities are present at all ages, but the period of greatest opportunity occurs in early childhood. It is here that the "motor feedback" system passes through the basic training stage. The kinesthetic fluency which the child achieves during the first two years probably sets his level of K sophistication for life. If there is any slowing down or mislearning in the motor feedback system at that time, he is likely to remain kinesthetically naive into his adulthood.

A poor K organization during those early years goes a long way towards setting the pattern for a lifetime description of "always being all thumbs", "never could learn how to dance", "never been much of an athlete", "I'm a duffer at everything I try", "spoils whatever he tries to fix", and hundreds of other expressions which are conversationally quite common among adult social groups. Not "learning to read and interpret" his own muscles in early childhood may well leave the individual a lifelong "poor kinesthicizer".

Kinesthetic organization is the "bread and butter" mode for movement efficiency. It is the staple upon which movement must thrive. Everyone must achieve it to some degree to survive. Kinesthetic organization can also be plotted on a continuum from very naive to very sophisticated and each individual can be placed somewhere along the line.

Kinesthesia follows tactuality in the developmental order and becomes the system for achieving purposeful transport. It adds to the foundation for audition and vision and relies, for its own development, upon the preceding structures of Gustatory, Olfactory, and Tactual modes. As kinesthesia emerges the individual begins to move through space with a purpose, general and specific, constantly reducing the number of movement errors as he develops. Kinesthesia permits him to refine and sharpen his gross patterns of movement into delicately complex patterns of fine performance. Walking is refined to running, running is refined to racing another child. A large repertoire of motor skills is encouraged through the usual course of development. Eventually, he is expected to swim, ride a bicycle, do cursive writing, build craft projects, throw a ball with accuracy, pitch a tent, dance with a partner, tackle a runner and countless other actions.

All of these rely upon the sophistication of his kinesthetic organization at the time he is expected to conform to such events in life. If he brings a low order of kinesthesia to that life-demand, he must bumble through or devise some conforting escape route.

If his K organization is of high order, he comfortably experiences satisfaction and moves into the next performance echelon. His level of kinesthetic organization can serve as a lifelong asset or a lifelong liability. One of the major reasons that our national leaders on fitness deplore the sedentariness of the population comes from their recognition of the generally low order of kinesthetic organization which prevails among our citizens. When muscles are involved the percentage of the population who can be classified as skilled performers is always a minor figure.

A poor kinesthetic organization within an individual denotes a perceptual immaturity or a perceptual disturbance for movement patterning at a muscular level. In the general literature on neurologic dysfunction the most appropriate synonym for a disturbance to kinesthetic perception is apraxia. The accepted meaning for **apraxia** is an inability to voluntarily produce a desired or requested pattern of movement. While the neurologically impaired patient may perform the same desired action on a routine automatic basis during the regular course of living, he is unable to cognitively process it voluntarily upon request. At a visual level, when attempting to imitate a demonstrated action he becomes confused in his imitative patterning "as though he does not know what to move next". Movements become dyssynchronized and the patient is bewildered and confused. He has a perceptual disturbance which prevents kinesthetic organization.

This type of perceptual disturbance is often found in neurologically impaired children who have no significant neuromuscular problem. Their awkwardness and clumsiness is manifest only when they must cognitively process muscular patterns, but they may generally give the impression that they move about with reasonable agility. Many times, however, the neurologically impaired child walks but does not know he is walking, he climbs but does not know he is climbing, bends but does not know he bends and so on. The motor patterns have been habituated at a non-cognitive level and as a consequence, the feedback system necessary for refining muscular patterns to resolve movement problems does not efficiently serve the child. Perceptual immaturity in kinesthesia may also be found among the neurologically impaired children manifest, as the organization of muscular patterns, at a lower level of efficiency than is necessary for the task. The general effect becomes one of "doing things the hard way" or managing a response that does "not quite get the job done". This concept of a kinesthetic perceptual disturbance may also be extended to the spastic and athetoid child. While their muscular involvement stems from a neurologic dysfunction, its total effect prevents a high order kinesthetic organization. The children with cerebral palsy who are severely involved from a muscular standpoint are most perceptually disturbed in relation to kinesthesia. Those who are only mildly involved may manage a relatively high order of kinesthesia but this will be dependent upon their early experiences.

A low level of kinesthetic organization is to be found among emotionally disturbed populations. Mentally retarded populations may also be expected to have a high incidence of perceptual immaturity in relation to kinesthesia. Despite a number of early efforts to establish a belief in good kinesthesia among the retardates there is a general acceptance of kinesthetic immaturity among these groups among present workers in the field.

Difficulties in cognitive processing of motor patterns appear to be a natural corollary among disability groups. This concept of kinesthesia may provoke no argument from workers in child and adult rehabilitation but we wish to stress the implications of this concept when it is applied to the generally accepted stereotype of the normal child in our society. The child who is non-handicapped is also scalable at many points along the continuum from naive to sophisticated in kinesthetic organization.

A high level of kinesthetic organization is not necessarily the natural byproduct of the customary experiences of the average child in our society. The attainment of the usual patterns of walking, creeping, running, climbing and so on is not to be taken as evidence that kinesthetic organization has in fact been achieved. Among a variety of deviant populations, there is ample evidence that basic motor patterns have in fact been established but there is also a high incidence of observation that these individuals have reduced abilities to organize appropriate patterns of movement to resolve simple obstacle situations. Similarly, the general observation that a child is "developing normally" is not synonymous with a high kinesthetic organization.

In casual day by day observations of normal children some will be noted to respond immediately and precisely to new learning which requires muscular reorganization and others will appear "dunce like" in their approach to motor tasks. The differences among children is an **established** fact but not an explained fact. The critical issue rests upon the extent of capability they hold for **processing information** throughout the proprioceptive system. Some process information efficiently and others do not. We feel that the differential is traceable to the degree that cognition has become an integral feature of their gross motor and fine motor patterning in the early stages of movement.

Kinesthesia, itself, emerges as a higher order functioning from the more primitive dimensions of Muscular Strength, Dynamic Balance, Body Awareness, Spatial Awareness and Temporal Awareness. The efficiency achieved in the primitive organization of the Postural-Transport Orientations is the crucial foundation for kinesthesia. Muscular Strength at levels below minimal requirements for age, sex, and task demands reduces the potential for proprioceptive cognition. Problems with Dynamic Balance scarcely leave the individual in a position to become an efficient kinesthicizer. The efficiency level of all five of the postural components contributes the potential for K. A disturbance to any of them reduces the possibility for full kinesthetic efficiency.

Kinesthesia probably bears the closest kinship to Time in the Transport Orientations revolving upon the common element of synchronization in movement. Each terranaut faces a kinesthetic future of greater or lesser extent if he expects to move with any degree of efficiency. His movements must come under his cognitive control if they are to advantageously promote his economical and efficient transport. He will have to acquire the kinesthetic "knack" for many, many patterns to remain abreast of his developmental timetable. Crawling, sitting, standing, walking, stooping, running, rolling will all become part of a K organization to be cognitively selected and produced in continued appropriateness to the situation he faces. He will wield a spoon, set a block on a tower, pull a toy, lift a game, pedal a bike, jump from a perch, climb a fence, walk a rail and fly a kite. Experience after experience he is initially naive and his muscles are untutored. As muscles learn their lessons each next encounter becomes easier and his muscles benefit from one experience to another constantly gaining more efficient patterns.

He will shove, push, pull, lift, kick, jump and throw. He will move continuously to perform, mastering some moves and remaining clumsy in performing others. Muscles learn bit by bit and day by day when to tense and when to relax. He will come to identify when a movement "feels right" and when it does not. He has no choice but to become a kinesthetic learner. The only question to be asked is whether he is an efficient kinesthetic learner or an inefficient one. He may be graceful or clumsy. He may be retarded or gifted; emotionally disturbed, neurologically impaired or behaviorally normal; poor or rich—his grace of movement and his efficiency of performance will continuously be dependent upon his acquisition of kinesthesia. He must build a conceptualization and a set of generalizations from his movements.

High K persons find it easy to translate learning demands into proprioceptive patterns and use these supportively for their learning. They learn quickly when the task is motoric and quickly grasp a new way of moving their hands and feet when novel demands are placed upon them. The low K person, on the other hand, is at a disadvantage when the learning demand takes on a muscular orientation. He may hold some efficiency in other modes but is less efficient when proprioceptive demands are made.

Cognition in kinesthesia is the crux of all motor learning. Only as the individual can perceive his own movements can he make the necessary modifications to improve his efficiency. Without the cognitive processing of feedback to recommend changes he will perpetuate a system of error. The high K person holds his proprioceptive system under excellent control. Because he can translate a given dilemma into cognitive-muscular terms, he can defeat a larger and heavier opponent, drive a golf ball as far as a heavier and larger player and sustain less fatigue in muscular affairs. Cognitive integration is more critical than muscle bulk when efficiency is a factor.

Whether or not kinesthesia has become an efficient source of information for the young child can be observed in the grace and speed he employs in learning new motor tasks. Eventually, most children learn to climb, ride bicycles, swim, write and so on. Despite adequate I.Q. some learn such things quickly while others do so only after much effort. In this area as well as many others, the differential in ease, grace and timing has been related to maturational variations. It seems a great deal more logical to ascribe such variations to differences in cogniting proprioception.

At this time we can only speculate as to reasons why some children would be more adept than others but at this stage speculations may hold great values pending the eventual clarification of this issue through well defined research. Our first speculation is that children who are slow to learn motor skills and manifest difficulty in figuring out "what to move and how to move it" express this kinesthetic inefficiency because one or more of the Postural Transport Orientations have not provided a sufficient founda-

To lift, carry and move is a typical sequence in the development of kinesthesia.

tion. As a consequence we would expect to find problems in Body Image present in their organization as well as some difficulties in Dynamic Balance. We also would expect problems in Spatial Awareness and Temporal Orientation as concomitant areas of dilemma. Our second speculation relates to opportunities for movement. Children, manifesting kinesthetic immaturity may be expected to reveal a history of limitations in exploring their surround whether this resulted from circumstances of illness or handicap, from lack of parental concern for movement exploration, from parental solicitousness for fear of injury or any other cause. The net result of any of these limitations has been an impoverishment of opportunities to practice many different forms of movement to build the cognitive processes for directing changes.

The child who kinesthicizes readily in the learning of the usual childhood skills becomes generally more proficient in any motor learning. Having acquired an effective proprioceptive feedback process, he tends to quickly reduce his motor errors. His muscular system becomes the servant to his learning. He has confidence in it and trusts to his ability to work out a comforting solution in his motor dilemma. Once he discovers the utility of feedback, he can rely upon it to support his learning at any age. A good child kinesthicizer becomes a good adult kinesthicizer. Kinesthesia may become a major mode of learning for some people who find their greatest efficiency derived from "getting the feel of it", "putting it through their muscles", or "working it through in motion".

Every attempt to teach an individual a more efficient system of moving in space must involve a cognitive association to movement on the part of the individual.

TACTUALITY is the process of cutaneous cognitive experiencing and therefore, externally related in contrast to KINESTHESIA as the process of proprioceptive cognitive experiencing and therefore, internally related. Both require cognitive awareness. Tactuality is the antecedent for kinesthesia. Tactuality puts the finishing touches on the early organization of near space and permits the individual to move purposefully into mid and far space. Kinesthesia permits the organism to move his TACTUALITY to other points in space. His world expands with tremendous increases in range as soon as he becomes kinesthetic. He can now direct his active touch in the solution of problems and in the arrangement of objects in his world to suit his convenience. TACTUALITY and KINESTHESIA are basic cognitive modes serving as major building blocks for the higher order symbolic functioning which will take place in the Auditory mode.

14

THE
AUDITORY
MODE

Sound is a constant in the life surround. It is a life companion with which the infant must become acquainted. He must come to learn the sound of himself, others and the world of objects. Sound moves and he moves. Another spatial interweaving process is inherent. Confronted with the immense complexity of the sound world, the human organism must contain the necessary mechanisms to promote its survival in an acoustic surround.

First the sensitivity channel for sound entry must be activated and energized. Sound stimulation must initially operate at a reflex level. To permit the learner to evaluate and assess sound values, the reflex response must be followed developmentally by a localizing process. To determine source in a complex surround the organism must be able to scan. Sound comes from space and is always directionally and distance related. It emanates from above-below-front-back-left and right and from all variations of the geometric coordinates. In the localizing process, the learner becomes aware of the space of sound, assigning it to some position related to himself.

On a survival basis, the localizing process is only intended to position a sound. The identification and evaluation of the sound is an informational process which must rely upon the companion function of other members of his percepto-cognitive system.

Since one characteristic of sound is its transport in space, it is subjected to other energy forms enroute causing it to vibrate through air. Dependent upon its emanating source, it may experience a short or long journey. It leaves a source and moves across space and as it moves it elevates to a peak and declines. At some point in its transport the intensity is maximal with a decline as it moves. This makes distance an important variable in sound processing. The basic survival sequence is alert-scan-localize. The alerting characteristic sensitizes the auditory mechanism to a state of readiness — the scanning potential permits a survey for survival values and the localizing process enables the individual to have awareness of distance to signal whatever adjustive mechanisms may be required. This primitive trio of mechanisms may preserve life only if they promote some form of movement in response to such localization. In other words, an immobile being is helpless in the face of auditory danger. Alerting, scanning and localizing must be accompanied by two additional features in order to have survival utility.

These three must be followed by a percepto-cognitive transduction of sound into information and evaluation of such information in movement terms if the auditory system is to fulfill its share of the adaptive process. Consequently, localization of sound must lead to discrimination, differentiation and eventual classification. Sound must be processed through the cognitive sequence of sensitivity-perception-symbolization-conceptualization and abstraction for survival value and for movement efficiency. To acquire value to the organism, sound must be labeled in some manner. In a myriad of sounds the infant must select and ignore in a constant stream of decision. He cannot manage **every** sound—although all sounds in his surround may enter. He must economically build two space fields for sound — a foreground and a background. The basic training in building foreground and background must serve a lifetime so the foundation must be adequate.

Those two fields will determine his attention. If he attends to the background he will be forced to give up the foreground. If he attends the foreground, he will have to assign background to secondary status. Foreground and background are auditory terrains and the auditing organism must acquire a flexibility of moving from one to another in milliseconds as his world of demand might dictate. No matter how engrossed he may be with a symbolic foreground, there is a continuity of scan within a background, alert to any possibility that an immediate shift might be required. For full efficiency he must be able to move facilely from one ground to another.

The young infant soon discovers that he himself is a source of sound. He can emit sound to signal danger, pain and discomfort as well as a state of contentment. He can use sound to reflect his feelings of the moment. But most dramatic of all—he can use sound to initiate movements in himself and among the humans in his surround. He becomes, in computer terms, a decoding and an encoding mechanism. He receives sound and expresses it. He projects himself vocally into space. He receptively acquaints himself with the four parameters of near-mid-far and remote space as he localizes sound sources at varying distances from himself. He expressively progresses to projectional efficiency in spanning the four parameters with his own voice. He cries loudly and babbles softly. As his development progresses, he will learn to whisper, talk in conversational tones, raise his voice to cover distance and shout across remote space.

An important outcome of the alerting-scanning-localizing trio is the development of listening. The child "tunes in" to his auditory surround. He remains alerted until his scanning device picks up a signal and then acts upon that pickup. In a multiple auditory surround the sounds do not travel in nice neat serial rows. They scramble in a bombardment profusion, each at its own rate of speed and each from its own directional source converging upon a mobile organism. To manage this bombardment in some orderly process of filing the sounds economically—some crowding out takes place like a stadium crowd converging on a single gate—some sounds must wait their turn and in the process may expire. The cochlear turnstile operates quickly, however, and sorts out the entrants in temporal order. On occasion single sounds may appear for entry, but the usual state of affairs is a multiplicity. Series of sounds are the characteristic of speech—so some system of storage and organization must also be a part of the design.

The scientific space world of audition has concentrated primarily on the physical characteristics of the receiving and expressing system. Each mechanical component of the auditory system has been studied in minute detail with an accumulation of precise anatomical detail and the functional relationship of parts. As is generally the case, two separate groups of investigators have been engaged in hearing research. One group has dedicated itself to the analysis of normal hearing, while the other has been concerned with various forms of deprivation. In large measure the focus has been upon the mechanics and physiology of hearing—more precisely fixated on acuity.

Several comments are necessary to establish a perspective for our considerations. In seeking precision of method and measurement the pure tone and the click have become the principal stimuli used in study and have been laboratory-oriented. True, many studies using speech have been employed but these, too, have been laboratory-oriented. The dynamics of audition in a moving organism in a variable sound surround have not attracted nearly as much attention as the sedentary listener in a controlled auditory surround. The mechanics and physiology are well defined—the dynamics are still only penciled sketches.

In recent years the concept of auditory coding has received increasing attention. A comment from Davis' (1961) discussion of the complexity of peripheral coding illustrates the general thinking on this question at that time:

> *Our broadest generalization concerning the peripheral code for auditory information is that it is not a single but an elaborate multiple set of codes. There is not only one but several acoustic transducer mechanisms each with its own code, and in the central nervous system there must be at least as many distinct neural receiving mechanisms, and also a mechanism or mechanisms for resynthesis.*

Cherry (1961), on the same symposium related to sensory communication, addressed himself to the concept of binaural fusion and discussed how a bilateral organism designed with two ears manages one sound:

> *If two earphones are driven with identical signals of any kind, the subject hears a single fused image located in the center of his head. If the interaural time difference...or the relative intensity...of the left and right hand signals is varied the image appears to move across the head laterally in a line between the two ears. The image does not appear to pass outside the head and has no angular direction, as in real life; it has only a lateral position left to right...*
>
> *...If, however, the left and right signals...are utterly different... say, two different voices or different noises, then no fusion takes place.*

Such circumstances prevail in the laboratory situation where rate, intensity and difference can be mechanically controlled but the intake of sound by the two ears is never exactly alike, in detail in real life. As Cherry (1961) has pointed out the signals differ not only in timing and average intensity owing to the spatial directions of sound sources but in other ways owing to head sound-shadows, reflections and reverberations and random sound contributions from the wind on our faces. In the face of all this variance the aural image remains fused and does not flutter in the wind of variance. A binaural fusion mechanism sorts data from both ears, "recognizes" commonalities according to circumstances. If one class of data is not available in the stimuli, the mechanism finds another. Cherry (1961) conceived of this fusion mechanism as a correlational model moving from left to right and right to left and noted some aural effects which can be related to such a modal (1) when the left or right ear only, but not both, is stimulated no centrally fused subjective image is formed; (2) when a complex source of sound applied binaurally has not frequency components below approximately 1200 to 1500 cps, it is an experimental fact that only the **envelopes** of the L and R signals fuse into a binaural image; (3) identical binaural pure tones above 1500 cps with no varying envelopes produce no fused image.

Steinhauser discussed the parallel between binaurality and binocularity in 1877. (Mach, 1906). Mach (1906) stated that the determination of position in space by means of the ear is far more uncertain and restricted to a much more limited field than that by the eye.

Research by Walsh (1957) has shown that sensitivity to binaural time difference is retained after the loss of the auditory cortex on one side. Under conditions of such loss the localization of sounds in a horizontal direction remains possible while the ability to localize sounds in the verical plane is lost.

Only if the two signals entering the right and left ear are totally unlike will there be a fusion failure. Otherwise the binaural fusion mechanism will operate to come to some kind of average to establish a single integrity. The design is for fusion with a range of operational freedom to move laterally more to the left or the right as an accommodative mechanism in the face of inevitable variance.

The comments of Cherry (1961) are again pertinent here:

> *The brain takes maximum advantage of the slight differences between the signals that reach the two ears — differences in timing, in intensity and in microstructure — and by processes of inductive inference breaks down the complex of sounds into separate coherent images,* **Gestalten** *which becomes projected to form the subjective "spatial world" of sound.*

Ronchi (1957) also views sound as a subjective phenomenon:

> *....Outside the mind there are vibrations. These, however, are not sound or noise, but a silent motion. Only when these vibrations have been received by an ear, transformed into nerve impulses and carried to the brain and mind, only then, internally is the sound created that corresponds to the external vibrations, and it is created to represent this stimulus as it reached the mind.*

The fact that each ear has neural circuiting in both cerebral hemispheres suggests that both hemispheres are required for maximum effectiveness of audition. The individual must distinguish between foreground and background, between speech and noise, localize source and direction and differentiate many other aspects of events in auditory space. It is likely that the more complex facets of audition require both ears and both hemispheres to function simultaneously.

The auditory development of children has not been subjected to the same type of careful observation and analysis as Gesell and others have given to vision, motor and other traits. Some work by Spencer (1958) in studying factors in auditory perception among preschool children, Birch and Mathews (1951) in hearing patterns among mental defectives and Myklebust's (1954) discussion of auditory disorders in children suggest that the full maturity of auditory functioning does not occur until the child is nearly seven years of age. It is interesting to note that visual fusion, laterality and a solid foundation of gross motor skills are similarly centered in that same time period. Even though the child has been hearing sounds since early infancy, has fully acquired speech during his preschool years and has been a listener for six years, all of these events are only preparatory to his maturity as an auditory organism. This apparent basic training period of six years is required to carefully prepare the child for an auditory lifetime. Pitch, loudness and timbre will have to be psychologically organized: frequency, intensity and complexity are physical attributes of sound which must be managed. Man is never able to manage all of the frequencies which exist—his range is from 20-20,000 but he is most sensitive to the speech range from 500-4000 cycles. By design man is equipped to be most sensitive to the range which will require his greatest auditory occupation during his lifetime—the spoken word.

Audition is a constant for man. It is a warning system, an alerting system, a scanning system to keep a constant notation of the activity in auditory space. It alerts the organism to possible danger, records changes in the acoustic surround and scans for sound which may have pertinence to its own value systems. One of audition's major services is to alert the visual mode to inspect detail for relevance. At times audition may directly provide information on danger causing the organism to react reflexively in its defense but for the most part the survival purpose of audition seems to be primarily a warning system to activate visual inspection for critical evaluation of whether threat or no threat is imminent and requires some form of defensive action.

Audition also aids in spatial orientation and is regarded as a distance sense spanning the six fields of space and noting the four zones of space. Reduction in acuity is manifest in two major forms of loss. First the individual loses some aspect of clarity and secondly, suffers some space loss in reduced ability to identify sounds from remote or far space. A hearing loss serves to reduce auditory space bringing the perimeters of efficiency closer to the individual.

Myklebust (1960) has described the behavioral effects of sensory deprivation on other modalities:

> *Although all sensory avenues are not being stimulated simultaneously, a specific sensory experience is interpreted on the basis of what has been learned from all sensory experience. When a certain sensory input is lacking, however, the experience gained from the remaining senses is structured differently.*

Referring specifically to deafness Myklebust described a reduction in "perceptual reciprocation" and referred to vision as being called upon to serve a dual role, fulfilling both foreground and background needs. The close senses also shift their roles becoming more supplementary and critical to the individual's learning and adjustment.

Movement inefficiencies have been noted among speech defective populations when motor tests were employed with comparative normally speaking groups. Patton (1942),

Bilto (1941), Karlin, Youtz and Kennedy (1940) and Albright (1948) all found their speech defective groups to be inferior to control groups on various tests of motor proficiency. Eisenson (1955) wrote that "it is reasonably safe to conclude that the evidence suggests that some degree of motor involvement is etiologically associated with defective speech development".

Myklebust and Boshes (1960) related psychological test findings to neurological findings and found significant problems in re-auditorization among children with disturbances in the occipital parietal and temporal parietal areas.

Deaf individuals may become "near spaced" in their adjustment in adopting Pattern I described by Meyerson (1955). They withdraw into a small safe circle of "fellow deaf" whenever possible. In Adjustment Pattern II the deaf become mid-space people teeter-tottering between the two worlds of the hearing and the non-hearing. For some, this works and for some not. The far spaced deaf person does not fool himself—travels in both worlds—but recognizes his limitations in each world (Pattern III).

It is probably true that the development of hearing can be sequenced on the same corporate scheme we have employed elsewhere. Initial hearing responses are diffuse. The diffusion (an absence of fusion) must then give way to a specific preparatory sequence of monaurality, then bi-aurality, then binaurality and finally fusion. This sequence would place auditory development in a consistent relationship to other percepto-cognitive modes. The coordinate systems of verticality, horizontality, and depth in the auditory process seem clearly established in auditory localization externally in geometric space and internally in physiologic space as described by Cherry (1961). One more positional statement is required before we plunge into our discussion of the auditory mode—the clarification of **listening**.

We differentiate sharply between hearing and listening considering hearing to designate the functional efficiency of the mechanisms of sound receipt and related to physical procedures while listening is a percepto-cognitive function of converting raw sound into meaningful information. Any form of impairment to tissue or structure in the sensitivity channel for sound results in an intake reduction but cannot be taken to infer a disorder in listening. A hearing loss, defined according to decibels and frequencies may be manifest in a variety of ways. The speech range for sound in decibels and frequency becomes the most critical variable across the auditory spectrum but a variety of other peculiarities may be noted in intaking efficiencies. Minor losses in high or low frequencies may be observed and variance in acuity across the frequency scale is probably more usual than a flat pattern of profiled equality. The mechanics of hearing are derived from structural integrity but the dynamics of listening are derived from percepto-cognitive integrity. The dynamics of listening become a matter of understanding the individual's regard for sound as an information resource in building his survival efficiency.

Consequently, our attention is directed primarily to the evaluation of the individual's functional efficiency as a listener regardless of the extent of his auditory acuity. Whether his acuity be totally adequate, moderately reduced, variably reduced, or seriously reduced to the status of deafness, he lives in a world of sound and must take information from that world of sound to promote his survival. Acuity reduction may distort the sound intake but the significance of such reduction can only be understood in terms of the effect of such reduction upon perception. It is the transduction of sound into meaningful information which is the critical human process. Auditory impairment reduces the data intake but it is the perceiving mechanism which determines the amount of data necessary for meaning to occur. An efficient perceiver can process less data into meaningful patterns while an inefficient perceiver requires much more data.

It is entirely conceivable that many people obscure the presence of an acuity problem because of their perceptual efficiency. It is not unusual to discover a variety of minor losses in various frequencies when an audiology student recruits a sample testing population to "practice audiometric procedures" in the college hearing clinic. Many of these people have been unaware of any auditory difficulty until the audiometric process reveals it. Their general perceptual efficiency probably obscured their awareness of such a loss. The customary explanation given to the "unaware-now-aware" testee is frequency-related indicating the types of sounds which are probably not being received such as violins, high pitched voices, organ tones, etc. Since the perceptual process relies upon many more clues than the single phenomenon of vibrations, it is usually very difficult to draw a one to one relationship between aural mechanics and a single sound. It must be remembered that auditory acuity is seldom checked with precise instruments unless there is good reason, from the individual's case history, speech, or present behavior to suggest the possible linkage of an acuity reduction. While there are many situations where audiometric study is routinely conducted, it is rarely routine in a typical elementary school population.

Regardless of the acuity level of the individual, the world of sound is a constant surround. Whether his intaking is adequate or reduced, the world of sound is still "out there" to be processed for information. The profoundly deaf person, despite his serious reduction in receipt must become aware that a sound world exists in which his participation has been limited. He must build a perception of the auditory world even though he does not personally receive it. He must come to an appreciation that various objects emit sound and people emit sounds whether or not he hears them. He must build an auditory space world from silent inference. If an individual's hearing loss is of such nature and degree that some form of amplifying unit will bring the intaking process nearer to normal levels he obtains such a booster unit. The benefit of the booster unit, automatically calibrated on a mechanical basis to increase volume, balance intake and so on, generally becomes a matter of perception. If a hearing aid enables the individual to secure more data and such increase is perceptually exploited to improve his information processing the booster is a positive instrument. If no change in perception occurs, there is little value to the volume boost. The value of a hearing aid is measurable in perceptual improvement not in elevation of an acuity level.

A hearing loss of any kind reduces the survival potential of the individual in Movigenic conceptualization of human performance and produces a survival vulnerability in the world of sound. The determination of the presence or absence of an acuity reduction is a necessary feature in survival study, but is truly secondary to the perceptual issue. The real issue centers on the question of how the individual processes sound, however much or little may enter, to promote his survival. Many people with acuity reductions gain more information from the world of sound than the unimpaired majority. What one gains from the auditory world on intake, is determined by listening efficiency far more than by auditory acuity.

Consequently, the Movigenic focus is upon **listening** as the percepto-cognitive transduction phenomenon.

The auditory development of a child begins in the fetal stage. Riesen (1950) noted a fetal response to noise at five weeks. Gesell (1939) indicated that an infant at one month heeded sounds and ceased activity if a bell was sounded. At two months of age the infant attends to voices and gives evidence of listening behavior according to Cattell (1948). At four months the infant will turn his head when a sound is heard. The localizing process is emerging. This receptive process serves as an introduction to meaningful expression which follows and merges with the development of listening. Words form and are monitored by the infant in inflectional pattern with a hand in hand mutual development of listening and speaking. The listening behavior of the preschool child has apparently been taken for granted by developmentalists since the literature is quite silent in this area. However, in keeping with the general principles of developmental progression we can assume that there is a general increase in listening span and that more and more complex receptions become possible both in relation to content and to temporal variations. The preschool period is perhaps the most critical period of all time periods in relation to listening. In a highly verbal society oral directions, oral admonitions and oral discussion of behavior probably can be rated as the principal shaping technique used by parents to teach appropriate forms of behavior. The age bracket from two to five is a saturating period of "do's and don'ts" as the parents attempt to define conformity patterns for the child. It is a time of listening to favorite stories being read, listening to records, overhearing adult conversations, being intrigued by unusual noise and sound-making toys, listening to corrections made of speech patterns and attempting to comply—it is the basic training period for listening. The child learns to listen in order that he might listen to learn. He literally practices listening—erring frequently in the early stages but progressively becoming more efficient. He listens to shadings in tone, modulations in sound, variations in timing, gradually organizing his auditory attention and sustaining efficiency. At times he is an eager listener and at other times his mother is "convinced" that he has a hearing loss. Listening development probably follows the same general pattern of temporalizing as the speech span. As single words are replaced by phrases and these in turn by sentences and eventually converted to sentenced conversational interchange, it is very likely that his listening efficiency follows the same buildup. He listens efficiently first to single words and gradually builds his efficiency to a greater intaking span. Observations of the parental verbal relationship to a young child will verify the tendency to rely upon single word communications gradually increasing the length as the child grows older. Although the young child may be bombarded with a verbal barrage, when the parent truly desires to "communicate" he or she resorts to brief explicit direct words. Parents do not resort to this brevity because they have been advised to do so by experts but rather from an intuitive recognition of the child's developmental limitation in the listening span.

A child's preschool listening efficiency develops according to the extent of listening demand which confronts him in the learning of behavior. If his parents are high auditory persons it is likely that the major communicative pattern is verbal and the child's psychological and social survival depends upon how well he "listens to what is going on". Because his parents translate their world into auditory symbols with ease and comfort listening will be a prized asset in that particular household. On the other hand, if his parents tend to be low auditory, quiet non-talkative, reticent people, the listening demand will not be as great. If he lives in a noisy environment where sound discriminations become a major system for sorting out the world of objects and people and defining their spatial relationships according to sound cues, the development of listening efficiency becomes important to survival. In a quiet surround where the noise level is relatively stable the listening demand is less. Listening efficiency is built in response to demand. If the child's comfort within that given environment demands that he become a good listener in order to fit the family pattern, it is likely that he will arrive at the kindergarten doorstep with a high degree of listening proficiency. If listening has not been a vital need in his preschool years, his basic training as a listener has probably not equipped him for the intense demands that lie ahead. Whether or not a child comes to school as a trained listener is directly related to the nature and intensity of the listening demands which have permeated his preschool years. The steady stream of bombardment from an acoustic world necessary to maintain the fitness of a processing system may or may not have been adequate for the building of auditory intaking efficiency. Once he enters school, the listening demand becomes a fixed critical and continuous process. Brown (1950) states that listening is the chief mode of learning in the early school years and that at least in primary grades, children tend to prefer gaining information from listening rather than reading. Horn (1937), Russell (1928), and Young (1936) all share in the belief that listening is preferred to reading in the early grades although this preference may diminish in the upper grades. The Commission on the English Curriculum (1952) as one of its conclusions reported that "pupils from preschool to college learn more frequently by listening than by any other means". Wilt (1950) discovered in his study that the majority of pupil time is spent in listening and Bird (1953) in several studies of college freshmen reported that listening was more important than reading for success in 38-42% of his groups.

In 1930 Rankin estimated that 70% of an adult's waking day is spent in verbal communication. Nichols (1957) found that white collar workers receive about 40% of their salary for listening. Lamar Johnson (1957) felt that the development of good listening skills is vitally important for every individual. Wendell Johnson (1949) declared that listening plays the key role in human relations. The Harvard Report on General Education (1951) includes the statement that listening is as important as speaking in the communicative process. Brown's (1950) research indicates that we listen almost three times as much as we read.

In 1952 Anderson compiled an exhaustive bibliography in the field of listening and found no more than 175 titles of which only 50 may be loosely classified as research.

Many of the early studies of listening employed a questionnaire form requesting subjects to estimate the amount of time they spent in listening; another form was the "charting" method asking subjects to keep track of time spent in listening; another form of study was the rating scale technique using observers to record the amount of time the subjects were observed to be occupied in listening. All of these techniques were essentially "estimations" and from that standpoint, suggestive, but not an accurate set of measures.

The two favored populations in listening research have been the adult and college student groups. (Heilman, 1951; Brown, 1950; Irwin, 1953; Cartier, 1952; Nichols, 1948; Bird, 1955) A few efforts have been directed toward the high school student. (Young, 1936; Schonell, 1942; and Monroe, 1932). Younger children have been less favored. Wilt (1950) reviewed elementary school curriculum guides and concluded that 58% of a child's school day is devoted to listening while only 4% of the day is devoted to activities, which could be construed as training in listening.

It was not until the late 1940's that tests were designed to specifically evaluate listening ability. The process was a matter of presenting auditory material and then questioning the comprehension of the subject. Rankin (1930) predated the general development of tests in his study of listening comprehension among fifth grade children finding that they comprehended only 73% of what they had heard. Brown (1950) reported on conducting a test of listening comprehension for college freshmen with the subjects able to comprehend only 40% of what they heard. In a study by Cartier (1952) 75% of a college group comprehended only 33% of what they heard. Irwin (1953) found that only 27% of his college subjects could successfully identify the main points in an informational lecture. When Brown repeated his technique on a group of junior high school students, he found that they comprehended only 60% of what they heard. Using third grade level information on a group of fifth grade children, Nichols (1950) found only 73% listening efficiency.

The general literature from the field of reading yields a number of studies related to listening usually designed to determine correlations between listening and reading comprehension. Correlations ranged from r. of 40 (Young, 1936), .78 (Goldstein, 1940), .60 and .82 (Larson, 1940). In several studies listening was equal or superior to reading when recall was tested. (Brown, 1948; Corey, 1934; Krawiec, 1946; Rulon, 1943; Spencer, 1940). Gates (1939) concluded that the ability to listen to a story and supply a reasonable ending was the best single predictor of success in learning to read.

Although the literature on listening is by no means extensive and the testing procedures which have been employed are open to a considerable amount of criticism, we are forced to a general conclusion that each population tested revealed varying degrees of listening inefficiency. Furthermore, the phenomenon of listening has not evoked a great deal of interest as a research topic.

Nichols and Stevens (1957) have discussed four false assumptions which they feel have limited the teaching of listening in schools and the same assumptions are probably responsible for the lack of research as well. They cited the following assumptions as false: (1) listening ability depends largely on intelligence; (2) listening ability is closely related to hearing acuity; (3) everyone gets so much practice in everyday situations of listening that training in the skill is unnecessary; (4) learning to read well automatically teaches us to listen.

The general impression gained from the literature is that the definition of listening and the concepts of the process of listening have tended to be vague and overgeneralized. Definitions are scarce, research is scarce — even theories of listening are scarce.

Fessenden's (1955) theory of listening represents one of the few available. He described seven levels of listening: (1) isolation of auditory stimuli; (2) identification of auditory stimuli; (3) integration of auditory stimuli with past experience; (4) inspection of an auditory stimulus; (5) interpretation; (6) interpolation; and (7) introspection. He viewed listening as an "amalgamation of physical and mental events".

> *Our process of thought as we listen is composed of many separate and independent concepts which seem to flow more or less smoothly into ideas and emotions. The several levels of listening...are not static levels but are levels in constant change and flux according to that which is determined by the total pattern of impulses at any given instance. In the course of a single minute of listening activity one might run the gamut of all seven of the levels; or one's mental habits might confine him to a single level in most of his listening.*

Optimal listening according to Fessenden would then be the ability to flexibly shift from level to level, interchangeably as necessary to the listening demand placed upon the listener in a given situation. When the listener cannot manage this flexible shifting, there is an attendant loss to his listening efficiency. If we follow his line of reasoning, it leads us to a conclusion that efficiency in listening is dependent upon adequate development of proficiency in each of the seven levels and that some or all of the levels are constantly called upon in the act of listening. Presumably, each level must possess its own characteristic proficiency in order to flow into the next high level without loss or interference. Listening, therefore, can be viewed from a perspective of a balanced integration among these seven levels each making its proportionate contribution in some manner in every listening situation. For optimal efficiency, all seven levels must be actively processing sound minute after minute if the individual is to gain appropriate information to promote his day by day social survival.

Fessenden's seven levels are cognitive functions and do not refer to the sensory characteristics of the auditory system. Perception and cognition are the vital forces which enable the individual to convert the raw data of sound waves into patterns of meaning. This conversion process sustained through time and multiple circumstances can be called **listening**.

Brown (1950) also focused upon the cognitive perspective in listening in his description of five basic skills required for efficiency in learning:

1. the ability to synthesize the component parts of what is heard to discover the central idea;

2. the ability to distinguish between relevant and irrelevant material;

3. the ability to make logical inferences from what is heard;

4. the ability to make use of contextual clues;

5. the ability to follow without loss, a fairly complex thought unit.

Eisenson (1955) has defined a normal listener as one whose "hearing, visual perceptive abilities, intelligence, expectations and motivations make it possible for him to wish to and be able to understand what the speaker is attempting to communicate". Meyerson (1955) offered the term "auding" as a descriptive term for listening to speech.

One of the most primitive purposes assigned to the auditory mode, is that of localization in space. Awareness of space becomes a vital element to support audition.

The sound from one of the six space fields enters the listener's nearer ear a fraction of a second earlier than it enters his farther ear. This minute difference serves as a first step in localizing the source. Held (1965) produced a decorrelation in this auditory localizing differential by equipping his subjects with a pseudophone. If subjects were allowed to move around in their environment they learned to make proper localizations. Those who remained immobile became auditorically confused. The pseudophones caused a double auditory image, diplophonia which in auditory terms is the equivalent of diplopia in vision. Held's experiments have clearly shown that active movement is essential to perceptual adaptation in the face of any auditory disarrangement. If the individual can move freely, his active movements produce auditional sensory feedback which eventually correlates and brings about an adaptation.

A stationary listener (head movements restricted) has difficulty telling if a sound is in front or back of him but has little difficulty in localizing front and back space sounds if the head is free to move. (Teuber, 1959)

Rayleigh (cited in Cratty, 1964) among others, discovered that the location of sounds could be made with greater accuracy when they were produced at the sides of the body than when they were located at the front or the back of the head. Wallach (1940) has shown that the kinesthetic sensation produced by head movements integrates with auditory sensations to provide perceptions of auditory space.

For survival purposes, the auditory alerting process serves to identify distance around the perimeter. Near sound of an emergency nature is reacted to by startle and simultaneous activation of protective mechanism. For near sound—the waves of sound span time too quickly for the visual mechanisms to be set in action to evaluate the threat so the protective mechanisms must activate defensively without critical reflection.

If a sound is localized as emanating from left back space at the far perimeter, the survival response is to turn the neck and head to visually scan and fixate in order to evaluate the potential danger of the stimulus. If sound is grossly localized as being in back space without a lateral orientation, a mislocalization would require a correction of a head turn, increased scanning time or a full body rotation. This loss of time because of inefficiency would increase the vulnerability of the organism if the stimulus were a dangerous one.

On the basis of these studies, a listener is a "full body listener". Listening is not an isolated function of the auditory channels. It is very likely that some degree of postural malalignment is occasioned by listening habits. The most obvious illustration comes from the possible inequality between the two ears on a strict acuity basis. If one ear has better acuity, the individual must seek to spatially set his "better ear" in the most advantageous listening position. Consequently, he will either have to station himself spatially at a postural angle to the sound source so as to "center" his better ear or place himself under muscular tension while listening because of reduced efficiency. Straining to hear, involves muscular tension throughout the body. (Smith, 1962) The net effect of either form of adaptation is the introduction of postural malalignments.

Wallerstein (1954) has suggested that the rise in tension may be associated with increasing comprehension or organization of incoming verbal material. Such organization is felt to take place during attentive listening.

It is also highly probable that the rather common visual disorder of ambliopia (suppressing one eye) has an auditory counterpart. In the same manner as the human performer may find it to his temporary advantage to rely upon monocular processing, he may also find it profitable to rely upon monaural listening.

It is also possible that the strong unilateral preference which is so common in this society carries with its development an almost automatic buildup of auditory inequality. If auditory testing were to be concentrated upon listening rather than acuity, we suspect that a differential would probably be routinely in evidence. The individual traveler must achieve his binaurality on a developmental basis building it in the yard work of an acoustic surround. Voices and other Gestalten can be separated by the listener with one ear alone but with reduced effectiveness. (Cherry, 1961) Optimal auditory efficiency can only be achieved on a binaural fusion basis. Anything less than this reduces the listener to a functional status below the caliber of his basic anatomical design.

Listening Demands are Variable

In any given momentary listening situation, the efficiency the individual brings to the situation becomes the critical determinant of whether or not he can successfully resolve the listening demand. Each listening situation has its own unique composite of elements. The garage mechanic listening to a motor to diagnose some irregularity, is in a different listening demand than when this same mechanic listens to the customer's description of complaints. Listening to unfamiliar material differs from listening to familiar material. Listening to words in general conversation differs from listening to a technical lecture. The first grader faces a different demand in listening when his teacher describes a new concept versus listening to his mother's admonitions about his behavior. Listening to a foreign language differs from listening to your native tongue. Each listening situation is a demand. If the individual by virtue of experience, opportunity and background can bring an adequate degree of efficiency to that demand, the net result is successful resolution. At any moment that the efficiency level is not equal to the task, the successful processing of the demand is aborted to some extent. Listening inefficiencies result in misperceiving and error.

Research in hearing has also revealed a developmental phenomenon in relation to sensitivity to certain frequencies at different ages. In the early periods of development when the psychosexual identifications are being established, all children show a preference for high frequency sounds and a dislike for low frequencies. As they develop their sexual identifications girls retain their initial sensitivity to high frequency and boys switch to greater sensitivity to low frequency as a form of basic training for the adolescent emergence of the low frequency masculine voice. Since there is no sexual attraction during the latency period preceding adolescence, both sexes tend to be relatively frequency-insensitive to each other's provincial range. With the pubertal change frequency sensitivity changes for purposes of mating and each sex becomes more sensitive to respective vocal frequencies. This heightened sensitivity holds sexual significance during the reproductive span and shows evidence of decline when the mating period is terminated. The typical presbycusic loss is noted in the high frequency range for males and the low for females as a signal of the decline of the mating period. It appears entirely logical that auditory sensitivity has design values from many other perspectives than the simple matter of defining and localizing sounds. As a part of dynamic mobile man, it must serve his needs on all fronts of life exploration. The auditory like all other components of Movement Efficiency must contribute to his fulfillment.

Auditory-Expressive

The human organism is capable of emitting sound. The mechanical equipment to produce sound is composed of a larynx, diaphragm, nasal passage, oral cavity, tongue and so on. The selection of which sounds will be produced becomes a matter of the dynamics of the individual terranaut. During infancy, the vocal explorations become the tuning process for eventual regulation of those sounds into meaningful units. The sequence in which this occurs, has been exceptionally well documented in a wide variety of investigations during the past two decades. Unless the infant suffers a significant acuity loss, the natural design of his mechanical vocal equipment will yield a sound production which will eventually become recognizable speech. Even deaf infants are known to engage in vocal exploration as if they were preparing for speech and then progressively become aware that they cannot monitor their own sounds and use the process only sparingly. The emission of sound, however, is a basic characteristic and some sound production is continuously noted under certain conditions among deaf populations of all ages. Basically, the expressive element in the Auditory mode is manifest in two ways. Voice production requires the self-monitoring of the individual to regulate the volume of the sound being emitted. The clarity of the sound in terms of distinctive phonemes may be more a matter of mechanical efficiency of tongue, nasal passages, vocal folds and so forth. The second way it is manifest is in terms of rate of emission.

The absence of clarity in the word sounds of little children is a twofold dilemma. In a simultaneous process they have mechanical immaturities on a natural developmental basis in tongue, larynx, etc. and also experience an immaturity in the monitoring process. Progressively, both issues are resolved as their developmental timetable is enacted. Most children monitor their own speech for clarity and appropriate volume by the time they have reached their third birthday. Some word sounds may continue to be difficult but by and large the average youngster is a quite well organized communicator at an early age. When sound substitution problems persist as a general characteristic after that time this should be considered as evidence of a lag in the organization of the auditory and become an indication for a need for auditory organizational training and tongue exercises. Expressive auditory performance also includes singing and the use of voice to produce sounds other than words.

The general characteristics of speech from a developmental standpoint, has been so extensively investigated and diseminated by so many competent researchers in the field of speech and hearing that there is little point to citing well known data in this discussion. We only wish to comment on several points about the auditory-expressive phenomenon which have special pertinence to our concept of movement.

We suggest that an individual's expressive span is a reflection upon his receptive span. When the child can speak a three word phrase it is very likely that he can also only "listen" a three word phrase. As he expands his "listening" span, a corresponding increase occurs in his ability to sustain his auditory expression. People who speak in short, crisp sentences or phrases probably listen in the same manner whether they are adults or children. We also suggest that the listen-express span of the individual is related to a general characteristic of sustenance or span throughout all modal performance.

An interesting sidelight on the listen-express ratio is to be found in the high verbal characteristic of American society. Most parents bombard their children with a barrage of words from early infancy. Everybody is always talking. Observation of this phenomenon of verbal barrage leads to the suggestion that the typical state of affairs is that most people are more concerned with what **they will say next** than with what they are being told. Listening for many people is simply the interval between their own utterances. They await their turn to talk.

Within the context of Auditory-Expressive reliance upon vocal expression as a source of information must also be included. There are those people who acquire information from the procedure of orally expressing their own thoughts. It is only as they express their thoughts aloud that they seem to learn. These are people who seem to require a personal reverbalization to check their learning. Having received some bit of information at a receptive level they must repeat it aloud or produce a rephrasing or a digest to insure themselves of its import. For such performers the oral repetition of rephrasing has value to their learning. At times high Auditory-Expressive people, "talk their way out of a paper bag" not knowing where their words may eventually lead but holding a confidence in their own ability to "make it come out alright". They learn as they talk more so than learning as they listen.

Another note of concern must be registered on the topic of confusion between the two behaviors of speech and language. Speech is the anatomically mechanical process of giving voice to the language which has already been organized somewhere in neurologic space. Speech is the vocal expression of language. To confuse the two terms by interchanging them is to reveal a lack of understanding of the true nature of each.

To conform to the communication practices defined by his society it is imperative that the child learns to speak the phonemes according to vocal expectancy. It is communicative facility and social acceptance which govern our concern for enunciative clarity. If a child or adult mispronounces or confuses a phonemic organization but the listener comprehends the utterance, there is really no reason for concern. If the listener, however, does not grasp the communique because the word or words are not clearly spoken, an auditory blurring occurs and there is reason for concern. As an active communicator there will be many, many listeners who will confront the speaker. Enunciative clarity, therefore, becomes critical to communication with those listeners who are not accustomed to making allowances for enunciative error. Parents may have little difficulty understanding their child's speech and even come to a point of tolerance where the phonemic error is essentially ignored because the parent has become accustomed to supplying the correct sound — not to the child — but within their own listening.

It is only as the child must communicate with less tolerant listeners that he must achieve a clarity. The design of the listening process seems to have taken into account the many possible articulation errors which could occur and provided a form of auditory editing which will correct the pronunciation for the benefit of the listener. The listener often edits a vocal communique as though he were proofreading. He deletes, changes verb position, supplies missing phonemes and substitutes others. He arranges it in the order and clarity which is necessary for **his** comprehension. When a listener is unable to perform such editing upon an unclear presentation, it is likely that communication breaks down.

As we have noted before, the expressive element in the auditory mode is pertinent to the cognitive system only insofar as the individual employs his own vocal effort for information getting purposes. If he uses vocal sound, however expressed, to convey information or reach out for information for himself, then we truly regard auditory-expressive within the concept of the Auditory in the Percepto-Cognitive system.

Blind children who utilize their own vocal efforts as sonar devices to orient themselves spatially, fall within this concept. Any individual who characteristically must hear himself say a thought in order to learn it is also included in such a group. The subvocal reader comes within this classification.

Essentially, the modes within the Percepto-Cognitive system are of import to movement only as channels of information to the MOVER. They are intended to serve him in **acquiring** information to be processed toward his enhancement and advancement. Consequently the major emphasis in the Auditory mode is upon the receiving process with the expressive process holding a secondary import.

Both the receptive and expressive levels of auditory functioning must achieve efficiency if the organism is to benefit fully from the auditory component in his organismic design. A good speaker who is a poor listener is less than fully efficient. A good listener who is a poor speaker is also less than optimally efficient. Only as both elements achieve efficiency can the organism move in space with the proficiency which his design promises.

While the auditory aspect of man is considered a hand in hand pair with the visual aspect, we hold it to be less economic than vision. It is truly more symbolically influential in man's explorations within himself and his external world than the gustatory, olfactory, tactual and kinesthetic but remains secondary to vision in range, amplitude, speed, coverage and so on. Light travels faster than sound and requires greater processing speed from the mechanism of receipt. Although there are undoubtedly many authorities in the field of speech and hearing who would cast their ballot emphatically in favor of audition as man's most useful modality, our vote clearly favors the visual.

All modes prepare the way for the supremacy of the visual, as we interpret the modal system. Man's auditory functioning is magnificent but remains as a pre-climactic mode reaching deeply into cognitive space, secondary in importance to the headline act in the Percepto-Cognitive system.

The auditory mode is survival oriented, of particular import in a panasonic world of verbal bombardment. Efficiency in the auditory mode is critical to man's symbolic fluency. Sensitivity to auditory information is a vital component of movement. Sound moves and travels. Man moves and travels. A transport unity must be achieved. The acoustic world must be organized by the learner if he is to move with efficiency in physical and cognitive space.

15

THE
VISUAL
MODE

Vision is many things to many people. The understanding of vision has advanced a long distance since the Helmholtzian era when the prevailing model of vision compared the eye to a camera. What once appeared in historical distance to be only a physical orb, has been refined and elaborated into the full specimen of the human organism. As the lenses of improved knowledge about the nature of man have cleared the apparent blur which once was thought to be vision, the cleared image was discovered to be a total dynamic organism. As the scientific study of man has continued there has been a theoretical reversal. In full face confrontation, the dynamic organism has demanded regard for his totality in identifying his vision rather than allowing it to be identified in a segmented manner. Where formerly the needs of the organism as a dynamic mobile unit promoting its survival in an energy surround were regarded as secondary to the study of the mechanics of the optical structures, the scientific perspective has changed to the study of the way a given individual utilizes vision. Optical structures are not to be ignored in the study of vision. However, instead of holding the center stage position in the spotlight, the circle has been expanded to encompass a great many more elements within a dynamic organism. The reversal may best be illustrated by a short statement from MacDonald (1964), "...eyes do not tell people what they see. People tell eyes what to look for." It is the peopleness in vision that has now come into focus. There are those, however, among many branches of professional work who still accord the primary position to mechanical structures of the eye. In a large measure, these two viewpoints of relative emphasis in regard to the dynamic qualities of the viewer are derived from a division of opinion on the question of whether vision is learned or is innate. Those who advocate the "innate" belief tend to regard visual states as inevitable consequences of some type of genetic factor, as a typical expression of genetic difference and hold an attitude of "what must be — must be". Those who believe that vision is a "learned" phenomenon in a dynamic organism and that an infant actually learns how to see probably derive their first supporting note from the work of Stratton (1896) who inverted the physical world for himself and several subjects by means of a special optical device. In spite of the fact that the world of objects was made to look upside down, it took a comparatively short period of time for the wearers of these devices to redefine their upside down world into patterns which could be employed by them in daily living without significant interference with typical behavior. More recently, the work of Hebb (1958) has lent further confirmation to the belief that vision is learned. As Getman (1965) has stated, "Even the anatomically complete and healthy eye must learn to perform and it is these performance skills which receive primary attention".

Ronchi (1957) has attempted to revise the development of physical optics to what he calls the science of vision of energy optics. Mechanisms are involved but are "predominantly psychological in nature".

Ronchi views vision as a tripartite relationship drawn from physics, physiology and psychology but being predominantly psychological in nature. The observer rather than the mechanics is all important in seeing. He states that the "figure that a seeing individual beholds before himself in a field containing sources of visual waves is a creation of his own mind". The observer constructs an "effigy" by combining all the factors at his disposal. The "effigy" relies on: (1) modulated nerve impulses; (2) muscular information connected with the mechanisms of accommodation, convergence, and temporal parallax; (3) previous knowledge of observed objects and previous experience with them; (4) imagination and initiative of the mind itself. Ronchi's description of the dynamics of mind is of interest:

> *This whole mass of factors is analyzed with a precision and rapidity that are marvelous...by the mind...If it blunders too often, it is adjudged abnormal and what it says it sees is called an hallucination. Sometimes, it succumbs to errors that are committed more or less by everybody under the same conditions and then it is said to be subject to an illusion. At other times, it makes a mistake that it notices; it corrects the created effigy and says nothing even if a bit surprised at first. Most of the time it fashions an effigy that it does not subject to any criticism or control. For the effigy serves it well enough and it is satisfied. It believes that the figure it sees is the actual reality, forgetting that it has itself created the figure and given it brightness and color. (p. 120)*

Pieron (1952) described vision as a photochemical process in reception with supplementation by other sensory processes and cognitive modifications. Bartley (1951) has presented an explication of the psychophysiology of vision dealing with optical mechanisms related to acuity and clarity in terms of refractive error; the anatomical mechanisms of focus, rods, cones and so on; photochemical mechanisms related to light gradients; neural mechanisms in the retina, optic nerve and the periodic fluctuation related to the alpha rhythm and finally, the ocular motor mechanisms of eye muscles, convergence and accommodation.

Gesell (1949) regarded vision as having the peculiar function of assisting the organism in its adjustments to the plane and solid geometry of space. He said at one point:

> *No one of the major fields of behavior—motor, adaptive, language and personal-social is normally devoid of visual content or visual controls. So interfused are vision and action systems that the two must be regarded as inseparable. To understand vision, we must know the child; to understand the child, we must know the nature of his vision.*

An evolutionary point of view was expressed by Fay (1955):

> *The original purpose and design was to survive, reproduce and conquer the environment which acted upon the mobile unit structure. The light perceptive values of the eyes became intimately integrated with the need for adjustment and focus, to better serve their visual protective exploratory function. Perhaps the least important of their presently considered value was that of detailed object awareness. The sensitivity to light as an adjunct of the sun and stars and its differentiation from darkness with its uncertainty as to warned approach of impending catastrophe, was more important in a neuromuscular integration of defense, than one of appreciation of reading and the comparative values of detail.*

Gesell (1949) identified three basic fields in which every child organizes his visual space world: (1) SKELETAL in which the child seeks and holds a visual image; (2) VISCERAL in which the child discriminates and defines an image; and (3) CORTICAL in which the child unifies and interprets the image. He further emphasized that these fields develop jointly but by no means uniformly, the ratio varying with the advancing stages of the individual child's growth. Gesell referred to the term "visual image" not as a light scatter on retina, but as a perceived image in the broadest sense of complementation from such features as memory, feelings, attitudes, etc.

Skeffington (1965) has for many years presented a schematic model which holds vision to be an emergent from the dynamic overlapping of the (1) vestibular anti-gravity patterns of the organism, (2) centering, (3) identification and (4) the speech-auditory processes.

In the four overlapping circles of Skeffington's schematic model the manner in which the individual operates as a proprioceptive, kinesthetic and balanced organism in its continuing conquest of gravity, is interwoven with the manner in which he converges both the physical alignment of his eyes and his total body alignment. The viewer selects from a total space volume an area for attention and meaning and centers upon that area. The physiology of his inner optics operate to accommodate to his viewing. His anti-gravity response and centering enter into a transactional merger with his identification of his selected view and the speech-auditory process enables him to call upon his prior experiences to complete the process. The emergent from this dynamic interaction is referred to as vision.

Getman (1965) has presented a schematic model for the visuomotor primacy in the acquisition of learning skills according to a conceptualization of developmental sequences of organismic performance. In the Getman model innate response systems form the base line for the pyramidal model leading in a sequence of refinements to general motor systems, special motor systems, ocular motor systems, visualization systems and finally, vision.

Riesen (1958) has conceived of form vision as requiring a sensory-sensory integration that involves learning according to a contiguity principle. The development of such vision, must await differential excitation from contours, corners and edges. Such differential excitation serves to load certain loci on the retina differently than others.

Harmon (1958) has divided vision into primary and secondary functions. The primary function of vision, biologically, is related to space determinations and the space movements of the organism. Only as a "higher" function of abstracting and symbolizing space and space movements for later refacilitation and redirection of movement comes into the need system of the organism does the secondary "image" function of vision come into existence.

Vision has been defined by Emery (1962) as a process whereby data are received and integrated with other inputs into the brain and with stored information, the meaning is abstracted and the organism institutes the appropriate output whether the output be movement, visualization or projection. After the initial output, there is always some resultant input or feedback through some or many sensory paths, which tell the person whether or not the output satisfied the situation. In this process, a continuous check is being made on the rightness of actions. Riesen (1958) referred to the organism as abstracting "meaningful segments of spatial mosaics" from the visual environment by selective "attention".

The dynamics of a single act of "seeing" have been described by Harmon (1965) as a five-step process. First, the light gradient on the retina must trigger the body to come to a point of balance with both light and gravity so we can have a supporting base from which to aim accurately at our task. This is a system of "coming to attention"—"coming to balance" preparing the organism to act. It is the positioning of the body in comfort with gravity and light. This is the "tonus of attention" which Harmon has described elsewhere. (Harmon, 1958) The second step in the "seeing" process requires the cooperation of the head, neck and body to establish a frame of reference—the visual space—in which to accurately direct our movements in performing our visually-centered task. In this step the organism sets its own coordinates on visual space and centers itself on the task to the best of its current organization ability. As a third step, the organism defines its surround. It determines its whereabouts, locating itself in a surround containing certain boundaries and locates the specific placement of the task. The fourth step is an emphatically percepto-cognitive action, in which the performer defines the details of the task describing to himself the "what-to-do-ness" of the situation, establishing the relationship of one detail in the task with another and making a judgment of the relationship of that task to other significant objects in that surround. Finally, the vision directs each step in the performance of the task.

This sequence of steps is repeated billions of times by a mobile organism acting in an illuminated surround. Only as this sequence occurs with economy and comfort, does the individual perform with meaning and purpose. What one sees at any given moment, is dependent upon his readiness to see, his ability to come to balance for action, his awareness of his surround, his ability to relate his sighting in the context of that surround and finally, his ability to visually direct his resolution of the demand. It is a dynamic sequence of "seeing" on the street, in the country, in a classroom, behind a steering wheel, in a museum, in a grocery store—whenever and wherever the performer looks.

Furthermore, this sequence must occur with "least effort" and without interfering with necessary postural and performing actions in relation to sound, heat, gravity and counterbalancing actions. There must be a synchrony throughout the organism for the "seeing" to be most profitable to the viewer. As Harmon (1965) has pointed out, "...we use some of the same nerves and same muscles for light response, for a balancing response, for gravitational response and for other non-visual concurrent responses". If these multiple responses are not synchronized or labor under some degree of interference, the major penalty is paid by the visual system in the form of reduction in meaningfulness and some form of visual maladaptation.

Ronchi (1957) further elaborated on his concept of the "effigy" in vision.

> *...For vision of the external world to take place (by contrast with dreams and hallucinations) there must be a body emitting radiation,*

which is propagated in the surrounding space, transmitted to an eye and absorbed by it. A stimulation of the peripheral sense organ thus occurs and impulses are generated which, by way of the optic nerve carry to the brain and mind not only the news that the radiation has arrived at the eye, but also the characteristics of the stimulus. Then the mind goes into action. It analyzes this "information" inferring therefrom whatever it can with regard to the form and position of the emitting body as well as its external properties. Having completed this operation, the mind portrays the conclusion with a model, a figure, an effigy....

Having finished this task, the mind confronts the luminous colored effigy and says that it "sees the object" which emitted the radiation (p. 69-70)

In his presentation of a dynamic theory of vision Harmon (1958) defined eight specific roles for visual processes. These roles are listed below along with the supporting citations which were used by Harmon:

"Visual processes enter into:

1. localizing the organism in space (Fincham 1951, Lashley 1951)

2. adjusting the organism in efficient relationship with that which it wants or needs to manipulate (Duke-Elder 1942, Lashley 1942, Magnus 1924)

3. holding the organism in support (Harmon 1945, Magnus 1924)

4. identifying significant forms, objects, events or symbols in the surround (Adler 1950, Vernon 1937, Marshall and Talbot 1942)

5. synthesizing and unifying other sensations and experiences with the immediate visual ones to derive meaning (Renshaw 1951, Allport 1955, Pitts and McCulloch 1947, Pratt 1950)

6. directing action (Pitts and McCulloch 1947, Lashley 1942, 1951)

7. recording significant aspects of experience for later use in making performance or problem solving more efficient (Von Foerster 1949, 1950 Stevens 1951)

8. establishing needed and satisfying equilibria (Duke-Elder 1942, Magnus 1924, Cannon 1932)"

As we regard vision, at this moment in time, it is divided into three areas of consideration. the first area can be designated as "physiologic optics" embracing the consideration of the anatomical, muscular and neurologic aspects of the eyeball and its multiple components and processes. Cornea, lens, pupil, retina, extraocular muscles, fovea, optic nerve are the key terms in defining that area of concern. Those who limit a concept of vision to such anatomical boundaries, must of necessity, regard the orb itself as most significant. The physiologic adequacy and the state of health of the two eyeballs becomes the prime concern. Within that boundary, the concept of the eye as a camera, is fenced. Hereditary states, genetic predispositions, tumors, rods and cone equations and so on become a part of this view of vision. Acuity is the second significant concern after the anatomical adequacy has been confirmed. Here the distance measurement is used to determine whether lenses might have any value to the viewer. Essentially, from an acuity standpoint, the population of the world divides into the near sighted, far sighted and those who are presumed to see well at any distance. Corrective measures run to surgical intervention of some kind, prescription of correcting lenses and muscular exercises.

A second area of consideration may be given the general designation of **functional vision**. This conceptual framework leads to concern for the manner in which an individual makes use of his sight in gaining information. Advocates of this general thought believe that visual problems commonly identified as myopia, hyperopia, astigmatism, anisometropia represent adaptations or solutions to stressful conditions which the individual could not resolve in any other way. Here the belief subscribes fully to Harmon's statement that "stress alters function and function alters structure". The individual builds a "visual problem" for himself in the experiential vicissitudes of life.

The wonder of a lens becomes a cornerstone to this conceptual edifice. The primary therapeutic course again rests upon lenses as corrective and/or supportive aids to a greater visual efficiency. There is concern for appropriate alignment and teaming of eyes, scanning, fixations, saccadics and so on.

This aspect of vision continues the orientation to the orb and retina but expands its scope into the domain of perception and cognition. There remains, however, a solid anchorage to the lens.

A third area of consideration is the concept of **visual perception** which, according to the literature, is represented as a step beyond the first two concepts moving vision squarely into the mysterious domain of neurologic space. The vast majority of studies conducted in this area, can be classified as continuing the orientation to the retina but the total behavior of the organism has increasingly risen in interest.

The perceptual viewpoint on vision has been the subject of much investigation.

Gibson (1950) described the visual world as extending in distance and depth, being upright, stable and without boundaries, colored, shadowed, illuminated and textured, composed of surfaces, edges, shapes and interspaces—and most significant—as containing things that have meaning. He also emphasized that this visual world was not open-spaced "air" but was rather the objects in that world as they are related to each other. He viewed visual space as a continuous background surface.

Gibson divided the perception of the visual world into two types: (1) the perception of the substantial or spatial world and (2) the perception of useful and significant things to which we ordinarily attend. The first type composed of color, textures, surfaces, edges, slopes, shapes and interspaces form a more or less constant background for experience and provide a fundamental repertory of impressions to guide present and future perceptions. This he termed the **literal world**. The second type of perception is composed of objects, places, people, signals and written symbols. It is constantly shifting and dedependent on what the perceiver may be doing at the moment. It is too complex to manage economically and consequently, the perceptions must be selective. The selectivity leads to distortions.

Gibson believed that spatial behavior is intimately connected with spatial perception and, therefore, the visual impressions of the developing child gained their solidity and depth from the association of his visual impressions with his movements in relation to those visual impressions.

He also commented on the visual-postural relationship in his discussion of the necessity for retinal motion and muscular impressions to be coordinated as a mediating process to achieve proficiency in the spatial behavior of the body.

Ames and Ittelson (1950) have expressed the view that a visual perception "no matter how well structured is not a disclosure of the external situation, but is rather a prediction made by the organism of what it is probably looking at, i.e., a perception is a prognostic directive for purposeful action" From the series of studies they conducted they raised serious questions about the generally accepted automatic physiologic qualities of the accommodation and convergence mechanisms in the eyes which imply a waiting eye ready for light with all of its behavior automatized by design properties. They conceive of dynamic man as holding an intimate directive role in relation to his own physiology, "the world he is related to, the world he sees, the world he is operating on and the world that is operating on him is the result of a transactional process in which man himself plays an active role".

Cantril (1959) conducted a series of studies of binocular rivalry and fusion using a stereoscope with picture stimuli in which each eye was shown a different picture. The eyes tend to fuse them together or impose one over the other. Subjects looking at two faces of football players saw only one face, that is, a new and different face composed of the better features of the two faces. South African whites viewing a colored face and a white face saw more colored faces than white ones. Psychologists when viewing a picture of Madonna and child and a picture of a nude female, saw one or the other and often got impressions of the nude dressing and the Madonna undressing. Mexican and American children exposed to stereoscope pictures of a bull fighter and a baseball player, tended to have opposite responses. The American children most frequently saw the baseball player and the Mexican children the bull fighter. As Cantril pointed out, "...a person sees what is 'significant' with significance defined in terms of one's relationship to what he is looking at".

In a study on sailors Cantril and his associates found that aniseikonic spectacles through which a person viewed is distorted almost beyond recognition, did not distort officers as much as they did enlisted men for the sailors who wore them. Neuropsychiatric patients viewing their own images in mirrors while wearing aniseikonic spectacles tended to see gross distortions in themselves. Normal subjects in the same experience tended to minimize distortions in their own images. They also found that a person tends to see only minor and detailed changes in himself but see major changes in a stranger.

In another series of tests using a "distorted room" (a purposely constructed distorted room that will appear like a regular square room when viewed monocularly from a certain point thus making the objects or persons in the room look distorted), Cantril and his group found that happily married couples reported the room distorted but held the image of their mate to be undistorted. The same "holding against distortion" occurred with the parents of young children when viewing their child in the room. What we perceive, according to Cantril, is in large part our own creation and depends upon the assumptions we bring to a particular occasion. We give meaning and order to our sensory impingements in terms of our needs and purposes and this process of selection is actively creative.

Wittreich (1959) conducted further experiments using the Cantril approach and found similar results. He pointed out that aniseikonic lenses used to view one's self and strangers resulted in seeing changes in one's own image mainly in the form of minor details while the changes in the "other person" were in terms of overall size and shape.

It is indeed a rarity to find a report on visual perception which takes into account the refractive status of the individual subject. It appears that the basic assumption of universal homogeneity in regard to the eye is automatic. Visual assumptions of distortions, rod tilting, form perceptions, adaptation to inversions and prisms and other phenomena have been reported with little or no accounting for the pre-experiment visual efficiency of the subject. There is rarely an accounting of whether the subjects wore lenses or did not wear lenses before, during or after the experiments.

The investigators in the field of visual perception have generally tended to represent a belief that light gradients upon a retina are secondary to other factors in the perceiving of the visual world. Murphy and Solley (1957) emphasized that the viewer perceives "as he wishes to perceive". Bruner (1950) and others spoke of "internal directing states", Cantril (1959) refers to assumptions, and the Gestalt group (Koffka, 1935; Koehler, 1929) analyzed organizational processes which essentially had little to do with the retina. What occurs in visual perception may have relatively little to do with specific light gradients. An exception to this general perceptual consideration is to be found in studies of strabismus.

McLaughlin (1964) has described the strabismic person as receiving a second image—an unreal one—which he learns to ignore because it confuses his perceiving. He refers to strabismus as a sensory-deprivation experiment per individual in which "a period of forty years is not uncommon". After conducting a variety of experiments, he concluded:

> *Strabismus appears to be the only disorder of visual perception in which the patient's reliability as a scientific observer and his ability to report his visual experience are unimpaired.*

The selection of strabismus or constant esotropia is apparently a clear choice of the individual. There is no middle ground. The "unreal" image present in the early stages of strabismic selection is eliminated and the organism accepts monocularity as **his** system for seeing.

These three areas of consideration, physiologic optics, functional vision and visual perception have each produced an immense body of literature and will undoubtedly continue to evoke more and more study. There is yet a fourth area of consideration which must be delineated—that of the Movement Efficiency of vision. Ronchi (1957) has said that the science of vision is "not a chapter of physics, nor of physiology, nor of psychology. It is a complex science that must take into account the contribution of all three of these disciplines."

It is this general concept of the integration of many aspects of a dynamic mobile organism seeking to economically promote an optimal survival in an energy surround that we feel must enter into the consideration of vision. In attempting to place vision into the model of Movement Efficiency there are a number of areas which must enter into the picture.

It is inevitable that a concern for the optimal development of a learning organism must turn attention to the relationship of vision and the most important occupation of the young elementary child — reading.

The study of vision and the process of reading has occupied an historically honored role in the world of educational research. In no other aspect of the total school process has the study of vision been a part of educator concern as it has in the field of reading. The evaluation of a child's visual efficiency prior to his entrance into first grade remains a rarity in our society. The customary referral for visual care for children is derived from two sources: (1) the annual cursory school vision examination, and (2) a concerned teacher confronted with a child who is not responding as expected to the reading process. Visual defect has long been considered as a possible source of reading difficulty.

The study of eye movements as they relate to reading has been the subject of much research. (Tinker, 1959; Laycock, 1955a, 1955b; Gray, 1956; Gilbert, 1959a, b, c, and many others) Though there is a general similarity in patterns of eye movements, the individual appears to have a pattern which is characteristically specific to himself. Accuracy in focusing and ability to track horizontally, vertically and diagonally as well as perception and comprehension of the material bear upon the unique eye movements of the individual. Research shows a reduction in the number of fixations and duration of fixations as the organism advances towards adulthood. Tinker (1959) expressed the belief that training of eye movements are not necessary for reading improvement. It is rather that the eye movements will automatically improve as reading improves according to Tinker.

Forgays (1953) found a difference in the accuracy of word perception when words were exposed in the right and left fields of vision with greater accuracy occurring in the right field. Neurologic dominance and perception in right and left visual fields were also studied by Leavell and Beck (1959) among retarded readers. They reported seven conclusions from their data:

1. Inferior readers are superior in left visual fields.

2. Left-handed and left-eyed subjects see significantly better than mixed dominance subjects in left field at 1/25 second exposure.

3. Both left-handed left-eyed and right-handed right-eyed subjects see significantly better than mixed dominance subjects in left field at 1/50 second exposure.

4. The theory of equipotentiality between left and right hemiretina is not confirmed.

5. Subjects with established dominance see significantly better in right visual field than subjects with mixed dominance at 1/25 second exposure.

6. Established lateral dominance appears to favor efficiency in peripheral vision in both lateral halves of the visual field.

7. Other factors as reading fluency and education level may be related to peripheral visual efficiency.

The superiority in the right visual field of subjects with established dominance over those of mixed dominance suggests that cerebral dominance is a factor in peripheral vision. The notions of Delacato (1963) on cortical hemispheric dominance in relation to the reading process are also in this direction.

Speed of perception in reading is also influenced by restrictions in the central field of vision. (Eames, 1957) Beck (1960) found no significant differences in reversal errors in a monocular-binocular pair of equated groups and also no difference between dominant and non-dominant eyes, or in children with mixed laterality. Berner and Berner (1921) differentiated between dominance and binocular vision control. They concluded after investigating eye-hand confusion tendencies in 500 subjects that: (1) no confusions are likely to occur when the controlling eye in binocular vision is on the side of the preferred hand, (2) confusions will occur when the controlling eye is on the contralateral side, and (3) when two hands are used, confusion symptoms are more likely to occur if the controlling eye is on the opposite side from the preferred hand.

Benton, McCann and Larsen (1965) studied children lacking in binocularity for their ability to read. Children having one blind or enucleated eye and children having constant esotropia with no fusion, showed a relative absence of reading difficulty. They went on to study 250 children who showed signs of mixed dominance or incomplete dominance. They developed an eye-patching regimen over a period of six months to establish eye dominance and reported that 87% of their cases made significant improvements in their reading achievement.

The studies cited above represent an exceptionally small sampling of the vast body of literature in the field of vision and the reading process. The area of speed reading which has become prominent in recent years also is a fertile field of reporting on vision and reading. Taking data from all sources into consideration, it seems reasonably clear that it is possible to learn to read in the absence of binocularity. We would hesitate to suggest an automatic correlation between visual defect and potential reading problem. We are inclined to think that learning how to read has little to do with the state of one's vision. However, continuing to read, once basic techniques have been established, and sustaining an efficiency in reading with expansion in comprehension, rate and range of reading are in large measure based upon the visual efficiency the reader brings to the task. The primary act of reading may be learned regardless of refractive state but if one wishes to sustain his efficiency through time, his visual state will become a critical factor.

The relationship which exists between posture and vision must be regarded as another significant aspect of a movement orientation. Gesell (1947) commented that the changing space structure of the child's visual domain "is primarily determined by growth factors which shape the basic postural orientations of the organism" (p. 17) As we have continued to emphasize, the neophyte organism must build a visual space domain.

Harmon (1958) refers to the eyes as the pilot mechanism for the head and the head in turn is the pilot mechanism for the body—all working to bring the total organism to a spatial position where it can align with gravity in an organization which can be maintained with least effort. Duke-Elder (1942) spoke specifically of the "intimate association between movements of the eyes and changes in posture". A close functional correlation exists between the extraocular muscles and the labyrinths which record the movements of the head in space and the muscles of the neck which register movements of the head with respect to the trunk. Evidence cited by Harmon (1958) on the dioptric system of the eye and exploration of the architecture of the retina and the optic tract supports the notion that the eye serves the organism as a "sighting" mechanism for at least the body-posturing function of photostatic centering and balancing with the visual field. Gesell (1957) stated that "...a primary function of vision is to direct movement".

Grossfeld (1951) regarded visual space as a "system of reference at rest relative to the gravistatically fixed parts of the body". Vision is therefore localized in the frame of this system of reference.

> *...visual objects have in fact no other shape beside their gravistatically established order and consequently, no abstract shape of an object is independent of gravitational structure and interrelations. Localization, as space vision, is not photic but is by itself, a gravistatotonic process. To localize in space, in a visual field, means to localize in an optic extension of the somatic gravistatic equilibrium.*

Vernon (1952) spoke of the accuracy of the individual's sense of spatial orientation and accuracy of movement being dependent upon the maintenance "of the habitual relationship of the main coordinates of the visually perceived field with both kinesthetic and labyrinthine sensations (the latter producing together the vertical gravitational sense)". Vernon went on to say:

> The individual's feeling of stability depends upon the stability of this framework. If some part of the sensory data which constitutes the framework is impaired, or conflicts with some other part, stability is so far affected that the individual is disorientated, that is to say, he loses his impression of an exact and enduring position of his body in space. (p. 91)

As the coordinate system of the optics of the eye transforms the light pattern in projecting it to the retina the organism derives its frame of reference of apparent visual space. (Harmon, 1958)

The relationship of vision and posture has also been considered by Vernon (1952).

> The distance receptors impose an additional set of space coordinates upon the postural system, which in turn continually modified the coordinates of the space receptors... The direction of movement on the retina imposes a directional orientation in the posturing system. Conversely, the gravitational system imposes an orientation on the visual field. (p. 125)

Lashley (1942) lends further support to the posture-vision linkage:

> The visual system is primarily concerned with spatial orientation and for its transition from a sensory to a motor pattern can be most adequately conceived as an interplay of polarized systems or of interweaving dynamic patterns in which the spatial properties of the visual stimulus are translated by integration at a series of levels into modifications of the general pattern of postural organization. (p. 321)

Another citation from Vernon (1952) has bearing upon the point we are trying to clarify:

> For the moment, I wish to emphasize only the existence of these systems of space coordinates. Their influences pervade the motor system so that every gross movement of limbs and body is made with reference to the space system. The perceptions from the distance receptors, vision, hearing, and touch are also constantly modified and referred to the same space coordinates. The stimulus is there, in a definite place; it has definite relations to positions of the body, and it shifts with respect to the sense organ but not with respect to

general orientation, with changes in body posture. (p. 126)

Grossfeld (1951) described visual space as the transformation of two kinds of field energy, the electromagnetic field energy (light) and the gravitational field energy (physical space). Light and physical space are physical realities representing two kinds of field energy but our idea and designation of both come from the specific sensations they cause in us. Grossfeld went on to point out that "physiology of space in establishing this relation between physical and visual space gives the reason why, in modern physics, the field of gravitation is designated by the same word 'space' as is visual space".

Sherrington (1915) emphasized that "spatial perceptions are by no means purely visual but are rather 'visual-muscular labyrinthine'" and these concern the attitude of the whole body in relation to gravity and the task.

Two of the pioneers in the study of postural alignments and the relationships of these alignments to visual function were Lowman (1918) and Mills (1919). Their studies, demonstrating improvements in visual efficiencies through orthopedic treatment, went by essentially unnoticed by the majority of professionals engaged in visual care. As vision specialists exhausted other preoccupations and began to consider performance and vision as intertwined and interwoven, the contributions of these two men could be viewed in new perspective. The improvement or reduction of various forms of visual distortion by means of special exercises or activities aimed at achieving efficient skeletal alignment and optimal response to gravitational pull was recognized by these men more than 50 years ago, but it took many more years before others came to the same conclusion. (Harmon, 1965)

The answer to the question, "What is vision?" is not a matter of a simple direct statement. Theories are as plentiful as the number of authorities who set themselves to the task of answering the question. For some the answer is one of structure and physiology. For others it is a combination of physiology and perception. For still others, perception is the dominant word in defining vision. It may be images, effigies, mosaics, gradients, proton scatters, pulses along a neural path—on and on. It is likely that the answers lie within some composite of all of these in some magnificent matrix which defies reduction to a simple sentence.

From the authoritative opinions we have already cited, a number of elements can be defined in the construction of an answer. It is clear that vision is a dynamic, persistent ongoing behavior in a light sensitive organism seeking information. Vision is learned by an inquiring traveler to serve his needs. Each organism builds a visual domain—a visual space—defining such a domain in a gravitational field. Vision has survival value. It directs movement, localizes space, identifies significance and unifies data from other sources. It records data for retrieval in time. Vision and postural transport are significantly interrelated. We may even speculate that vision is something quite different to each individual viewer. Vision is, perhaps, what each individual defines it to be for his own purposes.

Projected by developmental momentum, the infant is thrust upon an illuminated world and utters his cry of recognition. Equipped by design to receive variations in light gradients, gifted with a retina and blessed with computational potential, he enters a technicolored expanse of space filled with objects—millions and millions of objects. His assignment is a singular one if he is to adapt, advance and exercise control over that luminant world—he must discriminate, differentiate, localize, organize, categorize, conceptualize and synthesize—he must collect information—he must find meaning for himself to promote his survival in a brightly lighted world. That luminant world is filled with a constant stream of data which must somehow be converted into information having value to the organism.

What a wondrous array of sights are displayed before the infant viewer—all his to take in and use. From the first burst of light to the last, his career as a seeing organism will consist of viewing, observing, peering, discerning, inspecting, checking, peeking, staring, glancing, gazing, squinting and noting. A tremendous amount of organizing must be undertaken as he grows in stature as a viewer. The demand to look is a constant demand. Gesell (1947) said of the infant viewer, "He is born with a pair of eyes but not with a visual world". It does not take him long, however, to set himself to the task of acquiring a visual world. The development of his visual world is influenced at every turn by antecedent and current movement demands and patterns. By the age of four months, the infant has become an avid "looker" and most of his waking day is spent looking at his world. (Gesell, 1947) From a steady stream of electrical pulses, he gradually builds a visual space world. Sherrington (1940) noted the mysteriousness of vision in his comment:

> *Electrical charges have in themselves not the faintest elements of the visual...have nothing of "distance", nor "vertical", nor "horizontal", nor "color", nor "brightness", nor "near", nor "far", nor visual anything—yet they conjure up all of these.*

All colors in the spectrum will become a part of his visual world. He will see beauty and he will see ugliness. At times the light will be too bright and at times too dim. There will be happy sights and sad sights. Panoramas will stretch before him and stark singularity will be his target at other times. Always there will be a background—always a foreground and always a texture to his world. He will achieve a visual appreciation of the circular, squared, triangular, rectangular, trapezoidal, hexagonal and cubical forms in the object surround. In remote space, he will follow a bird in flight, study cloud formations, watch a sunset, wish upon a star, be amazed by lightning flashes, consider the Milky Way, observe a distant herd of cows from the window of a speeding car and watch a kite dance in the wind. In far space, he will catch a fly ball in centerfield, watch a squirrel in a tree, see a movie, notice traffic signs and billboards, see a duck swim in a pond and observe traffic patterns. In mid space, he will find a favored cereal, the candy shelf and the ice cream freezer among the laden counters of the supermarket. He will toss a ball toward a target, watch favorite television programs, see a friend, look at flowers, note the hand position on a clock face, see the picture on the wall and observe the demonstrations of his teachers. In near space, he will inspect his bottle and rattle, study his food on the high chair tray, see the details of his mother's face, watch a tear roll down a cheek, follow a rain drop's course down a window pane, struggle with a puzzle, look at a picture — and most wonderful of all — discover that the little black marks on the page are intended to present him with information. Information will come from all sides and from all distances extended beyond his own reference point. Everywhere the data are present — if the observer will note them and use them to his advantage.

As a general rule, we can say that the world of space is laden with information which changes very little with the passage of time. The same world was there for ancestors, grandparents, parents and our current neophyte traveler.

Some new sights have been added by new inventions, different clothes and so on but the basic structures have remained the same. Essentially we may think of a visually stable world which yields more and more information day after day to the new inhabitant. The world changes little — the observer simply becomes more astute in his searching for information. The visual repertoire probably increases in supergeometric proportions as the viewer becomes more adept. The details were there all the time. He only comes to note more of them as he develops. That his luminant world is in actuality laden with information is an independent discovery that must be made by each observer individually. As soon as this discovery is made the eyes become more than anatomical units in a physiologic system — they become dynamic mobile tools for seeking and acquiring valuable information. The discovery of visual information changes a passively receptive being into a vigorously active searching being alert on all sides to possible sources of information. This particular discovery of the information potential to be tapped by looking is perhaps the critical turning point where sight becomes vision — where the purely sensory process becomes subservient to the percepto-cognitive process. This turning point may be achieved at different points in the developmental timetable by different travelers. If this discovery is made after age two, a significant reduction in visual efficiency may be anticipated. The neophyte traveler must discover very early in his experience that his eyes are under his control and can be directed to seek information.

If the discovery is delayed, the visual organization for efficiency does not occur along the expected lines promised by the design of the organism. At any given point in life, it should be possible in some manner to ascertain whether an individual viewer is getting as much information from his world as is visually possible. The discrepancy between what he sees and what he should be seeing or could be seeing must then be reflected in his total efficiency as some form of loss.

There are a number of events in the early motor period of the infant which might be classified as foundation stones for visual efficiency. The sucking reflex may be regarded as a convergence phenomenon drawing the total organism into a muscular convergence for survival purposes. From the convergence of fetal posturing the infant is designed to gustatorily converge to insure his survival. The rudiments of visual convergence may well be founded in the sucking reflex since the tongue itself has been shown to bear such a striking relationship to "tracking" behavior. Secondly, we may cite the tonic-neck-reflex patterning which enables the infant to sight down a line toward his extended hand. We have often been impressed by the possibility that the line of sight which may be measured from the interpupillary point of the infant and his outstretched hand in the TNR position is approximately the same line of sight which has been defined by Harmon (1958) as the comfortable line of sight for the six year old in the standing position holding a book to read. This line of sight described by Harmon as the optimal distance from eye to page for arms extended to hold a book, seems to us, to be the natural anatomic arc circumscribed by the arms when the extended arms of the TNR are eventually joined together at the midline by the infant in his effort to bimanually manipulate toys as he inspects them. It is suggested, therefore, that the TNR response serves as a second basic training element in the development of visual convergence. Since joining of the two hands at the midline for the tactual-kinesthetic and visual explorations of toys and other objects seems to be an inevitable successor to the TNR, this behavior must also be regarded as contributory to visual convergence. As a matter of routine every action of the infant which engages his visual attention upon an object held at midline by his two hands becomes a visual training exercise aimed at developing a convergence efficiency. While there are hundreds of experiences in which the infant will shift his gaze to the right or to the left, follow a moving target from the left field into the right field, track an object from the up vertical to the down vertical and so on, these all appear to be secondary experiences in visual performance calculated mainly to establish the periphery and expand the visual range. The critical experiences are those which contribute to convergence for in this manner the organism is expressing its essential unity. As Gesell's (1947) developmental study has pointed out the infant passes through a monocular stage, then a bi-ocular period and finally a binocular period eventuating in the normal course of development into a fusion capability. The design scheme of his visual patterning matches the general sequence of the total organism and seems only to be a final repetition of a basic scheme of monolateral organization leading to eventual reciprocal interweaving around a midline.

Vertical tracking of a target is probably closely related to the efficiency of the total vertical organization of the mobile organism. It is very likely that good horizontal visual tracking is intimately linked with the development of the horizontal coordinate which we have previously discussed. It is interesting to note that the advent of fusion in the child's visual performance seems to be chronologically related to the time span devoted to the acquisition of the "Z" axis in his general patterning. It is as though his visual system has carefully read the script of his total developmental drama and emerges upon the scene on proper cue to support the next dramatic scene. Developmentally, it seems clear that when a greater degree of visual proficiency seems called for to insure the next developmental advance the visual timetable rises to the occasion and stands ready to serve the organism.

If all goes well in the total scheme of development from infancy to the fifth, sixth or seventh year, it would seem reasonable to assume that the natural design of the visual systems would comfortably bring the young child to the academic task as a binocularly efficient fusing being organized to sustain convergence as necessary in the regular demands of daily living.

We may regard his visual system as passing through an organizational period in the four zones of space as well. Initially his vision is organized in near space and progressively expands to establishing clarity of detail in mid, far and remote space. Again, we may consider that if all goes well in the visual experiencing the earthling should arrive at first grade age with a reasonable degree of visual proficiency in all four zones of space. He should experience little difficulty with resolving the details of the near-point task, manage the clarification of objects and people in mid space and identify and localize with clarity that portion of his world which occurs in far and remote space.

For all practical purposes, we can consider his basic training in visual efficiency to have been completed by the time he has reached his seventh birthday if his visual experiencing has been comfortable, economic, progressive and developmentally expansive during the formative years. Visual development after that time can probably be considered as a refinement devoted to sharpening minute detail through continuous multiples of near space behavior, intensifying the details of mid space, expanding the range of far space and exploring the enormous potential of remote space. After the seventh year, it is likely that the mechanics of the visual system have nothing more to learn — they simply serve the organism to expand upon and extend his information getting capability. Like all other motor systems within the organism, the visual system can now be assigned to the level of habituation while cognitive expansion becomes the focus of developmental movement. By this time the organism has learned to look and now can devote his full energy to looking to learn. By this time he has learned to scan and can direct his scanning toward a search for increased information. By this time convergence is an habitual state throughout the organism and it automatically serves the informational process. By this time his eyes team readily and he has a comfortable and sustaining state of bilateral consistency in the visual system. He looks where he wants to look. He shifts comfortably from near space to far space as he needs to for the demands which may confront him moment after moment. He can sustain near-point activities over a protracted period of time benefiting from the input and find an expression of far point activity to counterbalance the near-point containment.

This is the state of visual efficiency which seems to be his heritage according to his anatomic design. This is the promise laden in the first burst of radiant energy which greets him upon emergence from the womb. This is how it should be if all goes well along the developmental timetable from infancy onward. Seven years, however, is a long span of time and as we have already seen there is much, much groundwork to be done to lay a proper foundation for visual efficiency. Literally, we may speak of ten components of Movement Efficiency which are all necessary to ensure this ideal state of visual efficiency. In some manner the degree of efficiency achieved in each of the previous ten components we have discussed has a direct bearing upon the eventual efficiency of the visual system. The workload imposed upon the organism to achieve a comfortable and economic organization of so many components is a far more formidable task than we have ever assumed. In our present society, few children achieve this state of ideal visual efficiency. The penalty of civilization—modern and complex as it may be—is exacted upon the visual system. It is a regrettable commentary upon the complexity of modern civilization that only a small percentage of children reach the period of academic demand in an ideal state of visual efficiency.

Civilization has changed man's survival meridian from the horizon to the printed page and within this achievement resides the explanation for an essentially "visually inefficient" society. It is perhaps more pertinent to concentrate upon the delineation of the dynamics of a visual problem than to focus upon a discussion of what is considered to be the normal dynamics of vision.

In a study of the incidence of visual defects among 160,000 Texas school children conducted by Harmon (1942), it was pointed out that while only 20% of the kindergarten children showed measurable visual deviations, the percentage rose to 40% by the time that group reached second grade and increased to 60% upon testing in the fifth grade. Six out of every ten elementary school children revealed a measurable visual problem by the time they reached the fifth grade. This does not mean that corrective lenses were supplied. It is simply a clear cut study of incidence. In 1965 we sampled 2,000 elementary school children in the Oconomowoc, Wisconsin school system asking teachers to simply report the number of children in each class who wore lenses. The incidence rose in progression from 2% in the kindergarten to 32% in the sixth grade. This study did not investigate the nature of the visual problems, it simply sought an incidence figure in the belief that a progressive incidence would be observed. By implication the 32% figure represents only those children who have been professionally examined and found to require lenses.

Stockwell (1952) reported that 45.5% of the 960 children she studied had deficient vision to the extent of requiring lenses. Braly (1937) found 38% of his deaf population required lenses and Myklebust (1960) placed the incidence of visual disorders among deaf children at 40-50% and noted hyperopia as being of highest incidence. The general incidence among other disability groups tends to fall within the 30-50% range. The usual technique for defining the incidence of visual problems is to rely upon a criterion of wearing lenses or requiring lenses upon examination. This criterion imposes upon the survey a lens-orientation which tends to ignore the concept of visual efficiency as it relates to sustaining such efficiency on a continuing basis over years of performance. Harmon's study has pointed to a cumulative progression through the grades. It seems from the studies cited and many others that the development of a visual problem is the inevitable fate of at least a majority of the nation's population. As we continue our efforts to study the nature of visual efficiency in complex mobile organisms, it becomes increasingly clear that the individual who escapes the development of a visual problem becomes more and more of a rarity in our society. Consequently, the dynamics of visual deviation become more critical to our effort to understand human performance than the dynamics of normal optics.

Opinions on the critical period in development for the onset of visual problems vary. Those who believe in a genetic factor suggest that a visual problem is some obscured consequence of heredity or at least "genetically plotted". Gesell (1947) in his developmental studies emphasized the critical period at ages four and five when the child was defining a lateral world as being the main period of definition. Skeffington (1964) and his optometric colleagues, while not ignoring the possibilities of earlier incidence, view the intensity of containment in the "socially compulsive near-centered task of school work" to be the primary period for the development of visual problems. Vision specialists also hold the belief that a visual problem may develop at any point in life and we will comment further on this point later in this chapter. Now, however, we wish to express a belief that the primary source of a visual problem can be assigned to that early period in life when the child is acquiring a vertical orientation to his world of space. Our reasoning follows along these lines: if the organism relies upon visual steering to guide his body in transport through space, his alignment for postural transport is immediately linked with his visual system in an interaction in which both vision and postural alignment are simultaneously productive in achieving efficiency in movement.

As we have already pointed out, it seems abundantly clear that the organic architecture intended an emphatic development period to be devoted to the building of the vertical coordinate. The total convergence of the organism is continuously constructed along a vertical midline in a massive array of movement learning during the first four years. When proper centering on a task and alignment of the mobile unit are not a continuous by product of the visually steered movement explorations, the penalty for malalignment and miscentering is exacted upon the vertical coordinate. An improperly organized or skewed vertical orientation, in our thinking, becomes the seed bed for the visual problem. The exact nature of the visual problem may be deferred in its delineation until the organism has been placed under an adequate amount of stress to call forth the more discernible aspects of a visual problem but the foundation for its existence is laid in the gravitational vineyard where the earthling builds his vertical orientation. While we are in accord with the incidence figures showing the critical import of the "socially compulsive near centered task" as a culprit in the staging of a visual problem, we are inclined to regard this period as the stress period enacted upon an organism that is more or less economically and comfortably oriented in the vertical. Under the stress of containment within the "near centered task" experienced by the learner, the adequacy of his vertical organization becomes the critical indicator of the speed with which the individual must seek to find a resolution. We suggest that those children holding a well-defined vertical coordinate can tolerate more stress for longer periods of time than those who have an inadequate vertical. Any deviation in the vertical organization is an invitation to a visual problem. Stress quotients being equalized, the child with the poor vertical is more susceptible than the one with the good vertical to the onset of a visual problem.

The development of the horizontal coordinate for action emerges from the vertical. If the vertical is not properly established the developmental momentum pushing the child into horizontal emphasis places the child into an organization conflict between visceral and skeletal components. This is the conflict period which according to Gesell (1949) forces some children to resolve this dilemma through the route of myopia and others to resort to strabismus.

Incidence figures on visual problems in children show a progressive increment with each passing grade level. (Harmon, 1958) Each grade year shows a higher percentage of problems. It takes longer for academic stress to take its visual toll upon some children than others. We suspect that the progressive increase is linked to the vertical coordinate. The better verticals take longer to show the signs. We do not mean to ignore the fact that some children seem to "escape" this elementary dilemma until high school years or even college or later adulthood.

In a nation of people so dedicated to the achievement of literacy among all of its members, it is probably not possible to avoid the development of visual problems among all of its members. We can no longer ask the question, "Does this person have a visual problem?" with any degree of security that a yes-no possibility exists. The more appropriate question to be asked is, "What type of a visual problem does this person have?". Civilization in our Space Age era has changed the terrain of survival from the horizon to the printed page, the column of figures, the telephone and the speedometer. It is indeed a rare individual who can escape from some form of visual problem. The absence of a set of lenses worn before the eyes or on the eyes does not constitute a mark of freedom. Noting such an individual who has been "cleared" by visual examination and who can boastfully claim that there is "nothing wrong with his vision" one must reserve judgment relying upon the phrase, "the world has not yet demanded a high degree of visual efficiency". The individual by many different routes may well have avoided a visual containment and achieved success by general, social and economic standards. We can only suggest that "he has not yet been put to the test".

Any individual whose efficiency in visual performance does not enable him to function with equal and sustained skills in all four space zones, near, mid, far and remote, under survival stress as we have defined it, has a visual problem. His visual problem may vary in degree and kind — it may be present under only certain circumstances — it may be in the early stages of development — but it is an inevitable product of a symbolically oriented world.

There is a high degree of predictable certainty that the thousands of babies born this day will acquire a visual problem by the end of the third grade or be well underway in the development of such a problem.

According to the line of reasoning, we have presented in our discussion of the Percepto-Cognitive systems any interference with the rich, full development of the gustatory, olfactory, tactual, kinesthetic and auditory modes, will result in some diminution of the full achievement of visual efficiency. The emergence of an optimal state of visual efficiency relies upon each of the lesser modes contributing the full measure of its design to the perfect utilization of vision as the ultimate synthesizer of survival information.

In a world filled with prejudice, distrust, absence of respect, declining morality, inequalities, and a persisting state of imminent disaster, full visual efficiency is difficult to develop. Where the available statistics reveal a staggering incidence of visual problems among our nation's school children visual efficiency can scarcely be expected to flourish. Where available authoritative opinion places the incidence of significant postural deviation at 90% of our population and we have related posture to vision, it is difficult to imagine the rare person who has escaped a visual problem.

Harmon (1959) has estimated that the average school child spends approximately 80% of his school day engaged in near point tasks at desk or table top level and must make both a visual and a postural adjustment to this containment. In the discussion to follow we must rely heavily upon the comments of Harmon who has devoted many years to the study of this topic in building our argument.

Organizing and establishing an adequate visual base with the body's basic responses to gravity and proper alignment of supporting structures (head, neck, trunk, etc.) and of moving parts (such as eyes and hands) in a semiflexible machine such as the human body is a function of the light gradient over the total visual field.

Whether organization is achieved properly and with least effort so that the child has available a maximum of resources for performing the purposeful part of the task depends upon the way the total brightness pattern is organized over the entire visual field. The more unbalanced this brightness pattern is, the more effort it takes to stay in balance with the task; the more stress producing misalignment there is between body parts, then the less energy and physiologic equipment there is available for the performance of the learning task. (Harmon, 1958, p. A33)

When a close visually centered task is sustained, such as in school tasks, in drafting and accounting room, etc. the first functions of vision are optokinetic and body balancing, localization and centering on the task. Full resolution follows these, not as a first function of the details of the task, but as a result of the functions of establishing the eye and body balances necessary to center on the task and establishing the necessary frames of reference for direction of performance. In fact some of these centering and balancing functions would seem to have their sensory origin, not even in the central areas of the retina, but in the periphery. (Harmon, 1958)

Because of the close relationship of bodily actions and meaningful vision—both in the higher integrated functions of perception and in the power processes of feedback between eyes, trunk, neck and labyrinth—adverse stress in any segment of this complex produces adverse functioning throughout the complex. (Harmon, 1965)

Misdirected, misapplied or too little or too much stress leads to uncommunicable and unreal meanings and eventually to malconditioning to maladaptations and finally to warping of structure—all to the detriment of the "seeing" individual. (Harmon, 1965)

Harmon (1958) has provided data to show that certain **constant** relationships exist in the forward inclination of the head and trunk in sustained close visually centered activities as a result of body balancing and orientation reflex mechanisms. When stimulated to such activity the trunk and the head lean forward out of the perpendicular to a position where they can be supported in this inclination with a minimum expenditure of energy and means of minimum activity of the muscles supporting the weight of the head and trunk against the pull of gravity.

> *Visual definition of space, localization, size, orientation and three dimensional form and relationship in a learning task is largely a function of contrast in either light or color. Consequently, uncontrolled contrasts or lack of appropriate contrasts — such as overly "flat" lighted fields — which might not interefere with passing recognition of known things or symbols can distort localization, orientation, form, size and other visual characteristics needed for acquisition for full meaning in a sustained learning situation. (Harmon, 1958, p. A31)*

The necessity for giving consideration to the manner in which a task area is illuminated is related to the binocular function of the learner. An established opthalmological principle states that a difference of intensity of illumination between the two eyes amounting to over 12% leads to suspension of vision in the less illuminated eye. (Harmon, 1958) This principle holds practical significance for the desk top performance of the elementary, secondary and collegiate learner as well as for all adult workers whose daily work demands a containment at table top for long periods of time. An improperly lighted work surface whether it be in the first grade or the executive offices becomes an invitation to visual stress for the performer. The shadows, glares, and variances which unfortunately are often a part of the performer's regular working surround may create a sufficient variation to establish intermittent spans of performance time when one eye is suspended and other spans when both eyes are equally illuminated. Under equalized illumination, the worker can bring to the task a binocular function which is automatically more advantageous than a monocular function. In variable lighting surrounds, the most efficient learner is likely to experience varying degrees of discomfort and associated reductions in perception, comprehension and interest. In a similar surround an inefficient learner already struggling with content which is difficult, has his learning problem compounded by an illumination hazard. He becomes the victim of an error in engineering for human dynamics and is forced to contend with a hidden foe of which he is unaware. His energy for the task is dissipated in a search for visual comfort instead of being totally directed toward acquiring the advance in knowledge to which his task has invited him. Under such obstacles, he must either seek visual comfort or struggle with his learning under adverse conditions. For the majority of our nation's children social and economic demands do not permit a clear choice possibility. The learner must usually attempt to achieve the visual comfort and ALSO achieve the learning. In such a dilemma the compromise rarely favors the individual's achievement of greater efficiency. The typical result is to reduce visual efficiency and also to reduce learning efficiency. It is true that the individual does resolve his immediate problem. The long term consequences of his resolution are not immediately apparent, of course, but the toll is cumulative.

The work of Hebb, Riesen, Senden, Ronchi, Harmon, Gesell and many others accounts for a sizable weighting for the concept that vision is learned. Since we have already cited observations supporting the notion that each of the five previously discussed modes are learned and functionally organized the belief that vision is learned is harmonious with a general notion about the Percepto-Cognitive system. Each notion is relatively supported by the observations on the total. Accepting this belief of learningness leads to the suggestion that, in simple terms, vision may be learned at varying levels of efficiency from the very onset of retinal stimulation. It may be learned well or it may be poorly learned. Gesell (1957) has shown that the development of vision follows along the general principle of sequential progression. It is possible therefore, to consider various genetic factors, neurologic impairments, metabolic inadequacies and structural deformities as interferrents to the learning process. Learning to see may be adversely affected by physical or physiologic influences but regardless of the presence of such characteristics the infant viewer is still compelled to organize a visual domain. He must learn to see—whatever might be the organic state of his visual system. In general the incidence of such congenital interference appears to account for only a small percentage of the visual problems among our population. The usual state of affairs is that the infant enters an illuminated world with an unimpaired, naive, visual system.

Where and when does a visual problem originate? It must in some manner be generically related to the child's general state of learningness and derive from some effort to find significance.

Thrust into an illuminated world the newborn is under some degree of constancy of visual demand. He must sort out "the shadows, nuances, edges, contours and corners". He must seek information about variations in light gradients. The first critical period for the development of a visual problem is therefore designated as the first three months of life when the infant becomes a viewer. The second critical period for visual distortion may be assigned to the time span covering the intense struggle for gravitational control. When the visual system must be in readiness to steer the organism, define approach targets, avoid transport obstacles and contribute to the extension of the personal coordinate reference system the visual patterning must be appropriately interwoven with other processes. The efficiency with which the individual achieves a comfortable neophyte travel status in a gravitational field is in large measure determined by the adequacy of infantile visual learning. As we have previously noted that critical period may extend from the first year to the seventh year. The efficiency of the vertical coordinate becomes the primary target area for visual problems which may originate in the time span of the coordinate reference system.

Riesen's (1958) studies of visual deprivations among infant primates is of special interest here. Without a patterned visual environment in early infancy eye movements remained infantile. When the infant primates were brought into light after seven months, alternation of fixations and exotropia were pronounced. In further research, he found that when one eye was deprived of form stimulation during the learning of a discrimination the task learned remained specific to the uncovered eye.

A patternable environment becomes critical to visual development for the infant-toddler-preschool child. It is necessary for visual space computing.

Whatever the circumstances of viewing may be during this preschool period, we are inclined to believe that the thousands upon thousands of visual experiences which must inevitably be brought into some composite organization if we are to speak of the child as learning to see, must present varying degrees of difficulty for the child. He must continue to "push his vision" farther and farther out into space building clarity of detail in near, mid, far and remote space. This extension would logically seem to be a matter of many instances of indistinctness. In any of the space zones objects may be tilted, lighting may be insufficient, moving objects may travel too fast and so on. It is a period of visual space training when many errors occur but also many successes. Progressively the ratio of successful resolutions to failures turns in favor of the successful. Some degree of distortion is always present in the world. The path to visual efficiency is not an easy one. The world of objects, energies and people is unfortunately not organized into simple, separate, neatly packaged light gradients for the infant. He must work at building vision and he must labor diligently if he is to succeed. Distortion, imperfection, dulling, dimming, distance are universal obstacles to be managed on the road to visual efficiency. Why then do some children pass through this stage relatively unscathed while others seem to lay a solid foundation for inefficiency? While it is entirely possible to consider a number of explanations for this happening, we wish to underscore a concept of **cognitive effort** as being significantly related to early inefficiency. When the event, object, circumstance, person, scene and so on confronting the neophyte viewer is accompanied by any negative the possibility of such a view contributing to a visual problem is dependent upon the value placed upon the view by the viewer. When the view is important to satisfy whatever needs may be activated at the moment, the youngster will do whatever he must do to clear the image—he will twist his head, bend his neck, close one eye, move to another vantage point and so on. We hold forth the contention that the preschool child with a visual problem has literally been confronted with too many distortions which were imperative to resolve but could not be comfortably resolved due to insufficient organization of all other components of movement efficiency. Because he placed a personal value upon the resolution, he did whatever he had to for success. His visual problem becomes the price of the need for information regardless of distortion.

The next critical period is usually described as the "socially compulsive near centered task" and refers to the intensive containment of the elementary learner in a visual space which Halstead (1947) has regarded as an area of persistent visual demand for which the human organism is "biologically least equipped". As soon as the learner enters the academic process he is committed to a confinement in near space. The visual demand becomes intensively near.

When a persistent visual demand exceeds his capability (the range of visual freedom he has achieved prior to the demand) the "looking" or "minding" efficiency he has attained by that time and the supportive strength in terms of efficiency of the other five information channels — he is confronted with two basic alternatives. He may elect to quit the demand or find some method of adapting. If the elected course is to quit, he must withdraw, cease and escape. In this manner he can retain whatever visual efficiency he had prior to the demand, but he must then face the consequences of his escape. For the school child, the decision to quit the excessive visual demand may be manifest as distractibility, negativism, rebellion, lapses into day-dreaming or other forms of behavior which indicate his giving up on the task. The adult uses the same general pattern of escape mechanisms at a more sophisticated level. Such behavior in a school child is intolerable and a host of forces are generated to devise some means to return him to the task since his containment within the task is necessary to his academic advancement. Usually, the escape process simply moves the child "from the frying pan into the fire". The preferred course of action is to meet excessive visual demand by adaptation.

Such a course has less social consequences but greater personal consequence. The personal consequence is incurred in the form of a postural warp and a visual problem. The demand is a survival demand in the jungle of academics. Each student becomes keenly aware of his demand to conform to expectancy, match his peers, satisfy his teacher and live up to the expectations of his parents. He soon learns that the academically oriented near-point task is a way of life and represents his way to "make a living" in the world of school. When the print becomes fuzzy or the graphic signals jump, he tries to clear the image. He explores various methods of "hold on to the task" as he struggles for competency. He intensifies his scanning and searching. He tilts his head to find a better light angle. He bends intently into the task and increases bodily tension. He wiggles himself into a temporarily more comfortable position to reduce his muscular tension and to find a comfortable visual angle. He twists toward a light source or away from it. He tries to avoid glare. He tightens and loosens his whole system. He is in the midst of a survival struggle. His "life" depends on his success. He must achieve. His parents have told him so in words or attitude. His teacher conveys the urgency. His classmates exert their competitive influence. He gets the message. He fights for his academic life. His struggle is further complicated by his physical confinement to a desk. For the most part, the rules of the game contain him in his two foot square of "classroom learning space". Release from this confinement may be planned by his teacher at intervals but as a general rule, his self-initiated escape from his "space" is frowned upon. His academic sentence is to hard labor at gaining information from little black marks printed by others which are called numbers, words and letters or to black marks made by himself to represent the same trio. The battle is to achieve meaning. He **must** learn his trade. His promotion in the shop depends upon it. The adults before him have already plotted the course for many years to come. If he wishes to stay in the mainstream of education he must fulfill the job specifications. The specifications are for achievement.

So here is our young warrior thrust upon the battlefield of academics into armed combat with graphic symbolism. His five previous years of basic training were designed to prepare him for this battle. His conquest depends upon whether he has learned his lessons of performance well or whether his basic training contained all the necessary prerequisites.

Essentially the child is challenged by the question of whether his visual efficiency has now emerged to a position of primacy and whether all other processing modes were efficiently established in a progressive pattern of ascending complexity, each fitting into its proper position of emphasis and each having contributed toward the development of the next mode. If this organization of efficiencies has been properly prepared in the five year basic training, he enters the battle optimally prepared. Unfortunately, the likelihood of such efficiency organization decreases as a host of preschool circumstances contrive to make him a casualty of civilization before he ever enters the battlefield of the elementary school. Having already become a casualty of civilization as a result of forces beyond his capability, he must struggle diligently lest he becomes another listing — as a casualty of education.

Critical periods for visual stress can occur at any time after the elementary school period. Visual containment tends to intensify as the natural sequence of academic work progressively occasions greater amounts of time to be spent in the acts of reading and writing. Always there is the question of whether the individual's current state of visual efficiency is adequate to the task which confronts him. If the efficiency is adequate, the containment is tolerated and successful resolution occurs. If the efficiency is not adequate, the containment becomes a stress, not only upon the visual system but upon the entire percepto-cognitive system and some adaptation must take place. Faced with some degree of prolonged stress, the organism searches for some way to come to balance. He must search for comfort.

Apell and Streff (1964) reported a longitudinal study of the infant's visual development from the crib to the classroom. According to their study the child goes through the stages of being astigmatic, myopic, anisometropic, strabismic and so on. If these persist, the ocular defect is established. In this exploratory process the infant and toddler samples deviational states as though he were evaluating the beneficial potential of each, discarding one after another — or retaining the deviational state which appears to have value. As he resolves each dilemma of asymmetry which confronts him, he sorts out the deviational listing in relationship to himself. What continues to have value is retained — what proves to be of no significant value is dismissed.

What Apell and Streff have described for the young child is probably the usual course of reaction to visual stress at whatever age it may confront the dynamic organism. The individual attempts to resolve his dilemma through a variety of visual adjustments as though he were fully aware of all the possibilities which could be employed and finally selects a particular visual state which accomplishes the resolutions he desires. The individual **selects** a visual problem after a period of search and achieves a compromise within himself. In selecting a particular visual state, he accepts it as a solution to a pressing problem but at the same time, reduces his general visual freedom. When he selects myopia, he gives up sustained clarity in the far field. When he selects astigmatism, he reduces his total range. As he selects a problem, he automatically reduces his overall freedom. We think of this selection process as a matter of accepting the limitation upon full efficiency in favor of resolving the immediate persisting stress.

There is a common belief that the wearing of lenses is a signal that the wearer has a visual problem. We regard the incidence of visual problems, however, to be much greater than those represented by lens wearers. It is possible for an individual to be unaware that he is less efficient than he could be. If his solution to visual stress has produced a degree of comfort which sustains him over time he may feel no visual discomfort and consequently seek no help. Not every visual problem demands a search for lenses but every visual problem results in some diminution to visual efficiency.

The presence of a visual problem is a significant indication that the total organism has met with some form of adverse stress which could not be resolved comfortably and economically by the matrix of efficiencies available to the organism. Every disability group that has been studied in relation to incidence of visual defects has shown a significant percentage of cases with noted ocular distortions. The figures on postural deviation point to 90% or more of our population to have such a problem. Harmon's figures show a gradual rise in percentages of visual problems among normal elementary children. There is some likelihood that any impairment to sensory functioning in any cognitive mode will eventually be manifest in the visual system. Similarly, we would suspect that any form of interference with postural organization will be manifest in the visual system. We are inclined to the belief that the visual system will bear the eventual penalty for any deviation in development. Bartley (1951) wrote, "Although it has usually been supposed that discomfort localized in the eyes must originate there, some evidence suggests that much of the localized discomfort is a function of the organism as a whole, becoming localized when visual achievement becomes unsatisfactory."

The intimate linkage of vision with the total muscular system leads to the conclusion that an ocular defect is replicated throughout the organism. The strabismic patient is strabismic throughout his performance range. It is logical to believe that the solution of strabismus which seemed most valuable to the organism to resolve his dilemma in clarifying the world and bringing that external world into some state of balance for him also required a head to foot adaptation. He did not limit his adaptation to his visual system. If he had limited his resolution simply to vision he would not have solved his conflict but simply have further confused the issue of adjustment by setting other systems to imbalanced function. He must find a state of balance for today's problem whatever the long range cost might be. His problem is **now** and his solution must be now. Long range consequences cannot be evaluated at a conscious level. His solution is always dictated by a survival need.

Our concern for the incidence of visual problems is not based upon physiologic considerations in the sense of deficiencies, but rather based upon a concern for the consequences of a visual problem upon the achievement of optimal Movement Efficiency. Man is anatomically designed as a binocular organism capable of fusing information from bilateral circuits into meaningful action patterns. What has usually been referred to as visual fusion is but an introductory step to a higher order fusion which we designate as "cognitive fusion". Each modality approaches its optimal functioning level by achieving a character of fusion, e.g., binaural fusion, bimanual fusion. Man seems therefore destined to achieve a fusional integration at all levels if he is to fully express the potential of his design. When fusion in any mode is not achieved, the penalty is paid in terms of reductions in information processing. Failure to achieve a consistent state of binocular matching of the two circuits means that the organism is functioning at a lesser level than his design potential and as a consequence, some reduction in efficiency is inevitable.

When we speak of the visual mode as the highest order modality in the percepto-cognitive system, we prefer to discuss it as a system of visual dynamics, certainly incorporating the general mechanics of sight but not limited to a light gradient relationship. Visual dynamics relates to the full range of experiencing which may occur for an individual in which the visual system plays a primary, secondary or even remote role. Vision may operate as a directing force or as a confirming agent for all other modes.

We view vision as the synthesizing agent for experiencing in all modes. Vision becomes the mechanism which converts all other modal information to a common denominator — visualization. Visualization is the common denominator for all modal information if it is to be integrated with the growing body of knowledge accumulating in the curious learner. It is the tool used by the human organism to create the effigies of which Ronchi speaks, from whatever modal source they may be derived.

Reading a description of a scene, an encounter, a landscape, a phrase enables the reader to conjure up the effigy suggested by the words. Sounds can also trigger pictures. Touches can serve to stimulate a mental picture. A smell or a taste can produce a mental picture. In the case of reading, there is an external stimulation impinging upon the retina but the light scatter from the printed page is quite different from the mental picture called forth by the light. In the other examples given, there need be no light gradients involved and yet a visualization can take place. One may read an adventure story and become muscularly fatigued by kinesthetic empathy with descriptions of vigorous physical activity. The smell of food may produce a full image of the cooking or the finished food placed invitingly upon the plate. Pictures may portray a garden scene so realistically that one may smell the flowers from the canvas. A picture of food on a sign or a magazine page may conjure smell, taste, texture and so on. An extensive list of examples could be drawn where visual stimulation serves to call forth gustatory, olfactory, tactual, kinesthetic and auditory responses as well as where stimulation of any of the other five modes serve to call forth a visualization. Many taste patterns are acquired on a visual association basis with that which appears inviting more likely to be perceived as tasty. Similarly, many smell experiences are governed by an object "looking as if it would smell that way". Illustrations of intramodal associations could go on and on. The marvel of the retina is a further illustration of visual primacy. Even when a stimulation is auditory, gustatory, kinesthetic and so on — retinoscopic study has revealed that a color shift occurs in the retina to signal the occurrence of cognition. The chemico-biologic response to cognition is observable in the retina. It would appear that by design there is a visual process — a sort of seeingness — that is a part of all perception regardless of the modality involved. It is as though the organism "sees what it tastes, smells, hears, touches and feels". Even though no light scatter from the external world is involved, the retina participates in the experiencing. Cognition retinoscopy continues to show a definite color shift when mental closure is achieved and a dulling when search for meaning or absence of meaning is present. It is probably true that the cognitive efficiency of all six percepto-cognitive modes is measurable in terms of retinal chemical responsiveness. All modes are probably visual in final analysis. The efficiency of any single mode or combination of modes in the performing individual will depend upon the complexity of the development of visualization. All modes are related to visualization.

We do not think of visualization as a process for manufacturing images which have any form of metrics involved but rather as a system for creating the effigies of Ronchi, the "computations" of Skeffington, the "spatial mosaics" of Riesen, and the "mental manipulations" of Zimmerman (1954).

We regard visualization as the dynamic emergent of "cognitive fusion". Visualization is the word we should like to apply to the total buildup of behavior in an attentive listener which culminates in a nod of comprehension, a facial expression of cognitive grasp, a verbalization of "I see", "I understand", "Now I get it" and so on. It is the "closure" and the gestalten of the Gestaltists—the hypothesis confirmation of Postman—the "pooling and weighting" which Helson describes—the functional emergent from the cell assemblies and phase sequences of Hebb — the product of the transactionalists. Visualization is built from all of these and incorporates them all—and more. Visualization becomes the agent for synthesizing, revising, retrieving, computing, evaluating and designing.

As a consequence of our belief about the nature of visualization, we are inclined to add to our earlier statement "children learn to see in order that they may see to learn" — "towards the building of visualization which will enable them to mentally manipulate that which they cannot see". What in earlier experiences had to be physically present to be touched, tasted, smelled, felt, heard or seen eventually arrives at a point where effigies of all sensory experiencing can be conjured up for the individual by a sequence of graphic symbols arranged on a printed page.

The entire scheme of development of visual dynamics appears to be a matter of learning to progressively look at less and see more.

Visualization is, by design, the most economic, most flexible, most expansive and swiftest mode for processing information. All other modes contribute to its development and it, in turn, enriches and expands the functional efficiency of all others. Visualization is cognitized vision—cognitized audition—cognitized tactuality — and so on. Thus, the task of the individual is not only to become an astute observer, a careful viewer and an organizer of visual space but to extend his development beyond such accomplishments into the realm of visualization—where his entire percepto-cognitive system may express its full potential.

Visualization becomes the major tool for fashioning the terrain of cognitive space. It is the key to movement efficiency.

We can say again that vision means many things to many people. It is like a crystal chandelier glittering in different colors as the spotlights of concern play upon it.

Wherever one stands and however one looks the view may be different. Each theorist, investigator or clinician has a particular cognitive stance and the view varies in color and shade.

Our major concern is to place the visual mode at the pinnacle of the Percepto-Cognitive hierarchy. All modes are beholden to the visual.

We are reminded again of Gesell's statement that the understanding of the child will help to understand his vision and his vision will help us to understand the child. We cannot depart from the discussion of the Percepto-Cognitive modes without indicating our firm belief that the understanding of the nature and quality of each learner's visual efficiency, as we have defined the terms, must become the matrix from which the full comprehension of learning will eventually be derived.

The core components of Movement Efficiency have been discussed and elaborated. Eleven foundation stones give movement efficiency substance and solidity. We can turn now to the components which enrich the basic structures and provide the learner with the degrees of freedom to move toward the full expression of his capabilities.

16

DEGREES

OF

FREEDOM-

BILATERALITY

A dynamic mobile organism undertakes a prodigious assignment when he initiates the task of fashioning a meaningful organization in the world of space. He is faced with a constant stream of variabilities from a multiple energy surround which must somehow be stabilized for his security and yet must allow for the constancy of variation that is a necessary part of his advancement to a more and more complex state. There is permanence and temporariness. There is static-ness and dynamic-ness. There are similarities and differences. There are quiet and noise, lightness and darkness, softness and hardness. Objects move swiftly and slowly. Some are fixed in place and some move. He lives in a polarized world where some form of a continuum stretches between the polar opposites constantly. We may even speak of the learner traveling on a terrain with acres upon acres of continua with which he must become acquainted. Not only must he become acquainted with an immense number of polar opposites but he must also acquire the capability to move freely on those continua in either direction. The learner must be free to move. When he is bound tightly in ignorance, his movement is limited. When he is imprisoned by bias and prejudice he loses degrees of freedom. Man requires ranges, ratios, proportions, amplitudes and scope. He is a composite of gradations and gradients of performance. He must be able to emphasize, underline, stress and accent. To do this he must acquire a range of performance in all domains and fields of space. He must travel freely without encumberance, emphasizing what is important as he moves, accenting, highlighting, stressing and underlining the special and the significant. He must sort, discriminate, classify, rank, scale, grade, evaluate and arrange. To exercise such a range of action, he must be free to move.

Four components which seem most directly to permit man the full freedom to move have been designated under the general heading of Degrees of Freedom. **Bilaterality** grants a freedom to movement. **Flexibility** gives the range for adapting in a multivariant world and **Rhythm** provides the grace and ease of movement that is necessary to economically promote efficiency. **Motor planning** provides the learner with freedom to direct his own performance towards his survival ends.

Bilaterality

The study of unilaterality has engaged the attention of investigators far more than bilaterality. Hundreds of studies of handedness have been conducted to establish the incidence of right handedness and left handedness as well as to speculate upon the causative factors. Whether handedness is genetically determined or learned in a family context remains an unresolved issue. (Gaddes, 1966)

Dennis (1935) observed fraternal twins and concluded that laterality preferences were due to innate factors. Lederer (1939) studied infants during the first two years of life and found no clear signs of handedness. Gaddes (1966) has pointed out that the source of handedness cannot be proven at this time. Each viewpoint, constitutional factors, Mendelian trait, fetal position, social learning and so on has its respective group of authoritative advocates.

Jones (1931) computed a dextrality ratio in five tests on preschoolers from 18-66 months which allowed them to resolve the task with one hand, both or in alternation and found that girls used the right hand oftener than boys and further, that the use of the right hand increased more with age for girls than it did for boys. The sex difference was attributed to faster maturation among girls.

One factor of spatial orientation for the young child resides in the unilateral preference of the parents. In hundreds of different relationships, the preference of the parent determines the contralateral orientation of the child. In dressing the child, feeding him, bathing, washing face and hands the right handed parent tends to orient the child's position for the parents' ease and comfort in ministering to the child.

The exact contribution of this parental lateral orientation to child ministration is probably unmeasurable but the persistence of this "dis-centering" phenomenon merits consideration in the study of techniques for optimizing the movement efficiency of children. The frequency with which this unilateral orientation causes a torqued postural alignment for the child in literally thousands of prosaic child-rearing situations suggests at least the possibility that such practices may have consequences which have thus far been completely ignored in the study of child development.

The incidence of right hand-preferred people and that of left hand-preferred has continued to run the same general 85-15% ratio in most studies which have been conducted. As investigators changed their focus from the handedness to the sidedness of man seeking to establish an incidence of unilateral preference for handedness, footedness, earness and eyeness, the discovery of a nagging percentage of cases was always present who gave evidence of a right side preference in a foot or an eye and a left side preference in an ear and a hand and multiple varieties of criss-crossing preferences. From such findings arose the concept of mixed dominance implying that the individual had localized certain preferences in the right hemisphere and others in the left hemisphere. For those who subscribe to the theory of cerebral dominance, a finding of mixed dominance became an inevitable etiologic significance in accounting for a wide variety of problems in performance.

The recent symposium on hemispheric relationships (Mountcastle, 1962) indicates that investigators are now principally concerned with the interaction and interrelatedness of the two hemispheres and that the traditional concept of cerebral dominance is losing favor. Pribam (1962) proposed the notion that one side of the brain provides for stabilization in space and the other stabilization in time. Others seem to accept the notion that the right hemisphere is devoted to spatial relationships while the left is devoted to language relationships. There is now some belief in the symmetry of the two hemispheres and there are those who believe in asymmetry.

Tschirgi (1958) and Mach (1959) suggest that a true bilateral symmetry in the brain would pose a dilemma of differentiation to the brain and that evolution, therefore, is dedicated to increasing the asymmetry as an aid to differentiation of stimuli. Tschirgi particularly has expressed the belief that "awareness of spatial position is...dependent upon asymmetry of the perceiving system". Tschirgi continued his argument by expressing the belief that man is only just beginning to develop a functional difference between the two hemispheres and that his universe has only dimly achieved three dimensions. He felt that man may now be able to truly distinguish "left from right" but that he frequently made mistakes. Mach believed that man's ability to differentiate between the two modes of horizontal orientation depended upon some sort of proprioceptive difference and "possibly in the last resort on some kind of chemical difference".

It seems safe to conclude at this point that investigators have reached no true concordance of fact on either the concept of handedness or the activity relationships of the two hemispheres. There is common agreement on the fact that man is a bilaterally equating organism when it comes to his eyes and his ears and legs but disagreement when it comes to his hands. Common observation indicates that there are children and adults who are left handed, right handed or so called ambidextrous. Acuity measures continue to reflect a "better eye" or a "better ear". However, one might observe the unilateral preference, item by item there are those who are successful performers and those who are unsuccessful. We are concerned with setting forth the notion of a bilateral equation throughout the human organism. Any finding of inequality is disturbing to the equation unless the individual organism has counterbalanced the inequality in one system by adapting another system to serve "above and beyond the call of duty". It is likely that the organism continues distorting one system after another— always to insure the equation of a previous system and as a consequence falls within Harmon's (1958) statement that "an organism grows along a line of stress in order to avoid a stress".

The loss of the well balanced bilateral equation serves always to restrict the organism and thereby, reduce the freedom of movement. Any life circumstance which causes the individual to operate in spatial computing with any less than complete bilateral equalized consistency in the two visual circuits is definable as a loss of degrees of freedom to utilize the full potential of the visual mechanism in acquiring information of value. Any differential in auditory circuiting must also be regarded as a reduction to the information getting potential. In a similar manner, the emphatic development of manual unilaterality with assignment of the contralateral hand to the status of a passive companion of only complementary value must also be viewed as a reduction to freedom of movement.

It is likely that the average individual in our society is unilaterally skillful, possessing a wide variety of competencies on the right side, hand and foot and very few if any competencies on the contralateral side. The non-preferred arm and hand may be used as a carrier of bundles, books, packages, umbrellas, etc. in order that the preferred hand may be available for any tasks requiring dexterity. The loss of the preferred hand because of sprain, break, shoulder separation, etc. usually has the effect of causing the person to become relatively helpless and to require special help in buttoning clothes, dressing, washing, bathing, feeding, brushing of teeth, turning of door knobs, lighting of matches, writing, etc. The inefficiency of the contralateral side is painfully manifest. A similar impairment to the non-preferred side presents some inconvenience but does not reduce the individual to helplessness. Most of our society now must be regarded as survival oriented with efficiency on one side of their bodies with a state of inefficiency on the other. We must hope as a nation that if danger is to be thrust upon us individually that it comes on the side where we are better prepared to meet it. Danger approaching from the contralateral side will be met with reduced reaction time, less efficiency and less sustaining power. Our hope lies in our ability to define danger in sufficient time to turn our bodies to the preferred side so we may bring the higher efficiency to bear. Yet by anatomical design we are equipped as bilaterally equating.

Only as some degree of equality is achieved in the functional efficiency of both sides of a bilateral organism can we establish a true freedom of movement. Freedom to move comfortably, economically and with survival security must characterize the efficient mover on both sides of his body and in the top and bottom vertical halves.

The critical value of this concept of bilaterality is best illustrated by the skilled performer whose grace and ease of movement is a delight to observe and a sight for which large audiences of spectators will be content to pay sizable sums for choice viewing seats.

The major league baseball player who can move with approximately equal facility to the right and left, covers his assigned "territory" on the playing field with no blind spots. The player who loses several seconds in initiating movements towards his contralateral side may have an imbalance on his field coverage so that the ball continues as a "hit" instead of becoming an "out". The moment another player comes on the scene who can demonstrate this equality of coverage on both sides, the "unequal" player finds himself in a "substitute" rather than "regular" player status. The boxer who cannot develop a bilateral punching ability with some degree of power poses only a one sided threat to his ring opponent. The dancer who cannot cast off nearly equally well with the left as well as the right, loses the picture of grace for all movements on the contralateral side. The basketball player who can shoot for baskets with either hand poses a more difficult problem to an opposing guard than the unilateral player. In athletics bilateral efficiency has value.

The swing of a golf club and a bat are both bilaterally oriented tasks in which the contribution of both hands or sides are critical to the convergence of directional force upon the ball. Example upon example may be cited where equality of contribution in some form of equation from both sides is a requirement for performance efficiency.

Bilateral efficiency is a prized achievement recognized by coaches and spectators alike as being of value to the movement freedom of the performer. It produces a better state of balance and permits greater agility. It is true that there are many stellar athletes who do not possess it but the performer who does is of greater value to his team and to himself.

The infant starts life as a bilateral being and oftentimes does not select a preferred side for performance until six or seven years. Failure to establish a manual preference by age three is usually viewed with some alarm by those who are "dominance oriented". Our own clinical experience over the past ten years with children who had not yet established a "handedness" has indicated the efficacy of a bilateral approach to such a problem. The children have been given an intensive series of activities which required both hands to be used simultaneously in performance followed by emphasis upon activities which required alternation of hands. This was followed by unilateral activities on either side. Under this approach the child selected his preferred hand with few signs of regression. The approach was modeled as a developmental recapitulation following the usual infant progression from simultaneity to alternation to unilateral preference. We are in full accord with the establishment of a unilateral preference in performance because engineering principles dictate that a bilaterally equating machine must have a triggering side to establish a pattern of motion. We are, however, in disagreement on the question of ignoring skill development on the contralateral side. Children should have many opportunities to explore the use of both sides in skill learning. Some skill patterns may be more efficient if triggered from the contralateral side and others more efficient from the ipsilateral side. Living in a multivariant world there is no forecasting of the direction of thrust that problems will have as they approach. We must be bilaterally prepared. This appears to be a critical point for loss of freedom for modern man.

The human body is a bilaterally equating organism moving around a center axis. For greatest efficiency of movement, the total organism must operate as a coordinated unit. If the body is not smoothly working as a bilateral mechanism, other means of maintaining its equilibrium must be substituted. Not until the weights of the body have been shifted from positions involving adverse strains to positions of better balance, and the strains removed, can effective responses and coordination take place in postural patterns. Postural patterns in the human body imply an active process in maintaining balance.

The organism is not one solid structure but a jointed structure with many movable parts. As any part of the body moves, the total body acquires a new shape and a different distribution of its weight. The center of gravity shifts with this new weight distribution in order to maintain the condition of having equal amounts of weight on all sides of it. (Broer, 1960; and Metheny, 1952) The further these parts move from the axis, the greater the power needed to hold them in balance. The body feels free when the midline is at right angles to the earth, but it is off-balance when the midline varies from its perpendicular position. (Radler and Kephart, 1960) The adjustment is made by allowing some other part of the body to move in the opposite direction from the original movement so that the weight is still evenly distributed from the center. Strain will result if the requirements for the additional force is too great, and strain contributes to the breakdown of the organic machine. To have a minimum of stress and strain, the structure must be balanced as a unit in relation to external forces along with internal forces. (Todd, 1929)

The learner is a dynamic bilateral equation in active physical movement. There is a constant seeking to hold alignment on the central axis as the two sides of the organism engage the environment in the management of daily confrontations. The careful observation of characteristic patterns of movement in the learner will reveal the manner in which the individual has organized the various segments and body planes to maintain the bilateral equation with some degree of comfort.

The walking gait, crawling, rolling, jumping and hopping patterns of the performer carefully observed reflect the equation in dynamic action. The manner in which the individual addresses himself to a manipulative task on a desk or table-top and sets himself for performance as a bilateral being is also reflective of the bilateral organization of the individual. Both sides must make a contribution. If one side is the lead side and used as the major performing agent, it is critical to observe the countering action of the immobile side. The full understanding of human motion in all of its respective segments can only occur when evaluative concentration is also given to the relatively immobile side in unilateral performance. Each side has a role to perform. A proper state of immobility or complementation may be crucial to the efficiency of the unilateral performance.

Two specific motor tasks, rolling and vertical repetitive jumping may be singled out as examples of performance which require a bilateral balance to hold alignment. In rolling the total body is in contact with a surface. In repetitive rotations the individual will be able to maintain an accuracy in direction toward a target only as both sides of his body make an equalized contribution to the act. Unequal thrusting patterns in rotating the body will cause the roller to veer off a direct line. Vertical repetitive jumping also requires the two sides to operate with equality if the jumper is to remain in a single landing area. Inequality of sides in such jumping will cause the jumper to veer toward the left or the right or require him to constantly adjust for the inequality. These two tasks require vertical orientations in different relationships to gravitational pull and afford an excellent opportunity to observe the bilateral equation in dynamic action.

Curran's (1965) study of the rolling patterns and vertical jumping patterns (on a trampoline) of third and fourth grade children is an example of such observations. She found that none of the 37 children could accomplish a non-deviating roll. All veered off-course to some extent. One third of her group were able to correct their positioning as they rolled but two thirds veered significantly off course and were unable to make adjustments to their errors. When the same children were placed on a trampoline and requested to repetitively jump vertically, maintaining the same specific landing spot on the canvas 95% of the group revealed a significant deviation from the canvas midpoint. She noted that her findings were unrelated to sex, handedness or trampoline sophistication. A similar set of findings have emerged from a replication of this same design with 250 high school girls. (Barsch, in progress)

The general conclusions from these two studies suggest that a majority of children and adolescents are not bilaterally equated to a degree that would allow them to move freely in comfort and ease holding an accurate alignment on the vertical axis in gross motor tasks. The inability to obtain a balanced contribution of both sides in gross performance may well be viewed as a possible factor in explaining the significant incidence of postural deviations among the nation's children and adults.

Freedom to move in any direction with balance and grace is promised by the skeletal design of the learner. The balanced contribution of both sides to the maintenance of alignment on task is essential to efficiency of performance and the sustained comfort of the performer. Only as the learner can sustain alignment can he insure directional accuracy and be regarded as efficient.

Bilaterality gives the performer degrees of freedom in adaptation and promotes the fulfillment of his potential, not only in the physical world but in cognitive action as well. He must come to recognize "both sides of an argument", "determine and evaluate alternatives" and "make choices". With cognitive bilaterality the individual can select, exercise an option, note a preference, show partiality, decide between, divide, segregate, cull out and glean. When cognitive bilaterality is absent the individual may be indecisive, rejecting, opinionated, stubborn, "one-sided", biased, prejudiced and disdaining. Choice has little meaning unless there is a clear cut understanding of the relative merits and values of both alternatives.

If we desire to insure the neophyte traveler of the full measure of freedom in his performance, those who provide him with an environment for learning must make certain that ample opportunity is provided for the exploration and development of both physical and cognitive bilaterality. Emphasis upon bilateral activities can be expected to yield dividends in tactual, kinesthetic, auditory and visual processing and place the learner in a more comfortable and advantageous relationship to the demands which confront him. Bilateral emphasis will increase his range of freedom for movement in comfort and alignment. To further increase his freedom to move in grace and ease attention must be directed to the component of Rhythm.

17

RHYTHM

Rhythm can be defined in a number of different ways but each variation conforms to a general similarity. Rhythm in speech is defined as an ordered recurrent alternation of strong and weak elements in a flow of sound and silence. In biological relationships, rhythm is a regular recurrent quantitative change in a variable biologic process. A novel, play or movie may be considered to have rhythm if it "moves along well". However it may be defined, some extent of recurrence is involved and some kind of beat is necessary to establish the time spanning.

Some authors have taken a broader viewpoint. Driver (1936) defines rhythm as a "ceaseless ever-varying movement of an intangible force interwoven with all that can be comprised in the word 'Life'". Rhythm is a cadence, a lilt, a swing and a tempo — all at one time. The general literature on rhythm is mainly devoted to considerations of musical performance and the dance. Throughout the literature however, there appears to be a general agreement upon the point that "muscles are made for moving and rhythm is movement".

There is also concordance of thought on the belief that a child's body possesses instinctively the essential elements of rhythm which is a "sense of time". Dalcroze (1921) and many others believe that "when we compare the functions of the ear with those of the muscular system, we arrive at the conclusion that the first place in the order of elementary music training should be accorded to the muscular system". Execution (movement) should precede the perception of rhythm. "Move to acquire rhythm" seems to be the thought.

The human organism receives rhythm as a biological grant. Circulatory, respiratory, digestive and neurologic patterns of rhythm are built into the design of the developing fetus. There are many meters of rhythm, which although different in tempo, function in a synchrony as a part of the totality we can designate as biologic rhythm. It is expressed as a pulse, a heartbeat, a brain wave, a metabolism, a breathing rate and so on. The vast majority of infants enter the world of terrestrial space with an integrity in biologic rhythm.

Many prosaic events contribute to the child's learning of rhythm. Parents make their contribution by the many ways they "impress" patterns of accentuation upon their offspring—often unintentionally — but nonetheless rhythmic whatever the basic intent might be. It may well be that the first impression of external rhythm occurs in the uterine movement occasioned by maternal walking and moving during the gestational period. Once born, the infant becomes a part of the totality which can be designated as cosmic rhythm but it is the typical day by day experiences of infancy which perhaps have greater initial value to the building of the rhythmic pattern. Being held and carried for feeding, stroked in bathing, caressed and patted, responding to the body rhythm of the carrier are all a part of the initial "impressing". The meter of parental voices, the ticking clock, the radio, stereo, TV, household noises of food preparation, affectionate vocalizations of mother and father, his own vocal explorations in lalling and babbling all help to establish an auditory tempo for the new world he has entered. The patting of his body to comfort him, the rhythmic stroking as he is bathed, the rocking motion set to lull him to sleep and a variety of regularities in touching patterns help to found a tactual rhythm. His own reflexive, seemingly diffuse, thrashing of arms and legs set up a proprioceptive patterning. Lights and shadows dancing before his eyes in the normal course of a luminant day from sunlight, mobiles, revolving lamps, objects dangled before him, pendula and people moving about serve to set a visual rhythm. Soon he begins his own system of rhythmic expression with his rolling, crawling and walking—all in some pattern of effort, fruition and rest. He will ride a tricycle, travel up and down a stair, build and rebuild his block towers, fill and refill containers, scribble and scribble again, play pat-a-cake, listen to lullabyes—all in some form of pattern and each event contributes. Everything he does will progressively become more accentuated and rhythmic as he learns to move in a world of space and discovers the existing patterns in the world about him.

Rhythm in human performance can be classified in three different states. We may refer to a performance as **rhythmic** when a specific sequence is followed in order with no incidence of delay or interference or when a regular beat or cadence can be defined within sustained action patterns. Any disturbance to the flow of a motor act, speech pattern, thought flow or language expression which serves to interrupt or interfere with regularity, interval span or sequence but still permits the completion of the intended action may be classified as **dysrhythmic**. When no flow of action is manifest and no pattern of regularity can be observed, the classification of **arhythmic** may be assigned to that specific bit of behavior. One of those classifications is pertinent to all movements of the mobile organism. Two general possibilities exist. We may refer to an individual as characteristically dysrhythmic when a disruption or distortion of pattern can be observed in muscular patterning, ocular motilities, speech, graphic expression and general postural and manipulative transport. Such a classification infers that some degree of success can be achieved in performance but a regular cadence, beat, accent or flow cannot be observed and consequently, there is always some question as to whether a successful outcome can be expected. The presence of dysrhythmia is automatically an indicator of efficiency loss. If design intention is to establish a rhythmic flow of action emerging as an inevitable outcome from an efficient organization of all components, a designation of general dysrhythmia is a sign of failure to achieve the optimal state and some degree of general inefficiency must be attendant upon such failure. A positive rating of **rhythmic** is an indication that general movement patterns have achieved a grace and flow which enable the individual to perform efficiently in the desirable sequence and at a desirable rate so as to promote a total Movement Efficiency.

It is possible however, that the three classifications may be assigned differentially to specific functions. Under such possibility, we may consider an individual to be a collective composite of the three different rhythmic classifications. He may give evidence of good rhythm in gross transport patterns moving his full body through space; show a dysrhythmia when asked to manipulate fine objects on a table top task and show an inability to demonstrate any form of rhythm when ocular motilities are tested. This allows for two types of classification in the area of rhythm; a general classification which refers to an overall impression regarding total performance and a specific classification which refers to the patterning of particular portions of the performance pattern on a head to toe basis.

The greatest degree of inefficiency is manifest in the individual who is classified as **arhythmic**. If such a classification is deserved it indicates that all previous components are poorly organized and the individual has no amplitude or range of performance. Arhythmic individuals may have some success, but it is likely that their success is accidental and fortuitous since there is no way of predicting a temporal patterning of behavior. Dysrhythmic performers are also inefficient since they cannot follow the principle of economy and comfort but they do maintain some semblance of success. It is usually a question of achieving "the hard way", with an "unorthodox method", at expense to other components in the system, etc. They may achieve and they may perform but their temporal sequencing is unpredictable and so is the quality of performance. The rhythmic individual performs with a consistency of grace and ease operating always in a state of comfort and in an executional state of least possible effort. In general parlance, the rhythmic individual makes "difficult tasks appear easy". In performance terms, the rhythmic individual achieves an executional ease and comfort which is admired by those who observe the actions. The most obvious illustration for this point is the corps of performing artists who attract observant audiences to applaud their grace.

At one extreme we may place the arhythmic and at the other extreme the optimally rhythmic performers. In a normal curve of distribution on this rhythm scale, it is likely that we can place the vast majority of our population within the massive middle category of the dysrhythmic. On such a curve, some may be placed nearer to the positive extreme and some placed nearer to the negative extreme. It is our contention that one's placement along this continuum is dependent upon the degree of efficiency which has been achieved in all of the other components which go to make up Movement Efficiency.

There are four fundamental aspects of rhythm with which we must be concerned in relating rhythm to Movement Efficiency. First, there must be a recognition of the **cosmic rhythm** of the universe — the regulated order of day and night, seasonal changes, rotations and revolutions, perennials and hundreds of other examples of rhythmic pattern. There are many different tempos all bound together in a rhythmic matrix that allows for variation in accentuation and rate but retains a fundamental unity. This totality becomes a cosmic rhythm surround into which the neophyte traveler is thrust at delivery. This is a fixed rhythmic matrix, the tempo of which is beyond modification by man. Second, the **biologic rhythm** of man must be considered. This rhythmic system is a built-in regularity of respiration, heart beat, pulse rate, brain waves, digestive actions and so on. This is a universal heritage for the human being. While it is probably true that the biologic rhythm of each being is unique unto itself in the respective tempos of each element, there remains a universal characteristic pattern for all humans. Any significant deviation in biologic rhythm becomes a matter of grave concern for the vitality of the organism. Although there is recognition of the refined uniqueness of each individual when minute considerations are given, there is an expectancy of a general pattern characteristic of the species which is regarded as necessary to the physiologic integrity of the human organism. A deviation in biologic rhythm which is distressing to the physiologic integrity must activate survival concerns. The vast majority of infants, fortunately, enter the world of space containing a functioning biologic rhythmic pattern which conforms to initial standards for physiologic integrity.

The first two rhythm systems have a certain invariant quality. Cosmic rhythm is fixed and to a certain extent biologic rhythm must be thought of as fixed. Therefore, the newborn infant begins life in an internal and external milieu of fixed rhythms. Invariant, though each rhythmic system may be, there has been an historical harmony between the two which has enabled the human organism to adapt biologic rhythms to the cosmic pattern in the ageless melody of life.

It is the final pair of aspects of rhythm which we must regard as the dynamic challenge for a mobile, information processing organism seeking to promote an economic and comfortable survival in a multiple energy surround. Each organism must develop a rhythmic pattern of postural and manipulative transport and expressiveness in a gravitational field to insure the most economic advancement towards more and more complex levels of behavior. The acquisition of this kind of patterning can be referred to as

performance rhythm. This type of rhythm is constructed into patterns of varying tempos by the human performer as he moves and acts. Day by day the infant, child, adolescent and adult introduce some new temporal element into performance rhythm as they explore, enact and learn. The patterns may be many and varied, they may be clearly articulated or poorly articulated, all may be synchronized with all others or minor dyssynchronies may be present—but **performance rhythm** is **acquired** and **developed** by an active mobile organism processing information on a minute by minute, day by day basis.

A fourth element is derived by an active organism from an external world where sounds, sights and touches may occur in cadences which need to be perceived according to their temporal order. This is the process of perceiving rhythm in an active external surround. This fourth type of rhythm may be designated as **perceived rhythm**. A "sense of rhythm" has often been used to define this fourth type. Seashore's (1936) definition conveys the idea.

> *The sense of rhythm is an instictive disposition to group recurrent sense impressions vividly and with precision by time or intensity or both in such a way as to derive pleasure and efficiency through the grouping. It is a complex process and involves literally the whole organism in the form of responsiveness to measured intervals of time or tone.*

Perceived rhythm includes not only the perception of beat and tone in musical selections, but any ordered pattern in the environment. The blinking lights on an electric billboard, the drip of a leaky faucet, the click of a typewriter, Morse code, the hum of an airplane motor, and threads of cars winding over the spool of the hill all are included under this category. Wherever there is recurrency, wherever there is regularity of interval, wherever there is beat and wherever there is movement according to some defined order—there is rhythm. Wherever there is rhythm the perceiving organism may process it to his adaptive advantage.

The component of Rhythm within the complex of Movement Efficiency is a fourfold integration of four rhythm systems synchronized in a harmonious dynamically interweaving action enhancing the human performer as he acquires more and more knowledge of the Universe and his personal unique relationship to that Universe. Cosmic rhythm and biologic rhythm operate as the first interweaving action establishing a foundation pattern for the more complex weaving process that comes from a dynamic being acting in a dynamic surround. Perceived rhythm and performance rhythm then become the shuttles on the loom to weave a complex changing pattern according to experience and opportunity. In the symphony of life cosmic and biologic rhythm may be the underlying theme while perceived and performance rhythms serve as variations upon the theme. A disturbance to any of the four rhythms introduces some degree of discord into the performance of the organism and results in some penalty to Movement Efficiency.

It is very likely that a musical time signature such as 3/4, 6/8, 2/4 and so on could be assigned to any recurrent series of movements made by the human performer. Throughout the course of a typical activity week an individual probably moves according to all defined time signatures at one time or another in response to the multiple demands he encounters. The component of Flexibility bears directly upon the component of Rhythm in providing for a wide range of tempos. The more variations the individual may be able to temporally express, the greater will be his freedom in Flexibility.

Observation of human behavior will also suggest that the descriptive language of the composer which indicates the spirit of a given passage may also be employed to characterize human performance in certain circumstances. The terms "largo", "andante", "allegro", "allegretto" and so on all might just as readily be used to define either the characteristic demand of a given situation, e.g., a "largo" situation in which ponderous tones and prolonged intervals characterize events or the particular rhythmical attitude of the performer in a given situation, e.g., performing in "allegro" fashion. The circumstance of a characteristically "largo" individual confronted with an "allegro" situation suggests an obvious performance dilemma.

Whenever the rhythmic demand of a situation cannot be met by the rhythmic capability of the individual the performer is faced with an "adapt or quit" decision. He either "gets on the beat" or "he is out of step". This may occur when the demand is musical, social, graphic, athletic or cognitive.

The general performance patterns of the individual may be characterized as rhythmic, dysrhythmic or arhythmic but can only be judged when a temporal standard is set by some arbitrary system. It is when the human performer must adapt his movement to an existing beat that the more subtle manifestations of movement discord become apparent. Skating to music, dancing, singing with an orchestra, doing acrobatics to music and so on are examples of a need to reciprocally interweave **perceived rhythm** with **performance rhythm** for manifest temporal synchrony. High school and college band directors are acquainted with the nagging percentage of musicians who have an accurate sense of timing when the band rehearses sitting down but who experience varying degrees of frustration when they must march and play their instruments at the same time. Holding body rhythm in keeping with a drummed cadence, moving in alignment and retaining a rhythmic beat for the performance of their respective instrument requires a comfortable interweaving between performance and perceived rhythms.

An individual may perceive rhythmic patterns in the "out thereness" of his world and may even move in what might be classified as a reasonably rhythmic manner but until he can reciprocally utilize both perceived and performance rhythm in purposeful adaptive patterns, we cannot speak of him as being a truly rhythmic person.

Rhythm in Gross Movement

The infant traveler equipped with a muscular system and propelled by developmental momentum to achieve a progressively more complex orientation in terrestrial space faces a lengthy checklist of movement patterns which must become part of his motor repertoire if he is to move with efficiency. He will roll, crawl, walk, hop, jump, skip and run. He will push, pull and lift. He will throw, bat, catch and kick. If we could actually tabulate the number of muscular contractions which occur in the average three year old's body in the course of a normal "play" day the count would be a staggering amount. He is designed to move and he enacts his design.

Each move has some temporal duration. A move starts, proceeds and ends. In the basic infant training sequence each set of muscles is provided with its unique opportunity to become organized. Each set joins with other sets in patterns of relatedness. He not only must learn to walk but he must establish a temporally related pattern to his gait. Muscular timing is an elusive goal which remains just outside his grasp for months and sometimes years.

The difference between the awkward efforts of first attempts at any coordinative effort and the ease and efficiency of perfected movement is basically a matter of acquiring a more appropriate pattern of timing and intensity in the related time and stress values of the movement phase. The awkward initial efforts of the neophyte walker, runner, writer, mechanic, dancer, skater, acrobat become progressively more graceful and comfortable as the "timing" improves. When the flow of energy is properly related in time, efficient and satisfying movement results.

Rhythm in Speech

Each neophyte space traveler is expected to adopt a rhythmical pattern for his vocal speech which is consonant with cadence and flow of those around him. As an ongoing and related obligation to the acquisition of appropriate sounds and combinations of sounds for oral speech, and the patterns of formulation for language development the child must also acquire a meter. A good deal of time in early development is devoted to progressive modeling of halting, hesitant, inaccurate soundings into the flowing pattern of sustained conversational speech. The flow is so characteristically identified with geography, culture and parental rote that any pattern which does not match expectancy is regarded with some degree of diagnostic suspicion. In general daily living, one will observe conversational speakers who utter their words with machine gun rapidity and frequently stumble in their pattern or elide words, omit endings and so on in their haste. At another point on the speech meter continuum are those people whose rate of speech produces lengthened time intervals between words so that the listener grows impatient waiting for the full sentence to be completed. Some children and adults talk too fast and others speak too slowly. The vast majority of people speak within a middle range characteristic of their milieu. One of the major problems in acquiring a mastery of conversational language in tongues other than one's mother tongue is the matter of achieving a rhythmic pattern of difference. Language students seeking to learn French, Spanish, Russian and so on and Europeans or Orientals who seek to learn English share the common problem of attempting to transfer the rhythm of their own language to the "new" language and thereby move clumsily in their early learning efforts. The oddity noted by the listener is related to the imposition of an unnatural cadence upon a language which the listener expects to hear in a customary meter.

Errors in rhythmic patterning occur in the stutter and the stammer which can be characteristically designated as dysrhythmic. Explosive utterances observed in children and adults with cerebral palsy are a further illustration of a dysrhythmic pattern of movement.

Not only must oral speech be rhythmical for proper expression and attractiveness to a listener, but it is also important that language formulations must have some pattern of flow. The speaker who speaks in phrases which never seem to be connected to an ongoing meter, uses incomplete sentences, repeats portions of thoughts, returns references to earlier words within the same conversational utterances and seems to indulge in a form of grammatical leap frog by darting hither and yon, produces a dysrhythmic pattern for the listener. For such a speaker the listener must be prepared to zig and zag in many directions if he wishes to "follow the thought". In such haphazard patterning the net impact upon the listener is one of dysrhythmic thought. When the rhythmic rate of expression is equal to the rhythmic rate of listening a counterpoint is established and a communication harmony occurs as a result of a patterned interweaving between a speaker and a listener.

The acquisition of rhythm in speech patterning is developmentally expansive. In progressive increments the youngster achieves improved beat, cadence and accent. Nursery rhymes, simple songs, alliterative sentences, riddles and behavioral mottoes which become a natural part of his pre-academic experiences all contribute to the patterning of his speaking rhythm. Breaks in rhythm occur when new words must be mastered for incorporation into expressive vocabulary. In states of anxiety or joy and under stress, the rhythm of speech is disturbed and becomes a manifest symptom of distress or exhilaration by breaking into regular patterns or introducing a different rate.

Rhythm in Graphic Expression

Graphic expression in drawings, printing, writing, coloring, finger painting, and easel painting require rhythmic flowing patterns. Unless a patterned flow is achieved in the graphic expression some degree of inefficiency will be noted within the performance that is directly traceable to a characteristic dysrhythmia or even an arhythmia. At an extreme level, the athetoid, ataxic and spastic child attempting to achieve graphic flow is under most duress to maintain rhythm. At the opposite extreme, microscopic inspection of handwriting has been useful in noting tremors or spikings traceable to some degree of systemic dysrhythmia. Under certain conditions, tremors which would be unnoted by the naked eye in handwriting samples are revealed when magnified and have proven to have diagnostic value of a very subtle nature.

In each instance of new learning in graphic expression, one of the critical variables in the learning is the extent of rhythm previously achieved by the learner. The learner who can be classified as rhythmic in a wide variety of performance areas brings to the task the full impact of a rhythmic background and has a headstart in learning the next necessary pattern of rhythm. The child who is manifestly dysrhythmic in a number of performance areas enters the next task at a disadvantage. Having failed to achieve rhythm in other movements, the demand to establish cursive rhythm presents a stressful challenge.

In musical performance rhythm is the ability to maintain an accurate beat while performing other activities at the same time. (Drake, 1957) Tests of rhythm for children which have been statistically subjected to normative efforts are relatively rare. The Seashore Rhythm Test and the Drake Musical Aptitude Test stand out as principal instruments in this field. Both are intended as musical screening devices and are not concerned with motoric performance unrelated to music. The Drake Test involves the subject in sustaining a given rhythm after the stimulus fades and permits a wide variety of response possibilities such as clapping, tapping, moving the feet and so on. The Seashore Test is directed toward auditory perception of rhythm in terms of similarities and differences. A measurement of rhythm in the operational definition contained in the concept of Degrees of Freedom is non-existent.

Drake (1957) defined three elements which he felt to be essential for a successful musical performer: (1) he must feel a rhythm strongly; (2) maintain a set tempo despite distractions; and (3) maintain a set tempo with accuracy before he can take musical liberties with rhythm in the form of rubato, accelerando and other deviations from equally divided beats. Although Drake was primarily interested in the performing musician, the same three elements may be considered in defining rhythm for the dynamic, mobile human organism. First, a basic internal rhythm must be brought to a level of awareness in the human mover so that he is conscious of flow and regularity in his movements. Secondly, he must be able to maintain his pattern in a flow despite noises, intervening views, and any form of shifting in his energy surround. He must walk as smoothly on crowded sidewalks as on open country roads. He must walk as rhythmically in a dimly lit surround as in a bright one. Noises which are unrelated to his transport must not be allowed to interfere with his pattern of movement and so on. The third element is of particular interest to our concern with Movement Efficiency. Unless the performer has established a basic rhythm in walking, running, crawling, hopping, manipulations, speaking, writing and so on he cannot successfully explore multiple variations in tempo in any of these skills. He cannot experiment with variations in walking until he has first established a rhythmic gait. He cannot test out various writing tempos until he has set a basic pattern of writing. The flexibility in active response which can become a part of his performance range by varying tempo can only be derived from a well-founded rhythm.

The influence of musical accompaniment as a reinforcement for rhythmic movement has long been recognized. Coaches have often found percussion and musical backgrounds to be an asset in athletic training procedures. Dancing instructors obviously rely upon such measures.

Recently, Rieber (1965) had studied the effects of music on the activity level of 5 and 6 year old children in a specially designed playroom. Two recorded selections of classical music, one slow and soothing and one fast and exciting, were played while the child was in the playroom. Activity rate was measured on the basis of length of time a child engaged in contact with each toy. Some periods of play were performed without music. Results indicated that activity rates were significantly higher during the time when music was played than during the quiet periods and that the fast music generated a higher activity rate than the slow music. Studies of this type are a rarity. Freeburne and Fleischer (1952) tried a variety of musical selections with college students seeking to determine whether music in a background would speed up or slow down their reading rates. Jazz music increased the reading rates but all other types of music had no significant influence on rate. Simons (1964) reported that infants from 9 to 31 months of age showed an increase in activity level when music was played. Physiologic differentials were found in children using GSR measures for varying types of music by Zimny and Weidenfeller (1962).

Cotton (1965) described an intriguing concept called "rhythmical intention" employed therapeutically by Professor Peto in Budapest. Children with cerebral palsy are taught to speak aloud a verbal direction for their own movements. Directed by a therapist the child says, "I lift my arms above my head" as he attempts the movement and then counts in rhythm as he proceeds. The rhythmic counting serves to aid in the achievement of the movement. In this manner, children are learning to move actively, unaided by the hands of a therapist and in an interaction not yet fully understood the rhythmic speech and counting association is producing exciting results. All type of movement patterning including writing and craft is based upon this concept of "rhythmical intention" at the Institute for Movement.

Delacato (1959) has advanced a theory of tonality related to the right hemisphere and acting upon his theory has advocated a "tonal deprivation" for children during the critical period of learning to read. Our own clinical experience has been in the opposite direction — that of enhancing the learning of reading with musical and metronomic procedures.

Another perspective on the components of rhythm in Movement Efficiency can be derived from an application to the domain of **cognitive space**.

Rhythm may also be viewed as a reach-grasp-release phenomenon. Inability to establish a smooth flow of reaching-grasping-releasing and reaching again may be viewed as a form of dysrhythmia in processing. (Barsch, 1965) If there is any interference with the R-G-R sequence in walking the walker is dysrhythmic. If this is a problem to the individual in manipulative tasks he may be classified as dysrhythmic. Dysrhythmia in speech may be due to temporal sequencing problems in the R-G-R pattern. Every muscular performance may be viewed according to the R-G-R sequence.

We may refer to an individual as being "in grasp" when he is unable to disengage himself from a given thought or topic and dwells upon it conversationally, in personal thought or in active behavior. It is a form of perseveration but not necessarily manifest as a repetition of identicalness. It is rather a holding on a topic, talking or thinking it over, examining many aspects of it and generally conveying the behavior of being unable to "move on" from that particular cognitive spot. Perhaps, "cognitive marking time" may be an apt term for the concept we are attempting to clarify. The individual "takes many steps in the same place", but does not actually move in any direction. In general conversation, this behavior is often described as "beating a dead horse", "sewing the same button over and over again", "gilding the lily" and other phrases of like content. The individual is unable or does not wish to release a particular construct, idea or point. Arguments are frequently "in grasp" behaviors when no advance is made. Being "in grasp" may be a positive or negative behavior.

On a positive level, being "in grasp" may be termed persistence, patience, endurance, ambition and dedication. On a negative level being "in grasp" may be called stubbornness, petulance, preoccupation, pedantic, insistence and so on. This concept is related to rhythm because it is analogous to establishing a monotonous cadence having little or no variation.

Cognitive rhythm is expressed as a flow of thought—moving and directing man's actions to a forward plane. Cognitive rhythm is also expressed as a fluidity in considering the past, evaluating the present and planning for the future. Some people can think in "allegro" and "andante" rates while others are of the "largo" variety. Reaching, grasping, releasing—to reach again is the rhythm pattern for inquisitive man. To make that R-G-R sequence of true value to man, we must insert a label for the cognitive accent in processing. The sequence is more meaningful when we express its rhythm as reach-grasp-cognite-release (store) and reach again. This is inquiry. This is search. This is the melody of knowledge.

Most adults in our society become passive appreciators of rhythm as they observe it or listen to it but rarely maintain an active proprioceptive relationship to rhythm except as they may walk, talk or write. Exhortations for adults to become active participants in regular rhythmic exercise have become standard fare in all advertising media. Sedentariness is a popular preoccupation with rhythmic expression assigned to a tapping toe or an occasional clapping. A proprioceptive enrichment to man's expression of the full quality of his movement design becomes progressively obscured and submerged by a welter of passive luxuries which flood the American scene. The flowing rhythmic movement of early childhood which seems to occur as a natural heritage suffers varying degrees of dyssynchrony as postural deviations, visual problems, listening problems, tensions, anxieties, fears and spatial ignorance become the dysrhythmic counterpoint in developmental momentum.

In prosaic daily experience we encounter people who "live" at an apparently faster pace than others as well as those who appear to be "slow-movers" more deliberately paced and operating at a slow pace. The basic rhythm of daily living is probably related to the composite tempo of all systems within the body which are constituted in some form of temporal arrangement and is chemical in nature. To understand the regular rhythm of a single individual, a detailed analysis would be required of all temporally oriented systems of the body. Such a requirement is not easily met. Present limitations in the measurement of various temporal systems and the inherent difficulties in establishing an analytic synthesis of the various rhythm systems suggest that the full understanding of the rhythmic uniqueness of each individual lies within the realm of remote space at this point in scientific history. There is probably a considerable amount of agreement among scientists that the basic rhythmic systems of the organism are manifest in the overt behavior of the individual but the definitive measures to validate such a belief are not yet available.

If we wish to optimize the utilization of each traveler's full potential for graceful, comfortable and economic movement, attention must be given to establishing activities and opportunities that will most rapidly contribute to the child's learning of the appropriate muscular "timing" which lies in the space between awkwardness and grace. The child must learn at the earliest possible moment that he can personally represent rhythm. He can direct his movements according to cadences. His experiences in space must be filled with opportunities to discover various time intervals in his own movements according to measured beats. He must perceive rhythm and he must express rhythm. He must become consciously aware of his own symphonic potential in space. As he acquires rhythm, physically and cognitively—as he discovers the economy of graceful movement—as he builds an extensive repertoire of many forms and types of rhythm—as he becomes aware of cosmic and biologic rhythms—as he orchestrates all of these awarenesses and knowledges—his degrees of freedom are multiplied and his performance range is expanded. He comes to a higher state of pleasure and enjoyment in his own capabilities.

As he moves, physically and cognitively, in rhythm he increases his amplitudes of performance and achieves Flexibility.

18

FLEXIBILITY

Flexibility, by any definition, has interested very few investigators. The polar opposite of rigidity has been of far greater interest. Rigidity is a term used in psychologic literature to mean many different things. Broadly, the term has been applied to stereotyped or persistent behavior in perception, thinking, motor activity and attitudes. Each investigator, in his own way, has given the term a specific meaning in relation to his findings among a particular population. In the literature on the organic or the psychotic patient, rigidity has been used interchangeably with perseveration to indicate that the patient is "locked into" a particular form of response and is incapable of changing his response within the boundaries of the particular situation. It is generally applied to describe the fact that the patient is unable to shift to any other course of action than a single given bit of behavior. The general thought seems to be that such "holding on" is due to neurologic impairment or a psychotic fear of what a shift might bring about. It is looked upon as a pathologic persevering which extends well beyond the boundaries of the situation. Inherent in this viewpoint is the belief that a release or a shift is regarded as so formidable and threatening to the patient that such an action is to be avoided at all costs. The persistency of behavior, on the other hand, is regarded as a positive, non-pathologic behavior which falls more in the category of an insistence upon a particular pattern of behavior with a disregard of information from the surround which would suggest a modification of response. Whatever may be the definition employed by a particular investigator, there can be no question that the concept of rigidity is regarded as a negative behavior wherever it might be found. It is reported as an inevitable associate of neurologic or emotional pathology and an impressive list of authoritative documentations support this contention.

From a pathologic standpoint, rigidity is regarded as a deprivation of behavioral freedom which is so binding upon the individual that there is only **one** course of action and if that one course of action cannot be employed with success, a chaotic state is inevitable even if such a state is expressed as a complete state of passivity.

Such rigidity has been defined in studies of perception among pathologic populations where perceptual shifting has been manifestly inefficient. It has been noted in motor studies where only one type of response could be initiated by the performer regardless of variation in demand. Studies of conceptual behavior among disturbed populations have also been reported as lacking in freedom to move in other directions than a fixed pattern. There is little doubt that rigidity, however defined, does represent the opposite end of the continuum from flexibility. Our view of the polarization is to place looseness, vagueness, indefiniteness and like terms at the opposite end of the continuum and to regard flexibility as a midpoint suggesting the possibility for the individual to travel freely between both negatives. Flexibility is neither the rigid, unyielding position at one extreme, nor the completely vague, indeterminate, indecisive and unclear position at the other end. It is rather a recognition that in certain instances, rigidity may be a desirable characteristic and in other instances vagueness and indecision may be an inevitable component of a given situation. The flexible individual may experience both ends of the continuum in the course of a lifetime but characteristically resides in the middle of the polarization free to move in either direction as a situation may dictate spending brief moments at either end but never a long enough time in either place to warrant an identification. The flexible individual is adamant and zealous when the situation demands, vague and confused upon occasion but if a tabulation is made of his general state of behavior, he is characteristically ready to move in any direction having committed himself to neither polar position.

When we speak of flexibility we associate it with terms like plasticity, tractability, formativeness, formability, malleability, elasticity, resilience and give. We do not regard this component as a negative in any sense. It is a freedom enabling the individual to achieve an adaptive latitude, offering a space and spread for adjustment and indicative of a spaciousness in performance.

Flexibility has been related to a definition of looseness of the joints and the accompanying increase in the range of movement possible in body parts associated with those joints. Two flexibility factors have been identified by psychologists—trunk and leg. There may be other factors but as Guilford (1959) has pointed out, flexibility tests have been neglected in practically all studies of psychomotor dimensions.

Guilford (1959) has referred to **semantic spontaneous flexibility** as the ability or disposition to produce a diversity of ideas when free to do so and to **figural spontaneous flexibility** as a tendency to see rapid alternations in perceived visual figures.

Adaptive flexibility is a freedom from persistence of approaches permitting the dynamic organism to restructure his response and the situation according to principles of economy and comfort.

Developmental Perspective on Flexibility

The infant terranaut is thrust upon a multivariant world of tremendous complexity.

His survival depends upon his ability to adapt to the vicissitudes of life. There can be no guarantee for any infant that the prosaic world will be to his constant liking and comfort. The world cannot move in complete subservience to his wishes moment after moment. Others will pose obstacles. Others will express desires. Demands will differ. Demands will frequently be inconsistent. In such a complex of variance socially, psychologically, economically and physically one beacon signal keeps flashing the message to the terrestrial traveler — adapt!

As a dynamically adapting organism the earthling must acquire a range of performance that will allow him alternatives in behavior. It is a common expectancy of early childhood that the world "must move in a certain way to insure the comfort of the immature and the insecure". Progressively, however, there is a more complex expectancy that the petulance, impulsivity and insistence of the young child will give way to the adaptive willingness of the older child and the eventual mature pattern of adaptive alternatives in the adults.

Whereas initially the infant sees only one possibility for action and is chaotically distressed if his single course does not produce results, he must develop a repertoire of possibilities for the solution of any given problem. This repertoire allows him to draw upon other methods for solution if the first selection is blocked in some manner by life circumstances.

What a tremendous list of problems can be written for the life of any individual from birth to old age. Thousands upon thousands of problems, thousands upon thousands of dilemmas — all posing the single question to the performer — "do you have more than one possibility for solution or are you restricted to a single course?".

Perhaps the earliest learning for flexibility occurs when the mother does not get around to changing the diaper immediately upon soilage and when the bottle is not produced on exact schedule. As he grows his hunger may not be satisfied upon immediate cry and he must learn to wait. Even more so he must come to accept a variable meal time according to the schedule of his parents. He must find more than one way to play in the sandbox, more than one direction to ride his bike, more than one type of play activity and a dietary variation in which every meal will not be the same. He will find that other people than his mother can read a story to him, that others can tuck him in at night, that the little boy's hat in the coloring book can be made any one of twelve colors from the crayon box and that there are many different flavors of cookies. He will learn that prayers can be said in many places and do not have to be limited to church, the bedside and at table. He will learn that he can play in his yard or the neighbor's yard and that he can enjoy himself at play in many places. He will learn to be first, second, third and to be denied and see all different possibilities. He will learn to talk and to listen and to appropriately define which shall be his role moment after moment.

When he arrives at school age, he will discover that he may print or write cursively to convey his thoughts, that he can leave a small margin or a large margin, that he can expect a spelling test on Friday but that sometimes he may see an educational movie instead. Week after week, month after month he will be given more and more opportunities to learn flexibility. He will learn to walk swiftly and slowly and discover that he is in control of that rate and can govern it as he desires. He will come to know that he can run, crawl, hop, skip or roll to a desired goal and that the choice is his. He will learn to whisper, shout and talk in a quiet tone according to circumstance. He will face hours of playtime with a wide assortment of possible occupations and select day after day a different set. He will learn to cry when he is hurt or give many other signs of discomfort and discover that he has a repertoire of such behaviors at his disposal. He will discover that ice cream is enjoyable whether it is chocolate, strawberry, vanilla or any other flavor. The opportunities for flexibility are countless and they are his for the learning. Every time there is the choice to be rigid or to be indecisive or to carefully evaluate alternatives. If he characteristically learns rigidity he becomes constricted and restricted. If he characteristically learns indecisiveness he loses direction and momentum. His advancement into complexity can only be truly served as he learns to live with different possibilities to achieve a desired goal.

His cognitive world will be filled with thoughts and ideas which diverge, digress and deflect. His physical world will slope, tilt, incline, decline, twist and turn. He must slant, stagger, reverse, invert, interweave, separate, intersect, intertwine and so on.

As a general organization he may become structured as a "tight case" which will make him rigidly fixed in space capable of moving only within a narrowly defined circumscribed area. He may also become a "loose case" in which event he is characteristically lacking in any form of boundary tending to be unpredictable and disorganized. His most comfortable position will lie somewhere between these two extremes. As a tight case, he will move only a small step at a time. As a loose case, he will be inclined to take giant steps with no thought of where they might take him.

Students in college courses frequently receive a survey of pertinent theories in the field, each having its respective set of studies supporting the particular theory and then are left to make their own decisions regarding which theory seems to them to hold the greatest merit. There are many theories of learning and many theories of perception, any one of which may prove valuable in explaining a particular circumstance. Since no theory has as yet proven itself champion over the others, although all are contenders, the student is left with a demand for theoretical flexibility. Any single theory may serve the purpose according to a given situation. The student of human behavior must be able to skip gingerly from theory to theory to meet his own explanatory need. If a student becomes deeply committed to a particular theory he will find a variety of human behaviors which defy explanation unless another theory can be used in supplementation. Shifting from one theory to another to explain behavior must be guided by a principle of economy and comfort. It is becoming more and more fashionable to declare one's self to be an eclectic. The usual connotation of this reference is that the individual referrent regards theories as a behavioral smorgasbord to be sampled for taste and possible application but affords none of the theories sufficient evaluation to arrive at an intelligent choice. To be a sampler is not an indication of flexibility. To have a profound understanding of several theories and to move freely from one to another **based upon theory comprehension** in seeking to explain observed behavior **is** an example of flexibility.

In the one case we think of an indecisive shopper buying five brands of the same product and trying each one on the same wash to determine which one produces greatest "whiteness". In the other case, the choice is made among several theories each carefully understood to have unique pertinence.

In the field of physical education, the term agility is a compatible substitute for physical flexibility. The usual definition of agility is the ability to change the direction of the body or parts of the body rapidly. It may involve small ranges of movement as typing or playing the piano or it may involve large ranges of movement as in a zigzag run. There is always contained in this concept the idea that the directional shifting is fully under the control of the individual and utilized by the individual selectively and consciously for the purpose of solving the problem. The repertoire of moves are available for use by the organism as demands are placed upon him. There is a range of movement possibilities. The greater the agility of the athlete, the more value does he have to a variety of performances.

Art teachers strive diligently to free their students to explore many different media and to liberate them from confining boundaries of traditional form. Music instructors seek range of performance in their pupils. Everywhere we look flexibility is a desired freedom. Ability to approach a goal from many different routes is preferable to being a one-track person. To use either hand alternately or simultaneously gives flexibility.

Loss of flexibility can be illustrated in the development of a visual problem. The range of freedom for visual adaptations is greatest in the young child. When the child, adolescent or adult builds a visual problem the net effect is one of reducing the degrees of freedom in visual performance. The individual gives up freedom to move visually in favor of a state which eliminates stress but also reduces range and amplitude.

Flexibility can be lost in an auditory limitation, tactual deprivation, kinesthetic insensitivity, unalterable food preferences and in many other ways. The net effect is always a limitation upon the individual's ability to move in whatever direction can be desirable to optimally promote his survival. Our term flexibility is most akin to the physical educator's agility. It is the ability to shift direction in movement, cognitive or physical with grace, ease, comfort and economy.

Flexibility is manifest in those people who play life situations "by ear" prepared for whatever eventualities may arise, confident of their own abilities to "rise to the occasion". It is manifest in a high regard for conformity as a general pattern of behavior with the freedom to create responses above and beyond conformity if the need arises. It is leading in one instant and following in another when the cause is just. It is freedom to dwell upon history, live energetically in the present and plot optimistically for the future. It is a freedom of movement in the three time zones. It is a freedom to move efficiently in the six fields of space. It is a freedom to move through all the domains of space.

Cognitive flexibility allows for a change of opinion when the evidence dictates such a change. It is perhaps in cognitive flexibility that man achieves his highest level of function. It is within cognitive space that his most significant adaptations are made. As he can achieve a cognitive flexibility he can accept an idea other than his own, that he can attempt to see the value in another person's viewpoint and that he can adapt his oral or written communication to a level where he can assure meaningful interchange. He can speak simply or be complex. He can be precise on occasion or be vague when his own thinking is unclear. He can talk to children and to adults. He can play and he can work. He can be profound and he can be facetious. He can be serious and satirical. He can move freely in cognitive space whatever the terrain may present. He can shift directions with agility. He can be spontaneous or ponderously deliberate. The important element in flexibility is a shifting power. It is the system for comfortable adaptation. It is learnable. The opportunity is present in constant streams of experience. Flexibility is a key factor in Movement Efficiency. It presents the human organism at his adaptive best. Freedom to move in any direction with security of purpose is a cherished goal for every traveler. Whatever needs to be done to insure such freedom for every earthling, is an obligation upon our teaching society. Anything short of cognitive and physical flexibility is a penalty and a restriction upon the organism's freedom to move. Free movement with purpose along the terrain of life's continua must be incorporated as a daily learning opportunity.

The flexible learner is prepared to advance his complexity through his own efforts to plan. Motor planning becomes his final component.

19

MOTOR PLANNING

The epitome of human performance is expressed in the component designated as MOTOR PLANNING. It is the final enriching element in dynamic mobile man. It is the "sapiens" in **homo sapiens**. Once again the label is intended to include a wide range of human behavior—well beyond the immediately obvious relationship to muscular functioning. The single title **Planning** might serve alone to convey the conceptualization of this component except for our insistence that Movement is the irreducible factor in human performance in all four domains of spatial function. To maintain that emphasis, we prefer the term Motor Planning as the nomenclature for this component.

We conceive of this component as containing a combination of Motor Planning at the physical and cognitive levels of behavior. It is never one or the other but always a fusion of both in its expression.

Motor planning is the ultimate intent in human design. It is through this component that man expresses intelligence. It is within this expression that man synthesizes the contributions of all other components to his functional advantage in adapting the universe to his use, in promoting his survival in a multivariant energy surround and in fashioning an existence of comfort and economy.

It is the dynamic functional expression of this component which enables man to invent, institute, develop, initiate, design, contrive and construct. He can be described as a planner, promoter, architect, conspirator, programmer, organizer and executor because he is capable of motor planning. He can outline, diagram, chart, plot and cast. He can initiate, program, execute and evaluate. He can originate, generate, formulate, fabricate and manufacture. He can advocate, espouse, campaign and crusade. He can induce and deduce. In his adventuring in Cognitive space he can consider, contemplate, reflect, cogitate, deliberate, and meditate. As he moves in his complex world, he may hypothesize, speculate, postulate and conjecture. He may develop notions, ideas, fancies and concepts. As a seeker and promoter of knowledge to support his comfort and economy in survival behaviors he is able to survey, investigate, examine, probe and explore. He can inquire, search, inspect and rummage. He can sift and winnow the unessential from a multiple world in defining and delineating that flow of information which has value to him. He can coax, cajole and persuade. He can appraise, evaluate and analyze. All of this represents a descriptive listing of behavioral planning and the product of this final component — Motor Planning.

When man is unable to plan, we describe this dilemma as being perplexed, confused, bewildered, baffled, perturbed and dismayed. This list of adjectives can be selectively employed to characterize the dynamic situation of mobile man meeting a movement dilemma which, at least temporarily, defies resolution.

It is Motor Planning under the direction of a human performer with hammer and chisel that converts a massive block of granite into a masterpiece of form. The human performer faces a blank canvas and with oils and brushes expresses in color and form an enduring conceptualization that generations of viewers can admire. The plot of the novelist and the playwright, the meter and rhyme of the poet, the melody of the composer, the reporting of the journalist and the design of the architect all occur as a result of Motor Planning. Barren hillsides become homesites because man can plan. Slums give way to housing developments, conservation projects become national parks, roadways become super highways and tunnels burrow through mountains because man can plan. The corrugated washboard gave way to the automatic washer and dryer, television signals are reflected off a Telestar, a death rate is reduced by immunization and an astronaut walks in outer space because man can plan. Man has advanced the complexity of his civilization generation after generation from primitive simplicity to modern complexity because he can invent, project, dream, diagram, plot and execute. He can devise an easier way, a more comfortable transport and a more economical system. As man has planned he has discovered ways to transport himself over increasingly larger distances in less and less time. As he has planned he has found it possible to do more things for his convenience and comfort in smaller and smaller units. Historically mankind is beholden to famous planners who influenced the course of human development and every scholar of civilization becomes keenly aware that the history of mankind is truly written by individual men who brought dreams to a reality or at least near reality stage during their own lifetime. Each age has produced intellectual giants whose motor planning capability became the vehicle for man's transport to the next higher level of complexity. These are the honored names that the student becomes acquainted with in his elementary, secondary and collegiate years. The contribution of these great names has been well documented but it is the unsung hero of planning — the average teranaut — the individual dynamic human organism — that must concern us here. Every learner is an architect, inventor, developer, planner, enterpriser, promoter and organizer. Each learner builds a world of space for himself — accurately or inaccurately, concise or vague, clearly or dimly, loosely or tightly, well organized or poorly organized. However, it may eventually be organized he is the personal architect and inventor of his own world. As the totality of mankind is dependent upon planning to promote its advancement to new stages of complexity, so also is each individual learner dependent upon the efficiency of his Motor Planning to promote his personal advancement to more complex and yet economic behaviors.

Developmental Perspective

Close observation of the infant and toddler will reveal many occasions when his desires to move are not matched by his ability to direct his body parts in appropriate movements. He obviously wants but does not know how to move to achieve his goal.

It is a rather common sight to observe the very young child standing helplessly before the latch of a garden gate, a door knob, any obstacle or obstruction unable to resolve the dilemma. He may whimper, cry, or stand bewildered awaiting "rescue" by someone else **who can** solve the problem for him. This is an instance of inability to motorically plan and execute.

Motor planning is a lifetime objective for the human organism. If he is to move with purpose to acquire information, he must have direction, support and thrust. To define direction, provide support and insure momentum some degree of planning is necessary very early in the child's life. He must discover how to move an arm and a hand to grasp what is attractive and appealing to him. He must discover how to move his legs, supporting his weight to move his body weight through space. To get where he wishes to go he must **plan** to move.

A major portion of his waking hours during the first two years of life are devoted to inventory of his motoric assets so that he might call upon that inventory as he is confronted by motor dilemmas. He must learn how to plan the movement of his arms and legs to climb a stairs, crawl under a fence, fetch an object that is partially hidden under the davenport, and how to walk up and down a hill. He must plan how to move his legs to cover distance quickly and how to walk slowly beside his mother. He must plan how to place the fourth block on his tower, to hold a crayon, turn the pages in a book, scoop food with a spoon and move his arms to put on a jacket. Day after day he improves his ability to plan his moves and as he improves he wastes less effort, moves more directly and comfortably. He plans how to get where he wants to go by moving forwards, sideways, backwards, upwards and downwards. He learns to bring the toys he wants to the place of play and in that manner plans in advance. As he grows muscularly stronger and moves in better balance through known space he is aided by an improved appreciation of time and a better understanding of his own body. He learns how to exert more force from his leg muscles to jump higher and farther and to reach further into space. He learns how to stand on stools and chairs to increase his own height to obtain desired objects which are located beyond his unaided reach. He learns how to move the primary pencil to form a "d" in a different way than he forms the "m". The jungle gym, the playground slide and the whirl-a-round are managed successfully when he plans how to shift his body positioning.

He plans in advance to purchase a gift for Mother's Day, figures out a way to fix his coaster, and works on projects for his merit badges in the Scout troop. As an adult, he can plan a career, save money for a vacation and endure an apprenticeship.

Always he is a planning-being capable of plotting his patterns of movement so as to attain a goal. He plans physically and cognitively. In the final analysis his physical planning is a cognitive act and he is inevitably an expression of his intellectual design.

At a negative level the research has pointed out the extreme dilemmas faced by the neurologically impaired, the emotionally disturbed and the mentally retarded in respect to their ability to plan.

In the general field of neurologic dysfunction for both children and adults the inability to motor-plan is covered by the term **apraxia**. The term is usually defined as an inability to voluntarily perform a requested action but to possess the action itself in daily usage when specific cognitive direction of the action is a natural part of the activity. A **lingual apraxia** is an inability to voluntarily place the tongue to promote proper articulation while still giving evidence through normal vegetative processes of chewing and oral management of food that the tongue musculature is unimpaired.

On many occasions in clinical work with neurologically impaired children, a child has been observed to watch another child's motor performance with great interest and then make the attempt to imitate what he had seen. As he started his imitative effort, an expression of bewilderment came over him as he struggled to plan what part of himself to move first, how to move it and how to complete the action. All observers were in agreement that the imitative child clearly intended to imitate but was bewildered in his cognitive motor planning. The term **apraxia** seemed a natural label for this lack of performance.

Apraxia is one form of difficulty on the negative side between the polar opposites of planning and non-planning. At the opposite extreme are those beings who are unable to plan and as a consequence lack the ability to set goals and achieve any purpose in their behavior. The non-planning-being lacks purpose and direction and as a result must be impulsive, random and confused. Lacking in direction, such a being has no real system for identifying himself as a part of a spatial surround and as a consequence is considered to be "lost in space". The learner must plan his actions if he is to be regarded as a purposeful being. He plans in order that he might act with the greatest economy.

As a planning being he is capable of revision of plans if the initial plan is not a success. He becomes a planning being during infancy and expresses his proficiency as a planner throughout his life. He may err and miscalculate and thus behave in ways which are less than economical but he does possess the capability to critically review his own actions and modify his behavior. He can operate in a context of alternatives which allow him to behave in different ways according to the situation in which he finds himself. He may plot ways to escape. He may devise a plot to circumvent obstacles and he may choose to defer his actions to another time. He plans how to spend his money and he plans how to spend his time. If he does not plan, time is upon him in an urgency of the present and he is impulsively at the mercy of each impinging gradient of energy.

Throughout his life he is the victim or the victor of his own planning. When he plans wisely and moves with economy to enact his plans he is pleased and benefited. When he is unwise and his execution lacks economy he finds himself disappointed and frustrated. As he plans — he moves, sometimes wisely and sometimes foolishly. Every learner is eventually the product of his planning. His life is made up of errors and accuracies. When he analyzes a situation accurately and moves in response to his analysis, he achieves success. When his moves are directed by misperceptions he is frequently caught in a dilemma. He may move in a particular way and invoke sharp and severe criticism. He may choose to follow a certain cause and discover later that he has chosen unwisely. He may read social signs which appear to be to his advantage and move in accordance with his reading only to become painfully aware that he has done a poor job of interpretation. As he plans inaccurately he may suffer a broken ankle, a strained back and a wounded pride. Here the feedback mechanism is persistently active to help him become aware of the errors of his ways. The crushed ice cream cone will help him plan how to hold it more carefully the next time. The bruised knee will help him to recognize how to move his feet more gracefully and securely the next time. For most of life's encounters there is always a "next time" enabling the traveler to benefit from his previous experience.

The story of his success as a mobile organism will in large measure be recorded in terms of his planning. From infancy until his adulthood there will be an expectancy that he will become progressively more adept. The impulsive uncritical behaviors of his childhood are expected to be gradually replaced by planful and organized behavior. When he is a young child he is permitted the luxury of indulging in a "trial and error" form of behavior seeking to find a successful technique for organization. As he advances in complexity "trial and error" behavior is expected to subside and be replaced by careful analysis and planning before he sets himself into motion. It is generally expected that he will make less and less mistakes as he grows older and wiser. The wisdom of age is perhaps best characterized as moving slower but with wiser planning so as to minimize possible error.

As he plans it is also expected that he will reduce time of response. As he critically evaluates and brings a greater experiential background to bear upon the problems which confront him, it is expected that he will rid his behavior of extraneous and uneconomic responses and rest his performance on the least number of efficient moves necessary to resolve his problems. There is a "hard way" of doing things and an "easy way". Both may result in successful performance. One way achieves success but with much wasted and unnecessary effort and the other is direct and efficient. The difference results from wise planning.

If we consider all travelers to be learners of spatial transport then it is possible to conceive of grading their travel planning in the usual letter grading of A, B, C, and D. In the same manner as classroom teachers and college professors devise some system of differentially grading student performance, we may employ such a conception to the component of Motor Planning. The A learner may be characterized as most directly and economically presenting a digested and integrated organization of the expected content. No wasted effort is noticeable. The essentials have been covered precisely and the expression is clear. He has reviewed the content, selected wisely and interpreted the "heart of the matter". The B learner has achieved nearly the same economy but is lacking in precision and tends to incorporate certain unessentials in a "not quite" fashion even though his performance is consistently better than average. His performance is generally characterized by a lack of precision although his content is accurate. He has planned and selected but has some degree of vagueness in interpreting the "heart of the matter". The C learner is unpredictable. In some respects he is accurately "on target" and in other respects he has missed the point. He has interpreted "the heart of the matter" in some instances and has also evidenced some degree of confusion. The D learner gives evidence of a very hazy grasp of the situation and is frequently wandering in confusion in the general area of the content.

Each of these labels may be used in defining the Motor Planning ability of the individual. Each organism experiences all four gradings in relation to motor planning according to the situations and experiences of his life. Life is a continual struggle to merit an A rating as a planner. The most beautifully designed buildings often reveal a particular flaw which resulted because the architect did not account for some trivial factor in human engineering.

Inefficiency in planning results in a great deal of discontentment among troops, employees, volunteers and participants. The ability to take into account a wide variety of possibilities characterizes the effective planner.

Motor planning at the physical and cognitive level is an unescapable component of man's ability to move towards economic complexity. He must be a planner as a young infant, as a toddler, as a second grader, an adolescent, a young adult and as a senior citizen. He must be a planner whether he is deaf, blind, physically handicapped, emotionally disturbed, culturally disadvantaged, or mentally retarded.

As he plans, the learner achieves the cognitive excellence of his human design. The ability to plan how to move, what to move, why to move, where to move and when to move is a critical component in the composite of Movement Efficiency.

Our choice of the term Motor Planning is an arbitrary one but it seems most appropriate to the concept of freedom we wish to convey. If we are correct in our assignment of this component to the status of the final synthesis of movement, the implications for providing, guiding and directing the neophyte traveler to the discovery of such freedom are lucidly clear for parents, teachers, counselors and any professionals who are in a position to influence development.

To achieve the synthesis we have described, all learners must be given an appropriate program of activities and experiences to promote such a happening. A space-oriented curriculum must be considered.

20

DEFINING

A

CURRICULUM

The previous chapters of this book have set forth the formulations of the theory of Movigenics. The premise of the learner as a space-oriented organism seeking to establish efficiency in physical and cognitive movement has been set in a model of ten basic constructs, (1) the organism is designed for movement (2) the objective of movement is survival (3) movement occurs in an energy surround (4) the mechanism for acquiring information is the percepto-cognitive system (5) the terrain of movement is Space (6) developmental momentum thrusts the learner toward maturity (7) movement occurs in a climate of stress (8) feedback is essential to efficiency (9) development occurs in segments of sequential expansion, and (10) communication of efficiency is derived from the visual spatial phenomenon called language.

The discussion of these ten constructs was intended to establish a cognitive orientation to movement eventually culminating in a clear image of man's symbolic capabilities serving as the principal constructional element in building an efficiency in space.

Defining the learner as a space-oriented being requires a working model of space. In Chapter III space was defined as **an abstraction derived from the relative intervals between and among objects requiring always a referent and a terminal point.** Within this space model the four domains of space: physiologic, physical, milieu and cognitive, four zones of space: near, mid, far and remote and six fields of space: up, down, back, front, left and right were designated as the organizational units of construction.

In Movigenic theory, the learner is viewed as continuously **engaged in an** effort to achieve grace, ease, comfort and efficiency in both physical and cognitive movement. Movement Efficiency is a matrix composed of fifteen component parts divided into three organizational units within each performer. The basic anatomical, physiologic and neurologic design of the organism is intended to unify all fifteen components into a harmonious and efficient pattern of interrelatedness and interdependence. The five components: Muscular Strength, Dynamic Balance, Body Awareness, Spatial Awareness and Temporal Awareness contribute to the establishment of Postural-Transport Orientations for the learner at all ages. The Percept-Cognitive Modes, gustatory, olfactory, tactual, kinesthesia, auditory, and visual combine to provide the organism with an efficient system for acquiring information to promote his optimal survival. To insure ranges and amplitudes in function the Degrees of Freedom, bilaterality, Rhythm, Flexibility and Motor Planning serve the learner in enriching his constructional effort.

The singular intent of this book has been to identify the constructional elements which must be considered in providing a curriculum for Movement Efficiency. These elements have been presented. Each of the constructs, domains, zones, fields and components must find its expression in a curriculum which is intended to achieve its desired goal—the efficiency of the learner. These must now be woven into a pattern of activities and experiences to insure the objectives.

In its simplest form the term "curriculum" is used to describe a series or a sequence of events occurring with particular emphasis over a specified period of time, offered in gradients of quality and quantity to produce a desired result. The usual expectancy when the term is applied is for a booklet or a collection of specific activities complete with equipment and instructions to be available as a **curriculum guide**. Very specific instructions for equipment, activity sequences, remedial procedures and workbooks are intended in the subsequent volumes of the PERCEPTUAL-MOTOR CURRICULUM series but within the scope of the present volume we must limit our specificity to the elaboration of a set of "guidelines to curriculum" and hope that the foregoing chapters have provided the "instructors" with the necessary background to bring the "guidelines" to a practical level.

It is imperative that these guidelines be set forth to clearly establish the formal for interweaving all of the constructional elements into a practical model for the teacher.

GUIDELINE #1

It is critical for the teacher to adopt an abiding orientation to the learner as a spatial organism and to utilize a spatial orientation in evaluating the performance of the learner. The first step in adopting such an orientation requires the teacher to carefully observe and record the characteristic patterns of movement employed by the child in managing his actions in physical and cognitive space. The observations must be recorded in terms of EFFICIENT-INEFFICIENT. The customary evaluative terms "successful-failing" must be relegated to a secondary consideration. The teacher must become more interested in whether the learner is performing with efficiency than whether he is successful or unsuccessful. The efficiency of his performance will become the critical indicator of his potential to advance to more complicated behaviors in the future. Progressively more efficient patterns can scarcely be expected to emerge from inefficient foundations.

GUIDELINE #2

Complexity is the goal and the product of efficiency in learning. The teacher must continuously question whether the learner is actually becoming a more complex organism day after day as a result of his learning. The judgment of complexity, however, cannot be limited to a consideration of reading paragraphs, sentences and spelling words. The complexity which must increase is that of processing information from all fields and zones of space through the utilization of all six channels of the Percepto-Cognitive system. The question must be asked in terms of increased complexity in processing gustatory, olfactory, tactual, kinesthetic, auditory and visual information from near, mid, far and remote space in whatever direction it may be moving.

GUIDELINE #3

Activities must be planned to give the learner ample opportunities to explore his muscular relationships, varying positions of balance, all parts of his body, all positions of space and varying relationships to time.

GUIDELINE #4

Activities must be provided for the learner to explore the utility of ALL SIX perceptual modes in gaining information about his world. Arrival at the kindergarten, the third grade or even the senior high school is no guarantee that the learner has achieved efficiency in all areas of modal processing.

GUIDELINE #5

Activities should be provided to deliberately vary the zones of stimulation presenting opportunities in wide assortments of target sources from near, mid, far and remote space.

GUIDELINE #6

Once a basic learning of a task has been achieved the learner should be exposed to multiple variations in performance of the learned task. He may perform it slower or faster, forward or backward, right-side up or upside-down, in many different settings and contexts, etc. Varying the performance permits the learner to embed the learning and to integrate the particular information solidly. If minor variations in orientation cause the learner to "give up" his learning the teacher may conclude that it was not truly established as an integrated bit of information.

GUIDELINE #7

It is the learner who must construct his own Movement Efficiency. The teacher must therefore, provide him with an ample range of variations so that he might continue to test his learning under varying conditions and varying forms of deliberately induced stress. Each learner must discover **his** range of performance. To discover such range, he must have opportunities to explore differences in his own performance process.

GUIDELINE #8

All movement must be cognitively directed. The learner's achievement of awareness of movement and the development of his abilities to plan his moves appropriately becomes a critical goal.

GUIDELINE #9

A spatial orientation can be applied to all types of performance. The skills of reading, writing, arithmetic and spelling can be considered as spatial orientations. The use and structure of language can be regarded as spatially defined.

GUIDELINE #10

A space-oriented approach to teaching does not require the teacher to discard existing practices and methods. It is rather a matter of restructuring existing procedures to emphasize the spatial orientation and suggests the diversification of activities **within** existing and effective techniques.

These ten guideline points may all be unified into a single composite directive. The synthesis of Movigenics is intended to establish a model for observing and evaluating the performing efficiency of the learner. Every transaction with his environment provides the learner with some form of spatial information to be utilized in building a more complex level of behavior.

The Movigenic viewpoint on curriculum extends well beyond the customary usage of the term. The parent of the infant can be regarded as an instructor providing a sequence of activities and experiences to assist the neophyte in acquiring spatial competence. The parent of the pre-school child is also an instructor providing a curriculum. The pre-primary teacher in the cooperative nursery school structures opportunities for the learner to explore space and develop perceptual-motor competence. The occupational therapist and the physical therapist relating to the learner in a clinical setting also structure a program of spatial learning. The speech therapist, the remedial reading instructor, the mobility instructors of the blind, the psychotherapist, the school and clinical psychologist can all be regarded as instructors within a space curriculum. The formal programs of school define the classroom teacher as an instructor offering a curriculum of space orientation. The concept of curriculum is not limited to the activities which occur in a classroom. Many, many instructors are available to assist the learner in his effort to achieve Movement Efficiency.

The obligation to master space is equally in force for those learners who are generally classified as special children. The child who is classified as neurologically impaired, cerebral palsied, blind, deaf, emotionally disturbed, physically handicapped, aphasic or mentally retarded is also a space traveler. The deeper understanding of the dynamics of deviancy in each of those conditions can be achieved by studying the development of these children from a space-oriented point of view. A single viewpoint to replace the customary separation into seemingly discrete categories provides a system for examining the similarities among these various child problems rather than emphasizing the differences. The net loss, whatever name be given to the condition or category of the child, will be recorded in terms of reductions in spatial efficiency.

Throughout the text, a developmental perspective has been the principal focus of the presentation. The emphasis upon the infant was intended to demonstrate the possibility that the inefficient learner at later ages is operating in his current affairs with a set of inefficiencies which were built into his movement patterns during his formative years. The consensus in the field of remediation points to a need to give attention to the failing learner in those areas of performance which developmentally were intended to establish the base for mounting a lifetime of advancing complexity. The foundations for efficiency are built in the early laboratory of childhood. It is there that we must diligently search for a deeper understanding of learning.

In a very real sense every child contains the corporate structure of his own society. He is a geometer, physicist, engineer, biologist, zoologist, botanist, physician — he is an individual incorporation of all men. He is a prosaic living example of the organization of mankind. His day by day struggles represent the complex struggle of his society. He moves to learn as have all men before him. The tally sheet of his achievements will be marked in spatial encounters. He moves in space. It is the terrain of learning. He moves and he perceives, He perceives and he moves. He is a perceptual-motor being. All of his learning is perceptual and all of his learning is motor. Only as we come to understand the remarkable complexity of his perceptual-motor unity, will we find the ways to assist him to achieve the highest possible level of Movement Efficiency.

The goal of all teachers must be to provide the learner with those opportunities and experiences which will enable him to transport himself physically and cognitively, in comfort and ease so as to promote his optimal survival...he is a space traveler seeking the route to competency...as are we all.

BIBLIOGRAPHY

Abbe, M. THE TEMPORAL EFFECT UPON THE PERCEPTION OF TIME, Jap. J. Exp. Psychol., 4:83-93, 1937.

Abbe, M. THE SPATIAL EFFECT UPON THE PERCEPTION OF TIME, Jap. J. Exp. Psychol., 3:1-52, 1936.

Adler, Francis Heed PHYSIOLOGY OF THE EYE. C.V. Mosby Co., 1950.

Adrian, E.D. THE BASIS OF SENSATION. SOME RECENT STUDIES OF OLFACTION, Brit. Med. J., 1:287, 1954.

Adrian, E.D. SENSORY MESSAGES AND SENSATION. THE RESPONSE OF THE OLFACTORY ORGAN TO DIFFERENT SMELLS, Acta Physiol. Scand., 29:5, 1953.

Adrian, E.D. THE PHYSICAL BACKGROUND OF PERCEPTION. Oxford, The Clarendon Press, 1947.

Albright, R.W. THE MOTOR ABILITIES OF SPEAKERS WITH GOOD AND POOR ARTICULATION, Speech Monogr., XV:164-172, 1948.

Allport, Floyd H. THEORIES OF PERCEPTION AND THE CONCEPT OF STRUCTURE. New York, John Wiley and Sons, 1955.

Ames, A., Jr. VISUAL PERCEPTION AND THE ROTATING TRAPEZOIDAL WINDOW, Psychol. Monogr., V. 65, No. 7, (324) 1951.

Ames, Albert, Jr., and Ittelson, William H. ACCOMMODATION, CONVERGENCE AND THEIR RELATION TO APPARENT DISTANCE, J. Psychol., 30:43-62, 1950.

Ames, L.B. THE SEQUENTIAL PATTERNING OF PRONE PROGRESSION IN THE HUMAN INFANT, Genet. Psychol. Monogr., 19:411-460, 1937.

Ames, Louise Bates THE DEVELOPMENT OF THE SENSE OF TIME IN THE YOUNG CHILD,

J. Genet. Psychol., 68:97-125, 1946.

Anderson, H.A. NEEDED RESEARCH IN LISTENING. Elem. English, 29:215-224, 1952.

Ashby, W.R. DESIGN FOR AN INTELLIGENCE AMPLIFIER, Shannon, C.E. & McCarthy, J. (Eds.), Automata Studies. Princeton, Princeton University Press, 215-234, 1956.

Ashby, W.R. DESIGN FOR A BRAIN. New York, John Wiley and Sons, Inc., 1952.

Ashby, W.R. DESIGN FOR A BRAIN, 2nd Edition, New York, John Wiley and Sons, Inc., 1960.

Austin, T.R., and Sleight, R.B. ACCURACY OF TACTUAL DISCRIMINATION OF LETTERS, NUMERALS AND GEOMETRIC FORM, J. Exp. Psychol., 43, 1952.

Austin, T.R., and Sleight, R.B. FACTORS RELATED TO SPEED AND ACCURACY OF TACTUAL DISCRIMINATION, J. Exp. Psychol., 44:283-287, 1952.

Ayers, A.J. DEVELOPMENT OF THE BODY SCHEME IN CHILDREN, Amer. J. Occup. Ther., 15:99, 1961.

Bain, A. THE EMOTIONS AND THE WILL, 4th Edition. London, Longmans, Green and Co., 1899.

Bakan, P., and Weiler, E. KINESTHETIC AFTER-EFFECT AND MODE OF EXPOSURE TO THE INSPECTION STIMULUS, J. Exp. Psychol., 65:319-320, 1963.

Baker, Lawrence M. GENERAL EXPERIMENTAL PSYCHOLOGY. New York, Oxford University Press, 1960.

Barcroft. J. FEATURES IN THE ARCHITECTURE OF PHYSIOLOGICAL FUNCTION. New York, MacMillan, 1934.

Barndt, Robert J., and Johnson, Donald M. TIME ORIENTATION IN DELINQUENT, J. Abnorm. Soc. Psychol., 51:343-345, 1955.

Barnett, S.A. EXPLORATORY BEHAVIOR, Brit. J. Psychol., 49:289-310, 1958.

Barsch, Ray, H. THE CONCEPT OF LANGUAGE AS A VISUAL SPATIAL PHENOMENON. Academic Therapy Quart., 1:1. 2-10, 1965.

Barsch, Ray, H. THE CONCEPT OF REACH-GRASP-RELEASE AS A VISUAL, AUDITORY

AND TACTUAL PROCESS. J. Genet. Psychol., 106. 237-243., 1965.

Barsch, Ray H. THE PARENT OF THE HANDICAPPED CHILD: A STUDY OF CHILD-REARING PRACTICES. Springfield, Charles C. Thomas, (in press) 1967.

Bartley, S.H. THE PERCEPTION OF SIZE OR DISTANCE BASED ON TACTUAL AND KINESTHETIC DATA, Psychol. Journal, 36:401-408, 1953.

Bartley, S. Howard THE PSYCHOPHYSIOLOGY OF VISION, Stevens, S.S. (Ed.). Handbook of Experimental Psychology. New York, John Wiley and Sons, 921-984, 1951.

Bauer, H.J. DISCRIMINATION OF TACTUAL STIMULI, J. Exp. Psychol., 44:455-459, 1952.

Bayley, Nancy. THE DEVELOPMENT OF MOTOR ABILITIES DURING THE FIRST THREE YEARS - A STUDY OF SIXTY-ONE INFANTS TESTED REPEATEDLY. Monogr. Soc. Res. Child. Develop., 1:1-26, 1936.

Bayley, Nancy. MENTAL GROWTH DURING THE FIRST THREE YEARS—A DEVELOPMENTAL STUDY OF SIXTY-ONE CHILDREN BY REPEATED TESTS, Genet. Psychol. Monogr., 14:1-92, 1933.

Bayley, Nancy. THE DEVELOPMENT OF MOTOR ABILITIES DURING THE FIRST THREE YEARS, Soc. Res. Child. Develop. Monogr., 2, 1935.

Beck, Harry S. THE RELATIONSHIP OF SYMBOL REVERSALS TO MONOCULAR AND BINOCULAR VISION, Peabody J. Educ., 38:137-142, (1) July, 1960.

Bekesy, G. von. CURRENT STATUS OF THEORIES OF HEARING. Science, 123, 779-783., 1956.

Belmont, Lillian and Birch, Herbert G. LATERAL DOMINANCE, LATERAL AWARENESS, AND READING DISABILITY. Child. Develop., 36:57-71, (1), 1965.

Bender, L. and Silver, A. BODY IMAGE PROBLEMS OF THE BRAIN-INJURED CHILD, J. Soc. Iss., 4:84-89, 1948.

Bender, M.B., Fink, M. and Green, M. PATTERNS IN PERCEPTION ON SIMULTANEOUS TESTS OF FACE AND HANDS, Arch. Neurol. Psychiat., 66:355-362, 1951.

Benton, Arthur L. RIGHT-LEFT DISCRIMINATION AND FINGER LOCALIZATION. New York, Hoeber Medical Div., Harper and Row, 1959.

Benton, A.L., Hutcheon, J.F. and Seymour, E. ARITHMETIC ABILITY, FINGER LOCALIZATION CAPACITY AND RIGHT-LEFT DISCRIMINATION IN NORMAL AND DEFECTIVE CHILDREN, Amer. J. Orthopsychiat., 21:756-766, 1951.

Benton, A.L. and Schultz, L.M. OBSERVATIONS ON TACTUAL FORM PERCEPTION (STEREOGNOSIS) IN PRE-SCHOOL CHILDREN, J. Clin. Psychol., 5:359-364, 1949.

Benton, C.D., McCann, J.W. and Larsen, M. DYSLEXIA AND DOMINANCE, J. Pediat. Ophthal., 53, July, 1965.

Berner, G.E. and Berner, D.E. RELATION OF OCULAR DOMINANCE, HANDEDNESS, AND THE CONTROLLING EYE IN BINOCULAR VISION, Amer. Med. Ass. Arch. Ophtholm., 50:603-608, 1921.

Bilto, E.W. A COMPARATIVE STUDY OF CERTAIN PHYSICAL ABILITIES OF CHILDREN WITH SPEECH DEFECTS AND CHILDREN WITH NORMAL SPEECH, J. Speech Dis., VII: 187-203, 1942.

Birch, H.J. DYSLEXIA AND THE MATURATION OF THE VISUAL FUNCTION, J. Money (Ed.), Reading Disability, Progress and Research Needs in Dyslexia. Baltimore, Johns Hopkins Press, 1962a.

Birch, H.J. PSYCHOLOGICAL MATURATION OF NORMAL AND BRAIN DAMAGED CHILDREN. Address to American Academy for Cerebral Palsy, Miami, Florida, 1962b.

Birch, H.J. and Belmont, L. AUDITORY-VISUAL INTEGRATION, INTELLIGENCE AND READING ABILITY IN SCHOOL CHILDREN, Percept. Motor Skills, 20:295, 1965.

Birch, Herbert G. and Belmont, Lillian. AUDITORY-VISUAL INTEGRATION IN BRAIN-DAMAGED AND NORMAL CHILDREN, Develop. Med. Child Neurol., 7:135-144, 1965.

Birch, H.G. and Belmont, Lillian. AUDITORY AND VISUAL INTEGRATION IN NORMAL AND RETARDED READERS, Amer. J. Orthopsychiat., 34:852, 1964.

Birch, H.J. and Lefford, A. INTERSENSORY DEVELOPMENT IN CHILDREN, Monogr. Soc. Res. Child. Develop., 28:No. 5, 1963.

Birch, J.W. and Mathews, J. THE HEARING OF MENTAL DEFECTIVES, Amer. J. Ment. Defec., 55:384, 1951.

Bird, Donald E. BIBLIOGRAPHY OF SELECTED MATERIALS ABOUT LISTENING. Education,

75:334-359, 1955.

Boag, Audrey K. and Neild, Margaret. THE INFLUENCE OF THE TIME FACTOR ON THE SCORES OF THE PRIGGS DIAGNOSTIC READING TEST AS REFLECTED IN THE PERFORMANCE OF SECONDARY SCHOOL PUPILS GROUPED ACCORDING TO ABILITY, J. Educ. Res., 55:181-183, (4) December-January, 1962.

Boring, Edwin C. SENSATION AND PERCEPTION IN EXPERIMENTAL PSYCHOLOGY. New York, Appleton-Century-Crofts, 1942.

Bornstein, W.S. THE LOCALIZATION OF THE CORTICAL TASTE AREA IN MAN AND A METHOD FOR MEASURING IMPAIRMENT OF TASTE IN MAN, Yale J. Biol. Med., 13: 133-136, 1940-1941.

Boyd, W. FROM LOCKE TO MONTESSORI. New York, Henry Holt and Co., 1914.

Braly, K. INCIDENCE OF DEFECTIVE VISION AMONG THE DEAF. West Trenton, N. J., New Jersey School for Deaf, Tech. Series 4, 1937.

Braun, H. W. PERCEPTUAL PROCESSES, J.E. Birren (Ed.), Handbook of Aging and the Individual. Chicago, University of Chicago Press, 543-561, 1959.

Breckenridge, Marian and Vincent, E. Lee. CHILD DEVELOPMENT, PHYSICAL AND PSYCHOLOGIC GROWTH THROUGH THE SCHOOL YEARS. Philadelphia, W.B. Saunders Co., 1955.

Brieson, Hans V. A DISCUSSION OF STRESS AND EXHAUSTION AS A PRIMARY AS WELL AS A CONTRIBUTING ETIOLOGIC FACTOR IN ORGANIC NEUROLOGICAL DISEASE, Milit. Surgeon, 101, 1947.

Briggs, G.E. and Brogden, W.J. THE EFFECT OF COMPONENT PRACTICE ON PERFORMANCE OF A LEVEL POSITIONARY SKILL, J. Exp. Psychol., 48:375-380, 1954.

Briggs, M.H. and Duncan, R.B. ODOUR RECEPTORS, Nature, 191:1310-1311, 1961.

Briggs, M.H. and Duncan, R.B. PIGMENT AND THE OLFACTORY MECHANISMS, Nature, 195:1313-1314, 1962.

Brock, Timothy C. and Del Giudice, Carolyn. STEALING AND TEMPORAL ORIENTATION, J. Abnorm. Soc. Psychol., 66:91-94, (1) 1963.

Broer, Marion R. EFFICIENCY OF HUMAN MOVEMENT. Philadelphia, W.B. Saunders

Co., 1960.

Brown, James. THE MEASUREMENT OF LISTENING ABILITY. School and Society, 71: 69-71, 1950.

Brown, J.J. COMPARISON OF LISTENING AND READING ABILITY. College English, Vol. X: 105-107, 1948.

Brown, James. EVALUATING STUDENT PERFORMANCE IN LISTENING. Education, 74: 316-326, 1955.

Bruner, J.S. and Goodman, C. VALUE AND NEED AS ORGANIZING FACTORS IN PERCEPTION. J. Abnorm. and Soc. Psychol., 42:33-44, 1947.

Bruner, J.S. and Krech, D. PERCEPTION AND PERSONALITY: A SYMPOSIUM. Duke University Press, 1950.

Brunnstrom, Signe. CENTER OF GRAVITY LINE IN RELATION TO ANKLE JOINT IN ERECT STANDING, APPLICATION TO POSTURE TRAINING AND TO ARTIFICIAL LEGS, Physical Therapy Review, 34:109-115, (3) March, 1954.

Brunswik, E. ORGANISMIC ACHIEVEMENT AND ENVIRONMENTAL PROBABILITY, Psychol. Rev., 50:255-272, 1943.

Brunswik, E. PROBABILITY AS A DETERMINER OF RAT BEHAVIOR, J. Exp. Psychol., 25: 175-197, 1939.

Brunswik, E. PSYCHOLOGY IN TERMS OF OBJECTS. Proceedings of the 25th anniversary celebration inaugural graduate studies. Los Angeles, University of Southern California Press, 1936.

Burklen, K. BLINDEN PSYCHOLOGIE. Leipzig, Johann Ambrosius Barth, 1924.

Cannon, W.B. THE WISDOM OF THE BODY. New York, W.W. Norton and Co., Inc., 1932.

Cantor, G.N. and Girardeau, F.L. RHYTHMIC DISCRIMINATION ABILITY IN MONGOLOID AND NORMAL CHILDREN, Amer. J. Ment. Defic., 63:621-625, 1959.

Cantril, Hadley. PERCEPTION AND INTERPERSONAL RELATIONS, Amer. J. Psychiatry, 114:119-126, 1959.

Cantril, H. THE NATURE OF SOCIAL PERCEPTION, Trans. N. Y. Acad. Sci., 10:142-153, 1948.

Carmichael, L. THE ONSET AND EARLY DEVELOPMENT OF BEHAVIOR, L. Carmichael (Ed.), Manual of Child Psychology (2nd Edition). New York, John Wiley and Sons, Inc., 60-185, 1954.

Casler, Lawrence. A STUDY OF THE EFFECTS OF EXTRA TACTILE STIMULATION ON THE DEVELOPMENT OF INSTITUTIONALIZED INFANTS. Genet. Psychol. Monogr., 138-175. 1965.

Castner, B.M. THE DEVELOPMENT OF FINE PREHENSION IN INFANCY. Genet. Psychol. Monogr., Vol. 12, 1932.

Cattell, Psyche. TESTS OF INTELLIGENCE. A. INFANT INTELLIGENCE SCALE. A. Weider (Ed.), Contributions Toward Medical Psychology, 688-701, 1953.

Cheatham, P.G. and White, C.T. TEMPORAL NUMEROSITY AS A FUNCTION OF FLASH NUMBER AND RATE. J. Exp. Psychol., 44:447-451, 1952.

Cherry, Colin. TWO EARS—BUT ONE WORLD. Walter A. Rosenblith (Ed.), Sensory Communication, 99-117, 1961.

Clark, Legros, W.E. OBSERVATIONS ON THE STRUCTURE AND ORGANIZATION OF OLFACTORY RECEPTORS IN THE RABBIT. Yale J. Biol. Med., 29:83-95, 1956.

Clark, Legros, W.E. INQUIRIES INTO THE ANATOMICAL BASIS OF OLFACTORY DISCRIMINATION. Proc. Royal Soc. Ser. B. 146:299-319, 1957.

Cleghorn, T.E. and Darcus, H.D. THE SENSIBILITY TO PASSIVE MOVEMENT OF THE HUMAN ELBOW JOINT. Quart. J. Exp. Psychol., 4:66-77, 1952.

Cofer, C.N. and Appley, M.H. MOTIVATION: THEORY AND RESEARCH. New York, John Wiley and Sons, 302-366, 1964.

Cohen, L.A. ROLE OF EYE AND NECK PROPRIOCEPTION MECHANISMS IN BODY ORIENTATION AND MOTOR COORDINATION. J. Neurophysiol., 24:1, 1961.

Corah, N.L. ATTENTION AND KINESTHETIC FIGURAL AFTEREFFECT. Amer. J. Psychol., 74:629-630, 1961.

Cotton, Esther. THE INSTITUTE FOR MOVEMENT THERAPY AND SCHOOL FOR "CONDUCTORS", Budapest, Hungary, Develop. Med. and Child Neurol., 7:437-446, 1965.

Cratty, Bryant J. MOVEMENT BEHAVIOR AND MOTOR LEARNING. Philadelphia, Lea and Febiger, 1964.

Cratty, Bryant J. and Hutton, Robert. FIGURAL AFTEREFFECTS RESULTING FROM GROSS ACTION PATTERNS. Res. Quart., 35:147-160, 1964.

Cruickshank, W.M., Bice, H.V. and Wallen, N.E. PERCEPTION AND CEREBRAL PALSY: A STUDY IN FIGURE-BACKGROUND RELATIONSHIP. Syracuse, Syracuse University Press, 1957.

Cruickshank, William. PSYCHOLOGY OF EXCEPTIONAL CHILDREN. New Jersey, Prentice-Hall, 1963.

Curran, Jeanne. A PRELIMINARY INVESTIGATION OF BILATERALITY AMONG ELEMENTARY SCHOOL CHILDREN. Unpublished master's thesis. University of Wisconsin, Madison, 1965.

Dalcroze, Jacques. EMILE, RHYTHM, MUSIC AND EDUCATION. London, Chalto and Windus, 1921.

Davids, Anthony, Kidder, Catherine and Reich, Melvin. TEMPORAL ORIENTATION IN MALE AND FEMALE JUVENILE DELINQUENTS. J. Abnorm. & Soc. Psychol., 64, 1962.

Deach, Dorothy F. THE GENETIC DEVELOPMENT OF MOTOR SKILLS OF CHILDREN TWO THROUGH SIX YEARS OF AGE. Doctoral dissertation. Ann Arbor, Univ. Michigan Press, 1950.

Delacato, C.H. THE TREATMENT AND PREVENTION OF READING PROBLEMS. Springfield, Illinois, Charles C. Thomas Co., 1959.

Delacato, Carl H. THE DIAGNOSIS OF SPEECH AND READING PROBLEMS. Springfield, Illinois, Charles C. Thomas, 1963.

Dennis, Wayne. LATERALITY OF FUNCTION IN EARLY INFANCY UNDER CONTROLLED DEVELOPMENTAL CONDITIONS. Child Develop., 6:242-252, 1935.

de Vries, H. and Stuiver, M. THE ABSOLUTE SENSITIVITY OF THE HUMAN SENSE OF SMELL. In Walter A. Rosenblith (Ed.), Sensory Communication. New York, Wiley and Sons, 159-167, 1961.

Disher, D.R. THE REACTIONS OF NEWBORN INFANTS TO CHEMICAL STIMULI ADMINISTERED NASALLY. Ohio State Univ. Stud. Contr. Psychol., 12:1-52, 1934.

Dolphin, J.E. and Cruickshank, W.M. THE TACTUAL-MOTOR PERCEPTION OF CHILDREN WITH CEREBRAL PALSY. J. Pers., 20, 1952.

Driver, Ann. MUSIC AND MOVEMENT. London, Oxford Univ. Press, H. Milford, 1936.

Duffy, E. MUSCULAR TENSION AS RELATED TO PHYSIQUE AND BEHAVIOR. Child Develop., 3:200-206, 1932.

Duke-Elder, Sir W. Stewart. TEXTBOOK OF OPHTHALMOLOGY. Vol. 1. C.V. Mosby Co., 1942.

Eames, Thomas. THE RELATIONSHIPS OF THE CENTRAL VISUAL FIELD TO THE SPEED OF VISUAL PERCEPTION, Amer. J. Ophthalm., 63:279-280, 1957.

Elliott, Rogers. PHYSIOLOGICAL ACTIVITY AND PERFORMANCE: A COMPARISON OF KINDERGARTEN CHILDREN WITH YOUNG ADULTS, Psychol. Monogr., V. 78, No. 10 (587), 1964.

Eisenberg, P. and Reichline, P.B. JUDGING EXPRESSIVE MOVEMENTS. II. JUDGMENT OF DOMINANCE FEELING FROM MOTION PICTURES OF GAIT, J. Soc. Psychol., 10:345-347, 1939.

Eisenson, Jon. THE NATURE OF DEFECTIVE SPEECH, WILLIAM M. CRUICKSHANK (Ed.), PSYCHOLOGY OF EXCEPTIONAL CHILDREN AND YOUTH. Englewood Cliffs, N.J., Prentice-Hall, 184, 1955.

Emery, Leonard. VISUAL PROCESSES AND VISION SCREENING, Claremont Reading Conference 26th Yearbook, 1962.

Escalona, S. EMOTIONAL DEVELOPMENT IN THE FIRST YEAR OF LIFE, M.E. Senn (Ed.), PROBLEMS OF INFANCY AND CHILDHOOD: TRANSACTIONS OF THE SIXTH CONFERENCE. New York, Josiah Macy, Jr. Foundation, 11-92, 1953.

Fairbanks, G. and Bebout, B. A STUDY OF MINOR ORGANIC DEVIATIONS IN "FUNCTIONAL" DISORDERS OF ARTICULATION: 3. THE TONGUE, J. Speech Hearing Dis., XV: 348-352, 1950.

Farber, I.E. and Spence, K.W. CONDITIONING AND EXTINCTION AS A FUNCTION OF ANXIETY, J. Exp. Psychol., 45:116-119, 1953.

Farrell, Muriel. UNDERSTANDING OF TIME RELATIONSHIP, FIVE, SIX AND SEVEN YEAR OLD CHILDREN OF HIGH IQ, J. Educ. Res., 46:587-594, (8) April, 1953.

Fay, Temple. THE ORIGIN OF HUMAN MOVEMENT, Amer. J. Psychiatry, 644, 1955.

Fertsch, P. HAND DOMINANCE IN READING BRAILLE, Amer. J. Psychol., 60:335-349, 1947.

Fessenden, Seth A. LEVELS OF LISTENING — A THEORY. Education, 75:288-291, 1955.

Festinger, Leon. COGNITIVE DISSONANCE. Stanford Univ. Press, 1962.

Fincham, E.R. THE ACCOMODATIVE REFLEX AND ITS STIMULUS. Optical Developments. Chicago, Bausch and Lomb Optical Co., 1951.

Fischer, L.K. THE SIGNIFICANCE OF ATYPICAL POSTURAL AND GRASPING BEHAVIOR DURING THE FIRST YEAR OF LIFE. Amer. J. Orthopsychiat., 45:368-375, 1958.

Fisher, M.B. and Birren, J.E. AGE AND STRENGTH, J. Applied Psychol., 31:490-497. 1947.

Fisher, S. and Cleveland, S. BODY IMAGE AND PERSONALITY. New York, Van Nostrand Co., 1958.

Fischgold, H. and Lairy Bounes, G.C. REACTION D'ARRET ET D'EVEIL DANS LES LESIONS DU TRONC CEREBRAL ET DES HEMISPHERES. Rev. Neurol., 87:603-604, 1952 (abstract).

Fitts, P.M. and Crammell, C. LOCATION DISCRIMINATION II. ACCURACY OF REACHING MOVEMENTS IN 24 AREAS. USAF Air Material Command Technical Report 5833, 1950.

Fitzgerald, J.E. and Windle, W.F. SOME OBSERVATIONS ON EARLY HUMAN FETAL ACTIVITY. J. Comp. Neurol., 76:159-167, 1942.

Forgays, D.G. DEVELOPMENT OF DIFFERENTIAL WORD RECOGNITION. J. Exp. Psychol., 45:165-168, 1953.

Fox, Margaret and Atwood, Janet. RESULTS OF TESTING IOWA SCHOOL CHILDREN FOR HEALTH AND FITNESS. J. Health, Physical Educ. and Recreat., XXVI. 7, 1955.

Frank, L.K. TACTILE COMMUNICATION. Genet, Psychol. Monogr., 56:209-255, 1957.

Franz, S.I. THE CONSTANT ERROR OF TOUCH LOCALIZATION. J. Exp. Psychol., 1: 83-98, 1916.

Franz, S.I. DIFFUSION EFFECTS FOLLOWING LOCALIZED TACTILE TRAINING. University of California at Los Angeles Publications in Education, Philosophy and Psychology, 1:129-135, 1933.

Freeburne, C.M. and Fleischer, M.S. THE EFFECT OF MUSIC DISTRACTION UPON READING RATE AND COMPREHENSION. J. Educ. Psychol., 43:101-109, 1952.

Freeman, G.L. THE ENERGETICS OF HUMAN BEHAVIOR. Ithaca, Cornell University Press, 1948.

Fuller, R. Buckminster. VISION 1965-summary lecture. The American Scholar, 35,2: 206-218, 1966.

Gaddes, William H. THE NEEDS OF TEACHERS FOR SPECIALIZED INFORMATION ON HANDEDNESS, FINGER LOCALIZATION AND CEREBRAL DOMINANCE. William M. Cruickshank (Ed.) The Teacher of Brain Injured Children. Syracuse, Syracuse University Press, 207-218, 1966.

Gardner, R.W. and Long, R.I. CONTROL, DEFENCE AND CENTRATION EFFECT: A STUDY OF SCANNING BEHAVIOR, Brit, J. Psychol., 53:129-140, 1962.

Gardner, R.W. and Schoen, R.A. DIFFERENTIATION AND ABSTRACTION IN CONCEPT FORMATION, Psychol. Monogr., V. 76, No. 41, 1962.

Geldard, Frank A. ADVENTURES IN TACTILE LITERACY, Amer. Psychol., 12:115-124, (3), 1957.

Geldard, Frank A. CUTANEOUS CHANNELS OF COMMUNICATION, Walter A. Rosenblith (Ed.), Sensory Communication. Massachusetts Institute of Technology Press, 1961, 73-87.

Geldard, Frank A. THE HUMAN SENSES. New York, John Wiley and Sons, 1953.

Gesell, A.L. THE TONIC-NECK-REFLEX IN THE HUMAN INFANT. J. Pediat., 13:455, 1938.

Gesell, A. THE EMBRYOLOGY OF BEHAVIOR. New York, Harper and Row, 1945.

Gesell, Arnold and Ames, L.B. THE ONTOGENETIC ORGANIZATION OF PRONE BEHAVIOR IN HUMAN INFANCY, J. Genet, Psychol., 56:247-263, 1940.

Gesell, A. and Ilg, Frances L. CHILD DEVELOPMENT. New York, Harper and Bros., 1949.

Gesell, Arnold, Ilg, Frances L. and Bullis, Glenna E. VISION: ITS DEVELOPMENT IN INFANT AND CHILD. New York, Paul B. Hoeber, Inc., 1949.

Gesell, Arnold and Ilg, Frances L. THE CHILD FROM FIVE TO TEN. New York, Harper and Bros., 1946.

Gesell, Arnold and Amatruda, Catherine S. DEVELOPMENTAL DIAGNOSIS. New York, Hoeber, 1947.

Getman, G.N. HOW TO DEVELOP YOUR CHILD'S INTELLIGENCE. LuVerne, Minn. Published privately by the author, 1962.

Getman, G.N. THE VISUOMOTOR COMPLEX IN THE ACQUISITION OF LEARNING. In Jerome Hellmuth (Ed.), Learning Disorders. Vol. I. Seattle, Special Child Publications, 49-76, 1965.

Ghent, Lila. DEVELOPMENTAL CHANGES IN TACTUAL THRESHOLDS ON DOMINANT AND NON-DOMINANT SIDES. J. Comp. Physiol. and Psychol. 54, 1961.

Gibson, Eleanor and Olum, Vivian. EXPERIMENTAL METHODS OF STUDYING PERCEPTION IN CHILDREN, Paul H. Mussen (Ed.), Handbook of Research Methods in Child Development. New York, John Wiley and Sons, 311-373, 1960.

Gibson, J.J. A CRITICAL REVIEW OF THE CONCEPT OF SET IN CONTEMPORARY EXPERIMENTAL PSYCHOLOGY, Psychol. Bull., 38:781-817, 1941.

Gibson, James J. THE PERCEPTION OF THE VISUAL WORLD. Boston, Houghton Mifflin Co., 1950.

Gibson, James J. THE USEFUL DIMENSIONS OF SENSITIVITY, Amer. Psychologist, 1-15, 1963.

Gibson, J.J. OBSERVATIONS ON ACTIVE TOUCH, Psychol. Rev., 69:477-491, 1962.

Gibson, James J. THE CONCEPT OF THE STIMULUS IN PSYCHOLOGY, Amer. Psychologist, 15:694-703, (11), 1960.

Gibson, J.J. ADAPTATION, AFTER-EFFECT AND CONTRAST IN THE PERCEPTION OF CURVED LINES, J. Exp. Psychol., 16:1-33, 1933.

Gilbert, L.C. SACCADIC MOVEMENTS AS A FACTOR IN VISUAL PERCEPTION IN READING, J. Educ. Psychol., 50:15-19, (1) 1959.

Gilbert, L.C. SPEED OF PROCESSING VISUAL STIMULI AND ITS RELATION TO READING, J. Educ. Psychol., 55:8-14, (1) 1959.

Gilbert, Luther C. GENETIC STUDY OF EYE MOVEMENTS IN READING, Elem. Sch. J., 6:328-335, 1959.

Gilliland, A.R., Hofeld, Jerry and Eckstrand, Gordon. STUDIES IN TIME PERCEPTION, Psychol. Bull., 43:162-176, (2) March, 1946.

Glanzer, M. CURIOSITY, EXPLORATORY DRIVE AND STIMULUS SATIATION, Psychol. Bull., 55:302-315, 1958.

Goldstein, Harry. READING AND LISTENING COMPREHENSION AT VARIOUS CONTROLLED RATES. Contribution to Education—No. 821. New York: Bureau of Publications. Teachers College, Columbia University, 1940.

Goldstone, A., Boardman, W.K. and Lohamon, W.: KINESTHETIC CUES IN THE DEVELOPMENT OF TIME CONCEPTS. J. Genet. Psychol., 93:185-190, 1958.

Goodenough, Florence L. MENTAL TESTING. New York, Rinehart, 1949.

Gray, Wm. S. A STUDY OF READING IN FOURTEEN LANGUAGES. Monog. Fundamental Educ. Scott-Foresman Co., 1956.

Grossfeld, Henry D. VISUAL SPACE AND PHYSICAL SPACE, J. Psychol., 32:25-33, 1951.

Guilford, J. P. PERSONALITY. New York, McGraw-Hill Co., 1959.

Guilford, J.P. A SYSTEM OF PSYCHOMOTOR ABILITIES, Amer. J. Psychol., 71:164-174, 1958.

Guilford, J.P. PRINTED CLASSIFICATION TESTS. A.A.F. Aviation Psych. Program Research Reports No. 5, Washington, D.C., Government Printing Office, 1947.

Gutherie, E.R. THE PSYCHOLOGY OF LEARNING. New York, Harper and Row, 1952.

Gutteridge, M. A STUDY OF MOTOR ACHIEVEMENTS OF YOUNG CHILDREN, Arch. Psychol., 34:5-178, (244) 1939.

Halpern, L. OPTIC FUNCTION AND POSTURAL ATTITUDE, Neurology, 4:831, 1954.

Halsey, Elizabeth and Porter, Lorena. PHYSICAL EDUCATION FOR CHILDREN. New York, Holt, Rinehart and Winston, 1958.

Halstead, Ward C. THE BRAIN AND INTELLIGENCE. Chicago, University of Chicago Press, 1947.

Harmon, Darell Boyd. NOTES ON A DYNAMIC THEORY OF VISION, VOL. I, Third revision published by the author. Austin, Texas, 1958.

Harmon, Darell Boyd. LIGHTING AND THE EYE. Illuminating Engineer, Sept. 1944.

Harmon, Darell Boyd. BODY RESTRAINED PERFORMANCE AS A CONTRIBUTING CAUSE OF VISUAL PROBLEMS. Paper presented to Southwest Congress of Optometry. Fort Worth, 1965.

Haworth, B. DYNAMIC POSTURE IN RELATION TO THE FEET. Clin. Orthop., 16:74, 1960.

Head, Henry. STUDIES IN NEUROLOGY. VOL. II. London, Oxford University Press, 1920.

Hebb, D.O. A TEXTBOOK OF PSYCHOLOGY. Philadelphia, W.B. Saunders Co., 1958.

Hebb, D.O. ORGANIZATION OF BEHAVIOR. New York, John Wiley and Sons, 1957.

Held, Richard. PLASTICITY IN SENSORY-MOTOR SYSTEMS, Scientific American, 84, 1965.

Held, Richard, and Freedman, Sanford J. PLASTICITY IN HUMAN SENSORIMOTOR CONTROL, Science, 142:455-462, 1963.

Held, Richard, and Rekosh, Jerold. MOTOR-SENSORY FEEDBACK AND THE GEOMETRY OF VISUAL SPACE, Science, 141:722-723, 1963.

Hellebrandt, Frances A. STANDING, A GEOTROPIC REFLEX, THE MECHANISM OF THE ASYNCHRONOUS ROTATION OF MOTOR UNITS, Amer. J. Physiol., 121:471-474, 1938.

Hellebrandt, Frances A., Brogdon, Elizabeth and Tepper, Rvbye. POSTURE AND ITS COST, Amer. J. Physiol., 129:773-781, 1940.

Hellebrandt, Frances A., and Brogdon, Elizabeth. THE HYDROSTATIC EFFECT OF GRAVITY ON THE CIRCULATION IN SUPPORTED, UNSUPPORTED AND SUSPENDED PATTERNS, Amer. J. Physiol., 123:95-96, 1938.

Hellebrandt, F.A. and Franseen, E.B. PHYSIOLOGICAL STUDY OF THE VERTICAL STANCE IN MAN. Physiol. Rev., 23:220-255, 1943.

Hellebrandt, Frances A., Schade, M. and Carns, M. METHODS OF EVOKING THE TONIC NECK REFLEX, Amer. J. Phys. Med., 41 (3), 1962.

Hellebrandt, Frances A., Outz, Sara Jane, Partridge, Miriam J., and Walters, G. Etta. TONIC NECK REFLEXES IN EXERCISES OF STRESS IN MAN, Amer. J. Phys. Med., 35: 144, 1956.

Heller, T. STUDIEN ZUR BLINDEN-PSYCHOLOGIE. Leipzig Wilhelm Engelman, 1895.

Helson, Harry. THE FUNDAMENTAL PROPOSITIONS IN GESTALT PSYCHOLOGY. Psychol. Rev., 40:12-32, 1933.

Helson, Harry. ADAPTATION LEVEL AS A FRAME OF REFERENCE FOR PREDICTION OF PSYCHOLOGICAL DATA. Amer. J. Psychol., 60:1-29, 1947.

Hoagland, H. THE PHYSIOLOGICAL CONTROL OF JUDGMENTS OF DURATION: EVIDENCE FOR A CHEMICAL CLOCK, J. Genet. Psychol., 9:267-287, 1933.

Hohman, L.B., Baker, L., and Reed, R. SENSORY DISTURBANCES IN CHILDREN WITH INFANTILE HEMIPLEGIA, TRIPLEGIA AND QUADRIPLEGIA, Amer. J. Phys. Med., 37: 1-6, 1958.

Hooker, D. THE PRENATAL ORIGIN OF HUMAN BEHAVIOR. Lawrence, Univ. Kansas Press, 1952.

Horn, Ernest. METHODS OF INSTRUCTION IN THE SOCIAL STUDIES. New York: Charles Scribner's Sons, 1937.

Hovland, C.L. and Riesen, A.H. THE MAGNITUDE OF GALVANIC AND VASOMOTOR RESPONSE AS A FUNCTION OF STIMULUS INTENSITY. J. Gen. Psychol., 23:103-121, 1940.

Hurlock, Elizabeth. CHILD DEVELOPMENT. New York, McGraw-Hill, 1956.

Huxley, Aldous L. THE DOOR OF PERCEPTION. New York, Harper, 1954.

Irwin, Charles E. EVALUATING A TRAINING PROGRAM IN LISTENING FOR COLLEGE FRESHMEN. School Review, 61:25-29, 1953.

Irwin, Charles E. AN ANALYSIS OF CERTAIN ASPECTS OF A LISTENING TRAINING PROGRAM AMONG COLLEGE FRESHMEN AT MICHIGAN STATE COLLEGE. Speech Monographs, 20:122-123, 1953.

Ittelson, W.H. THE AMES DEMONSTRATIONS IN PERCEPTION. Princeton, Princeton University Press, 1952.

Ittelson, W.H. THE CONSTANCIES OF PERCEPTUAL THEORY, Psychol. Rev., 58:285-294, 1951

Ittelson, W.H. and Kilpatrick, F.P. EXPERIMENTS IN PERCEPTION, Scientific American, 185:50-55, (2) 1951.

Jasper, Herbert. RETICULAR-CORTICAL SYSTEMS AND THEORIES OF THE INTEGRATIVE ACTION OF THE BRAIN, Harry F. Harlow and Clinton N. Woolsey (Eds.), Biological and Biochemical Bases of Behavior. Madison, University of Wisconsin Press, 1958, 37-61.

Jensen, K. DIFFERENTIAL REACTIONS TO TASTE AND TEMPERATURE STIMULI IN NEWBORN INFANTS, Genet. Psychol. Monogr., 12:367-479, 1932.

Johnson, Lamar B. GENERAL EDUCATION IN ACTION. Washington, D.C. American Council on Education, 139-173, 1952.

Johnson, Wendell. DO YOU KNOW HOW TO LISTEN? ETC. 7:3-9, 1949.

Jones, F.P. and Narve, M. INTERRUPTED LIGHT PHOTOGRAPHY TO RECORD THE EFFECT OF POISE OF THE HEAD UPON PATTERNS OF MOVEMENT IN MAN. J. Psychol., 47:247, 1959.

Jones, F.P. and O'Connell, D.N. POSTURE AS A FUNCTION OF TIME. J. Psych., 46:287, 1958.

Jones, H.E. DEXTRALITY AS A FUNCTION OF AGE. J. Expe. Psychol., 14:125-143, 1931.

Kane, Robert K., and Meredith, Howard V. ABILITY IN THE STANDING BROAD JUMP OF SCHOOL CHILDREN 7, 9 AND 11 YEARS OF AGE, Res. Quart., 23:198-208, 1952.

Karlin, I.W., Youtz, A.C., and Kennedy, L. DISTORTED SPEECH IN YOUNG CHILDREN, Amer. J. Dis. Child., 1203-1218, 1940.

Karlin, J.E. FACTOR ANALYSIS IN THE FIELD OF MUSIC, J. Musicology, 3:1, 1941.

Kelly, Ellen D. TEACHING POSTURE AND BODY MECHANICS. New York, A.S. Barnes and Co., 1949.

Kephart, N. THE SLOW LEARNER IN THE CLASSROOM. Columbus, Ohio, Merrill, 1960.

Kirchner, Glenn and Glines, Don. COMPARATIVE ANALYSIS OF EUGENE OREGON ELEMENTARY SCHOOL CHILDREN USING THE KRAUS-WEBER TEST OF MINIMUM MUSCULAR FITNESS. Res. Quart., 28:1, 1957.

Knapp, Robert, R. THE EFFECTS OF TIME LIMITS ON THE INTELLIGENCE TESTS OF MEXICAN AND AMERICAN SUBJECTS. J. Educ. Psychol., 51:14-20, 1960.

Koehler, W. GESTALT PSYCHOLOGY. New York: Liverright, 1929.

Koffka, K. PRINCIPLES OF GESTALT PSYCHOLOGY. New York, Harcourt, 1935.

Kohler, W. and Dinnerstein, D. FIGURAL AFTER-EFFECTS IN KINESTHESIS. In Albert Michotte (Ed.), Miscellanea Psycholgia. Paris, Libraire Philosophique, 196-220, 1947.

Krawiec, Theophile. A COMPARISON OF LEARNING AND RETENTION OF MATERIAL PRESENTED VISUALLY AND AUDITORIALLY. J. Gen. Psychol., 34:179-195, 1946.

Krech, D. PSYCHOLOGICAL THEORY AND SOCIAL PSYCHOLOGY. Theoretical Foundations in Psychology, Harry Helson (Ed.), New Jersey. Van Nostrand Co., 656-697, 1951.

Kraus, Hans and Kirschland, Ruth. MINIMUM MUSCULAR FITNESS TESTS IN SCHOOL CHILDREN. Res. Quart., 25:2, 1954.

Laidlow, R.W. and Hamilton, M.A. A STUDY OF THRESHOLDS IN APPERCEPTION OF PASSIVE MOVEMENT AMONG NORMAL SUBJECTS. Bull. Neurolog. Instit. New York, 6:268-273, 1937.

Larson, Robert P. and Fedder, D.D. COMMON AND DIFFERENTIAL FACTORS IN READING AND HEARING COMPREHENSION. J. Educ. Psychol., 31:241-252, 1940.

Lashley, K.S. THE PROBLEM OF CEREBRAL ORGANIZATION IN VISION. Heinrich Kluver (Ed.), Visual Mechanisms. Biological Symposium. Vol. VII. Jacques Cattell Press, 301, 1942.

Laycock, Frank. MOTOR AND PERCEPTUAL SKILL IN READING MATERIAL WHOSE MEANING IS UNIMPORTANT. J. Exp. Psychol. 320-330, 1955.

Laycock, Frank. SIGNIFICANT CHARACTERISTICS OF COLLEGE STUDENTS WITH VARY-

ING FLEXIBILITY IN READING RATE. J. Exp. Educ., 311-319, 1955.

Lazarus, Richard and Alfert, Elizabeth. SHORT CIRCUITING OF THREAT BY EXPERIMENTALLY ALTERING COGNITIVE APPRAISAL. J. Abnorm. and Soc. Psychol., 69:195-205, 1964.

Lazarus, R.S., Speisman, J.C. and Mordkoff, A.M. THE RELATION BETWEEN AUTONOMIC INDICATORS OF PSYCHOLOGICAL STRESS: HEART RATE AND SKIN CONDUCTANCE. Psychom. Med., 25:19-30, 1963.

Leavell, U.W. and Beck, H. ABILITY OF RETARDED READERS TO RECOGNIZE SYMBOLS IN ASSOCIATION WITH LATERAL DOMINANCE. Peabody J. Educ., 37:7-14, 1959.

Lederer, Ruth Klein. AN EXPLORATORY INVESTIGATION OF HANDED STATUS IN THE FIRST TWO YEARS OF LIFE. Univ. Iowa Stud. Child. Welfare, 16:9-103, 1939.

le Lionnais, Francois. THE ORION BOOK OF TIME. New York, Orion Press, 1960.

Leuba, J.H. THE INFLUENCE OF DURATION AND OF ARM MOVEMENTS UPON THE JUDGMENT OF THEIR LENGTH. Amer. J. Psychol., 20:374-385, 1909.

Levy, S. FIGURE DRAWING AS A PROJECTIVE TEST. L.E. Abt and L. Bellak (Eds.), Projective Psychology. New York, Knopf, 1950.

Lewin, K. A DYNAMIC THEORY OF PERSONALITY. New York, McGraw-Hill, 1935.

Lewin, K. PRINCIPLES OF TOPOLOGICAL PSYCHOLOGY. New York, McGraw-Hill, 1936.

Lewin, K. FIELD THEORY IN SOCIAL SCIENCE. (Papers posthumously edited by D. Cartwright). New York, Harper, 1951.

Lindner, R.M. PSYCHOPATHIC PERSONALITY AND THE CONCEPT OF HOMEOSTASIS. J. Clin. Psychopath. and Psychother., 6: 517-521, 1945.

Lindsley, Donald B. THE RETICULAR SYSTEM AND PERCEPTUAL DISCRIMINATION. Herbert Jasper, et al. (Eds), Reticular Formation of the Brain, Boston, Little Brown and Co. 513-534, 1958.

Lowenfeld, Berthold. PSYCHOLOGICAL PROBLEMS OF CHILDREN WITH IMPAIRED VISION. William M. Cruickshank (Ed.), Psychology of Exceptional Children and Youth. Englewood Cliffs, New Jersey; Prentice-Hall, 1955.

Lowman, C.L. THE EFFECT OF FAULTY SKELETAL ALIGNMENT UPON THE EYES. Amer.

J. Orthosurg., 459-492, 1918.

Lowman, Charles and Young, Carl. POSTURAL FITNESS. Philadelphia; Lea and Febiger, 1960.

Luria, A.R. and Vinogradova, Olga S. AN OBJECTIVE INVESTIGATION OF THE DYNAMICS OF SEMANTIC SYSTEMS. Brit. J. Psychol., 50:89-105, 1959.

MacDonald, J.C. AN INVESTIGATION OF BODY SCHEME IN ADULTS WITH CEREBRAL VASCULAR ACCIDENT, Amer. J. Occup. Ther., 14:75-79, 1960.

MacDonald, Lawrence W. PROBLEM SOLVING AND THE VISUAL PROCESS, Optometric Extension Program Postgraduate Courses, 3, 8, 1965.

MacDonald, Lawrence W. TOWARD ORGANIZING THE VISUAL SPACE VOLUME: PRISM ROTATIONS, CHERROSCOPIC TRACING AND STEREOSCOPIC POINTER TECHNIQUES, Optometric Extension Program Papers, 35, 36, Series 2, No. 5, 1964.

Mach, Ernest. SPACE AND GEOMETRY IN THE LIGHT OF PHYSIOLOGICAL, PSYCHOLOGICAL AND PHYSICAL INQUIRY. Chicago, Open Court Publishing Co., 1906.

Mach, Ernest. ANALYSIS OF SENSATION. New York; Dover Publications, 1959.

Machover, Karen A. PERSONALITY PROJECTION IN THE DRAWING OF THE HUMAN FIGURE: A METHOD OF PERSONALITY INVESTIGATION. Springfield, Illinois; Charles C. Thomas, 1961.

Macy, Icie G. and Kelly, Harriet J. CHEMICAL AND PHYSIOLOGIC GROWTH. Paul H. Mussen (Ed.), Handbook of Research Methods in Child Development. 251-283, 1960.

Magnus, R. KORPERSTELLUNG. Julius Springer, 1924.

Major, D.R. CUTANEOUS PERCEPTION OF FORM. Amer. J. Psychol., 10:143-147, 1898.

Malmo, R.B. ACTIVATION: A NEUROPHYSIOLOGICAL DIMENSION. Psychol. Review., 66:367-386, 1959.

Maltzman, Irving and Raskin, David C. EFFECTS OF INDIVIDUAL DIFFERENCES IN THE ORIENTING REFLEX ON CONDITIONING AND COMPLEX PROCESSES. J. Exp. Res. Person., 1:1-16, 1965.

Marshall, W.H. and Talbot, S.A. RECENT EVIDENCE OF NEURAL MECHANISMS IN

VISION LEADING TO A GENERAL THEORY OF SENSORY ACUITY. Heinrich Kluver (Ed.), Visual Mechanisms: Biological Symposia. Vol. VII. Jacques Cattell Press, 1942.

Martin, W.W. SOME BASIC IMPLICATIONS OF A CONCEPT OF ORGANISM IN PSYCHOLOGY. Psychol. Rev., 52:333-343, 1945.

McAuley, J.D. WHAT UNDERSTANDING DO SECOND GRADE CHILDREN HAVE OF TIME RELATIONSHIPS? J. Educ. Res., 54:312-314, 1961.

McCaskill, L.L. and Wellman, B.L. A STUDY OF COMMON MOTOR ACHIEVEMENTS AT THE PRESCHOOL AGES, Child Develop., 9:141-150, 1938.

McFarland, J.H., Wapner, S., and Warner, H. THE EFFECT OF POSTURAL FACTORS ON THE DISTRIBUTION OF TACTUAL SENSITIVITY AND THE ORGANIZATION OF TACTUAL-KINESTHETIC SPACE, J. Exp. Psychol., 63:149, 1962.

McGraw, M.B. SUSPENSION GRASP BEHAVIOR IN THE HUMAN INFANT, Amer. J. Dis. Child., 60:799-811, 1940.

McGraw, M.B. BEHAVIOR OF THE NEWBORN INFANT AND EARLY NEUROMUSCULAR DEVELOPMENT, Res. Pub. Assn. Nerv. Ment. Dis., 19:244-246, 1939.

McGraw, Myrtle B. and Breeze, K.W. QUANTITATIVE STUDIES IN THE DEVELOPMENT OF ERECT LOCOMOTION. Child. Development, 12:267-303, 1941.

McLaughlin, Samuel C. VISUAL PERCEPTION IN STRABISMUS AND AMBLYOPIA. Psychol. Monogr., V, 78, No. 12, (589) 1964.

Meredith, Howard V. THE RHYTHM OF PHYSICAL GROWTH, University studies in child welfare, University of Iowa, 1935.

Merry, R.V., and Merry, F.K. THE TACTUAL RECOGNITION OF EMBOSSED PICTURES BY BLIND CHILDREN, J. Appl. Psychol., 17:163, 1933.

Metheny, Eleanor. BODY DYNAMICS. New York: McGraw-Hill Book Co., 1951.

Meyer, Edith. COMPREHENSION OF SPATIAL RELATIONS IN PRE-SCHOOL CHILDREN. J. Genet, Psychol., 57:119-151, 1940.

Meyerson, Lee. SOMATOPSYCHOLOGY OF PHYSICAL DISABILITY, Willian M. Cruickshank (Ed.), Psychology of Exceptional Children and Youth. Englewood Cliffs, New Jersey, Prentice-Hall, 1955a.

Mills, Lloyd. THE EFFECTS OF FAULTY CRANIOSPINAL FORM AND ALIGNMENT UPON THE EYES, Amer. J. Ophthal., 493-499, 1919.

Milne, L. J., and Milne, M. THE SENSE OF ANIMALS AND MEN. New York, Atheneum, 1962.

Money, J. READING DISABILITY. Baltimore, Johns Hopkins Press, 1962.

Montagu, M.F.A. THE SENSORY INFLUENCES OF THE SKIN, Texas Rep. Biol. Med., 11:291-301, 1953.

Morehouse, Lawrence E., and Cooper, John M. KINESIOLOGY. St. Louis, C.V. Mosby Co., 1950.

Morton, Dudley J. HUMAN LOCOMOTION AND BODY FORM. Baltimore, Williams and Wilkins, 1952.

Moruzzi, G., and Magoun, H.W. BRAIN STEM RETICULAR FORMATION AND ACTIVATION OF THE EEG, EEG and Clin. Neurophysiol., 1:455, 1949.

Mountcastle, Vernon B. INTERHEMISPHERIC RELATIONS AND CEREBRAL DOMINANCE. Baltimore, Johns Hopkins Press, 1962.

Murphree, D. MAXIMUM RATES OF FORM PERCEPTION AND THE ALPHA RHYTHM: AN INVESTIGATION AND TEST OF CURRENT NERVE NET THEORY, J. Exp. Psychol., 48:57-61, 1954.

Murphy, Gardner, and Solley, Charles. LEARNING TO PERCEIVE AS WE WISH TO PERCEIVE, Bull. Menninger Clinic, 21:225-237, 1957.

Myklebust, H.R. PSYCHOLOGY OF DEAFNESS. New York, Grune and Stratton, 1960.

Myklebust, H.R. AUDITORY DISORDERS IN CHILDREN. New York, Grune and Stratton, 1954.

Myklebust, H.R. SIGNIFICANCE OF ETIOLOGY IN MOTOR PERFORMANCE OF DEAF CHILDREN WITH SPECIAL REFERENCE TO MENINGITIS, Amer. J. Psychol., 59:249, 1946.

Myklebust, H.R., and Boshes, B. PSYCHONEUROLOGICAL DISORDERS IN CHILDREN, Arch. Pediat., 77:247-256, 1960.

Neilsen, J.M. GERSTMAN SYNDROME, Arch. Neurol. Psychiat., 39:536-559, 1938.

Neilsen, J.M., and Sult, C.W., Jr. AGNOSIAS AND THE BODY SHAPE, Bull. Los Angeles Neurol. Soc., 4:69-76, 1939.

Nichols, R.G. and Lewis, T.R. LISTENING AND SPEAKING. William C. Brown, 1954.

Nichols, Ralph. FACTORS IN LISTENING COMPREHENSION. Speech Mongraphs, 15:154-163, 1948.

Nichols, Ralph. NEEDED RESEARCH IN LISTENING COMMUNICATION. J. Commun., 1:48-50, 1951.

Nichols, Ralph and Keller, Robert J. THE MEASUREMENT OF COMMUNICATION SKILLS. Jr. Coll. Journ., 24:160-168, 1953.

Nichols, Ralph. THE COMPONENTS OF EFFECTIVE LISTENING. Education, 75:292-302, 1955.

Nichols, Ralph G. and Stevens, Leonard A. ARE YOU LISTENING? New York, McGraw-Hill Book Co., 1957.

Oakden, E.C. and Stuart, M. THE DEVELOPMENT OF THE KNOWLEDGE OF TIME IN CHILDREN. Brit. J. Psychol., 12, 1902.

Ourth, L. and Brown, K.B. INADEQUATE MOTHERING AND DISTURBANCES IN THE NEONATAL PERIOD. Child Develop., 287-295, 1961.

Parsons, Talcott, and Shils, Edward et al. TOWARD A GENERAL THEORY OF ACTION. Cambridge, Massachusetts, Harvard University Press, 289, 1962.

Passey, G.E., and Guedry, F.E. THE PERCEPTION OF THE VERTICAL. II. Adaptation in Four Planes, J. Exp. Psychol., 38:700, 1949.

Patton, F.E. A COMPARISON OF THE KINESTHETIC SENSIBILITY OF SPEECH DEFECTIVE AND NORMALLY SPEAKING CHILDREN, J. Speech Dis., VII:305-310, 1942.

Pavlov, I.P. CONDITIONED REFLEXES (TRANSLATED BY G.V. ANREP). London, Oxford University Press, 1927.

Phelps, Winthrop Morgan, Kipphuth, Robert J.H., and Goff, Charles Weer. THE DIAGNOSIS AND TREATMENT OF POSTURAL DEFECTS. Springfield, Illinois, Charles C. Thomas, 1956.

Phillips, Marjorie, et al. ANALYSIS OF RESULTS FROM THE KRAUS WEBER TEST OF MINIMUM MUSCULAR FITNESS IN CHILDREN, Res. Quart., XXVI:3, 1955.

Piaget, Jean. THE CONSTRUCTION OF REALITY IN THE CHILD. New York, Basic Books, Inc., 1954.

Piaget, Jean. LA CONSTRUCTION DU REEL CHEZ L'ENFANT (THE ORIGINS OF INTELLIGENCE IN CHILDREN). Neuchatel-Paris, Delachaux et Niestle, 1937.

Piaget, Jean. THE LANGUAGE AND THOUGHT OF CHILDREN. New York, Harcourt and Brace, 1928.

Piaget, Jean, and Inhelder, Barbel. LE DEVELOPPEMENT DES QUANTITES PHYSIQUES CHEZ L'ENFANT (2nd rev. ed.), Neuchatel-Switzerland, Delachaux and Niestle, 1962.

Pieron, Henri. THE SENSATIONS—THEIR FUNCTIONS, PROCESSES AND MECHANISMS. London, Frederick Muller Ltd., 1952.

Pitts, Walter and McCulloch, Warren S. HOW WE KNOW UNIVERSALS. THE PERCEPTION OF AUDITORY AND VISUAL FORMS. Bull. Math. Physics., 9:127-147, 1947.

Pratt, K.C., Nelson, A.K. and Sun, K.H. THE BEHAVIOR OF THE NEWBORN INFANT. Columbus: Ohio State University Press, 1930.

Pribam, Karl H. DISCUSSION COMMENTARY B. Vernon B. Mountcastle (Ed.) Interhemispheric Relations and Cerebral Dominance. Baltimore, Johns Hopkins Press, 107-112, 1962.

Radler, Donald H. and Kephart, Newell C. SUCCESS THROUGH PLAY. New York, Harper and Bros., 1959.

Rankin, P.T. LISTENING ABILITY—ITS IMPORTANCE MEASUREMENT AND DEVELOPMENT. Chicago Schools Journ. 12:177-179 January and 417-420 June, 1930.

Razran, G.. THE OBSERVABLE UNCONSCIOUS AND THE INFERABLE CONSCIOUS IN CURRENT SOVIET PSYCHOPHYSIOLOGY: INTEROCEPTIVE CONDITIONING, SEMANTIC CONDITIONING AND THE ORIENTING REFLEX. Psychol. Rev., 68:81-145, 1961.

Renshaw, Samuel. PSYCHOLOGICAL OPTICS. Vol. 10, 11, 12. Optometric Extension Papers, Duncan, Oklahoma, 1950-1951.

Renshaw, Samuel D. THE ERRORS OF CUTANEOUS LOCALIZATION AND THE EFFECT OF PRACTICE ON THE LOCALIZING MOVEMENT IN CHILDREN AND ADULTS. J. Genet, Psychol., 38:223-238, 1930.

Renshaw, Samuel D., and Wherry, R.J. THE AGE OF ONSET OF OCULAR DOMINANCE, J. Genet. Psychol., 31:493-496, 1931.

Renshaw, Samuel D., Wherry, R.J., and Newling, J.C. CUTANEOUS LOCALIZATION IN CONGENITALLY BLIND VERSUS SEEING CHILDREN AND ADULTS, J. Genet. Psychol., 38:239-248, 1930.

Richardson, Paul C. DEVELOPING NATURAL TIME EXPRESSIONS, Volta Review, 64: 543-545, 574, (9) November, 1962.

Richter, C.P. TOTAL SELF REGULATORY FUNCTIONS IN ANIMALS AND HUMAN BEINGS, Harvey Lect., 38:63-103, 1942-1943.

Rieber, Morton. THE EFFECT OF MUSIC ON THE ACTIVITY LEVEL OF CHILDREN, Psychon. Sci., 3:325-326, 1965.

Riesen, Austin H. RECEPTOR FUNCTIONS, Paul H. Mussen (Ed.), Handbook of Research Methods in Child Development. New York, John Wiley and Sons, Inc., 300, 1960.

Riesen, Austin H. PLASTICITY OF BEHAVIOR: PSYCHOLOGICAL ASPECTS, Harry F. Harlow and Clinton N. Woolsey (Eds.), Biological and Biochemical Basis of Behavior, Madison, Wisconsin, University of Wisconsin Press, 425-449, 1958.

Riklan, Manuel, and Levita, Eric. LATERALITY OF SUBCORTICAL INVOLVEMENT AND PSYCHOLOGICAL FUNCTIONS, Psychol. Bull., 64:217-224, 1965.

Roff, Merrill. A FACTORIAL STUDY OF TESTS IN THE PERCEPTUAL AREA, Psychometric Monogr., 41:8, 1953.

Rogers, James F. FORWARD. Phi Delta Pi Fraternity Symposium on Posture. New York, Comet Press, 1938.

Ronchi, Vasco. OPTICS, THE SCIENCE OF VISION. New York, New York University Press, 1957. (translated from the Italian version and revised by Edward Rosen.)

Rosenblith, Walter A. EDITOR'S COMMENT. Walter A. Rosenblith (Ed.) Sensory Communication. M.I.T. Press, 815-826, 1961.

Rosenzweig, M.R. CORTICAL CORRELATES OF AUDITORY LOCALIZATION AND OF RELATED PERCEPTUAL PHENOMENA, J. Comp. Physiol. Psychol., 47:269, 1954.

Rosenzweig, N. A MECHANISM IN SCHIZOPHRENIA: A THEORETICAL FORMULATION, AMA Arch. Neurol. Psychiat., 74:544-555, 1955.

Rosenzweig, S., A DYNAMIC INTERPRETATION OF PSYCHOTHERAPY ORIENTED TOWARDS RESEARCH, S.S. Tomkins (Ed.), Contemporary Psychopathology. Cambridge, Harvard University Press, 235-243, 1943.

Ross, A.O. TACTUAL PERCEPTION OF FORM BY THE BRAIN-INJURED, J. Abnorm. Soc. Psychol., 49:566-572, 1954.

Ruff, George E., and Levy, Edwin Z. PSYCHIATRIC RESEARCH IN SPACE MEDICINE, Amer. J. Psychiat., 115:793-795, 1959.

Rousseau, Jean Jacques. EMILE: CONCERNING EDUCATION. Boston, Heath and Co., 1883.

Rulon, Phillip J. COMPARISON OF PHONOGRAPHIC RECORDINGS WITH PRINTED MATERIALS IN TERMS OF KNOWLEDGE GAINED THROUGH THEIR USE IN A TEACHING UNIT. Harvard Educ. Rev., 13:163-175, 1943.

Russell, R.D. A COMPARISON OF TWO METHODS OF LEARNING. J. Educ. Res., 18:235-238, 1928.

Rushton, W.A.H. PERIPHERAL CODING IN THE NERVOUS SYSTEM. Walter A. Rosenblith (Ed.). Sensory Communication. M.I.T. Press, 169-181, 1961.

Satter, George, and Cassell, Robert. TACTUAL-KINESTHETIC LOCALIZATION IN THE MENTALLY RETARDED. Amer. J. Ment. Def., 59:652, 1954.

Schafer, V.G. and Gilliland, A.R. THE RELATIONSHIP OF TIME ESTIMATIONS TO CERTAIN PHYSIOLOGICAL CHANGES. J. Exp. Psychol., 23:545-552, 1938.

Scheck, M.G. INVOLUNTARY TONGUE MOVEMENTS UNDER VARYING STIMULI. Proc. Iowa. Acad. Sci., 32:385-391, 1925.

Schilder, P. THE IMAGE AND APPEARANCE OF THE HUMAN BODY. New York, Harcourt Brace and World Inc., 1950.

Schilling, Charles W. THE HUMAN MACHINE. Annapolis, Maryland, A Naval Institute Publication, 1955.

Schnore, M.M. INDIVIDUAL PATTERNS OF PHYSIOLOGICAL ACTIVITY AS A FUNCTION OF TASK DIFFERENCES AND THE DEGREE OF AROUSAL. J. Exp. Psychol., 58: 117-128, 1959.

Schontz, F.C. BODY CONCEPT DISTURBANCES OF PATIENTS WITH HEMIPLEGIA. J. Clin. Psychol., 12:293-295, 1956.

Sears, R.R., Maccoby, Eleanor E. and Levin, H. PATTERNS OF CHILD-REARING. Evanston, Row-Peterson Co., 1957.

Seashore, Harold G. THE DEVELOPMENT OF A BEAM WALKING TEST AND ITS USE IN MEASURING THE DEVELOPMENT OF BALANCE IN CHILDREN. Res. Quart., 18: 246-259, 1947.

Seguin, Edward. IDIOCY AND ITS TREATMENT. BY THE PHYSIOLOGICAL METHOD. New York, W. Wood and Co., 1866.

Selye, Hans. THE STRESS OF LIFE. New York, McGraw-Hill, 1956.

Sherrington, Sir Charles Scott. MAN AND HIS NATURE. New York, Cambridge University Press, 1940.

Sherrington, Sir Charles Scott. THE BRAIN AND ITS MECHANISM. New York, MacMillan Co., 1937.

Sherrington, Sir Charles Scott. OBSERVATIONS ON THE SENSUAL ROLE OF THE PROPRIOCEPTIVE NERVE SUPPLY OF THE EXTRINSIC OCULAR MUSCLES, BRAIN, 1915.

Shewchuk, L.A. and Zubek, J.P. DISCRIMINATORY ABILITY OF VARIOUS SKIN AREAS AS MEASURED BY TECHNIQUES OF INTERMITTENT STIMULATION, Canadian J. Psychol., 14:244, 1960.

Shirley, M. M. THE FIRST TWO YEARS: VOLUME 1. POSTURAL AND LOCOMOTOR DEVELOPMENT. Minneapolis, University of Minnesota Press, 1931.

Simons, G.M. COMPARISON OF INCIPIENT MUSIC RESPONSES AMONG VERY YOUNG TWINS AND SINGLETONS. J. Res. Music Educ., 12:212-226, 1964.

Skeffington, A.M. THE CASE OF THE COMFORTABLE HYPEROPE WHO FAILED, Optometric Extension Program Postgraduate Courses, 38:6, (38) 1966.

Skeffington, A.M. CLINICAL OPTOMETRY IN THEORY AND PRACTICE, Optometric Extension Program Postgraduate Courses, 37:118, (12) 1965.

Skeffington, A.M. THE CASE OF THE UNCHANGING FINDINGS, Optometric Extension Program Papers, 37:3, 1964.

Sloan, W. THE LINCOLN-OSERETSKY MOTOR DEVELOPMENT SCALE, Genet. Psychol. Monogr., 51:183-252, 1955.

Slocum, Helen M. THE EFFECT OF FATIGUE INDUCED BY PHYSICAL ACTIVITY ON CERTAIN TESTS IN KINESTHESIS, Dissert. Abstr., 13:1084-1085, 1953.

Smith, Karl U., and Smith, William M. PERCEPTION AND MOTION: AN ANALYSIS OF SPACE STRUCTURED BEHAVIOR. Philadelphia, W.B. Saunders, 1962.

Sokolov, E.N. NEURONAL MODELS AND THE ORIENTING REFLEX. Mary A.B. Brazier (Ed.) The Central Nervous System and Behavior. Josiah Macy Jr. Foundation, 187-276, 1960.

Solomons, Gerald, and Solomons, Hope C. FACTORS AFFECTING PERFORMANCE IN FOUR MONTH OLD INFANTS, Child Develop., 35:1283-1296, (4) 1964.

Spencer, E. AN INVESTIGATION OF THE MATURATION OF VARIOUS FACTORS OF AUDITORY PERCEPTION IN PRESCHOOL CHILDREN, Unpublished doctoral dissertation. Evanston, Northwestern University, 1958.

Spencer, E.M. THE RETENTION OF ORALLY PRESENTED MATERIAL. Programs announcing candidates for higher degrees, State University of Iowa. Series on aims and progress in research. No. 66, 1940.

Stagner, R. HOMEOSTASIS: CORRUPTIONS OR MISCONCEPTIONS? A REPLY, Psychol. Rev., 61:205-208, 1954.

Stagner, R. HOMEOSTASIS AS A UNIFYING CONCEPT IN PERSONALITY THEORY, Psychol. Rev., 58:5-17, 1951.

Steindler, A. KINESIOLOGY OF THE HUMAN BODY. Springfield, Charles C. Thomas, 1955.

Steindler, A. A HISTORICAL REVIEW OF THE STUDIES AND INVESTIGATIONS MADE

IN RELATION TO HUMAN GAIT, J. Bone Joint Surg., 35-A:540-542, 1953.

Stirnimann, F. LE GOUT ET L'ODORAT DU NOUVEAU NE, Rev. Franc. Pediat., 12:453-485, 1936.

Stockwell, E. VISUAL DIFFICULTIES IN DEAF CHILDREN, Arch. Ophthal., 48:428, 1952.

Stone, L. Joseph. AN EXPERIMENTAL STUDY OF FORM PERCEPTION IN THE THERMAL SENSES, Psychol. Rec., 1:235-237, 1937.

Stone, L. Joseph and Church, Joseph. CHILDHOOD AND ADOLESCENCE. New York, Random House, 1957.

Stratton, G.W. SOME PRELIMINARY EXPERIMENTS ON VISION WITHOUT INVERSION OF THE RETINAL IMAGE, Psychol. Rev., 3:611-617, 1896.

Strauss, A.A., and Lehtinen, L.E. PSYCHOPATHOLOGY AND EDUCATION OF THE BRAIN-INJURED CHILD. New York, Grune and Stratton, Inc., 1947.

Strauss, A.A. and Werner, H. DEFICIENCY IN THE FINGER SCHEMA IN RELATION TO ARITHMETIC DEFICIENCY. Amer. J. Orthopsych., 81:719-723, 1938.

Streff, John and Apell, Richard. OPTOMETRY'S VISUAL POSTURE. New York All-States Optometric Congress Transcript. Elmira, New York, 1964.

Swanson, R. PERCEPTION OF SIMULTANEOUS TACTUAL STIMULATION IN DEFECTIVE AND NORMAL CHILDREN. Amer. J. Ment. Def., 61:743-752, 1957.

Sweet, A.L. TEMPORAL DISCRIMINATION BY THE HUMAN EYE. Amer. J. Psychol., 66:185-198, 1953.

Tabori, P. THE BOOK OF THE HAND. Philadelphia, Chilton Co., 1962.

Tart, Charles T. TOWARD THE EXPERIMENTAL CONTROL OF DREAMING: A REVIEW OF THE LITERATURE. Psychol. Bull., 64:81-89, 1965.

Teuber, H.L. PERCEPTION. H.W. Magoun (Ed.) Handbook of Physiology. Vol. 3. Washington D.C. Amer. Physiol. Soc., 1595-1668, 1959.

Thurstone, L. L. SOME PRIMARY ABILITIES IN VISUAL THINKING. Psychometric Laboratory Report 59. Chicago, Univ. of Chicago Press, 1950.

Tinker, Miles. EYE MOVEMENTS IN READING. Educ. Digest, 35-37, 1959.

Titchener, E.B. EXPERIMENTAL PSYCHOLOGY OF THE THOUGHT PROCESSES. New York, MacMillan Co., 1909.

Tichener, E.B. A TEXTBOOK OF PSYCHOLOGY. New York, MacMillan Co., 1914.

Tichener, E.B. A BEGINNER'S PSYCHOLOGY. New York, MacMillan Co., 1915.

Todd, Mabel Ellsworth. THE THINKING BODY. Boston, Charles T. Branford Co., 1937.

Treisman, Michael. TEMPORAL DISCRIMINATION AND THE INDIFFERENCE INTERVAL: IMPLICATIONS FOR A MODEL OF THE "INTERNAL CLOCK". Psychol. Monogr. 576, 77:13, 1963.

Tschirgi, R. SPATIAL PERCEPTION AND CENTRAL NERVOUS SYSTEM SYMMETRY. Arch. Neuropsychiat., 16:364-366, 1958.

Van Vorst, R. SOME RESPONSES OF THE PSYCHOPATH AS INTERPRETED IN THE LIGHT OF LINDNER'S SUGGESTED APPLICATION OF THE CONCEPT OF HOMEOSTASIS, J. Clin. Psychopath. Psychother., 8:827-830, 1947.

Vernon, M.D. A FURTHER STUDY OF VISUAL PERCEPTION. New York, Cambridge University Press, 91, 1952.

Wallach, H. THE ROLE OF HEAD MOVEMENTS AND VESTIBULAR AND VISUAL CUES IN SOUND LOCALIZATION, J. Exp. Psychol., 27:339-368, 1940.

Wallerstein, Harvey. AN ELECTROMYOGRAPHIC STUDY OF ATTENTIVE LISTENING. Canad. J. Psychol., 8:228-238, 1954

Walsh, Geoffrey E. AN INVESTIGATION OF SOUND LOCALIZATION IN PATIENTS WITH NEUROLOGICAL ABNORMALITIES, Brain, 80:222, (II) 1957.

Walter, W. Grey. THE LIVING BRAIN. New York, W.W. Norton and Co., 1953.

Wapner, S., and Werner, H. EXPERIMENTS ON SENSORY-TONIC FIELD THEORY OF PERCEPTION. V. EFFECTS OF BODY STATUS ON THE KINESTHETIC PERCEPTION OF VERTICALITY, J. Exp. Psychol., 44:126, 1952.

Wapner, S., Werner, H., and Morant, R.B. EXPERIMENTS ON SENSORY-TONIC FIELD THEORY OF PERCEPTION. III. EFFECTS OF BODY ROTATION ON THE VISUAL PERCEPTION OF VERTICALITY, J. Exp. Psychol., 42:351, 1951.

Way, R. Bernard, and Green, Noel. TIME AND ITS RECKONING. Redhill, England, Wells, Gardner, Darton and Co., 1951.

Wellman, B.L. MOTOR ACHIEVEMENTS OF PRESCHOOL CHILDREN, Child. Educ., 13: 311-316, 1937.

Werner, Heinz. COMPARATIVE PSYCHOLOGY OF MENTAL DEVELOPMENT. Chicago, Follett Publish. Co., 1948.

Wertheimer, M. and Leventhal, C.M. PERMANENT SATIATION PHENOMENA WITH KINESTHETIC FIGURAL AFTEREFFECTS. J. Exp. Psychol., 55:255-257, 1958.

White, C.T., Cheatham, P.G. and Armington, J.C. TEMPORAL NUMEROSITY: II. EVIDENCE FOR CENTRAL FACTORS INFLUENCING PERCEIVED NUMBER. J. Exp. Psychol., 46:283-287, 1953.

White, C.T. and Cheatham, P.G. TEMPORAL NUMEROSITY: IV. A COMPARISON OF THE MAJOR SENSES. J. Exp. Psychol., 58:441-444, 1959.

White, Carroll T. TEMPORAL NUMEROSITY AND THE PSYCHOLOGICAL UNIT OF DURATION. Psychol. Monogr., V. 77, No. 12 (575) 1963.

Wiener, N. CYBERNETICS. New York, Wiley and Sons, 1948.

Wild, M. BEHAVIOR PATTERNS OF THROWING AND SOME OBSERVATIONS CONCERNING ITS COURSE OF DEVELOPMENT. Res. Quart., 9:20-24, 1938.

Witkin, H.A., Lewis, H.B. Hertzman, M., Machover, K., Meissner, P., Bretnall, L. and Wapner, S. PERSONALITY THROUGH PERCEPTION. New York, Harper and Bros, 1954.

Wittreich, W.J. VISUAL PERCEPTION AND PERSONALITY. Scientific Amer., 200, 1959.

Woodworth, R.S. EXPERIMENTAL PSYCHOLOGY. New York, Holt, 1938.

Wright, R.H. THE SCIENCE OF SMELL. London, George Allen and Unwin, Ltd., 1964.

Young, William E. THE RETENTION OF READING COMPREHENSION AND RELATION TO HEARING COMPREHENSION AND RETENTION. J. Exper. Educ., 5:30-39, 1936.

Zigler, M.J. and Barrett, Rebecca. A FURTHER CONTRIBUTION TO THE TACTUAL PERCEPTION OF FORM. J. Exp. Psychol., 10:184-192, 1927.

Zigler, M.J. and Northrup, K.M. THE TACTUAL PERCEPTION OF FORM. Amer. J. Psychol., 37:391-397, 1926.

Zimmerman, Wayne. HYPOTHESIS CONCERNING THE NATURE OF THE SPATIAL FACTORS, Educ. Psychol. Measurement, 14:396-400, 1954.

Zimny, G.H., and Weidenfeller, E.W. EFFECTS OF MUSIC UPON GSR' OF CHILDREN, Child Develop., 33:891-896, 1962.